MW00982173

LEGISLATED INEQUALITY

Legislated Inequality

Temporary Labour Migration in Canada

Edited by

PATTI TAMARA LENARD

CHRISTINE STRAEHLE

McGill-Queen's University Press

Montreal & Kingston • London • Ithaca

© McGill-Queen's University Press 2012

ISBN 978-0-7735-4041-5 (cloth)
ISBN 978-0-7735-4042-2 (paper)

Legal deposit third quarter 2012
Bibliothèque nationale du Québec

Printed in Canada on acid-free paper that is 100% ancient forest
free (100% post-consumer recycled), processed chlorine free

This book has been published with the help of a grant from the
Canadian Federation for the Humanities and Social Sciences,
through the Aid to Scholarly Publications Program, using funds
provided by the Social Sciences and Humanities Research Council
of Canada.

McGill-Queen's University Press acknowledges the support of the
Canada Council for the Arts for our publishing program. We also
acknowledge the financial support of the Government of Canada
through the Canada Book Fund for our publishing activities.

Library and Archives Canada Cataloguing in Publication

Legislated inequality : temporary labour migration in Canada /
edited by Patti Tamara Lenard and Christine Straehle.

Includes bibliographical references and index.
ISBN 978-0-7735-4041-5 (bound). –
ISBN 978-0-7735-4042-2 (pbk.)

1. Foreign workers – Canada – Social conditions. 2. Agricultural
laborers, Foreign – Canada – Social conditions. 3. Migrant labor
– Canada. I. Lenard, Patti Tamara, 1975-   II. Straehle, Christine

HD8104.L46 2012   331.6'20971   C2012-901914-3

Typeset by Jay Tee Graphics Ltd. in 10.5/13.5 Sabon

Contents

Abbreviations

CAISP	Canadian Agricultural Injury Surveillance Program
CATTAQ	Centre d'aide aux travailleurs et travailleuses agricoles
CEC	Canadian Experience Class
CIC	Citizenship and Immigration Canada
CLC	Commission for Labor Cooperation
CMA	Census Metropolitan Area
CSST	Commission de la santé et de la sécurité du travail
DOL	Department of Labor (US)
FARMS	Foreign Agricultural Resource Management Services
FERME	Fondation des entreprises en recrutement de main-d'oeuvre agricole étrangère
FFQ	Fédération des femmes du Québec
FSWP	Federal Skilled Worker Program
FWSG	Filipino Workers' Support Group
GFMD	Global Forum on Migration and Development
HRSDC	Human Resources and Skills Development Canada
ILO	International Labour Organization
IOM	International Organization for Migration
IWC	Immigrant Workers Centre
LCP	Live-in Caregiver Program
LIC	live-in caregiver
LMO	Labour Market Opinion
LRC	Labour Relations Commission
LSPP	Low-Skill Pilot Project
MFW	migrant farm worker
MPNP	Manitoba Provincial Nominee Program

NAFTA	North American Free Trade Agreement
NOC	National Occupational Classification
PNP	Provincial Nominee Program
PR	permanent residency
PTNP	Provincial/Territorial Nominee Program
SAWP	Seasonal Agricultural Worker Program
SINP	Saskatchewan Immigrant Nominee Program
TFW	temporary foreign worker
TFWP	Temporary Foreign Worker Program
UFCW	United Food and Commercial Workers
WALI	Western Agricultural Labour Initiative

Acknowledgments

First and foremost, we would like to thank the contributors to this volume, who, along with both of us, are concerned about the status of low-skilled temporary labour migrants in Canada. Their collective expertise is, we believe, represented in this timely volume. They have been a pleasure to work with.

At the University of Ottawa, we would like to thank Roland Paris of the Centre for International Policy Studies and Luc Juillet of the Graduate School of Public and International Affairs. Both Luc and Roland were enthusiastic about the project as a whole and provided us with financial support for two workshops inspired by the research that is reflected in this volume. We thank Cynthia Brassard-Boudreau for her help in organizing these workshops from beginning to end. We would also like to thank both Graeme Cook and Claire Tousignant for their assistance in running these workshops and Claire also for editorial assistance in preparing the final manuscript.

Thanks are also due to Jonathan Crago at McGill-Queen's University Press, who was supportive of this project from its inception, who was always prompt in answering our many queries about the volume, and who helped us to steer our original plan to fruition. We would also like to thank Will Kymlicka for very helpful advice on book publishing in general and on this book project in particular. Two anonymous reviewers provided very detailed comments on each chapter; the volume is certainly better for their efforts.

This volume was prepared with the financial support of the Canadian Social Sciences and Humanities Research Council (SSHRC) and with the help of a grant from the Canadian Federation for the Humanities and Social Sciences, through the Aid to Scholarly Publications Program, using funds provided by SSHRC.

LEGISLATED INEQUALITY

Introduction

PATTI TAMARA LENARD AND CHRISTINE STRAEHLE

Perhaps tired of newspaper headlines announcing that temporary foreign labour migrants in Canada are equivalent to "slaves" or that the programs enabling citizens of developing nations to labour temporarily in Canada are best described as enabling "exploitation express," the Canadian government has recently announced its intention to implement additional protections for these most vulnerable workers. Temporary foreign labourers in Canada are vulnerable for a host of well-rehearsed reasons: they are often poor and uneducated, they often do not speak English or French, they are often geographically removed from the larger community, they are not familiar with Canadian society and the rights to which they are legally entitled, and so on.[2] Concern with their vulnerability has increased along with the number of temporary foreign migrants labouring in Canada, which has expanded at an unprecedented pace over the past decade. For most of Canada's immigration history, temporary labour migrants have formed a small part of the total number of migrants admitted to Canada, most of whom were admitted with the intention of residing in Canada permanently and of becoming Canadian citizens. However, the transition to permanent residency and, ultimately, to citizenship can no longer be taken for granted. Of late, the Canadian government has moved toward increasing the number of temporary labour migrants for economic and political reasons; as several of the contributors to this volume observe, since 2008 the yearly number of admitted temporary migrants has exceeded the yearly number of admitted permanent migrants. The Canadian government has facilitated this transition by reducing the number of

bureaucratic hurdles employers must pass in order to be eligible to
hire temporary foreign workers, by expanding some already existing
temporary labour migration programs, and by introducing new programs that target low-skilled temporary migrants in particular. The
contributors to this volume offer a critical analysis of the programs
themselves, as well as of the general trend toward increasing the
number of temporary foreign migrants labouring in Canada. In particular, the contributors are critical of the government's enthusiasm
for expanding temporary labour migration programs for low-skilled
workers without seriously considering the long-term consequences
of this expansion for either the Canadian labour market or Canadian society more generally.

In this introduction to the volume, we first offer an account of
Canada's immigration strategy in general, followed by an analysis
of the political and economic motivations behind temporary labour
migration programs in Canada. Second, we offer a brief outline of
the programs in operation in Canada, programs that are subject
to detailed consideration in the chapters constituting this volume.
Here, we argue that the rapid expansion of temporary labour migration opportunities represents a major shift in Canadian immigration priorities. Third, we identify several themes that run through
the programs under consideration. As we explain below, the contributors are concerned specifically with the status of low-skilled
temporary foreign labour migrants in Canada, which renders them
vulnerable to exploitation in spite of apparent efforts made to protect them. The exploitation is enabled particularly by the program
provisions that make it very difficult for low-skilled workers to transition to permanent residency and citizenship. Thus low-skilled temporary migrants in Canada occupy a doubly unequal status vis-à-vis,
first, Canadian citizens and, second, high-skilled migrants, who in
most cases are able to attain, and indeed are encouraged to attain,
Canadian citizenship. Because the Canadian government is acting
specifically to increase the number of low-skilled temporary labour
migrants through its temporary work programs, and because these
programs often force these migrants into the bottom stratum of
Canadian society, this volume is concerned with the challenges low-
skilled migrants face in Canada. The contributing authors argue
overwhelmingly that the aggressive attempts to recruit high-skilled

workers to Canada, and to ensure that they stay once they arrive, have diverted attention from the pressing challenges that face low-skilled migrants in Canada. Deploying a range of distinct methodologies that we outline in brief, the authors converge to paint a depressing picture of the lives of low-skilled temporary migrants in Canada and highlight the urgency of working toward improving the conditions that shape their lives while here. Without immediate policy shifts, Canada risks jeopardizing what has otherwise been rightly interpreted as its just and fair immigration regime, which has, at least historically, been identified as a model to emulate.

TEMPORARY LABOUR MIGRATION IN CANADA

Canada is well known as a nation of immigrants. From its founding in 1867, Canadian governments have welcomed and encouraged migration both to expand the boundaries of the nation itself and, more recently, to ensure a vibrant and expanding economy.[3] The migration policies pursued to secure this expansion are of course not unblemished: notably, until the mid-1960s, Canada's immigration policies actively and overtly discriminated against racial and ethnic minorities perceived to be difficult to integrate into the Canadian community. The overt racism was consciously eliminated from Canadian immigration policy in the mid-1960s, partly in response to changing views of racial minorities and their capacity to integrate and partly in response to the "shrinking supply of immigrants from Europe and the rising demand and competition of skilled labour from the United States."[4]

Since the 1960s, independent immigrants[5] to Canada have been selected according to a policy colloquially known as the "points system," according to which potential migrants are assigned "points" for their level of education, for their facility in one or both of the national languages, and for their labour experience in certain designated occupations facing shortages in Canada, to name but the most important desired features. If they can prove that they satisfy enough criteria to accumulate the necessary number of points, migrants are considered for admission to Canada. The purpose of admitting migrants in this way is to ensure that they have the work and language skills they need to be successful in the labour market since labour market integration is believed to be among the best indicators of successful integration over time.[6] Whereas historically Canadian policy interpreted racial difference as an obstacle to successful integration, contemporary policy suggests that integration depends not on racial characteristics but on the capacity of migrants to rapidly join the labour market and, more generally, on the human capital that new immigrants bring to Canada. The purpose of the "points system" is thus twofold: to meet the economic demands of the Canadian labour market, which continues to rely on immigrant labour across a range of industries, and to ensure that migrants have the tools to integrate effectively into the Canadian political community.

Thus, although it would be a mistake to deny the tensions caused by immigration in the past, and even in the present, Canadians are generally proud of the reception offered to migrants who are easily integrated into the nation's social fabric and of the tolerance displayed toward the new ways of life that accompany these migrants. Canada's largest cities – and increasingly smaller ones as well – are defined by their cultural and ethnic diversity. The contributions that immigrants have made, and continue to make, to Canada's public culture, as well as to its economy, are formally recognized in the Multiculturalism Act (passed in 1988) and in Canada's constitutional acknowledgment of its multicultural dimensions. Canada has presented itself as a model for immigrant-receiving nations and has historically been regarded as such by others.

Recent changes to the program give increased jurisdiction to Citizenship and Immigration Canada (CIC) to privilege some applicants over others when they demonstrate skills that are deemed to be in short supply in the Canadian labour market. The changes have a twofold purpose: to better match immigration demand and stated labour needs in Canada and to reduce the backlog of immigrant applications, reported to be 900,000 in 2008.[8] The flexibility given CIC to "fast track" certain applicants is not the only recent policy shift that is intended to make high-skilled migration to Canada attractive. As Delphine Nakache and Sarah D'Aoust observe in their chapter, the expansion of the Provincial/Territorial Nominee Programs, according to which provinces can set criteria for migrants' admission according to their own labour market needs, has in many cases permitted provinces to compete for skilled migrants. In addition, the Canadian Experience Class enables foreign students who have graduated from Canadian universities, as well as skilled workers with experience in Canada, to apply for permanent residency from inside the country (whereas previously they had been required to leave the country in order to apply from outside). These programs are likewise intended to make Canada more competitive in the global market for highly desirable high-skilled workers.

As in the past, the Canadian government has been forced to acknowledge that Canada is competing with many other developed nations for skilled workers – for instance, the United States, the United Kingdom, and Australia – the result of which is policy shifts that are favourable to skilled immigrants: the barriers they face in gaining access to labour markets in wealthy nations are declining fast. Increasingly, these same nations aim to attract migrants with the promise of immediate access to permanent residency and near-immediate access to citizenship. Skilled migrants, then, have many options to choose from, and these options are continuing to improve. Multiple commentators have, of late, applauded the government's decision to expand the opportunities for high-skilled workers in Canada via programs that emphasize their capacity to fill immediate labour shortages (rather than selecting migrants who are more generally able to interact in the Canadian political and economic environment). However, few have raised the issue at the centre of the volume here, namely whether the expansion of *low-skilled* temporary labour migration poses urgent moral challenges that must be addressed.

TEMPORARY LOW-SKILLED LABOUR MIGRATION IN CANADA

Until recently, little attention had been given to the role played by low-skilled temporary labour migrants in Canada, largely because the total number of temporary migrants labouring in Canada had historically been relatively small. The first formal program of temporary labour migration, established in 1966, invited Caribbean citizens (and eventually Mexicans as well) to labour in Canada's agricultural industry; for many years, the number of migrants

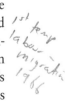

participating in this Seasonal Agricultural Worker Program was small. In the first year of its operation, 264 Jamaican farm workers travelled to labour in the Canadian agricultural industry.[9] After the Canadian government started experimenting with new programs, and expanded those already in operation, the number of all temporary migrants labouring in Canada rose to 250,000 in 2008. Moreover, the proportion of admitted low- versus high-skilled migrants is increasing as well: whereas in 2002 26.3 per cent of admitted workers were low-skilled, by 2008 34 per cent of admitted workers were low-skilled.[10]

Low-skilled temporary foreign workers do not operate in the same highly competitive sphere as do high-skilled workers. Instead, there appears to be an endless availability of low-skilled individuals who are willing and able to migrate from developing countries to fill labour shortages in developed countries. The need for labourers to fill low-skill jobs is great, and the number of workers willing and able to fill them is equally high. The oversupply of low-skilled workers produces the less than favourable conditions imposed on low-skilled temporary workers. Whereas high-skilled migrants are more or less interpreted to be future citizens of Canada, low-skilled migrants are generally encouraged to labour in the Canadian economy and then to return to their home country. Moreover, even the programs that allow low-skilled workers to transition from temporary to permanent status entail procedures for doing so that are often complicated and difficult to navigate. Let us offer a very brief overview of four programs for temporary foreign workers, which are explored in considerably more detail in the individual contributions to this volume.

The Seasonal Agricultural Worker Program. As we said above, the Canadian Seasonal Agricultural Worker Program has been in operation since 1966, when Canada began to invite Caribbean citizens to labour in its agricultural industry on a temporary basis. The program was expanded in 1974 to include Mexican citizens. These workers are permitted to labour in Canadian agriculture for eight months of the year (all visas expire by 15 December), and most do so in Ontario (although the number labouring in other provinces is increasing). They are permitted to return year after year, but whether they can do so is largely at the discretion of employers, who are permitted to request specific workers. The workers are generally not permitted to travel with their family, and historically preference has been given to labourers who have a family back home and who are therefore motivated to return to their country of origin upon completion of their contract. The program is operated on a bilateral basis (i.e., between Canada and each sending country), and the sending countries are intimately involved in running the program, as Patricia Tomic and Ricardo Trumper's chapter well illustrates. Governments of sending countries recruit labourers, ensure that the labourers are eligible to travel (e.g., by confirming that they have passed the requisite medical exams), and ensure that labourers leave Canada at the conclusion of their contracts. Although the program started small, it has been growing. Fewer than 300 workers entered Canada in 1966. By the mid-1980s over 6,000 were entering on a yearly basis, and by the mid-1990s approximately 12,000 were doing so. During the first decade of the twenty-first century, nearly 20,000 temporary foreign migrants participated in this scheme on a yearly basis.[11]

The Live-in Caregiver Program. The Live-in Caregiver Program (LCP) invites (mainly) women to provide domestic care to Canadian families. Caregivers are required to live in a family's home and to provide domestic care services, often to children and to the elderly. In exchange for providing live-in domestic care for a period of either twenty-four months or 3,900 hours over four years, domestic caregivers are permitted to transition to permanent residency and eventually to citizenship. The number of work permits issued by CIC under this program illustrates the LCP's popularity and the demand from Canadian families to hire a caregiver: CIC issued 21,489 caregiver work permits in 2006, compared to 10,148 in 2002 and 5,942 in 2000.[12] Also, according to CIC, most caregivers reach permanent citizenship: data from CIC show that between 2002 and 2009 the number of caregivers who received permanent residency rose from 3,063 to 6,272,[13] and estimates predict that 10,000 women will receive permanent residency through the LCP in each of the next ten years. Finally, government statistics show that 90 per cent of caregivers apply for permanent residency and that 98 per cent of them are successful.[14]

Pilot Project for Occupations Requiring Lower Levels of Formal Training. The Low-Skill Pilot Project began in 2002 as an expansion of the Temporary Foreign Worker Program (TFWP). In operation since 1973, the TFWP has historically targeted skilled workers, ranging from engineers to doctors to academics.[15] However, in response to labour shortages in industries that rely on low-skilled workers, the government expanded the program to enable Canadian employers to recruit low-skilled temporary labour migrants. Initially, employers wishing to hire such migrants under this scheme were required to meet fairly stringent criteria demonstrating their need for these workers (e.g., by following specific procedures to advertise jobs to Canadians and by providing evidence of their inability to fill jobs at reasonable wages). Since the pilot project's inception, the government has made it increasingly easy for employers to participate – for example, by extending the validity of visas from twelve to twenty-four months and by designating some occupations as "under pressure," for which work visa requests are formally expedited. The number of such occupations has quickly expanded: in 2007 twelve occupations were designated as under pressure, and one year later another twenty-one jobs were added to the list.[16]

Provincial/Territorial Nominee Programs. As the name suggests, Provincial/Territorial Nominee Programs (PTNPs) depart from the federal administration of temporary foreign labour migration to invite provinces and territories to "have a say about immigration into their territories."[17] Participating provinces and territories are permitted to identify selection criteria according to their own specific needs.[18] The first PTNP began in September 1998 in Manitoba, and the number of migrants participating in these programs across Canada rose quickly, increasing from 500 in 1999 to 22,000 in 2008. The government expects to admit a further 40,000 migrants on PTNP visas annually between 2010 and 2012.[19] Nearly all provinces and territories have developed PTNPs in association with the federal government to fill provincial and territorial labour shortages. For now at least, Alberta admits the largest number of migrants under this scheme.

For two reasons, the turn to low-skilled migration may seem to represent a kind of continuation of Canadian migration policy. First, labour demand in Canada is high in industries that employ low-skilled workers; to the extent that Canadian migration policy has been an attempt to respond to economic demands, it continues to do so. Second, it is largely believed that the success of the Canadian multicultural experiment is mostly a result of a system that privileges migrants who are likely to integrate effectively into the labour market. Canadians have historically perceived immigrants as contributors to the economy and to cultural life more generally, and this is largely because Canadian immigration policy has assured that immigrants don't "fall behind," find themselves in the bottom stratum of Canadian society, and end up being resented by nonimmigrant Canadians for occupying that status. The rationale for Canada's selective and targeted immigration policy has thus been the concern for integration of migrants into the Canadian social fabric. If the success of Canadian immigration policy can be attributed to the historical preference for high-skilled, highly educated migrants, if the success is attributed to the facility these migrants have in integrating, and if labour demand presently stems from industries that require low-skilled workers, then it is not inconsistent to resist admitting low-skilled migrants to Canada on a permanent basis and to instead admit them on a temporary basis. Doing so appears at first glance to serve both the economic demands to which migration responds and the integration concerns that certain categories of migrants appear to pose. These are the arguments that are deployed to justify the Canadian government's shift to low-skilled temporary migration.

However, describing the turn to temporary labour migration as consistent with Canada's historical immigration trajectory is deeply misleading for at least three reasons, which are explored by the contributors to this volume. First, the decisions about who to admit to Canada have historically been made by Citizenship and Immigration Canada, which has been guided both by a need to meet the economic demands imposed by the nation's labour market and by a sense of the individuals who can best contribute to the Canadian political community. In contrast, temporary labour migration programs as they are constructed in Canada have put the choice of admitted migrant almost entirely in the hands of prospective employers.[10] Although employers cannot be blamed for desiring migrants who will best contribute to their workforce, they also cannot be held responsible for their failure to select migrants who will contribute *more generally* to the wider Canadian political community. The extent of Canadian immigration policy's success, in other

words, is due largely to the centralized control exercised by the
federal government's careful selection strategies; a decentralized,
employer-based approach risks undermining this success. Second,
historically, immigrants to Canada have been thought of as proto-
Canadians – individuals who would in a very short time become
Canadian citizens.[21] As such, they have not only been provided with
resources in order to enable their integration but have also been
welcomed as full contributors to the Canadian community from the
time of their admission. The same is not true of temporary labour
migrants, even though many who first enter on temporary visas do
manage to transition to permanent status and others simply reside in Canada for an extended period of time.[22] In both cases, the
worry is that these citizens or residents effectively occupy a second-
tier status that relegates them to the margins of society. Third, temporary labour migration reintroduces, albeit implicitly, a racial
dimension to Canadian immigration that the state was proud to
dismiss in the mid-1960s. Although in principle temporary labour
migrants can hail from anywhere in the world, in practice they hail
from poor nations whose populations are often racially and ethnic-
ally distinct from the still largely white Canadian population. Thus,
although the Canadian immigration system has for the past half-
decade tried explicitly to remove race as an element in Canadian
immigration, temporary labour migration programs have reintro-
duced it; now, the poorest migrants are racially distinct, and since
(as the volume's authors indicate) many will find ways to remain in
Canada, the root of Canadian immigration success – avoiding the
perception that immigrants are necessarily poor and visibly distinct
– is at risk.[23]

Taken together, these three reasons suggest that the turn to temporary labour migration represents a radical shift in Canadian immigration policy, a shift that poses challenges thus far underacknowledged.
It is the goal of this volume to provide an assessment of the challenges this shift poses. In the next two sections, we summarize the two
challenges the authors identify: first, that low-skilled migrants are
treated as commodities rather than as individuals or even proto-
citizens; and second, that the injustice perpetrated on temporary migrants stems from their inability to access citizenship status
in Canada.

LOW-SKILLED MIGRANTS AS "COMMODITIES"

Although the programs in operation in Canada target a range of sectors, as the authors observe, they nevertheless raise similar concerns. One central concern is the determination to prevent low-skilled migrants from becoming full members of Canada, or at least to make doing so tremendously difficult. In the opening chapter, Nandita Sharma is critical of nationalism in general, and Canadian nationalism in particular, for the casual way that it distinguishes between insiders and outsiders and for the consequent designation of temporary labour migrants as foreign and therefore as legitimately subjected to differential and inferior treatment. The lived experience of temporary labour migrants, permanent residents, and Canadian citizens, all of whom share a geographical space, is defined by how they are categorized by the Canadian state. These categorizations mean that some individuals – citizens and permanent residents – are rights holders and experience the benefits of living in a liberal-democratic state, whereas temporary foreign labour migrants experience Canada as an authoritative state that dictates the conditions of their lives closely and restrictively since they do not have recourse to the same set of rights. Mobility rights are the most immediately affected by stipulations in the programs since temporary workers are mostly tied to the individual employers who hired them. Sharma's opening chapter provocatively concludes with a call for open borders, across which all persons should have the right to move freely. Although this ideal may seem unattainable, it provides a critical vantage point from which to observe the challenges that temporary labour migrants in Canada face as they navigate the restrictive conditions that shape their lives – conditions that seem to be in tension with the principles that define Canadian democracy.

These restrictive conditions derive from the priority given to domestic economic needs in constructing the temporary labour migrant programs and in shaping the conditions under which labour migrants live. Among temporary labour migrants in Canada, participants in the Canadian Seasonal Agricultural Worker Program face the most restrictive working conditions. As Patricia Tomic and Ricardo Trumper explain in chapter 3, there is a kind of tension at the heart of the program. On the one hand, the demand for the program stems from the pressures of capitalism, which necessitate access to "on-demand" workers available to labour in Canadian agriculture at a moment's notice for a predetermined period of time. The implication is that labour ought to be mobile so that it can meet this demand as efficiently as possible, and Tomic and Trumper evocatively describe the movements of labourers as they make their way to meet the demands of the Canadian agricultural market. On the other hand, even as they reflect a kind of mobility – they themselves are moving rapidly to their destinations in response to immediate demands for their labour – their own personal mobility is in fact highly restricted throughout the entire process. They are accompanied to the airport in their country of origin; they are accompanied from the airport of arrival in Canada to their place of work; their movements are highly constrained during their time in Canada as they labour; and finally they are returned to the airport at the expiration of their contract. The treatment to which they are subject provides a sharp illustration of the anxieties that motivate Sharma's introductory chapter.

Migrating agricultural workers, along with all temporary labour migrants, form part of what Kerry Preibisch and Jenna Hennebry refer to in chapter 2 as the "global migration industry," which enables the movement of citizens of developing nations to jobs in Canadian agriculture in particular and around the globe more generally. Workers are treated as commodities – not as human beings – that can be easily moved in response to labour market demand and then "returned" when they are no longer needed. Preibisch and Hennebry observe the pride Canada takes in its "success" in returning workers to their home country once their contract is completed (a reported 98 per cent of workers return home, which compares favourably with the relatively high overstay rate that accompanies a similar program in the United States, described below). The Seasonal Agricultural Worker Program (SAWP) is structured to enable the "circular" movement of labourers and therefore to generate what is often termed the "triple win": Canada benefits from the cheap labour, the workers benefit from having (for them) well-paid jobs on which they can depend, and the sending countries benefit both from the remittances that migrants send home while they labour abroad and from a convenient solution to their own labour market shortages.

Although Preibisch and Hennebry are critical of the program's operation for the ways that it privileges the needs of the employers –
who can choose their employees, for example – they observe that
to the extent that it can be described as successful (and for better or
worse the Canadian model is described as one that should be emulated),[24] its success is dependent on state involvement on both sides
of the border. In contrast, they are critical of one of the newest programs on the Canadian horizon, the Low-Skill Pilot Project (LSPP),
for its "hands-off," uncentralized approach to admitting migrants.
The pilot project is a response to ongoing employer demand for low-
skilled labourers, but it differs from the SAWP in the low level of government involvement in managing the program. Whereas the SAWP
is bilateral, the pilot project is "unilateral"; Canada advertises its
needs, and potential labourers can apply for the available positions.
There is, Preibisch and Hennebry observe, an absence of formal
organizational structures to regulate it and an absence of implemented protective legislation for workers who participate in this
program. Third-party actors have stepped into this administrative
"gap" to coordinate the matching of migrants to available positions,
and these third-party actors generally do not have the interests and
rights of the migrants in mind; it is not surprising that instances of
exploitation of temporary labour migrants have thus increased.

A comparison of the Canadian SAWP with a similar program in
the United States highlights the dangers that Preibisch and Hennebry
observe. The American H-2A visa program is a unilateral program
that invites migrants to labour in the American agricultural industry. In their comparative analysis in chapter 4, Christina Gabriel and
Laura Macdonald observe that the H-2A program's "unilateralism"
means that it is not overseen by the governments of the migrant-
sending states. As a result, the administrative gaps that Preibisch
and Hennebry observe, and into which unscrupulous recruitment
agencies step, emerge in sharp relief in the Canadian pilot project. The working conditions for temporary foreign workers in the
United States are widely known to be tremendously poor; the workers are largely unprotected (since neither the sending country nor
the receiving country has a particular interest in securing the protection of their rights); and the program produces high numbers of
illegal migrants. Participants will enter the underground economy

either because they are not guaranteed the opportunity to return in future years (and they prefer to stay illegally rather than risk being turned away if they ask for readmission), or because the jobs are so poor that it will often prove to be more lucrative to enter the underground economy, or both. The H-2A program, Gabriel and Macdonald observe, is widely perceived to be broken. The American experience with the H-2A program suggests that the Canadian SAWP to some extent may deserve the praise it garners in spite of its many defects. It should also teach us that the lack of administrative oversight of the Canadian pilot project is problematic: because of the absence of regulation, the LSPP may produce the same undesired consequences as does the H-2A program, and it may therefore fail to serve the stated goals of Canadian immigration policy.

The vulnerabilities to which agricultural workers are subject are equally highlighted in chapter 5, by Jenna Hennebry and Janet McLaughlin. Hennebry and McLaughlin focus in particular on the ways the health of temporary migrants who participate in the SAWP or as agricultural labourers as part of the LSPP is compromised by the conditions imposed on them as they labour in Canada. They point to multiple studies that indicate the poor health of migrants in comparison to Canadians more generally. A range of factors produce these poor health outcomes: migrants labour in conditions that are physically challenging; they labour in occupations that have relatively high rates of injury-causing accidents; they often labour in unregulated environments, with little training and insufficient access to protective equipment; they are housed in dwellings that are often genuinely hazardous to the health of migrants (e.g., they often reside in overcrowded and poorly ventilated environments); the regulations that govern the health and safety of temporary migrants are often nonexistent, and their workplaces are irregularly inspected (thus allowing frequent violations); and, importantly, the migrants often feel that their access to employment depends on their willingness to refrain from complaining about these conditions and about any ill health they experience as a result of them. To the extent that the Canadian government insists on hiring temporary workers, they argue, the government must be more scrupulous with respect to protecting migrants from the inhumane conditions they so frequently experience. The industries that employ temporary labour migrants have no incentives to refrain from subjecting them to exploitative conditions; it is the government's job to provide these incentives and thereby to minimize the exploitation of labour migrants who contribute in essential ways to the profitability of the Canadian agricultural industry.

In chapter 6, Christine Hughes focuses directly on the challenges faced by agricultural migrants who labour on farms in Quebec as participants in the Low-Skill Pilot Project. Like Preibisch and Hennebry, she is critical of the absence of oversight, which, in her view, enables the abusive treatment to which farm workers are often subject. Most workers are grateful for the opportunity to labour in Canada due to the real benefits they and their families derive from their participation. Many acknowledge that the long hours and challenging working conditions are part of the contract they have signed. However, some are also willing to express dissatisfaction with the conditions in which they labour, and a few are willing to publicly accuse their employers of exploitation or rights violations. These rights violations and exploitative conditions are confirmed by the information Hughes gathered from additional questioning of Guatemalan consular officials who suggested that migrants are pressed into offering positive evaluations of their Canadian experience out of fear that their critical responses may result in their ejection from future participation in the program. Hughes ultimately concludes, with Tomic and Trumper, that the challenges that migrants face stem from the employer-driven nature of the program. The program emerged in the first place to respond to employer demands, and the demands of industry are presented as an explanation for why government refrains from intervening to more effectively protect the rights of migrants labouring in Canadian industries.

LOW-SKILLED MIGRANTS AND THE PROBLEM OF MEMBERSHIP[25]

Above, we noted the expansion of Provincial/Territorial Nominee Programs, which allow provinces to set criteria that migrants must fulfil in order to be eligible to labour in a particular province. In most cases, migrants are required to meet criteria that designate them as "high-skilled" workers. Yet, as explained earlier, an increasing number of the workers admitted to these programs are low-skilled; as in other developed nations, Canada faces labour short-ages in both high- and low-skilled sectors. As Delphine Nakache and Sarah D'Aoust observe in chapter 7, although the programs do reflect specific provincial and territorial labour market needs, they are more or less united in reflecting a preference both for admit-ting high-skilled workers with the promise of permanent residency and citizenship and for admitting low-skilled workers on a limited, temporary basis. This policy priority is indicated by the restrictions placed on low-skilled migrants, which include the fact that they are not permitted to travel with their families if they cannot prove that they can support them and the refusal to grant the family members of low-skilled workers open work permits to enable them to provide for themselves (as is the case for the family members of high-skilled workers). Even so, low- or semi-skilled migrants to some provinces (e.g., Manitoba and Saskatchewan) have easier access to Canadian citizenship than others, and Nakache and D'Aoust are critical of these differences. They question the complexities that make it dif-ficult for migrants to know whether they are eligible for citizen-ship as well as the bureaucratic hurdles migrants must overcome in order to apply for citizenship in comparison to high-skilled workers. These hurdles create a hierarchy between migrants who are permit-ted to stay and those who are not rather than a system in which all migrants who arrive on temporary visas are able to apply for Can-adian citizenship.

That said, as Tom Carter observes in his comparison in chapter 8 of the Temporary Foreign Worker Program and the Provincial/Territorial Nominee Programs, for all of the faults attributed to the PTNPs, they fare relatively well in comparison to the TFWP, espe-cially as respects those low-skilled migrants admitted to the TFWP. Whereas migrants admitted to the TFWP are tied to one specific employer and have access to a relatively limited number of addi-tional rights while in Canada (and the specific rights to which they are entitled are difficult to discern, as Carter outlines), PTNP par-ticipants are instead typically entitled to those rights and privileges to which permanent residents are entitled, including those that are intended to facilitate and encourage integration into the larger Can-adian community. Since they are admitted to labour in a particular sector, rather than for a particular employer, their mobility is not constrained, unlike the mobility of migrants admitted to the TFWP. That PTNP participants are admitted, however, to a particular province, which is intending to fill specific labour shortages, has in practice translated into the provision of extensive services and benefits to them as an enticement to stay in the province to which they are initially admitted. Smaller provinces, which have not historically been immigrant destinations, are putting considerable effort into selecting immigrants who can be enticed to stay. Manitoba, for example, which has the longest-running and largest PTNP, puts considerable effort into selecting migrants who will have reason and motivation to reside permanently in Manitoba and then into providing them with the integration services that will facilitate their doing so. At least for now, as Carter reports, most surveyed newcomers in fact choose to remain in Manitoba as their community and cultural ties grow. That said, the PTNPs are still difficult to access for low-skilled migrants; except for Manitoba, the provinces and territories (which are permitted to delineate their own selection and program criteria) forbid low-skilled workers who are admitted to labour as part of the TFWP to apply for permanent residency through a transition to participation in the PTNPs.[26]

The membership problem may appear to be solved with the Live-in Caregiver Program since participants in this program are admitted with the knowledge that, as long as they fulfil their contractual obligations, they will be permitted to naturalize and, if they desire, to choose employment outside of the domestic care industry.[27] Like agricultural workers, they can be deported in the event of job loss; however, the timeframe in which they are required to find new employment in such cases is increasingly reasonable. As Abigail Bakan and Daiva Stasiulis observe in chapter 9, domestic caregivers in Canada report fewer experiences of discrimination than those who labour in Asian countries;[28] they attribute this relatively higher satisfaction to Canada's commitment to democratic and liberal principles. Moreover, as they acknowledge, domestic workers participate in the project as a means to an end – that is, with the purpose of gaining access to the larger pool of rights that accompanies citizenship status. Yet, they argue, the kind of restrictive legal conditions to which domestic caregivers are subject – most notably the requirement to live in the employer's household and the stipulation that every change in employer needs to be approved through a new work permit – cannot be justified in a free and democratic society. They advocate the removal of the live-in requirement for domestic workers as a way to capture the benefits of the program (caregiving for children and the elderly) while reducing some of the precariousness and vulnerability that now accompany domestic work. Otherwise, as Sharma also notes in the first chapter, Canadian immigration policy is aiding and abetting human rights violations by permitting the range of rights restrictions to which domestic caregivers are subject until they have fulfilled their contractual obligations.

As Sara Torres and her co-authors observe in chapter 10, domestic caregivers are indeed making a deliberate decision: they are choosing to escape poverty by participating in Canada's Live-in Caregiver Program despite its flaws. The (mainly) women who participate are often "underemployed" in the sense that they are often educated and skilled migrants who choose to participate in the caregiver program as a way to migrate permanently to Canada and, in time, sponsor their family members to join them. They often intend to transition out of the caregiver industry once their contractual obligations have been met. Yet even this transition is complicated by the challenges they face in entering the larger Canadian labour market. Those who have skills often put these skills on hold while they work as caregivers; as a result, when they enter the labour market, they are perceived to have experience that is no longer "up-to-date." Thus, once they have completed their contractual obligations, they find that their employment options are limited; many women find that they are effectively constrained to labour permanently in the poorly remunerated care sector. Similarly, the unnecessary delays in having their restricted visas converted into open work visas force women to continue labouring as caregivers while their applications to transition to permanent residency are considered. In general, Torres and her co-authors are critical of the Canadian government's transparent unwillingness to facilitate caregivers' effective integration into Canadian society once they have fulfilled their contractual obligations. The consequences of the government's inaction are ultimately felt in near perpetuity by ex-caregivers: the struggles they face construct trajectories of inequality that shape the futures of these women as long as they remain in Canada, which for most of them is for the rest of their lives. It is a mistake, in other words, to focus exclusively on the experiences of domestic caregivers – and of temporary workers in general – as they labour in their "temporary" positions. Torres and her co-authors highlight the importance of paying attention to the quality of the transition these workers make to permanent status: the (generally poor) future economic and social status of these workers is shaped almost irrevocably by their experience as temporary workers, an experience that as presently constructed translates into perpetuating their disadvantage in relation to high-skilled migrants admitted as permanent and in relation to Canadians more generally.

Both contributions to the volume that consider the Live-in Caregiver Program notice the ways that the program marginalizes its participants, in large part by reinforcing already existing gender and racial hierarchies. As Bakan and Stasiulis observe, domestic caregivers are nearly always women, and their employment typically permits a wealthier woman to continue to participate in the workforce. Additionally, today they are nearly always migrants from Asia, and so the dynamics in the household are such that they reinforce racial hierarchies; "brown" women labour in "white" homes. While labouring as caregivers, moreover, they often sustain two households: their own (in the home country) and the one in which they labour. The household, as Bakan and Stasiulis observe, is both a private environment and a workplace, which opens the possibility of employer abuse. The multiple dimensions along which caregivers are vulnerable to exploitation and discrimination also occupy Torres and her co-authors; domestic caregivers are women, they are often visible minorities, they are often poor (and from the global South), and they are often without social support.

As Jill Hanley and her co-authors observe in chapter 11, however, migrant organizations are working hard to protect the rights of both temporary and permanent migrants, with various levels of success. Temporary migrants are vulnerable, they observe, given the extent to which they (and their families) depend on their jobs to survive, the isolation and precariousness of their labour, and their apprehension with respect to their temporary status, a status that means they can be forced to return to their home countries at a moment's notice. All of these factors are obstacles to the effective organization of migrant workers into collectivities able to fight for the rights that they are often denied in practice, if not also in principle. Hanley and her co-authors consider the progress that has been made in organizing to protect the rights of domestic caregivers as well as the progress of those who participate in the SAWP and the Low-Skill Pilot Project. There is a host of organizations that focus their energies on multiple aspects of the migrant experience: labour conditions, conditions of migration, and the provision of social support to migrants who are often labouring in isolated and isolating environments. They suggest that the most pressing issue facing low-skilled migrants is ultimately their temporary status; without permanent status, their rights will continue to be at risk, and their motivation to challenge rights violations will be limited by their fear of deportation and therefore of losing jobs that are vital to their own livelihood and to the livelihood of their families.

METHODOLOGICAL STRATEGIES

The editors of the volume, trained in applied moral philosophy,[29] asked the contributors to consider whether there are morally troubling aspects of temporary labour migration policies as they operate in Canada and, if there are such aspects, to consider what *should* be done to remedy them. Our own perspective can be described as liberal-democratic, by which we mean to signal a commitment to a standard set of liberal and democratic norms that inform the way individuals should be treated by the state in which they live. In particular, we are guided by two simple premises: first, that all individuals are of equal moral worth; and second, that all individuals possess a right to participate in the political structures that govern their lives. From these premises, it may appear unsurprising that our starting point was a concern with the highly restricted set of rights to which temporary labour migrants are entitled. These restrictions suggested to us, first, that temporary labour migrants are being systematically denied the equal treatment entailed by a commitment to equal moral worth and, second, that they are clearly denied the opportunity to be self-determining in the way that democratic norms demand. The purpose of this volume is to offer a forum in which social scientists have an opportunity to examine the four temporary foreign worker programs currently in place in Canada from this perspective, thereby either assuaging or bolstering our concerns.

We have been troubled to see that our initial hypothesis finds significant support from across the range of disciplines and methodologies represented in this volume. That said, the critical conclusions that we present are more powerful for having been reached by scholars working in a host of disciplines across the social sciences. We invited them to provide the unique perspective of their disciplinary focus on this new and difficult moment in Canadian immigration history, and we did so without preformed views about the conclusions they might draw; these conclusions were largely not premeditated by us. The resulting volume is thus truly extraordinary. From a series of distinct methodological perspectives, the overwhelming conclusion is that these programs are flawed in precisely the ways we had worried based on our initial normative perspective.

The authors were asked to introduce their chapter by outlining the perspective taken in their analysis. Let us here preview the dominant methods readers will encounter as they travel through the chapters. Several of the authors take an intersectional approach to their analysis: intersectional analysis focuses on the marginalization experienced by individuals who find themselves "at the intersection of multiple categories of oppression."[30] These individuals – in the cases described here, poor foreigners (Sharma) and visible minority women (Bakan and Stasiulis; Hughes; Torres et al.) – face distinct difficulties, not simply as women, as racial minorities, or as members of the poor but also as individuals who inhabit more than one of these marginalized spaces at a time.[31] Many of the authors present data they have collected via qualitative research, including via extensive interviews (Torres et al.; Tomic and Trumper), participant observation techniques (Hughes), and critical ethnographic approaches (Preibisch and Hennebry; Hennebry and McLaughlin). The purpose of these techniques is, as much as possible, to understand the lives of individuals who live in circumstances distinct from our own and to represent them fairly and honestly – that is, to produce an "in-depth understanding" of the complexities of the lives that others live.[32] As these scholars observe, migrant workers live at the margins of Canadian society politically and socially as well as often geographically;

their research is an attempt to bring the "lived experience" of these workers to the consciousness of Canadians, who in general do not encounter those migrants who contribute such essential services to the Canadian economy. Several of the contributors engage in policy analysis, the goal of which is to evaluate the intended effects of policy, the actual effects of policy, and the unintended consequences of policy (Carter; Nakache and D'Aoust). These policy effects are evaluated in relation to Canadian immigration history; as this introduction has indicated, these policy shifts toward temporary labour migration mark a radical change in the Canadian immigration trajectory. Several chapters reflect what has been termed the "comparative turn in political science,"[33] according to which there is much to be gained from comparing in some cases the programs themselves (Hanley et al.) and in other cases the Canadian experience and the global experience (Gabriel and Macdonald; Lenard). On the one hand, these comparative evaluations illustrate the domains where Canada is doing well when its programs are compared with similar programs around the world and thus where Canada is a model to be emulated and where it has work to do. On the other hand, internal comparison of the programs' outcomes with Canadian's historically adopted immigration objectives suggests that Canada is moving away from the ideals that guided immigration in the past. The result is a volume critical of Canadian temporary labour migration programs, *even though* it must be admitted that in terms of global comparison, Canada comes closer than most nations to living up to liberal-democratic principles.

CONCLUSION

The chapters of this volume are motivated by the fact that the Canadian economy is increasingly turning toward temporary low-skilled migrants. With increasing frequency, these migrants fill jobs that are "permanent" in the sense that they are able to be filled only by reliance on a continuous stream of migrants. There is no sense that at some future moment, independently of migration, the Canadian economy will produce labourers to fill these positions. In light of this, the contributors express concern that the long-term impact of relying on temporary labour migration is unknown and unexplored, and they persuasively argue that more needs to be done to address these questions and the problems raised by temporary foreign worker programs. It is essential that we consider the wisdom of increasing reliance on temporary labour migrants, many of whom will ultimately reside permanently in Canada. Patti Tamara Lenard's concluding chapter invites readers to consider the Canadian programs in comparative perspective; there is much to learn from the ways other nations have either integrated or failed to integrate low-skilled migrant workers who arrive, initially, to labour on a temporary basis. Among the lessons to be drawn from the comparative analysis she presents, three stand out: (1) the right to access membership is essential to protecting migrants' rights during the time that they labour temporarily; (2) liberal-democratic states are limited in the extent to which they can "force" temporary migrants to leave since the principles that underpin liberal democracies grant increasing numbers of rights to temporary migrants over time; and (3) low-skilled migrants who are admitted on a temporary basis but transition to permanent status over time are disadvantaged by their inability to access the host of integration services and organizations that are more standardly available to permanent residents (by the time temporary migrants are "eligible" to be treated as permanent migrants, these services are difficult, if not impossible, to access, and thus they "integrate" less well than do migrants who do have access to the services). These lessons reveal that the anxieties raised by the contributors to this volume must be urgently heeded if Canada takes the premise of its history and of its previous immigration legislation seriously, namely that there ought to be no barrier to integration for those who come and work for the benefit of themselves and the Canadian nation.

The "Difference" that Borders Make: "Temporary Foreign Workers" and the Social Organization of Unfreedom in Canada

NANDITA SHARMA

INTRODUCTION

Throughout my years of teaching courses on social inequality, I have begun by asking students to think about the social processes that result in enormous disparities in people's ability to gain a livelihood and, consequently, to have secure access to food, shelter, good health, peace, joy, and even hope. Many of my students are aware of the importance of racism and sexism in creating these disparities. However, they are not quite sure what forms contemporary practices of racism or sexism take since many of the more recognized of these practices have been prohibited by law. In short, they want to know *how* discrimination is organized in a liberal-democratic society such as Canada, where citizens who are nonwhite, who are women, or who are other Others have (relatively) recently gained many of the civil rights and entitlements long denied them, including citizenship. When thinking about this question, students usually offer one of two main responses: some try to take comfort in the evolutionary view of ever-expanding civil rights, believing that those rights that are still denied to some will one day be bequeathed to them by a future, more enlightened government, whereas others believe that the various civil rights movements did indeed vanquish racism or sexism from the world. These latter students also believe that anyone who says otherwise is falsely crying racism or sexism for their own self-interest. Rehearsing the views of neoliberals, they say that any existing inequalities are the result of individual defects of personality or will.

To have students analyze their disparate questions and views, I ask the class to think about nationalism as a practice that organizes substantial inequalities. I do so to allow students to examine nationalism as one of the ideological (and policy) vehicles through which racialized and gendered inequalities are achieved in an era of so-called colour-blind and sex-blind state policies. I ask students to think about the limits of civil rights (i.e., the equalization of rights among "citizens" of a given national state) and the fundamental inability of noncitizens to remedy the discrimination caused by nationalism within the present system. I give students the example of how highly differential (im)migration statuses shape inequalities to show that one's life is significantly affected by the category in which one is placed, with the categories ranging from "citizen" to "illegal" or even "stateless" person.[1]

The most common response is astonishment and, at times, annoyance. For most of my students, nationalism is seen not as an ideology with the material force to produce significant inequalities. Instead, their identity as a national citizen (of one or another state) is something without which they cannot imagine their world or even themselves. Far from being a practice worthy of condemnation, nationalism is viewed as a source of pride for both their individual and group sense of self. It is certainly not considered to be harmful. This is as true for students from oppressed groups as for those from dominant groups. Following Thomas Hobbes, most students view the nation-state form of governance as necessary for keeping violent chaos at bay. Even after being shown the growing body of evidence documenting the effects of national forms of discrimination on wage levels, on access to healthcare, housing, and education, and on a sense of stability and security, many students believe that these disparities are simply natural, even desired, divisions. Their tautological argument is based primarily on the nationalist idea that the state, as the "representative" of the "nation," is responsible only for "its own citizens," not for "foreign noncitizens" (who, it is said, should rely on "their own" nation-state). After all, they correctly assert, not everyone can be "Canadian" (or any other nationality).

My point in discussing my students' views on the social inequalities organized through nationalism is to draw attention to the fact that despite the *acknowledgment* of gross inequalities between people falling into the two rough social categories of "citizen" and "foreigner," the differences between them are more often than not understood to be *just*. Unlike racism, which has largely become a term of (at least public) disapprobation since the end of the murderous first half of the twentieth century, and unlike sexism, which the feminist movement has long worked hard to make a pejorative identification, being a *nationalist* continues to be seen not only as unproblematic but also as a point of pride, even by those who otherwise believe quite strongly in social justice. This is of course wholly unsurprising. What Benedict Anderson calls "nation-ness" – that is, the belief that all people naturally belong to one or another "nation," one whose membership is always limited and one whose state (whether it currently exists or is awaited) is seen as sovereign over the separate affairs of each "imagined community" and the territory it claims – remains "the most universally legitimate value in the political life of our time."[2] It is this nationalist hegemony that results in the serious lack of attention paid to the effects of nationalism in the stratification of social formations.

Having said this, I am not arguing that racism and sexism are unimportant or that they no longer have any effect simply because the Canadian state has prohibited some of the practices associated with them and offered some social services to their victims or because most people recoil at being labelled a racist or sexist. Nor do I mean to imply that racism or sexism is any less important to the organization of our world than is nationalism. Not only are the practices of racism and sexism fundamental to the social organization of our world, but history has also shown us the danger of establishing a hierarchy of oppression, exploitation, and injustice. Instead, my purpose in talking about our general inability to recognize nationalism as a form of discrimination is twofold.

First, although racism, sexism, and nationalism are each comprised of a clearly defined set of ideas, it is impossible to fully understand any of them without taking an intersectional approach. Indeed, Étienne Balibar well notes that the ideas of "race" and "nation" are rarely very far apart.[3] And as feminist scholars have pointed out, neither racism nor nationalism can be fully comprehended without an examination of the forms of oppression and exploitation organized through gendered social relationships. Such insights are important not only for the scholarship on racism, sexism, and nationalism but also for the struggle for justice.

My second purpose in talking about nationalism is not only to see the forms of discrimination it organizes but also to have our understanding of nationalism (and racism and sexism) extend *beyond* seeing nationalism (and racism and sexism) as *only* a form of discrimination, one that can be remedied through the extension of civil rights (i.e., the rights of "citizens"). Instead, nationalism (and racism and sexism) is central to our *global* set of social *relationships*. Today, nationalism (and racism and sexism) is a key organizing basis for the existence of the always violent relationships of capitalist production. In short, fomenting, legislating, and systematically entrenching nationalist, racist, and sexist ideological practices are central to how capitalist social relations are *done*.

Nationalism (and racism and sexism) is central to the subordination of those classified by the Canadian nation-state as "temporary foreign workers." People placed within this state category are positioned not only as *noncitizens* in Canada but also as *nonimmigrants*: neither are they "citizens" nor are they "permanent residents" (i.e., "immigrants"). It is through this categorical slight of hand that "temporary foreign workers" can legally be tied to a particular employer as a condition of their entry and continued (lawful) stay in Canada. In short, "temporary foreign workers" are *made* unfree by Canadian immigration law. Yet, despite the fact that it is the differentiation of national status that organizes the unfreedom of "temporary foreign workers," nationalism is still not understood to be a leading factor in the creation – and continuity – of these conditions. In this chapter, I try to rectify this by looking at how the *absence* of an understanding of nationalism works to organize and reproduce inequalities. In particular, I look at how those classified as "temporary foreign workers" in Canada are represented as part of a "foreign" workforce instead of as an unfree section of the workforce available to employers in Canada.

Accounting for the absence of nationalism from our understanding of the subordination of "temporary foreign workers" in Canada is a necessary corrective to much of the scholarship in this area. Most studies situate the oppression and exploitation of "temporary foreign workers" within patriarchal and/or racist social relations, even when their focus is on the denial of citizenship status to those so classified. This has consequences for the demands made to end their subordination, the most often heard of which is the demand for the extension of citizenship (and permanent residency) to "temporary foreign workers." Although this would no doubt help the current group of "temporary foreign workers," such a solution prohibits an understanding (and critique) of the entire citizenship regime and its foundation in the nation-state's sovereign right (as enshrined in international law) to legally differentiate between citizens and those it categorizes as always already subordinate "nonmembers." Without a challenge to nation-state sovereignty, nation-states will remain empowered to continue to draw lines between people through their imposition of differential national statuses. This line may be pushed farther out (or contracted farther inward), but the line itself will continue to distinguish between those with rights and those without.

In contrast to this liberal view, I argue that the institution of citizenship is *fundamentally incapable* of meeting the demands for social justice made by those who find themselves cast as "foreigners." In this view, national citizenship is more than a political category: it is a mark of one's particular position within nationalized labour markets and, just as important, within the global market for labour power.[4] Citizenship regimes rely on the creation of "foreigners" to ensure competition throughout the system and to obtain legitimacy for the inequalities that result.

I begin my discussion of the difference that national borders make – and of the differential statuses they produce – with an examination of the ideological character of ever more restrictive immigration policies in Canada and the simultaneous and increasing use of "temporary foreign workers" programs. I discuss how such programs rely on the social organization of nationalized differences for their legitimacy and their ability to depoliticize the enormous gulf between the official narrative of "Canadianness" and life as it is actually experienced in Canada. I conclude with a discussion of the emergence of a politics of "no borders," which demands that people be given the freedom to move and, concurrently, the freedom not to be forcibly moved. Such a demand challenges our acceptance of the differentiation among human beings in terms of their receipt of rights and the stuff of life that is inherent in policies according them differential statuses of citizenship and (im)migration.

IDEOLOGICAL BORDERS

Since 1973 the Canadian state has considerably expanded both the scope and the scale of its "temporary foreign workers" programs. During this period, its discourse on immigration – alongside the discourse of the corporate-owned media and of the majority of public opinion poll respondents – has consistently pointed to immigration and immigrants as a serious "problem" for "Canadians."[5] A central theme in this anti-immigrant discourse is concern over the (falsely reported) negative effects of immigrants on the labour market position of "Canadians." Yet, although the dominant discourse in Canada has posited that immigration ought to be restricted so that "Canadian jobs" can be kept for "Canadians," the numbers of people officially admitted to Canada has markedly increased.[6] This is especially so in the case of people recruited to come to Canada specifically to work in the paid labour force. How do we make sense of this discrepancy between rhetoric and reality?

One way is to examine the categories of (im)migration through which people have been admitted. The most striking shift since the mid-1970s is that fewer and fewer people are admitted as "immigrants" – that is, as permanent residents. At the same time, there has been an enormous increase in the number of people admitted with the status of "temporary foreign worker." As of 1976 the majority (53 per cent, or 69,368 persons) of all (im)migrants entering Canada who stated their intention to work in the paid labour force were given the status of "temporary foreign worker." This figure compares persons admitted across the independent class, the family class, the refugee class, and the nonimmigrant class of "temporary foreign workers." Only 47 per cent (61,461 persons) were given the rights of permanent residency. By 2004 this figure had jumped both proportionately as well as numerically so that 65 per cent (228,677 persons) were given the status of "temporary foreign worker," whereas only 35 per cent (124,829 persons) came with the rights of permanent residency.[7]

This shift is even more noticeable when one compares only those in the independent class (who are admitted specifically for their labour power) with "temporary foreign workers" (who are also admitted for their labour power). In 2004 78 per cent (228,677 persons) of all those admitted specifically to work in the labour force were admitted as "temporary foreign workers," whereas only 22 per cent (64,374 persons) were granted permanent residency.[8] Thus the vast majority of people officially migrating to Canada since the mid-1970s have been made to work with the status of "temporary foreign worker."[9] For the most part, then, Canada's immigration system has moved away from admitting people as permanent residents and toward admitting people with only temporary, and largely unfree, status (which I discuss below). Canada has, in fact, a permanent and expanding system of "temporary foreign worker" recruitment.

In this regard, it is significant that although the numbers of "temporary foreign workers" are far greater than those of "immigrants," there is little, if any, attention paid to people who are placed in the former category within the anti-immigrant discourse. Instead, attention is disproportionately paid to those who come as *immigrants* (i.e., those who come with rights). If anything – and in glaring contrast both to those admitted under the refugee class, the independent (or skilled-worker) class, or the family class and to those with the status of "illegal" entrant – there is often an articulated demand for more and more people to be brought to Canada as "temporary foreign workers."[10] Indeed, even some self-styled advocates for (im)migrants argue that admitting people as "temporary foreign workers" is a "solution" to the "problem" of "illegal" migration to Canada.

Limits to (im)migration, then, lie in the ability of states not so much to restrict people's mobility as to restrict their rights and freedom once they are *within* nationalized labour markets. Anti-immigrant discourse, far from excluding new (im)migrants coming to Canada, has enabled national states to reorganize their nationalized labour markets in order to *include* a group of "temporary foreign workers" who are made vulnerable to employers' demands through their subordinated status as "temporary," as "foreigners," and as legally enforced unfree workers. The simultaneous presence of anti-immigration discourses and increases in the number of people entering Canada as noncitizens without permanent, full status is therefore not at all contradictory but instead reflects complementary processes. As Ghassan Hage comments, "anti-immigration discourse, by continually constructing the immigrants as unwanted, works precisely at maintaining [their] economic viability to ... employers. They are best wanted as 'unwanted.'"[11] However, it is crucial to recognize that, in this case, the "unwanted" are those who have the rights of permanent residents and that what is "wanted" is a legally subordinate workforce of unfree migrant workers made to labour as "temporary foreign workers." Placing people in this category gives both the state and employers greater power over this group of persons, the kind of power they cannot exercise over "citizens" and "permanent residents."

At the current historical juncture, when international migration is occurring at unprecedented levels (the United Nations estimates that every year over 200 million people migrate across national borders),[12] nationalism, with its legitimization of the subordination of those classified as "foreigners," is a driving force for neoliberal capitalist globalization. Whereas legally organized racism (discrimination against negatively racialized people) and sexism have mostly been defined as contradicting the "values" of "multicultural" and "liberal" states, such as Canada, nationalism continues to provide a legal avenue for making sharp distinctions among persons. As a result, national states and employers can continue to treat those cast as "foreigners" as unworthy of rights. The "global apartheid" that border control practices construct, therefore, exists not only at the level of *keeping out* migrants but also at the level of their "differential inclusion" as lawfully subordinated persons.[13]

This practice is brutally captured in the current "debate" (held largely between select academics and officials of either national states or international governmental organizations, such as the World Bank) about the "need" for a "trade-off" between the *numbers* of migrants that states admit and the *rights* that states afford them. The narrative used to legitimate such an approach goes something like this: national states, at least in the "rich world," can continue to admit migrants only if they further restrict their rights. Ironically, this approach to "managed migration" is a tacit recognition by national states that restrictive immigration and border controls are, in fact, ideological. Ultimately, what such approaches call for is the further entrenchment in the law of the idea that the rights and entitlements attached to the categories of "permanent resident" and "citizen" can be denied through the simple act of casting some persons as "temporary foreign workers."

In Canada unfree "temporary foreign workers" labour in a range of occupational sectors: they provide both relatively low-cost, low-skilled labour power and high-cost, high-skilled labour power (as well as various combinations thereof). However, important gendered and racialized differentiations are made between those who fill such occupations. Overall, men are highly overrepresented in professional occupations, whereas women are concentrated and overrepresented in the service – particularly the personal service – occupations, such as domestic work.[14] This is not atypical of the distribution of women and men within the Canadian labour market at large. Thus it seems that the "temporary foreign workers" regime reflects and further entrenches the gendered division of labour already in operation in Canada. Likewise, this system operates in a racialized manner. Consistently, in (relatively) high-skilled occupations, the vast majority of workers arrive from other "rich world" countries, whereas within certain of the lowest-paying occupations with the poorest documented working conditions, people from the "majority world," particularly women, predominate. Canada's "temporary foreign workers" regime, therefore, further exacerbates the already racialized labour market existing in Canada.

The category of "temporary foreign worker" shows how the maintenance of national borders occurs not only at the boundary between the Canadian nation-state and others but also *within* "Canadian" space. (Im)migration policy thus needs to be understood not only as a policy that allows the Canadian state to interface with other national states (and with the "nationals" of these states) through an international regime of border controls but also as a crucial part of shaping a society imagined as "Canada." In particular, immigration policy is a crucial component of how the Canadian state shapes a market for labour within its territorial boundaries. That it is able to do so with very little political disturbance is a testament to the naturalization of the "difference" between people categorized as "nationals" and those labelled "foreigners."

IMMIGRATION POLICY AND THE SOCIAL ORGANIZATION OF "NATIONAL" DIFFERENCE

Ideas of "difference" have their own materiality. Indeed, the process of capital accumulation has long relied on social and legal differentiations between people. The supposedly innate differences between women and men, between differently racialized persons, and between persons seen through the nationalist lens of belonging versus not belonging in "society" have all had an enormous effect on how one is positioned within the social relations of global capitalism. With the advent of national states and the implementation of border controls, it is immigration policies that have worked to materialize and regulate these differences.

This work has been done through the placement of people in hierarchically ranked categories of national belonging and not-belonging. This categorization has occurred in no small part through the differential gendering and racializing of migrating bodies, so much so that being granted citizenship or immigration (i.e., permanent residency) status has not meant that one is treated as a member of the "Canadian nation." A large majority of the research into Canadian immigration policies has focused on how sexist and racist practices continue to mark the boundaries of the Canadian "nation."[15] However, although the identification of someone as "foreign" is not necessarily affected by one's citizenship and (im)migration status, I wish to show that there are significant differences between being cast as a "foreigner" in Canada but holding the rights of citizenship or immigration (i.e., permanent residency) and being *legally* defined as a "foreigner" in Canada, as are "temporary foreign workers." That is to say, (im)migration status matters.

I begin this section, therefore, with an obvious statement of fact: "temporary foreign workers" are a creation of the Canadian state. That is, "temporary foreign workers" in Canada exist within a state bureaucratic classification scheme designed to hold people in a *particular* relationship of exploitation and social/political subordination.

Indeed, the category of "temporary foreign worker" was created precisely to produce this subordination and continues to be used in expanded form to ensure this outcome. This subordination is two-fold: "temporary foreign workers" are denied the ability to claim a large number of state-granted *rights and entitlements* to which those within the categories of either "citizen" or "permanent resident" have access. For instance, the vast majority of "temporary foreign workers" cannot claim unemployment insurance or provincial welfare assistance, even though they do contribute to these programs either directly through payroll deductions or less directly through general income taxes. This severely limits the ability of "temporary foreign workers" to decommodify their labour by accessing a social wage that would provide them with financial alternatives to working in the paid labour force.

Moreover, "temporary foreign workers" are legally denied some of the protections granted to "citizens" or "permanent residents." The most glaring example of this is how the Canadian state is able to legally bind "temporary foreign workers" to particular employers, in essence rendering them unfree. A result of their being tied to their employer and to a particular occupation is that they are also tied to a particular geographical location. If dissatisfied with a particular job or occupation or geographical location – for instance, when the wages one is paid are poor and there are better jobs elsewhere, when the working conditions or housing conditions on offer are substandard, or when the employer is not fulfilling his or her part of the labour contract or is being abusive – "temporary foreign workers" *cannot*, for the most part, leave their employment and seek alternative employment without the written permission of the Canadian state as represented by an immigration officer. If "temporary foreign workers" leave their employment without such permission, they are subjected to the deportation powers of the state. Not only do they lose their employment, but they also lose their legal standing in Canada. Importantly, according to section 6 of the Charter of Rights and Freedoms, such unfree conditions are considered *unconstitutional* when experienced by persons who hold "citizen" or "permanent resident" status.

Aside from being tied to their employer, "temporary foreign workers" – including those regulated by Canada's Live-in Caregiver

Program (LCP), the Seasonal Agricultural Worker Program (SAWP), or the even more restrictive Pilot Project for Occupations Requiring Lower Levels of Formal Training (the Low-Skill Pilot Project), introduced in 2002 – find themselves facing even further restrictions on their freedom and mobility within Canada. The LCP legally *requires* "temporary foreign workers" (who are mostly nonwhite women) to live in the same residence as their employer. Not only have there been well-documented cases of abuse arising from this condition, but such a stipulation also constitutes a clear violation of section 6 of the Charter of Rights and Freedoms if a person has the status of "citizen" or "permanent resident." Persons regulated by the SAWP often have curfews imposed upon them, are prohibited from receiving visitors of the opposite sex, and are often fired if they become pregnant.[16]

In the case of those employed through the Low-Skill Pilot Project, the Canadian state has written itself out of its responsibility to intervene in the conditions of work for those recruited through the project. This leaves these persons with no official recourse if their employer reneges on his or her part of the contract. Moreover, the contract that is drawn up (by employers with the assistance of the International Organization for Migration), which potential recruits must sign, contains terms for employment that, again, would be considered unconstitutional if they were imposed on "citizens" or "permanent residents." For the duration of their employment, workers are told that they should "avoid" joining any group or association, should not show any signs of what the employer considers "disrespect," and should not have sexual relations. The contract even contains a clause regarding the length of the person's hair![17] In short, Canada's "temporary foreign workers" programs create conditions to control workers and their entire personhood that the state or employers cannot legally apply to "citizens" and "permanent residents."

Understanding that people are not "temporary foreign workers" in any ontological sense but are, instead, captured by this state category is a necessary corrective to the two dominant narratives that try to secure legitimacy for their differentiation from "citizens" and "permanent residents." The first heavily racialized and gendered narrative represents "temporary foreign workers" as people who are *naturally inclined* toward work and working conditions that are seen as undesirable by "Canadians." A good example of such a tactic is the following 1973 statement by H.W. Danforth, the member of the federal Parliament for Kent-Essex, in which he tried to encourage Parliament to continue making "temporary foreign workers" available to agricultural employers:

> The attitude of this government has been that if you do not want to work, you should not have to do so. I raise this matter because the PM [prime minister] reaffirmed the position of the government that a Canadian should not have to work if he [*sic*] does not want to. Mr. Chairman, many people do not like to work in agriculture. They do not like the monotony, the conditions and the fact that you work sometimes in heat and sometimes in cold. That is all right; they do not like it and they should not be forced to work at it. We all agree with that ... How [then] do they [employers] obtain labour? Many of them have encouraged offshore labour over the years, which comes from three sources, the Caribbean, Portugal and Mexico. We need this labour ... and these people are used to working in the heat. They are used to working in agriculture, and they are satisfied with the pay scale ... Everybody is satisfied: the workers are satisfied, the primary producers are satisfied and the consumers of Canada are satisfied because we are getting the crops harvested.[18]

To legitimate allowing "offshore workers" (i.e., "temporary foreign workers") to labour under conditions considered unacceptable by "Canadians," Danforth mobilizes the interlocking ideologies of racism and nationalism, which posit that certain, mostly nonwhite, "foreigners" are a wholly different "type" of people – the "type" who are "satisfied" with what "Canadians" reject. This approach positions them as "naturally" inferior to "Canadians" (who in the historical narrative of "Canadianness" are usually seen to be white).

The second dominant narrative about "temporary foreign workers" insists that regardless of how difficult or even dangerous their work is or how little they are paid, they are *lucky* to work in Canada. This time, their "difference" is legitimated through ideas of their differential worth. Through this discourse, as Sedef Arat-Koc puts it, "immigration ceases to be viewed as a labour recruitment mechanism and becomes a system of 'charity.'"[19] Both of these legitimization tactics have come to form a kind of "common sense" by rendering *unpolitical* the very real differences legislated between "temporary foreign workers" and "citizens" or "permanent residents," who have the legal right to refuse work they find unsatisfactory and to choose both their occupation and their employer.

Interestingly, rendering the difference between citizenship and (im) migration status unpolitical does not mean concealing these differences, quite the opposite. Consider the following 1971 response by Prime Minister Pierre Elliott Trudeau to a question about the possibility of imposing unfree employment relationships on unemployed "Canadians": "No, ... the government will not commandeer the work force. The whole political philosophy of the government is based on freedom of choice for citizens to work where they want."[20] This statement highlights what is, ultimately, the crux of the issue. Trudeau acknowledged that the Canadian state could not render as an unfree labour force those categorized as *its citizens*. Within the twentieth-century (and now twenty-first-century) framework of liberal-democratic national states, "citizens" are *supposed* to be free. However, within this same framework, it *is* legally possible and socially permissible to exploit people as unfree labour in Canada and to grant them no "freedom of choice ... to work where they want" if, *and only if*, they are categorized as "temporary foreign workers." With this category in place, a system of unfree labour is able to proceed. With the organization of national difference through state categories, the Canadian nation-state can simultaneously be a liberal democracy *and* an authoritative state. How one experiences it depends on one's citizenship and (im)migration status.

The state-mandated category of "temporary foreign worker" is thus profoundly ideological. First, the category comes to stand in for the actual people whose lives are ordered by it.[21] Their histories, their reasons and desires for moving, their struggles, and their acts of agency – indeed, every aspect of their daily lives except their exploitation as labour – are subsumed under this state category. This may be why the state and employers often see people labouring as "temporary foreign workers" *only* as workers and find it difficult to accept that they are people with needs, wants, and desires that are as complex and rich as their own.[22] It is such social distancing that in part legitimates the ideological separation of "temporary foreign workers" from "the community" in which "Canadians" live and labour.

Second, much of the understanding (and even the study) of "temporary foreign workers" is done outside of a social relational framework. Consequently, this category appears to stand on its own. Yet naming someone a "temporary foreign worker" is an act of *comparison*. For example, what is conveyed by the idea that "temporary foreign workers" are "satisfied" with little or are "lucky" to have so little is that they are "satisfied" and "lucky" to have *less than* "Canadians." Abstracting the relationship *among* people classified as "temporary foreign workers" and "citizens" by paying attention to state categories, rather than to the persons captured within them, allows the state and employers (and certainly many citizens) to act as though there is no relationship among them.

Just as they are legally cast outside of the realm of citizens' rights in Canada, "temporary foreign workers" are also ideologically cast as existing outside of the "Canadian society" in which they live their lives and as outside of the "Canadian" labour market in which they work. The material organization of "temporary foreign workers" through Canadian citizenship and (im)migration policies is thus treated as existing in a field of analysis that is separate from other Canadian state categories of membership (and nonmembership). This obfuscates the full meaning of Canada's national borders and renders unpolitical the trope of Canadian citizenship.

NATIONAL SOVEREIGNTY AND GLOBAL CAPITALISM

People trapped in the working and living conditions of the Canadian state's category of "temporary foreign worker" are there because of the *biopolitical* logic of national state sovereignty that territorializes rights and even subjectivity. The internationally recognized right of national states to determine the membership of "their" societies creates the conditions by which a hierarchy of national rights and entitlements (or lack thereof) is organized. This unequal structure is deemed universally legitimate partly because of the enormous *affective* reach of ideas of nationness. Nationalism profoundly shapes *who* we think we are, *with whom* we feel connected, and concomitantly, *against whom* we define our "imagined community."[23] Nationalism thus allows for fellow-feeling and, equally, a feeling of estrangement from those deemed outside of the "nation." Just as importantly, nationalism allows for the historically novel idea – and thoroughly ideological one – that the ruled-over are the rulers. Nationalism, therefore, provides those recognized as "citizens" with a sense of power over "foreigners."

The concealment of the hierarchies among those defined as members of a "nation" is a crucial part of the ideological work that nationalism does. Yet the transformation of "classes into masses" obfuscates not only the gross inequalities *within* any said "nation" but also any similarities that exist *across* national divides.[24] Our sense of closeness with or estrangement from others is therefore not a geographical distinction but a *social and legal* distinction. As discussed above, although nationalism posits distinct and discrete spaces for "national subjects" and "foreigners," both always already exist in the *same* space.

There are two related ways to understand the character of this shared space. One is that "nationals" and "foreigners" exist within the same *nationalized* space, in which they are ideologically positioned as stark opposites. In this sense, "foreigners" are not alien interlopers into "national" space but are an intrinsic part of it. This is borne out historically, as there has never existed a national state comprised only of its "citizens." All have designated certain persons as social and/or legal "foreigners." Despite the organization of "difference" between the two – be it gendered, racialized, and/or based on citizenship and (im)migration status – people categorized as either "nationals" or "foreigners" often live side by side (sometimes in the same household!), work side by side, use the same transportation systems, pay the same taxes, and so on. In short, they live in the same nationalized space.

Another related way of looking at the shared character of space inhabited by "nationals" and "foreigners" is to recognize that they live together in a society that can be regarded only as *global*. In other words, in many respects, human societies today are neither scaled nor organized as "national."[25] Rather than viewing the global as something that national states regulate or, according to nationalists, keep at bay, it is more useful to recognize that global capitalist society is productive of nationalized spaces. Indeed, "nations" – particularly national states – were organized long after the advent of the global systems of capital, commodities, and labour.

Although dating the global character of capitalism is an imprecise task, Christopher Columbus's 1492 landing in the Caribbean was certainly a signal moment in the global circulation of people, plants, animals, ideas, and wealth. By the seventeenth century, with the emergence and expansion of a capitalist mode of production, all of those moving people, plants, animals, and ideas had been organized into a global arena of capitalist relationships of commodification and exploitation. People in what we now know as the Caribbean and the Americas were brought into this "new world" through the force of "blood and fire," as Karl Marx put it.[26] Significantly, no amount of fire and blood was spared for people in places now known as Africa, Asia, and the Pacific, as they too found themselves enclosed within a globalizing system of expropriation and exploitation. And, of course, terror, immiseration, and death were visited upon great numbers of people in Europe as well, even though some of the wealthiest and most powerful people and empires were also seated there. Left in the wake of European imperialism, then, was a global system of deep, often violent, sometimes cooperative, but always connected human relationships.

As Peter Linebaugh and Marcus Rediker show, it was within these connections that challenges to this emerging global system of capitalism also lay.[27] Indeed, the history of the formative period of capitalism is replete with numerous efforts to overthrow it. That these revolts were led by "motley crews" of people hailing from all parts of the world where capitalist social relationships had been imposed was an important part of why they were considered so very dangerous by the newly forming capitalist elite. For these elites, the sundering of the intimacies wrought by shared exploitation was seen as essential to the survival of capitalism. A major tool in this regard was the making of "difference."

Indeed, accompanying the process of capital accumulation, Sylvia Federici argues, was an "accumulation of differences and divisions within the working class, whereby hierarchies built upon gender, as well as 'race' and age, became constitutive of class rule."[28]

Nationalism also came to be a crucial "difference," for one of the ways that producers came to be convinced of their *dis*connection was through ideas of discrete, competing, and always antagonistic nationalized spaces and identifications. There was, of course, a structural element to the emergence of a nationalist subjectivity: the capitalist revolution (or, more accurately, *counter*revolution) relied on the growing power of the state to discipline and order workers.[29] The centralization of state power came to be regarded by ruling groups as the only institutional structure capable of safeguarding capitalist relations. As Federici puts it, "the state became the ultimate manager of class relations, and the supervisor of the reproduction of labor-power."[30] The national form of the state came to be seen as especially helpful in this regard.

National identities served to obfuscate the global character of power and of the relationship among people. Indeed, the nationalist notion that there *are* and *ought* to be differential rights for "nationals" and "foreigners" structured the devastating competition organized between people located in increasingly differentiated "national" labour markets. In this sense, "national" societies can be seen as ideological decompositions of a global society. The nationalization of society comprises a technique of ruling that both structures competition among producers and provides scapegoats (workers in other nationalized spaces or, in the case of immigration, workers deemed to be "foreign") for the "citizen" workers left reeling from this competition.

The realization that people do in fact exist within a global society is evidenced by their attempts at mobility within it. The grossly uneven and unequal spatial distribution of rights, security, peace, prosperity, and power more or less guarantees this. People's migrations are patterned in ways that are very much connected to these global inequalities. Citizenship and immigration policies are what allow national states to continually absorb – and ideologically decompose – these gross inequalities into a "flexible" workforce within nationalized labour markets. Indeed, immigration policies are the conduits through which the global movement of people is channelled for the benefit of both national states and employers hiring within nationalized labour markets. Thus such policies assist national states in organizing the circumstances through which capital can be accumulated within the territories they control. Indeed, the work that these policies do in the accumulation process helps to explain the tenor of most immigration policy changes in Canada since at least 1973 and the expansion of "temporary foreign workers" programs. It also helps to explain the expansion in the early 1970s of Canada's "temporary foreign workers" programs from agricultural and domestic labour to practically every occupational sector in Canada, the same period when the mobility of production sites became a growing strategy to maintain profit rates and to stifle the power of labour movements.[31]

NO BORDERS!

One very important challenge to the right of national states to accord differential citizenship and (im)migration statuses to persons is the emergence of a politics of "no borders." Such a politics coalesces around a struggle against the current international governance system and its denial of the free movement of people. An essential understanding of such a politics is that the border control practices of national states are not only a *reflection* of people's unequal rights (e.g., whose movements are deemed to be legitimate and whose are not) but are also *productive* of this inequality. By demanding that every person have the freedom to move and the concomitant freedom not to be displaced (i.e., not to have to move), "no borders" theorists/activists have *repoliticized* the very legitimacy of (im)migration restrictions. Far from reaffirming the significance of citizenship, even if it is understood "not [as] an institution or a statute but [as] a collective practice," as Étienne Balibar contends, those in the "no borders" movement also call into question the legitimacy of the global system of national states itself and the always already related global system of capitalism.[32] In making their demands, "no borders" movements bring to the fore the centrality of border controls to capitalist social relations, which are borne of – and still dependent on – practices of displacement, expropriation, and exploitation of commodified labour power.

There is a wide variety of individuals and groups who act on a "no borders" politics (sometimes only implicitly). They include groups of self-conscious activists directly confronting the state's imposition of barriers on people's mobilities (be they migrant detention camps, deportation schemes, harassment by police, or other coercive state practices). Examples of such groups are the Sans Papiers in France and groups inspired by their actions in other parts of Europe, such as the Sin Papeles in Spain. In Europe there is also a broader "no borders" network, a loose affiliation of individuals, sometimes in organizations, who reject any controls on people's migration and stage actions aimed at preventing deportations and other acts of solidarity with demonized and detained migrants.

Informed by a "no borders" politics, campaigns also exist that attempt to eliminate the use of (im)migration status as a tool of control of migrants. These include Don't Ask, Don't Tell campaigners calling for an end to citizenship and immigration status distinctions between people in the provision of social services and of state protections against patriarchal violence, substandard employment conditions, and so on. In Canada various No One Is Illegal formations in Montreal, Toronto, Vancouver, and elsewhere have been central to such organizing. Elsewhere, there exist groups such as Doctors of the World who provide needed medical assistance without applying status or residence restrictions on the provision of healthcare. Such groups often call for legalization (or regularization) of illegalized migrants as a means by which these migrants can gain rights and entitlements currently restricted to "citizens" and some "permanent residents."

Other groups include "sanctuary movements" that provide much-needed support in the form of information, shelter, water, and food to travelling migrants, trade unions that purposefully ignore a person's (im)migration status in their organizing drives or even specifically address the vulnerabilities faced by persons because of their "illegal" or "temporary" status, and other individuals and groups that argue for the abolition of the multiple borders that national states impose, such as borders created by laws regarding "official languages" and by other "banal" forms of nationalism.[33] These include groups such as No More Deaths, which works at the US-Mexico border, labour unions such as Justice for Janitors (part of the Service Employees International Union) in the United States and Canada, and the United Food and Commercial Workers union in Canada. These unions have crossed the ideological divide between "nationals" and "foreigners" to secure higher wages, better working conditions, and healthcare for any worker in the occupational sectors they organize. Indeed, such a rejection is what, in part, links disparate campaigns, groups, and individuals together within a "no borders" movement.

In eschewing national styles of solidarity and antagonism, the "no borders" movement acknowledges that a key aspect of the ideological work of nationalism is to make the global character of human (and other) relationships disappear. Many within the "no borders" movement, therefore, move from challenging national forms of "belonging" to trying to activate new subjectivities, ones that correspond to the global level at which human society is actually organized, in order to affirm a conception of freedom based on collective political action that supports commonality and equality. The "no borders" movement thus redefines society by positing it as a relationship not between "citizens" but between co-members of a global society.

The related rights to move and to stay are seen as necessary to the creation of this common world. Such rights are seen as operational only on a global scale and against the "nation." From an ecological perspective, we have long known that destructive (or helpful) practices in one part of the globe have effects, sometimes immediate, on all others. From a social perspective, creating restrictions on the movement of people (as well as plants, animals, food, fuel, medicines, ideas, and more) in a world that has long come to be shaped by such movements is tantamount to accepting the imposition of border controls of one sort or another. Such controls, as I've discussed above, are ideological: they do not prevent people's movement but serve to make legal and social distinctions between "nationals" and "foreigners."

Importantly, the rights to move and to stay are not framed within a liberal (capitalist) praxis, as are the rights of states, "citizens," and private property owners, or even within the ambiguous, often symbolic, and ultimately national arena of "human rights." Instead, the rights to move and to stay are understood as a necessary part of a contemporary system of *common rights*. Thus, although focused on realizing people's demand for freedom of movement (which includes the freedom not to be moved), "no borders" movements can be seen as part of a broader, reinvigorated struggle for a global commons.

According to Peter Linebaugh, there are four key principles historically evident in the practice of "commoning" (the practice of living in a commons) and in the rights held by commoners, rights that differ substantially from those allowed by the modern regime of citizenship or human rights.[34] First, common rights are "embedded in a particular ecology," one that is reliant on local knowledge of sustainable practices. In this sense, common rights are neither abstract nor essentialist but are based on one's actions. Second, "commoning is embedded in a labor process" and is "entered into by labor." Hence commoning, by definition, rejects class relationships centred on the dialectic of exploiters and producers. Third, "commoning is collective"; that is, it is a social practice. Fourth, commoning is "independent of the state" and the law. Commoners, it is said, cannot abide sovereigns of any sort. In sum, commoning is the realization of not only the political rights but also the social and economic rights of the commoners. Commoning as a practice, then, resolves the capitalist separation of falsely divided spheres. According to Linebaugh, common rights have historically included the principles of neighbourhood, subsistence, travel, anti-enclosure, and reparations.[35]

Significantly, the rights enjoyed by commoners are the rights of persons. In contrast to the rights of property, which are based on the right *to exclude* others from enjoying what has been privatized, the rights of persons include the right *not to be excluded*.[36] In a global commons, the common rights to move and to stay are necessary parts of these rights of persons. Holding such rights entitles one to fully enjoy the collective resources of society and not to be distinguished from others who also carry the rights of persons. I believe that such rights alone can provide the foundation for constructing a society of equals, a society without legal and social differentiations of citizenship and immigration status, such as the juridically unfree state category of "temporary foreign worker" and its operationalization of nationalism, racism, and sexism.

2

Buy Local, Hire Global: Temporary Migration in Canadian Agriculture

KERRY PREIBISCH AND JENNA L. HENNEBRY

INTRODUCTION

Across the high-income world, consumers are encouraged to "buy local" and choose food products that are grown, raised, or produced as close to home as possible. In Canada a growing movement in favour of local food has led to the rising popularity of farmers' markets, the reinvigoration of food cooperatives, and even changes in the procurement strategies of supermarkets.[1]

In a population galvanized by heightened awareness of environmental damage, popular books such as Alisa Smith and J.B. Mackinnon's *The 100-Mile Diet: A Year of Local Eating* (2007) have become bestsellers, and the term "locavore," a person who seeks out locally produced food, became the *New Oxford American Dictionary*'s word of the year in 2007. Moreover, the local foods campaign has become institutionalized as food policy at various levels of government. In 2007, for example, the Ontario provincial government committed $12.5 million to a Buy Ontario strategy aimed at increasing consumer demand for local foods and boosting sales of these products.[2]

Often absent from the discourse of the local food movement is the thoroughly global character of the labour force supporting agricultural production systems in high-income countries. Although campaigns aimed at directing consumer preferences homeward are often critical of global processes – including the globalization of agrifood markets, which has made supply chains more competitive and put pressure on small producers – markedly less attention has been devoted to exploring the increasingly global sourcing of workers that sustains local food systems. Yet an increasing share of Canada's food is produced, harvested, and packaged by international migrant workers, many of whom engage in circular, transnational migration between the Canadian farms where they work and their households within the global South. Each year this labour migration involves more than 50,000 flights between Canada and global destinations, millions of dollars of overseas money transfers, and innumerable international long-distance calls. Indeed, both the migrant system of labour serving Canadian agriculture and the global industry that facilitates and supports it remain largely invisible to most locavores.

This chapter addresses the global migrant system of labour supporting local food and agricultural production in Canada. We focus on two principal processes. First, by tracing historical developments in Canada's longstanding temporary migration program for agriculture, the Seasonal Agricultural Worker Program (SAWP), and changes brought about by the liberalization of immigration controls on temporary visa workers in low-skilled occupations since 2002, our chapter shows how international migrant workers (overwhelmingly nonwhites from the global South) are a growing component of the workforce in agrifood industries. Not only have the numbers of migrant workers increased dramatically, but their geographical distribution has also broadened across the country and across a wider range of industries. Moreover, we also show how the state, through the implementation of some policies and an unwillingness to institute others, has increased the availability of pools of highly precarious labour such as migrants without status or those facing contemporary forms of debt bondage.

The second principal process that we focus on in this chapter is the growth of a global migration industry that has facilitated the incorporation of migrants into the agricultural workforce and that supports a migrant system of labour. We explore the rise of third-party intermediaries in brokering the delivery of migrant labour to employers and also describe other components of the industry that have emerged to support international labour migration to rural Canada. Although these agents have undoubtedly facilitated the movement of migrant labourers into rural Canada, the absence of regulatory mechanisms has exposed some migrants to a range of abuses, including contemporary forms of debt bondage. The main argument we put forth is that the increasing numbers of migrant workers from the global South, the emergence of highly exploitative labour practices, and the growing and largely unregulated presence of private-sector agents in Canada's migration system have engendered greater vulnerability for those engaged in farm work and have further entrenched the position of this work at the bottom of Canada's occupational hierarchy.

The chapter is based on the authors' ongoing programs of research on temporary labour migration to Canada, primarily by persons employed in the agricultural sector. This research has included the collection of primary data using qualitative and quantitative methods, as well as extensive consultation of secondary data. Both authors have engaged in critical ethnographic approaches to studying temporary labour migration to Canada, involving prolonged and engaged field research in migrant-sending and -receiving communities. Subsequently, both authors have conducted research (independently and collaboratively) on migrant worker rights and health (Hennebry, Preibisch), the formation of migration industries (Hennebry and Preibisch), information and communication technologies, development, and transnationalism (Hennebry), gender as an organizing principle of migration and as a factor in shaping migrants' experiences (Preibisch), race and racialization (Hennebry, Preibisch), temporary migration and social inclusion and exclusion (Preibisch), the social relations of contemporary agricultural production in Canada (Preibisch), and comparative analysis of temporary migration programs (Hennebry, Preibisch). These studies have involved a broad range of participants – migrants, employers, community members, civil servants, and migrant advocates – in questionnaires, interviews, and focus groups, among other methods.

INTERNATIONAL MIGRANTS: A GROWING COMPONENT OF FOOD AND FARM INDUSTRY WORKERS

For centuries, successive waves of immigrants, temporary visa workers, and nonstatus migrants have comprised the agricultural labour market in Canada. As early as the late nineteenth century, First

Nations people living in Washington State and Chinese labourers worked as seasonal migrants in Canadian agriculture.[3] During the Second World War, interned ethnic Japanese immigrants and conscientious objectors of the Doukhobor and Mennonite faiths became important sources of labour; after the war, growers turned to displaced people arriving from western Europe and to Portuguese contract workers.[4] In this latter period, Mexicans, including Mennonites with previous settlement ties to Canada, also provided legal and unauthorized sources of labour for Canadian farms.[5] In addition, from 1954 to 1957 the Canadian government signed bilateral agreements with Portugal that provided the agricultural industry with an average of 1,000 workers each year.[6] These agreements served as historical precursors to the bilateral agreement signed with Jamaica in 1966 to bring workers to Ontario farms. This bilateral agreement formed the first of five to be signed over the ensuing years with Trinidad and Tobago (1967), Barbados (1967), Mexico (1974), and the Organization of Eastern Caribbean States (1976), which continue to operate in the present day. This set of agreements is now known collectively as the Seasonal Agricultural Worker Program, through which temporary visa workers – predominantly nonwhites from the global South – have become an institutionalized feature of Canada's agricultural labour force. In the following section, we briefly outline the main features of the SAWP before returning to its development from 1966 to contemporary times.

The Seasonal Agricultural Worker Program, 1966 to the Present

The SAWP is a set of bilateral agreements governing the managed migration of temporary visa workers from participating countries to Canada for employment in agriculture. The SAWP permits employers producing agricultural commodities designated as having seasonal labour demands to hire temporary visa workers from abroad to resolve purported labour shortages. Eligible employers must prove they have been unable to recruit Canadian workers and meet certain program requirements. When approved, they are able to hire international migrants who are issued work permits and entry visas that allow them to undertake contracts lasting from at least 240 hours within a period of six weeks or less to a maximum duration of

eight months between 1 January and 15 December. Employers pay
for approximately half of migrants' international airfare, provide
accommodation at no cost, and agree to provide free transportation
on a biweekly basis to migrants for the purposes of shopping.[7] In
addition to the program's role in resolving labour shortages in agriculture, the SAWP is often represented as a form of foreign aid for or
co-development with impoverished countries of the South.

Given the rising numbers of temporary visa workers in the sector,
trends we discuss below, and a generalized return to guest worker
programs across Western countries,[8] the SAWP has received growing attention in academic and policymaking circles.[9] The SAWP is
distinctive among temporary migration policies in North America aimed at the incorporation of migrants in low-skilled sectors
of the economy due to unique characteristics of the program and
its extraordinary "success" rate in returning participants to their
home nation.[10] First, the SAWP is characterized by a high level of
government involvement, owing to a bilateral framework that com-
mits the governments of Canada and migrant-sending countries to
greater responsibilities.[11] Migrant-sending countries undertake a
considerable portion of the management of the program, including
selecting and recruiting candidates to fill employer requests, preparing migrants through predeparture activities, organizing their international air travel, and providing government agents within Canada
to mediate employer-worker relations. In Canada the federal government's responsibilities in the SAWP include developing policy and
operational guidelines, authorizing recruited migrants for entry into
the country and issuing their visas and work permits, approving eligible employers to hire outside of the national labour market and
monitoring their compliance with the program policies, and participating in frequent negotiations with industry and the bilateral
partners. The federal government was formerly involved in more of
the operative tasks of the SAWP until 1987, when it authorized the
first private-sector organization run by employers – Foreign Agricultural Resource Management Services (FARMS) – to take over these
responsibilities in Ontario and lifted the quota on SAWP placements.
Today, FARMS in Ontario and the Fondation des entreprises en
recrutement de main-d'oeuvre agricole étrangère (FERME) in Quebec administrate approximately 80 per cent of the temporary visa

worker positions in the SAWP, including communicating employer requests to the sending countries and the Canadian authorities abroad and collecting employer signatures on standardized contracts. Together with their travel agency, CanAg Travel Services Ltd, these employer-directed companies coordinate the air travel of the SAWP's 25,000 participants.

The high level of government involvement has contributed to the SAWP's achievement of *circularity* – the return of migrants to their countries of origin following their contracts – a feature that has constituted the SAWP as a "success" within international policy arenas.[12] From a policy point of view, circularity through the legal channels of managed migration is a "triple-win" scenario: host countries are able to meet temporary labour needs without the long-term commitment implied by permanent settlement; sending countries are guaranteed to capture migrant remittances and relieve poverty and unemployment at home; and migrants move easily across borders to their overseas jobs with a fair expectation of when they will return to their households. Indeed, the SAWP moves some 25,000 migrants every year from Mexico and the Caribbean into Canada and, following the completion of their contracts, returns an estimated 98 per cent of them to their countries of residence.[13] The SAWP's high rate of return is attributable to a set of structural features and operational elements that work in tandem, of which greater government involvement is only one component. Since these features have received considerable treatment elsewhere, we briefly highlight the following here: highly controlled recruitment procedures that select candidates more likely to return, coercive elements that garner worker compliance, and economic incentives.

To begin, recruitment under the SAWP is controlled within migrant-sending countries by government departments that apply criteria designed to select candidates more likely to return home. In Mexico, for example, eligible candidates must be married and/or have dependants. Although single applicants are not discriminated against in theory, married candidates dominate the SAWP in practice. In a 2007 survey, 97 per cent of Mexican migrants were married.[14] As Tanya Basok points out, "Canadian immigration authorities try to ensure that seasonal migration does not turn into permanent settlement. Preference is therefore given to applicants who are married and have many children who serve as a 'collateral' against non-return."[15] Although Canadian government documents on the SAWP do not explicitly outline the use of targeted (or discriminatory) recruitment practices, bilateral partners seek to comply with the host country's policy imperatives. Additional recruitment policies further support circularity. For one, most migrant-sending states exercise policies to prevent couples from migrating together. Indeed, the separation of migrants from their families is a hallmark feature of most temporary migration programs.[16] This is enforced not only through recruitment policies but also through the tightly controlled travel of SAWP migrants and through rules governing employer-provided accommodation. Moreover, if migrants' family members arrive at the Canadian border, visa officials can deny them entry on the basis that SAWP workers do not have the means and ability to financially support their stay in Canada.[17]

As this last point suggests, circularity is also achieved through coercion. In addition to obliging temporary visa workers to migrate without their families, the SAWP is a system of "forced rotation"; that is, for migrants to participate each year, they must return to their countries of origin upon completion of their contracts. Further, migrants' mobility in the labour market is highly restricted by work permits that are valid with a single, designated employer; migrants cannot legally work for someone else without negotiating a transfer and receiving Canadian government approval to do so, a procedure that in practice is very difficult to accomplish. Following the completion of migrants' work periods, employers indicate whether they will reemploy each designated migrant for the following year and, if not, provide a reason for not recalling an individual. For Jamaican workers, failure to be recalled can result in indefinite suspension from the SAWP.[18] Although such failure does not result in automatic suspension in Mexico, it does damage a migrant's record and, if it happens again, can jeopardize a migrant's placement.

A further coercive feature of the SAWP affecting Mexican workers is end-of-year employee evaluations that employers submit to the Ministry of Labour offices in Mexico (as of 2011 via the Internet), which influence migrants' eligibility for future placements. Punitive government practices in response to poor evaluations act as powerful instruments of coercion of migrants' behaviour. These practices have included suspension from the program for one to two years, indefinite suspension, and assignment to a less attractive job, a less desirable employer, or a shorter contract.[19] Thus, whereas employers are at liberty to choose their employees, migrants have no voice in choosing their employers, their job profile, or their location.[20] In fact, some migrants believe that even asking the Mexican Ministry of Labour for a reassignment will jeopardize their placement in the program. Moreover, the Ministry of Labour at one time enforced an informal practice whereby it denied migrants' reassignment requests until they had completed three consecutive work seasons with the employer to whom they were first assigned.[21]

SAWP employment contracts also contain vaguely worded repatriation provisions that allow employers to arbitrarily dismiss workers and remove them from their property with no formal right of appeal.[22] In most cases, by the time migrants learn they have been fired, their return travel home has already been arranged by their corresponding government agent. Despite the fact that SAWP migrants may legally stay in Canada until the expiry of their work permits regardless of the employer's decision to rescind the contract, the option of staying in Canada presents various obstacles. Since SAWP participants are obliged to reside in employer-provided housing, loss of work almost always results in loss of residence.[23] Moreover, whether employers break migrants' contracts prematurely or migrants do so themselves – for example, when they become ill or injured or cannot tolerate the conditions of their employment or housing – the sending country's government agents place significant pressure on them to return. Even in cases where the employer has supported the bid of a SAWP migrant to remain in Canada for health reasons, such as to receive medical treatment for which they are eligible, government agents have insisted on deportation.[24]

Canada's bilateral partners engage in these and other coercive practices to ensure that temporary migration does not become permanent. For migrant-sending countries, temporary migration programs such as the SAWP generate much-needed foreign exchange through remittances and, by increasing their nationals' access to the labour market of a high-income country, contribute to longstanding problems in these countries of unemployment and uneven development. In the case of Mexico, although the economic benefits of Canadian jobs and remittances for migrant-sending countries pale in comparison to those generated through largely undocumented labour migration to the United States, the SAWP provides an example of what managed labour cooperation could look like. This is significant given recent negotiations in the United States around the expansion and reform of temporary migration programs encapsulated in the AgJOBS Bill that will result in an amnesty for millions of mostly Mexican undocumented farm workers while implementing mechanisms to expand that country's guest worker program. The phenomenon of migrant-sending governments around the world trying to leverage the economic benefits of temporary labour migration, as evidenced by their efforts to manage these flows through government agencies dedicated to the placement of workers abroad (e.g., the Philippine Overseas Employment Administration), is well documented in the academic literature.[25] In the case of Mexico, ensuring the smooth functioning of temporary labour migration is of particular importance in terms of its diplomatic relationship with Canada as a partner of the North American Free Trade Agreement (NAFTA).

However, the basis on which migrant-sending states participate with Canadian officials and employers in the SAWP is not just collaborative but also *competitive* due to mechanisms built into the program structure that ensure Canadian employers can access a competitive global labour pool. SAWP employers, rather than simply indicating the number of migrants they seek to hire, are able to choose from year to year the country that will supply them with labour.[26] SAWP bilateral partners are thus not awarded a set quota of job placements in Canada but must compete with one another for these placements, usually by seeking to provide the type of workers and government liaison services demanded by employers. Consequently, sending states often castigate SAWP workers who damage the "national brand" by underperforming, by going "AWOL" (or "absent without leave," the military term used in the SAWP when migrants abscond from their designated employer), or by violating Canadian laws. This usually involves deportation (if possible) and permanently removing the individual from future job placements in Canada. Collective reprisals, however, have also been carried out. When the Canadian high commissioner to Jamaica threatened that Canada would turn to other sources of labour if the numbers of

Jamaicans going AWOL under the SAWP continued to increase, the Jamaican government shifted recruitment to more rural areas and permanently suspended all workers who failed to be recalled by their employers.[27] Furthermore, when three SAWP migrants were accused of smuggling drugs into Canada in 2003, the Jamaican Ministry of Labour punished the migrants' entire home parish by banning its participation in the SAWP for the next three years.[28]

Economic incentives also ensure worker compliance. Eligibility for the SAWP hinges on "pro-poor" criteria: poverty, rural location, and low educational levels. As a result, most SAWP participants value their Canadian jobs very highly. Corroborated evidence suggests that most migrants must participate in the SAWP for several consecutive seasons before they are able to resolve their most pressing economic hardships, periods that are lengthened if they invest in their children's education.[29] Leigh Binford found low savings and limited productive investment among SAWP participants; in fact, close to one-third used a significant portion of their Canadian income to simply finance debts. He concludes that a number of factors encourage repeat migration among SAWP participants: (1) low Canadian wages prevent migrants from accumulating substantial amounts of capital; (2) the recruitment age of migrants means that most have young families that require ongoing, often increasing investments in food, clothing, healthcare, and education; and (3) the material improvements within migrant households become taken for granted, thus generating future migration.[30]

Since its inception in 1966, the SAWP has consistently provided a temporary workforce to Canadian food and agricultural producers without resulting in large numbers of Mexican and Caribbean workers seeking permanent settlement in the country. The program has grown considerably: whereas some 264 Jamaican workers were brought to Canada in the program's first year, over 27,000 positions had been confirmed by 2009.[31] This growth reflects the geographical extension of the SAWP across the country following its genesis in the orchards and tobacco fields of south-western Ontario. The SAWP is now available to eligible agriculture and food producers in all Canadian provinces, with the exception of Newfoundland and Labrador and the three territories. The most recent province to gain access to the program was British Columbia in 2004. Although the

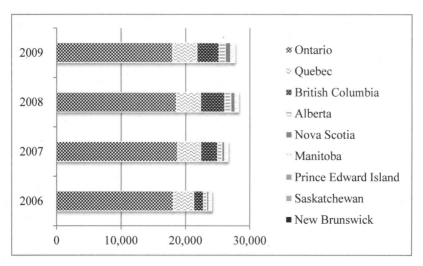

Figure 2.1
Number of temporary foreign worker positions on Labour Market Opinion confirmations under the Seasonal Agricultural Worker Program, by province, 2006–09

Source: Human Resources and Skills Development Canada, "Table 10 (Annual): Number of Temporary Foreign Worker Positions on Labour Market Opinion Confirmations under the Seasonal Agricultural Worker Program, by Location of Employment."

province has the third largest farm labour market in Canada, provincial authorities resisted employer lobbying to protect the employment of the domestic, largely immigrant workforce. Since most of this workforce is comprised of Punjabi-speaking Indian immigrants who entered Canada as sponsored family members, the immigration backlog and real decreases in the numbers of immigrants admitted under the sponsorship program gave credence to growers' claims of labour shortages.[32] Following the extension of the SAWP for Mexican workers in 2004 and Caribbean workers in 2008 in British Columbia, the migrant labour force employed in that province under this particular program grew considerably, from 47 migrants in 2004 to some 3,437 confirmed positions in 2009 (see figure 2.1).[33]

The NOC C&D *Pilot Project*

Prior to 2002 SAWP participants comprised the vast majority of noncitizen workers in agriculture. Some nonstatus workers were also employed in agrifood industries, largely people from countries without visa restrictions on entering Canada who overstayed or refugee claimants under deportation orders. This changed with the introduction of the Pilot Project for Occupations Requiring Lower Levels of Formal Training (National Occupational Classifications C and D), referred to hereafter as the NOC C&D Pilot Project, a federal government initiative to expand the temporary labour migration to Canada of workers designated as low-skilled. Implemented in 2002, the NOC C&D Pilot Project was a policy response to increasing employer demand created by the expansion of the Canadian economy in the first half of the 2000s.[34] Rather than replace the SAWP or the Live-in Caregiver Program, the NOC C&D Pilot Project operates alongside them, allowing employers in any sector or commodity to request temporary visa workers to fill "low-skilled" jobs, including for agricultural and food industry work.

The NOC C&D Pilot Project differs considerably from the SAWP (see table 2.1). The NOC C&D Pilot Project is not based on bilateral agreements but is a unilateral, immigration policy initiative of the Canadian federal government that allows eligible employers to hire workers for jobs designated as low-skilled from outside the country. As with the SAWP, most employers must prove that they have unsuccessfully tried to hire Canadian workers and must provide contracts that show that they are not undercutting Canadian terms and conditions of employment. Employers who receive positive or neutral Labour Market Opinions (LMOs) are given employment authorization to hire a specified number of temporary visa workers from any country in the world. Migrants are granted temporary visas and work permits that are valid for twenty-four months, after which they are expected to return to their home countries for at least four months before seeking reentry to Canada. Employers are required to pay for the full cost of migrants' return airfare, whereas migrants cover the costs of their accommodation, travel to their port of exit, medical examination, visa processing, and health insurance. Notably, the NOC C&D Pilot Project does not commit migrant-sending governments to participate in its governance or operation. Compared to the SAWP, the NOC C&D Pilot Project also implies a reduced role for the Canadian federal government. This policy change reflects a move away from resource-intensive, state-controlled temporary migration programs and, consequently, a wider role for market institutions in

Table 2.1
The SAWP and the NOC C&D Pilot Project compared

	SAWP	NOC C&D Pilot Project
Year implemented	1966	2002
Positions approved in 2009	27,654 migrants	10,359 in general farm duties; nurseries and greenhouses; harvesting; and food, beverage, and tobacco processing
Work permit type	Employer-specific	Employer-specific
Work permit length	≤ 8 months	≤ 24 months
Forced rotation	Migrants must return to home countries by 15 December and can return by 1 January	Migrants must return home for four years after accumulating four years of employment in Canada
Employment contract	Standard contracts, with sending country, employer, and worker as parties	Employers write contracts, with employer and worker as parties
Program structure	Federal bilateral agreements between Canada and sending countries formalized in memoranda of understanding	Federal program that approves employers' applications to hire workers from abroad
Countries eligible	Mexico, Jamaica, Trinidad and Tobago, Barbados, and the Organization of Eastern Caribbean States (nine members)	Any country
Employers eligible	Producers of a specific list of commodities considered to be primary agriculture	Any approved employer requiring workers in occupations designated as low-skilled
Worker recruitment	Government responsibility: sending countries fill grower requests, which are sent via authorized private-sector organizations	Employer responsibility: employers contact workers independently (often through recruitment agencies)
Role of sending country	Recruit workers, provide government agents in Canada that workers and employers can contact, and participate in annual and operational review meetings	No formal role, although some sending countries assist in recruitment and other operational aspects of moving workers into Canada
Main costs for migrants	Canadian visa, travel within home countries to/from airport, medical examination, portion of airfare, insurance, rent (British Columbia only)	Canadian visa, travel within home countries to/from airport, medical examination, insurance, rent, recruiter fee (if charged)
Healthcare	Access to provincial healthcare upon arrival and processing of documentation	Three-month waiting period for provincial access, private healthcare insurance
Contract dispute resolution	Contract stipulates that employers and employees can contact sending country's government agents to mediate	No intermediaries, problems to be worked out by employer and employee

Source: Revised from Preibisch, "Pick-Your-Own Labor," 412.

facilitating international labour migration.[35] In terms of agriculture and food industry jobs, the International Organization for Migration has assumed an important role in facilitating temporary migration under the NOC C&D, a role that, under the SAWP, is assumed by government agents from migrant-sending countries in collaboration with the Canadian government, a process discussed in greater detail below.

The NOC C&D Pilot Project was conceived as an employer-driven initiative based on market imperatives, and therefore no cap or quota was put in place to hinder its growth. Throughout the 2000s, the implementation of the project resulted in precipitously rising numbers of temporary visa workers. From just 2006 to 2007, the number of jobs approved by Human Resources and Skills Development Canada (HRSDC) to receive temporary visa workers more than doubled, growing from 12,304 to 32,277.[36] In the following year, this number doubled again to 66,400, partly due to policies within the 2007 federal budget that committed $50.5 million to facilitating and hastening the processing of employer requests for temporary migrant workers to fill "low-skilled" occupations.[37] Among these policies, the Expedited Labour Market Opinion consisted of a process that promised to process employer requests from Alberta and British Columbia for temporary visa workers *within five days* for a list of occupations recognized to have high and legitimate labour demands.[38] A second measure involved the development of "Regional Lists of Occupations under Pressure" for British Columbia, Alberta, and Ontario, which facilitated some of the job advertising efforts required of employers as a precursor to receiving approval to hire migrants. In Alberta a number of agrifood occupations were included in this list, including general farm work, harvesting, landscape and ground maintenance, and food, beverage, and tobacco processing. In addition, the Government of Canada extended temporary visas under the NOC C&D Pilot Project from an initial twelve months to twenty-four and, most recently, to forty-eight.

Farm and food industry jobs account for much of the employer demand for migrants under Canada's new temporary migration program for lower-skilled workers. Table 2.2 outlines the ten occupations that hired the highest numbers of temporary visa migrants in 2007 designated as "low-skilled," or National Occupational

Table 2.2
Top ten low-skill occupations (NOC C&D) hiring the highest number of temporary visa workers, 2007

Occupation	Total*
General farm workers	23,477
Babysitters, nannies, and parents' helpers	13,741
Food service counter attendants and food preparers	2,367
Harvesting labourers	2,228
Truck drivers	1,452
Light-duty cleaners	1,267
Labourers in food, beverage, and tobacco processing	1,065
Construction trades helpers and labourers	1,042
Industrial butchers and meat cutters, poultry preparers, and related workers	855
Food and beverage servers	524

* Data include entries under the SAWP and refer to the number of individuals entering Canada, not to the number of documents issued. Temporary residents are grouped according to the principal reason for residing in Canada during the calendar year. Entries include both initial entries and reentries.

Source: Citizenship and Immigration Canada, Facts and Figures 2008.

Classifications C and D. Of the ten occupations listed, six belong to the agrifood sector. Although available statistics make it difficult to estimate the number of temporary visa migrants employed annually in agriculture and food industry jobs, these industries count for a significant number of Canada's "low-skilled" migrants. In 2008 HRSDC approved 28,231 jobs under the SAWP and 11,160 under the NOC C&D Pilot Project for employment in crop production, animal production, and support activities for agriculture, food, and beverage manufacturing.[39] Food and agricultural industries that were excluded from the SAWP owing to the nonseasonal nature of their labour needs, such as mushroom and greenhouse production, are among the new employers of temporary visa workers in Canada.[40]

One of the most significant outcomes of the implementation of a new framework for facilitating temporary labour migration of "low-skilled" workers has been the emergence of escalating numbers of third-party agents offering recruitment services for employers, as described in the following section. The proliferation of the recruitment industry over the past decade has been nourished by the absence of a regulatory environment with mechanisms to register, monitor, and regulate the recruitment and employment of temporary visa workers. Indeed, when the federal government launched the NOC C&D Pilot Project in 2002, the initiative was narrowly aimed at facilitating the employment of workers from abroad and did not include protective legislation for migrants entering "low-skilled" occupations, many of whom took up employment in sectors with preexisting problems related to weak regulation and poor or non-existent enforcement of employment standards. Although comprehensive legislation has since been put in place in one province (Manitoba in 2009) and other measures have been proposed, these regulatory initiatives have been led by the provinces rather than by the federal government and have lagged in comparison to the pace at which policies have been developed to ease the processing of employer requests for temporary migrant workers. In the following section, we discuss the increasing involvement of third-party intermediaries in brokering temporary labour migration to the farm and food industry jobs and how this has increased the availability of pools of highly precarious labour, such as migrants without status or those facing contemporary forms of debt bondage. We also explore other aspects of the global industry that supports and facilitates international labour migration to Canada.

THE GLOBAL MIGRATION INDUSTRY'S AND CANADA'S LABOUR MIGRATION SYSTEM

With the expansion of temporary migration in Canada, and specifically with the implementation of the NOC C&D Pilot Project, a significant migration industry has emerged around labour migrants and employers. This migration industry is composed of a range of private agents and organizations with varying degrees of state involvement, collaboration, and regulation – and also with varying degrees of legality. This expanding migration industry profits from rising labour migration (largely from migrants themselves) and heightens the vulnerability of these migrants to exploitation and abuse. There are some services provided by the "legal," or legitimate, migration industry specifically for states (e.g., contracting out detention centres, deportation or removals, accreditation, and application processing), for employers (e.g., criminal record checks, LMO applications, and recruitment overseas), and for migrants (e.g., résumé writing,

job bank access, and migration consulting). And there are also services and agents who delve into the grey areas of the migration
industry, such as recruiters who charge exorbitant "resume prepar-
ation fees" but are really charging migrants for a work permit and
employment in Canada – a practice that is deemed illegal according
to international law. Finally, there are those agents who are firmly
in the grey areas, such as informal remittance-sending services or
money-lending services, and those agents who clearly fall into the
illegal range of activities that support labour migration, such as falsi-
fying documents, smuggling, and trafficking.

In agriculture, the agents that have taken on an increasing role in
mediating labour migration to Canada can be grouped into three categories according to the level of state involvement, collaboration, or
sanction under which they operate (see table 2.3). The first category
involves "state-sanctioned" actors that have been explicitly approved
or contracted by the state to carry out some service with respect
to temporary visa workers. These state-sanctioned actors include
international intergovernmental organizations such as the International Organization for Migration and national- or provincial-
level private organizations such as FARMS in Ontario and FERME
in Quebec – many operating at "arm's length" as privately incor-
porated bodies with government approval and extensive collaboration. Some of these organizations, such as the Royal Bank of Canada
(RBC), have been embedded into the structure of Canada's Temporary Foreign Worker Program (TFWP). For example, under the SAWP,
the RBC provides travel insurance to all of the program's participants under a closed tender. In addition, CanAg Travel – a travel
agency formed by the agricultural employers' organization FARMS
– is the designated travel agent for the SAWP's more than 25,000
annual return flights. As these two examples illustrate, private companies stand to make a considerable profit from labour migration to
Canada, at times free from competition.

Within this tier, the International Organization for Migration
(IOM) is a suprastate organization that has assumed a growing presence worldwide with respect to the provision of "migration management" services. As international labour migration grows across the
globe, the IOM has positioned itself as a "knowledgeable" and "valuable partner" in the area of migration management, helping private

Table 2.3
Summary of nonstate actors mediating temporary labour migration

State-sanctioned	• International organizations (e.g., International Organization for Migration)
	• Government-approved employment and migration agencies/ recruiters (e.g., in the UK, in Manitoba)
	• Sector organizations (e.g., FARMS in Ontario)
	• Government-approved training centres/accreditation and advertising services (e.g., www.jobbank.gc.ca)
	• Government-approved processing, transportation, holding, or detaining facilities/services (e.g., CanAg Travel)
	• Government-approved financial institutions and insurance companies (e.g., Royal Bank of Canada)
Quasi-sanctioned	• Nongovernmental organizations and unions
	• For-profit remittance service providers and other financial and communication services (e.g., Western Union)
	• Immigration lawyers (e.g., regulated by the Law Society of Upper Canada)
	• Immigration consultants, "job banks," and online employment/ immigration networks (e.g., JobsInCanada.com, Canadian-Nanny.ca)
	• Employment and recruitment agencies (e.g., ABC Nannies Canada Inc., AgCall Human Resources)
	• For-profit accreditation, CV and résumé preparation, eligibility assessment, criminal record checks, and training services (e.g., credential check)
Nonsanctioned	• Informal employment brokers and other intermediaries
	• Informal remittance services
	• Informal moneylenders
	• Document/identity forgers (e.g., false proof of marital status, training, and credentials; false work permits)
	• Smugglers and traffickers

employers in migrant-receiving countries to address labour shortages through employment of temporary visa workers while providing technical assistance to migrant-sending countries interested in expanding their worker-abroad programs.[41] In Canada, similar to in other migrant-receiving countries such as Spain, the IOM has had growing involvement in brokering temporary labour migration agreements for agriculture. In fact, the IOM has been involved in facilitating the recruitment and employment of migrant workers for Canadian companies in the food-processing and agricultural sectors. In particular, the IOM has been actively involved in recruiting temporary workers and facilitating their migration to Canada from

Guatemala (nearly 12,000 workers between 2003 and 2009) as well as from Colombia, El Salvador, Honduras, and Mauritius under the NOC C&D Pilot Project (some 1,000 workers in 2008–09).[42] IOM involvement in labour migration in Canada and other high-income countries responds to the requests of migrant-sending countries (or, in some cases, employers or industry associations) and of migrant-receiving countries (such as the agreements in negotiation with IOM–El Salvador and Canada) to put in place recruitment processes that place migrant workers with Canadian agrifood employers in jobs ranging from horticulture to meatpacking, often within the framework of bilateral labour agreements.

The IOM is an intergovernmental organization with significant legitimacy internationally: 127 states are members, a further 17 hold observer status, and the organization has offices in over 100 countries.[43] At the same time, the IOM – or "The Migration Agency," as the organization brands itself – is a private, nonstate actor that is not subject to the same accountability as an elected government. The intergovernmental organizational structure adopted by the IOM mirrors other global governance organizations such as the World Bank and International Monetary Fund yet represents a novel form of neoliberal governance indicative of the transformations of sovereignty that extend beyond capital flows to include the management of migration.[44] Migrant-receiving states such as Canada contractually employ the IOM to carry out a range of migration-related services that governments find themselves unable or unwilling to carry out for legal and political reasons. Being a nonstate actor enables the IOM to position itself in creative ways to carry out the transnational work of states "whilst turning a profit and employing the language of rights."[45] In positioning itself as an intermediary between nation-states, the IOM claims to represent migrant rights – which it may very well do in some cases – but it also works in the interests of states, which are its primary clientele (and which pay fees to the IOM for its services). The point here is not that the IOM makes a profit (although this is certainly something for which it has been criticized) but rather that the IOM is a nonstate actor that carries out services that were once state responsibilities (e.g., detention, deportation, and management of TFWPs) and therefore can be conceptualized as part of the growing migration industry within an increasingly neo-liberal model of migration management.

Not only have international private organizations such as the IOM and more regionally based associations such as FARMS stepped in to fill the administrative gap in facilitating migration, but many other for-profit businesses and services seeking to take advantage of Canada's expanding opportunities for temporary visa workers have also emerged to provide services to employers and migrants. These agents comprise the second category of the migration industry, made up of quasi-sanctioned actors and agencies that operate legally in Canada and, in some cases, have been given an explicit stamp of approval by a level of government or have been *implicated* into the structure of the TFWP. These include licensed employment agencies or recruiters such as Diamond Global Recruitment Group Inc. and Visa Solutions Inc. in Manitoba.[46] A great majority of these recruiting organizations operate transnationally, moving around the globe to provide international migrants for employers from a vast and competitive global labour pool. Globally, aside from increased involvement of transnational organizations, the trend for temporary migration programs seems to be to rely on industry or private-sector organizations to mediate the temporary migration process – for example, FARMS in Canada and HOPS Labour Solutions in the United Kingdom. As mentioned, the Canadian federal government characterizes the TFWP as employer-driven; thus there is no cap on admissions under the country's fleet of temporary migration programs, including the SAWP and the NOC C&D Pilot Project.[47] Even in the case of the SAWP, a temporary migration program in which government agents are heavily involved, the employer-run FARMS and FERME have assumed many of the program's operative tasks since 1997 that, in other migrant-receiving countries, are carried out by government agencies (e.g., job matching and worker transportation).[48] Since 2002 these organizations have also provided services to employers hiring migrants for farm and food industry positions under the NOC C&D Pilot Project.[49] Most recently, when the IOM instituted a fee for its placement of Central American workers in Quebec in 2011, FERME ended its relationship with the organization and opened its own offices in Guatemala to recruit migrants directly.[50] This and other examples reinforce the argument by one internationally recognized analyst of guest worker programs that Canada may be the country where the private sector most mediates temporary migration.[51]

These quasi-sanctioned and other non-state-sanctioned private agents have assumed a growing presence in Canada's migration system, particularly with the introduction in 2002 of the NOC C&D Pilot Project. Since the Government of Canada does not provide assistance to employers looking to find and hire workers from abroad (or to workers looking to find employers with permission to hire workers on temporary visas) under this new program, organizations such as Workpermit.ca and WorkVantage.ca have stepped in to fill the gap. These recruiting and employment agencies charge employers fees for registration, access to searchable databases of applicants, "dealing with legal issues," and navigating the work permit or immigration system. For example, AgCall Human Resources, a recruiting agency specializing in agricultural jobs, offers employers the following: "For just $299 your customized JobAd can run for up to 60 days, exposing it to thousands of interested candidates through our web site, e-mail newsletter, JobAlerts service, RSS feed and partnerships with other web sites. For $1,650 your organization can purchase an annual subscription to JobAds that allows you to make an unlimited number of posts during your subscription period."[52] Other agencies offer much more than searchable databases and job advertisements, such as Able Recruiters, which claims to take care of everything "from start to finish" in Canada as well as overseas. Able Recruiters offers to "arrange airport transit, accommodation and medical insurance" and ensures employers that "The Canadian government office in Asia works quickly and efficiently, as do we, to provide you with employees as soon as possible ... We can assist with airport transit, accommodation (if there is no accommodation on site available) and medical insurance arrangements."[53]

One of the most important services that recruiters offer is helping employers to fulfil the requirements for the Labour Market Opinion approval, which generally has involved providing proof of efforts to recruit Canadians or permanent residents through advertising.[54] In 2010 the advertising requirements obliged employers to: (1) advertise for a minimum of fourteen days through the national Job Bank (or the equivalent in Saskatchewan, Quebec, and the Northwest

Territories) during the three months prior to applying for an LMO; (2) conduct recruitment activities consistent with the practice in the occupation during the three months prior to applying for an LMO; and (3) demonstrate "reasonable, ongoing recruitment efforts which include communities that face barriers to employment."[55]

It is not clear, however, that the LMO application process is an efficacious labour market test. The 2009 report of the auditor general identified weaknesses in the practices for issuing LMOs that cast doubts on the quality and consistency of decisions being made by HRSDC officers.[56] The auditor general's report concluded that "CIC [Citizenship and Immigration Canada] and HRSDC have not clearly defined their respective roles and responsibilities in assessing the genuineness of job offers and how that assessment is to be carried out. As a result, work permits could be issued to temporary foreign workers for employers or jobs that do not exist."[57] These concerns were further outlined by the Standing Committee on Citizenship and Immigration in 2009 in a report on temporary visa workers that made six recommendations to the federal government with respect to improving the LMO process.[58]

Of significant concern is that recruitment companies engaged in providing services under the TFWP are unregulated in all but one Canadian province, Manitoba. This has created a number of challenges, including (1) recruiters charging excessive recruitment fees and/or failing to abide by the conditions of their service agreements, (2) lack of information on the employment of temporary visa workers, and (3) employers breaching the conditions of their employment contracts.[59] In terms of the first point, labour brokers have reaped considerable profit collecting fees for placing migrants in Canada or providing related services, often from both workers and employers. Fees have ranged from $2,000 to $25,000, in addition to fees charged to the employer.[60] Documented cases of migrants who financed these fees by mortgaging family assets and then felt compelled to work regardless of the circumstances of their employment (i.e., without employment authorization or under exploitative conditions) have arguably increased instances of contemporary debt bondage within Canada. There have also been documented cases of migrants being misled about immigration prospects, the nature of the work, and other matters, including exaggerating expected earnings. In addition, workers have been charged placement fees for nonexistent jobs or for jobs from which they are laid off shortly after arrival.[61] Migrants' needs to finance, at a minimum, the costs of their migration have grown the population of workers in Canada without employment authorization, as desperate individuals turn to the underground economy to find employment.[62]

Government failure to register employers of migrant workers and to monitor the treatment of these workers has also provided the scope for employers to engage in a range of exploitative practices. As the auditor general's report concluded, "there is no systematic follow-up by either department to verify that in their previous and current employment of temporary foreign workers, employers have complied with the terms and conditions (such as wages and accommodations) under which the work permits were issued. This creates risks to program integrity and could leave many foreign workers in a vulnerable position, particularly those who are physically or linguistically isolated from the general community or are unaware of their rights."[63] Documented abuses of temporary visa workers by employers have involved remuneration (e.g., paying workers lower wages than those indicated in the LMO, failing to pay overtime, and making illegal deductions), working conditions (e.g., exposing workers to undue health and safety risks, failing to comply with health and safety legislation, and providing cramped or degrading conditions), and/or issues related to migrants' mobility or immigration status (e.g., preventing migrants from leaving the property, withholding passports or other documents, and threatening workers with deportation).[64] At the time of writing this chapter, only Manitoba had implemented legislation prompted by problems seen throughout the country following the rise in temporary visa worker employment. Manitoba's Worker Recruitment and Protection Act replaced the province's Employment Services Act, which governed the activities of third-party employment placement agencies, in order to strengthen, modernize, and expand coverage so that it would encompass the protection of foreign workers from unscrupulous recruiters and employers.[65] Among the act's provisions, it is illegal to charge recruitment fees to temporary visa workers, and employers who collect fees from unlicensed recruiters are liable. Importantly, the act contains mechanisms to recoup these fees and indemnify migrants.

Outside of Manitoba, recruitment continues to be a lucrative business. Yet, arguably, those who profit the most, and who are indeed integral to the global labour migration system, are the providers of remittance-sending and long-distance telephone services, such as Western Union. Obviously, since the majority of SAWP and NOC C&D workers are married, sending money home is one of the most important ways that migrants support their families. A recent survey carried out among 600 migrant workers in Ontario found that the majority of migrants working in agriculture sent home money at least once a month.[66] Western Union and other for-profit industries, including remittance-sending services, phone card vendors, and immigration consultants, have also blossomed around the migration industry. In fact, prospective employers can even earn twenty AIR MILES® reward miles with the purchase of a six-month membership with Canadian Nanny.[67] SAWP migrants typically incur costs to open bank accounts in order to receive their wages (or they pay monthly fees even while the accounts remain inactive when they return home in the winter), to send money home (remittance sending costs migrants an average of $500 per year), and to make international telephone calls.[68] Temporary migrants and their families incur significant costs to migrate to Canada (both monetary and social),[69] particularly those whose "temporary" migration may span twenty years.

At the same time, the burden of these costs can render migrants vulnerable to exploitation and can further perpetuate the cycle of dependency created by circular migration. With respect to the SAWP, the evidence is not clear that temporary migration has positive and sustainable *development* effects, although the SAWP is clearly valuable for migrant families' *subsistence*. As mentioned earlier, few migrants purchase land or invest in income-diversifying or productive enterprises, and a great majority use remittances to meet subsistence and general consumption needs and to finance the costs of migration itself, including interest on loans, remittance sending, long-distance telephone calls, and transportation.[70] With the NOC C&D Pilot Project, these costs can be compounded by fees to unscrupulous recruiters, loan sharks, forgers, and smugglers who claim to provide would-be migrants with valid work permits or access to employment. Although these third-tier migration industries – clearly operating beyond the grey areas – are difficult to document, many argue that they have expanded worldwide, and as this chapter has shown, Canada is not exempt from this trend.[71] It is also important to note that migrating and participating in a temporary worker program does not assure that remittances lead to stay-at-home development. Without real job creation, temporary migration typically ends up subsidizing future migration or "making better migrants."[72]

CONCLUSION

The rising importance of temporary labour migration programs worldwide must be read within the context of global economic restructuring. New pressures under globalization have led states to engage in a number of strategies to protect their own position within the globalized political economy,[73] including using immigration policy as part of efforts to restructure labour-capital relations within their borders. In Canada the agriculture and food industry has lobbied the state to create the environment necessary to maintain and expand its position within the globalized food system. Temporary labour migration programs have been an important part of this globalization strategy and indeed of sustaining "local food" production in Canada.

At the same time, the Canadian TFWP has allowed for an expanded role for employers, industry associations, and private interests in Canada's migration system. In particular, private intermediaries and employment agencies have stepped in to provide services to employers and migrants, many of which operate transnationally through global communication networks such as the Internet and mobile phones. These processes mirror a global trend in which the number of migrant workers is at historic levels and private agents/agencies and migrant networks have become more important than public institutions in moving people across borders.[74] Yet, whereas social networks have received scholarly attention, "the role of private agents is among the most understudied aspects of international labour migration."[75] These global networks that intertwine with Canada's TFWP remain largely above scrutiny despite their potentially significant long-term consequences for Canada's local food system.

Mobilities and Immobilities: Globalization, Farming, and Temporary Work in the Okanagan Valley

PATRICIA TOMIC AND RICARDO TRUMPER

INTRODUCTION

Mexican workers have a history of migration from the country-side to the cities and also to the United States. This migration was exacerbated by the signing of the North American Free Trade Agreement (NAFTA) in 1994 and by the adherence of successive Mexican governments to neoliberal policies of free markets and integration into the American economy. Since there is little work to be found in Mexican cities, export of labour power to foreign labour markets, particularly to the United States, has continued to increase. Moving north has been normalized as a way of life for Mexican workers, with growing numbers of urban men joining the ranks of rural labourers who cross the border mostly illegally. At the same time, unlike in Europe, where the European Union has legitimized border crossings by citizens of signatory countries, the borders between the NAFTA countries have hardened and a combination of racism and the interests of the prison industry have resulted in the criminalization of illegal immigration from Mexico. However, the flow of migrants continues unabated. Mexican illegal migrants join the millions of migrants who serve the interests of global capital by offering cheap labour power. A minority of Mexican temporary labourers find their way legally into the United States through the H-2A visa program for temporary agricultural migrants.[1] In 2007 around 87,000 migrants were granted H-2A visas.[2] Others avail themselves of the

opportunity to work temporarily in Canada in the long-established
Seasonal Agricultural Worker Program (SAWP). Through the SAWP,
workers are transported year after year for limited periods of time
to work on Canadian farms and at nurseries under conditions that
Canadians refuse to accept. Based on our research on the SAWP in
the Okanagan Valley in British Columbia, in this chapter we look
at Mexican workers in movement. We are influenced by the "new
mobilities" paradigm, which incorporates mobility as a fundamental
idea to understand social phenomena in a global, networked world.[3]
We contrast the travel of Mexican workers to Canada with that
of the kinetic elites worldwide, who cross borders with ease, have
special privileges in airports around the world, are often fluent in
different languages, and feel at home wherever they go. We look
at mobilities together with immobilities.[4] We argue that temporary
Mexican farm workers, always ready to be in motion at the conven-
ience of Canadian employers, move in fits and starts through borders
that, although crossed legally, are constantly dangerous and risky for
them. We investigate how workers' travel to Canada is contingent
upon the immobilization of their families in Mexico, how sending
remittances back to Mexico is an essential aspect of their movement,
and how their return home at the end of each contract, sometimes
even at the will of the employer, are all done in accordance with the
conditions imposed by the SAWP. Further, we discuss how the SAWP
is designed to immobilize these workers while in Canada through
work contracts that tie them to a single employer and root them in
places where the gaze and power of the employer are ubiquitous.[5]

METHODOLOGY

This chapter emerges from a collaborative research project conducted
in the Okanagan Valley during 2008 and 2009 to study housing
conditions under the SAWP.[6] In this qualitative research, we interviewed officials from government and service organizations, from
farmers' organizations, and from community organizations, farmers,
union officials, and Mexican migrant farm workers in British Columbia. We used a combination of methods to secure participants.
We approached officials in key government offices and in organizations working on areas relevant to the project; we also contacted a

number of farmers in the area who hire Mexican temporary workers to request an interview and to obtain access to their workers for the same purpose. From these initial contacts, we used a snowball sampling technique to access other participants.[7] Many of the workers we interviewed were accessed through their employers, as most of them dwell in their employers' premises and spend most of their time in Canada within the confines of the farm. In some cases, the farmer chose the worker or workers to whom we had access, and on one occasion the farmer even drove the workers to a public place for us to conduct the interview while he waited.[8] Other interviews took place in public offices, community centres, private homes, and public places such as cafés, pubs, and restaurants. We conducted fifty-one semistructured interviews in total. The interviews lasted an average of one hour. Most of the interviews were tape-recorded and transcribed. Interviews with Mexican workers were conducted in Spanish (four members of the team were fluent in Spanish). Members of the team visited eleven dwellings where temporary Mexican farm labourers had been accommodated that year. Most of theses dwellings were located on the property of the employers, but not all. Immediately after a visit, we tried to record all the details of the housing conditions under which the workers lived. On some occasions we took pictures of the accommodations. Some of these visits coincided with interviewing workers and/or employers.

THE SAWP

The SAWP is a program for the temporary migration of agricultural workers to Canada that was established through bilateral agreements between Canada and a number of countries in Latin America and the Caribbean, among them Mexico. The SAWP is part of a larger system of temporary migration devised by the federal and provincial governments to plug labour holes in the Canadian economy. Temporary migration has surpassed the quota of immigrants accepted by Canada on a yearly basis. In 2005 temporary migration reached around 245,000 workers.[9] Temporary workers, specifically those who work under the Temporary Foreign Worker Program (TFWP), come to Canada under the sponsorship of the Immigration and Refugee Protection Act. Their participation in the labour market is restricted, and some of these workers are confined to designated locations while in Canada. There are a variety of programs for temporary migrants, with varying degrees of rights and restrictions for workers. Almost 10 per cent of the temporary migrants in past years have been agricultural workers who migrate seasonally to labour in occupations that Canadian workers are not willing to fill. In 2009 around 3,000 of the workers who travelled to Canada to work under the SAWP journeyed to British Columbia. Of these 3,000, about 2,000 went to the Lower Mainland and 1,000 to the Okanagan Valley. The large majority of the SAWP labourers in British Columbia are Mexicans.

The SAWP agreement has two key components. One is the workers' willingness to be on call to travel to Canada when needed by employers to work for periods ranging from a few weeks to a maximum of eight months during a calendar year. Workers must leave Canada at the end of the contract or when demanded by the employer. The second crucial constituent of the SAWP is the obligation of labourers to remain attached to an employer and to a place for the duration of the contract. Thus, workers must be mobile, travelling long distances to work on Canadian farms, yet they are immobilized once in Canada and restrained from changing employers at will, from travelling freely in the country, and from dwelling outside the premises assigned to them by their employers.[10]

MOBILITY

According to Alex Ferentzy, "Today, mobility is on the agenda, with researchers such as Zygmunt Bauman and Manuel Castells, each emphasizing the need to rethink the social world by putting movement, flows, and the very evanescence of social life at the forefront of sociology."[11] Manuel Castells argues that the globalized societies of today differ from others in the past in the ability of their members to be always on the move.[12] For him, "the space of flows ... links up distant locales around shared functions and meanings on the basis of electronic circuits and fast transportation corridors, while isolating and subduing the logic of experience embodied in the space of places."[13] His emphasis is on a world structured by the continual movement of people and data – a society of transient

individuals and codes in perpetual movement and ephemeral relations. In this world, individuals are continually moving through
corridors and nodes that they barely acknowledge. This is a world
where people and data move more or less unencumbered and where
people have few national identities – a world that, from a different angle, has been called a "liquid world." Others theorize spaces
of travel as "nonplaces" of fleeting encounters barely registered by
individuals who pass through them without noticing their surround-
ings or fellow travellers, nonplaces where time is constrained, empty,
and unnoticed – in other words, wasted.[14]

Although the examination of mobilities has exploded in recent
years in acknowledgment of the importance of movement, a significant part of the analytics of societies seen in constant flow through
nonplaces deals primarily with the kinetic elites, a sort of transnational group that seems to occupy the interstices of high mobility. The chief exponents of those in perpetual motion are people
who move through VIP lounges in large airports carrying business-
class tickets and special cards, like NEXUS, documents that grant priority status to their holders, enabling them to travel quickly and
with almost no interference by skipping the passengers in economy
class, who are constantly forced to line up in order to be humili-
ated and poked. Other representatives of this group are people who
today land their helicopters at the prominent heli-places built on
the rooftops of condo and office buildings in São Paulo and other
large populated cities to avoid what seems to be the undifferentiated
masses of sheep-like commuters stuck in traffic in the increasing network of roads and highways. Also, the users of cars in parts of the
global South, those who avoid the public transit system where the
poor move slowly and dangerously, may be considered part of the
kinetic elites in perpetual movement.[15] The corridors of hypermobility have become a global continuum in the life of the kinetic elites,
who are linked by fast travel and fast communications, who carry
several passports, and who experience constant stops at airports and
stays in hotel rooms equipped with their BlackBerries and iPhones,
laptops, and other electronic devices. This segment of the world
population, mostly white and inhabiting the "First World," shares
a cosmopolitan and commodified view of the world.[16] However,
although a new type of society has emerged – a society interlinked by

data and people's movement, flexible lives, and discourses of global citizenship – this reality is not universal. The majority of people in the world are tied to a place and nation, to a local landscape and village, to local factories and street corners, never accessing the corridors, nodes, and hubs of modernity that are familiar to and normalized by the globalized elites.

In this sense, social studies must also deal with the immobilities that have been selectively built into the world of globalization as a means to prevent the movement of many in order to preserve the interests of capitalism. In fact, Tim Cresswell warns that "any study of mobility runs the risk of suggesting that the (allegedly) immobile – notions such as boundaries and borders, place, territory and landscape – is of the past and no longer relevant to the dynamic world of the 21st Century."[17] Our analysis of temporary migration confirms Cresswell's view. In fact, boundaries and borders, place, and foreign territories are an everyday reality for Mexican migrant workers, legal and illegal, as well as for other migrants, for refugees, and even, sometimes, for those tourists who do not belong to the kinetic elites. For them, the images of hypermobility described in the literature on mobility do not apply. For some people, at least, the spaces of flows are ironically also solidified into harsh spaces of immobility. Here, we direct our attention to the around 1,000 migrants who work on farms in the Okanagan Valley of British Columbia, travelling to Canada for limited periods of time. They are a small part of a worldwide population that migrates around the globe, estimated at 200 million a year.[18]

MIGRANT TEMPORARY WORKERS IN CANADIAN HISTORY

The essence of Canadian capitalism has not drastically changed over time, at least in its use and discarding of migrant workers. The Canadian economy, particularly the agricultural sector, has historically been dependent on migrant workers, many of whom have been nonwhite and quickly discarded once they were no longer useful.[19] For white Europeans (a flexible construction), as for today's kinetic elites, there were few barriers to entering Canada in order to take up residence in the country. For nonwhites, however, movement and residence were much more limited. For example, at the turn of the twentieth century the Chinese were forced to pay a head tax to enter Canada. These were mostly "bachelors" who were expected to stay for a period that would not outlast their jobs. Immobilized by contractors and debt, prodded by family needs in China, outcast and isolated, they were paid less than whites to perform dangerous or unwanted occupations. The Chinese are particularly interesting for us because many found their way to the Okanagan, an agricultural area where they stayed when they found themselves unable to pay for tickets back to China. They lived in a ghetto area in downtown Kelowna. At one point, one-quarter of Kelowna's population was Chinese, but there is almost no historical record of their existence, despite their contribution to the region.[20] Whereas the names of prominent white men of Kelowna's past have found their way onto city streets and parks, none of the Chinese workers' names has been used for this purpose. Except a few records in the archives of the city and pictures in museums and on city and airport walls, the Chinese of this region have disappeared from the collective memory and history of the city.[21]

Perhaps the difference between the present and the past for migrants and sojourners is that whereas present sojourners and migrants are systematically sent back home after the working season is over, in the early twentieth century most Chinese bachelor migrants remained in Canada without their families, were isolated in selective areas, and had little or no contact with mainstream society, as demonstrated by Ross Huyskamp in his recent report to the City of Kelowna's Community Heritage Commission.[22] For example, in 1882 Prime Minister Sir John A. Macdonald expressed in Parliament his belief that the Chinese would not become permanent settlers because they had arrived without women or children. The expectation was that they would not have children with non-Chinese women. Thus they would become extinguished. This form of hypocritical eugenics was, to a large extent, successful in keeping Canada white until past the middle of the twentieth century. Immobile, alone, and with little means, the Chinese bachelors of the turn of the twentieth century withered away.[23]

Needed but unwelcome, these migrant nonwhite workers were, as they are now, made to travel to Canada under restrictive conditions. Ironically, these mobile peoples were and are immobilized once arriving in the country. The Chinese had travelled long days in the bowels of ships, hired by contractors who advanced them money to pay for head taxes charged according to racist legislation. Once in Canada they were subject to legislation that denied them citizenship and well-paid work. In fact, they were forced into dangerous jobs, banned from many occupations, condemned to Chinatowns and separated quarters in labour camps, placed in the basements of hospitals when sick, and interred in segregated graveyards.[24]

Other people of colour, such as Mexican, Filipino, Guatemalan, and Jamaican migrants, have replaced the Chinese imports of the turn of the twentieth century. Cresswell insists that the contemporary experiences of many mobile individuals are not as fluid, easy, and glamorous as those of the kinetic elites. In fact, for the Mexican migrant agricultural workers who travel to Canada every year for a limited sojourn under the SAWP and for the Guatemalan and Filipino workers who enter Canada under other types of temporary working visas,[25] the meaning of airports, passports, borders, aeroplanes, and communications with home is completely different from the meaning attached to these elements of experience when the traveller belongs to the contemporary kinetic elites.[26] Still, both groups – the kinetic elites and the migrant workers – experience mobility as a central aspect of their lives, and both experience mobility at an ever-increasing speed. In fact, one of the largest differences between the Chinese migrants at the turn of the twentieth century and the migrant workers of today is speed. And this is an important difference, no doubt. As Paul Virilio has pointed out, speed has not stopped increasing.[27] The ever-increasing speed allows neoliberal post-Fordist capitalism to recruit not only labour from faraway markets but also just-in-time labour. Like any other input in the productive process, workers arrive just when they are needed for exactly the time they are needed and are shipped back just when the job is done.[28] Concepts of nation, nationalism, and citizenship and the interests of capital contribute to keeping the movement of labourers under strict control,[29] whereas goods and capital itself move freely around the world. Whereas ships were the means of transportation used by immigrants and migrants at the turn of the twentieth century, the aeroplane is the instrument of choice to transport the present-day workers. For Mexicans, the airport of Mexico City is key for their travels.

WORKERS' MOBILITIES

The survival of Mexican workers and that of their families often involves movement, sometimes their migration from the country-side to cities and towns and sometimes their movement to a foreign country. For those who will move to another country, the first step is to decide whether to try Canada or the United States, legally or illegally. The decision to apply for a legal visa to Canada depends largely on the weight of the pros and cons in terms of risk and opportunity. The potential migrant must take into consideration all the alternatives. One is to cross the border illegally to the United States; a second is to try one of the few legal venues for working temporarily in the United States;[30] and a third is to apply for temporary agricultural work in Canada. Other possibilities are few. In fact, especially since the signing of the North American Free Trade Agreement between the Governments of Canada, Mexico, and the United States – which has resulted in the displacement of millions of people in Mexico – Mexican workers have been forced to emigrate north in increasing numbers,[31] while the borders between the signatories of NAFTA have been hardened through measures that include the mobilization of military personnel, the formation of paramilitary posses in the United States, and the construction of a continuous wall between the United States and Mexico.

Mobility is not a new phenomenon for Mexicans. Mexico has a long history of internal migration to Mexican cities and, at present, a practice of external migration to the United States.[32] Judith Adler Hellman argues that in Mexico migration has been normalized. She persuasively shows that everyday life has been adapted to the crossing of the American border by Mexican migrants, which is an increasingly expensive and dangerous excursion. In these trips, illegal migrants pay the *coyote* (smuggler) escalating fees, and they run the risk of being mugged, of getting lost or hurt, and of being caught and imprisoned in the vast and growing American industrial prison system. Given the criminalization of illegal migration to the

United States since the 1990s, "illegals" may not be able to go back to Mexico for long periods of time.[33] Nonetheless, there are positive aspects for those who choose to cross illegally to the United States. There are things workers who come to Canada under the SAWP cannot do, as tightly controlled legal workers, that they may do as illegal workers in the United States. For example, in the United States illegal workers are mobile, or relatively mobile. In Canada, in accordance with the norms of the bilateral agreement between the federal government and the sending country, temporary farm workers cannot change employers at will[34] and usually have difficulties leaving their place of employment after work since many, without access to means of transportation, must depend on their employers to leave the farm. In fact, the bilateral agreement requires employers to take the temporary foreign workers out only once a week for shopping and errands. We will return to this issue later. Moreover, illegals in the United States may stay in the country for long periods, whereas just-in-time legal workers in Canada must leave as soon as they are not needed. By 15 December, every foreign temporary agricultural worker under the SAWP must have left Canada.[35]

The above discussion shows how even in the context of the non-kinetic elites, there are different types of mobility conditions for migrants. In fact, the comparison between Mexican migration to the United States and to Canada shows differential conditions of motility marking the decisions taken by would-be migrants about choosing one country over the other in search of work. The process of migration to the United States, legal and illegal, has been institutionalized for so long and is so significant for the US economy that it has not been affected by the relatively small temporary migration of workers to Canada.[36] Yet in Mexico the waiting list of applicants for work in Canada is long. Indeed, there is a long list in Mexico of those willing to work for around $10 an hour on a farm in Canada, a salary that does not draw Canadian workers, even at times of high unemployment in the country.[37] This situation facilitates paying low wages to temporary foreign workers and, most important, submits them to strict discipline during their stay in Canada.

An international North American labour market for agriculture – comprising Mexican and Jamaican labourers in Canada and illegal migrants from Mexico, Central America, and other parts of the world in the United States – is made possible because there is a global labour force that is mobile enough to travel long distances to supply labour at cheaper wages than those paid to legal residents in Canada and the United States. Residence – the invention of nationality, borders, and belonging – is central to a process that fragments the labour markets in the global North in order to allow for differential wages.[38] Thus, unlike the unencumbered instant movement of data and capital,[39] the unhindered movement of American and Canadian tourists, and the mostly free movement of goods by truck, ship, and rail between countries, the mobility of Mexicans, especially poor Mexicans, is slowed down by borders and policies that immobilize them inside the foreign countries where they labour. In airports there is a gradation of speed, mostly determined by neoliberal parameters whereby the wealthier see their travel and controls facilitated while the masses are subject to slow movement and harsh surveillance.[40] Thus, although just-in-time migration implies that Mexican labourers can be deployed quickly when needed in faraway places, given their condition of being migrant nonkinetic elites from the global South, their travels are encumbered by the unequal forms of control and surveillance that characterize airports and borders, as well as by the slow pace of mobility to which they are subject within the airport. Moreover, for this group, the gradation of speed in transnational travel extends beyond the airport. In the case of Mexican temporary farm workers destined to Canada, it begins with a painfully slow bureaucratic process in Mexico of selecting the workers who will travel temporarily to Canada, where they will eventually end up in a condition of quasi immobility on Canadian farms and at nurseries. Indeed, the program in itself rests on immobility as much as on mobility.

IMMOBILITIES

Immobility takes different forms. According to the conditions established by the SAWP, workers are basically immobile once they arrive in Canada. In his study on greenhouses in Delta, British Columbia, Asoka Mendis addresses some of the SAWP's structural issues around mobility. He writes that in an industry characterized by periods of varying labour needs, "migrant workers find themselves in fairly rigid circumstances with respect to mobility – in essence unfree labour ... Contracts, agreed to between an employer and a worker before the journey to Canada, stipulate that the worker is obliged to labour for only that particular employer and must return to Mexico upon completion of the contract term."[41] The SAWP is also dependent on the marital status of the workers: they must be married; bachelors are not eligible to come. Most of them have children. However, families do not accompany the workers; they stay immobilized in Mexico. From the Canadian government's point of view, the separation is used as pressure to make sure that the workers return to Mexico every year. It also means that the costs of reproduction of the worker's family (e.g., schooling, health, food, and shelter) are not incurred in Canada. From the Mexican point of view, the state agrees to export a labour force of married people in order to secure regular remittances from Canada.[42] Around 20,000 married people with agricultural experience, without criminal records, and who have not been caught as illegal immigrants in the United States are chosen every year to work for minimum wages in Canada under the SAWP. In the case of Okanagan agriculture, in recent years around 1,000 mobile, just-in-time labourers have travelled thousands of kilometres from all over Mexico on an annual basis to sustain otherwise unprofitable, noncompetitive businesses.[43]

The lists of temporary workers who are hired to labour in Canadian agriculture are compiled from thousands of applicants, a large reserve army that serves as a disciplining force. One of the farm workers we interviewed in the Okanagan told us that he had heard many times, "if you do not want to work, go back to Mexico. There is a long line of people who want to come to Canada." Thus the successful applicants subject themselves willingly to a slow process that will accord them the right to a work visa under the SAWP program, a flight to Canada, and a job for a few months. First, workers approach an employment centre in the state in Mexico where they reside to learn whether they are eligible. If they are, they begin a long bureaucratic process. After completing a number of forms, they are sent for a medical check-up. Applicants go through this process at their own expense, undergoing medical tests and criminal record checks in Mexico, Canada, and the United States. They also have to pay to get their travel documents.[44] Only some have the means to afford the cost involved in the application. As a successful candidate said, "We are the ones who were able to pay the cost; those who are really destitute did not have the money and had to stay." Once the bureaucratic hurdles are cleared, the worker travels to Mexico City – at times, from faraway places – to catch a plane. All workers depart from Mexico City, whether they live in Nayarit or in Tamaulipas, in Monterrey or in Chiapas. The gathering of all workers in one airport facilitates the Mexican government's and the Canadian bureaucracy's efforts to coordinate the program; it is a long journey for many of the workers to get to the departure gates of the Aeropuerto Internacional de Ciudad de México. Some workers described the hardships of taking an interurban bus from their homes to Mexico City, travelling long hours to finally reach the airport, and even having to sleep in the waiting rooms at the airport while waiting for their flights. For example, the distance between Manzanillo in Nayarit – one of the Mexican states from which some of the SAWP workers in the Okanagan Valley originate – and Mexico City is 800 kilometres. The bus ride takes about thirteen hours and costs 640 Mexican pesos, more or less $60. This is a long overnight trip for someone who must then fly to Vancouver and from there to the Okanagan. In another example, a worker from Durango rides a bus to Mexico City that also takes about thirteen hours to cover almost 930 kilometres for around 600 Mexican pesos. Other labourers may live closer to Mexico City's international airport. The bus ride from Puebla to Mexico City, 120 kilometres away, lasts less than two hours; the trip from Guanajuato to the Distrito Federal, approximately 360 kilometres away, takes around four hours by bus and costs 350 pesos; Michoacán is 300 kilometres away from the Distrito Federal, and the journey may be made in four hours. These are often long, complicated, and slow trips that are far from the glamour experienced by the kinetic elites and by the global citizen. Worldwide, some workers who are integrated into the post-Fordist networked economies of a globalized neoliberal world are aero-mobile, whereas others, particularly industrial workers, use the bus for their insertion into the system.[45] Indeed, speed has accelerated for some social classes but remains at pre-globalization rates for many others. The Mexican workers who migrate seasonally to Canada move slowly through the corridors of the interurban bus systems in Mexico (as do many industrial workers), riding the most economical, uncomfortable, and sometimes dangerous buses to and from the airport in Mexico City.

And yet, after travelling by land all the way to the international airport in Mexico City, workers may be sent back home for several reasons: the farmers may not need them anymore; workers who are late getting to the airport may be replaced by other workers; and sometimes workers may even be attacked on their way to Mexico City. Also, the Mexican officials keep a reserve of workers in the waiting room at the international airport in Mexico City to make sure that the Canadian farmer will get all of his or her labour power just in time. A Mexican official explained to us that "there is always people we call reserves that the office sends in case someone is missing, perhaps someone who has been punished, someone who missed his or her flight, or someone who did not have a designated employer and in this way is accommodated." The Mexican government keeps a close watch on, and control over, the workers at the airport to complete its part of the bureaucratic process efficiently. In fact, its Ministry of Foreign Affairs maintains an office at the airport in Mexico City to process workers according to the instructions found in a passenger list prepared by the Mexican Ministry of Welfare, which, in turn, uses data collected by the airline selected by the Mexican government to transport the workers. This process was explained to us by a Mexican official in the following words: "There must be only one agent for transporting the workers to Canada ... if it is [a Mexican airline] it must be Mexicana the one to organize the flights ... they are the ones who inform [the Consulate] and the secretary of labour. The secretary of labour has a call centre to inform the workers. Transportation must be well organized because the number of applications must match the number of workers, both those asked by name by the employers [those who are returning to work for an employer at his or her request] and those who have not been named." Eventually, both the "named" workers and those who have not yet been informed of their placement board the plane that transports them to airports in Canada, from which they depart to farms and nurseries after clearing immigration.[46]

But unlike a tourist or a businessperson, who upon arriving in Canada and clearing immigration is free to move at will, the temporary workers are received by an official from the Mexican Consulate who, in turn, either hands them over directly to employers or directs them to flights to other city airports where employers or their representatives will be waiting for them. A Mexican official explained this protocol: "X is our official in charge of the airport logistics. He meets the workers on their arrival, and he is in direct communication with immigration offices to make sure transportation will work and that the workers arrive well and that they meet their employers." The same source added, "some farmers go to the airport to meet their workers, others buy tickets for connecting flights, and others hire transportation to the farms." This process is an early warning of the tight conditions under which temporary SAWP workers live and work.

Temporary agricultural workers are seemingly like any member of the globalized population, flexible people willing to take risks and make sacrifices in order to fulfil the many demands and pressures of life in contemporary society; they are prepared to travel far, to pass often through airports, to cross borders, to be on the road for months, to live in more than one country, and to separate from family, friends, and communities for long periods.[47] Like other globetrotting globalized and postnational elites and tourists, Mexican workers tighten their seat belts and follow all of the rituals of international flights. Yet, they hardly share similar experiences with the global elites who enjoy discursive entitlement to global citizenship, or with tourists enticed to travel and consume fun and dreams far from home. Many of the people who labour for Canadian farmers today possess Mexican nationality but few citizenship rights in either Mexico or Canada, nor do they hold global citizenship. Whereas kinetic elites feel at home in global spaces and often remember travel fondly, Mexican workers, who must work away from home but need permission from Mexican and Canadian governments to move, show little pleasure when they describe their temporary travels between countries in search of work. In today's global world, some people are able to move almost at will and to live, work, and enjoy life in different countries by choice, whereas others who are also in constant motion face many constraints, prohibitions, and hardships. Glenn Lucas, manager of the British Columbia Fruit Growers Association, states the conditions of Mexican workers' mobility in Canada: "There is very little risk, if any at all, of [Mexican workers] trying to stay [in the Okanagan] illegally." He added, "Mexico is their home and they know that they can return the next year without any problem."[48]

It is not surprising, then, to learn that after arriving at the airport in Vancouver, the Mexican workers destined for the Okanagan are carefully routed toward the sites where they will labour for the season. It is at this point that, according to the framework of the SAWP, the worker is subject to a process of immobilization. Indeed, the preconditions for the workers' immobilization have already been established by the regulations of the bilateral agreement between Canada and signing countries. As already stated, the temporary worker is tied by contract to a single employer, so changing employers is not easy; it must be sanctioned by the authorities of both countries and is subject to the worker's willingness to transfer.[49] A Mexican official explained that changing employers is nominally possible but so complex that it is generally shunned by workers, employers, and bureaucrats. Another form of immobility results from the housing regulations in the program. Priority is given to housing the SAWP workers on the work premises and within the sight of the employers or their representatives. Often the worker lives in a panopticon that is hard to escape, where the gaze of the employer easily reaches his or her workers and their living facilities.[50] Temporary foreign migrant workers labour under conditions close to the indenture systems of the past. They are tied to employers who have the legal ability to control all details of their lives while they honour the contract. Even when the employer does not use this power, the option is always present. Workers are also under the gaze of both the Canadian and the Mexican governments; both governments collaborate in making sure that the system of just-in-time labour implemented for the survival of the agricultural sector in Canada continues to operate rationally.

IMMOBILE IN THE OKANAGAN

The SAWP workers' immobility in the Okanagan embraces all aspects of their lives from the time of their arrival at the airport in Vancouver to the moment they depart Canada. Some Okanagan employers drive to Vancouver to pick up the workers at the airport and drive them to Kelowna, Penticton, or Osoyoos, adding four or five hours to a trip that started in different states in Mexico many hours before. When workers on their first trip to the interior are not picked up at the Vancouver airport but catch a connecting flight, Mexican officials may accompany them to the departure gates. A worker described this process, saying that "on arrival ... there is a roll call; we are placed in a room where there are bosses who ask for us from different corners." He also explained,

> a Mexican consul [consular officer] is waiting for us at the airport; he helps us to fill the visa form. They [immigration officers] place us in the room, and the Mexican consul is there only to give support to the officers and for interpreting. From there, we are sent to our destiny if we continue by air, or we are assigned to those bosses who are waiting for us at the airport ... In our case, the company pays for the flight to Kelowna. They are waiting for us at the airport. On arrival, they pick us up, feed us, and accommodate us in the trailers they have ready waiting for our arrival.

Most of the SAWP workers, at least in the Okanagan, are placed in accommodations on the farms, as this is the most efficient system from the point of view of the government. Although in British Columbia the Mexican workers pay rent, they do not sign rental agreements or have a say about their accommodations. In a few cases, employers forfeit the right to charge rent, but most workers pay 7 per cent of their monthly salaries for accommodation, up to a total of $550 for the season, as established by the contract. From our interviews with workers we learned that many of them must ask for permission to bring guests to the farm and must adhere to rules with respect to drinking, smoking, and having parties. Among the cases we studied, we found that one employer who hires a large number of workers locks the doors of the farm to impede the free movement of his workers. In another case, the workers have to ask the foreman, who has his own house on the same premises, for permission to open the gate if a vehicle brings visitors to their home. But in many other cases it is only the closeness of employers and workers that makes the situation difficult for people who feel powerless and who cannot dare to act as though they were in their own homes; after all, the landlord is the *patrón*, and the workers depend very much on their bosses' good will to be able to work in Canada. They also depend on their bosses for most of their everyday needs, including transportation, translation, information, the opening of bank accounts, access to a doctor, and buying medicines.[51]

The basic problem of immobility for many workers in the Okanagan is their location. In most cases, given that workers are without free access to means of transportation, moving from the place of dwelling to the city is a major problem. It is difficult to generalize, but from what we saw and heard during the time we conducted the research, it is safe to say that many workers are quite immobile on farms and at nurseries. The premises where they work and usually dwell are often far from town and in areas provided with little public transit given that the norm in the Okanagan is to be dependent on private transportation. And even when public transit is available, as was mentioned in our interviews, the cost of the bus ticket may be an issue for the worker. Thus, although some employers lend vehicles to workers who have a driver's licence – a minority – Mexicans frequently ride bicycles, sometimes in inappropriate areas for bikes, or depend on their employers for trips to do their banking and to shop for basic goods, phone cards, and presents for their families. One trip a week for these errands is the norm.

Thus, for people who work ten or twelve hours a day under the sun, there are few chances for leisure or relaxation. Most housing facilities do not include a conventional "family room," and the television sets are often placed in precarious positions in kitchens or bedrooms to be shared by several people. Lack of mobility makes it almost impossible to leave the house in order to escape to the corner store, a pub, a bar, or a coffee house, something that is normally taken for granted by resident Canadians. It is also difficult for workers to meet other people. Meeting other Mexican workers is more probable, but even this occurrence is often reduced to once-a-week chance encounters while waiting to be picked up by the boss in the lobby of the supermarket or at Value Village (nicknamed "*la segunda*" by the workers), where workers buy second-hand items for themselves and to take home. In fact, agricultural temporary workers see the Canadian world from a distance while passing by at great speed in cars they cannot drive; from a distance too, they see restaurants and coffee shops they cannot patronize and offices and factories where they cannot apply for work. They are noncitizens, temporary guest workers living in a hostile world that looks down on them and that will not accept them as permanent residents even though this world can hardly survive without their labour power. Clearly, they do not belong to the population of people with transnational identities who have been liberated by travel. These temporary workers certainly travel, every year if permitted, but they do so on different grounds. Once in Canada, Mexican workers are immobilized on farms they have not chosen, share their accommodations with other Mexican workers without any say, work in fields in the company of others in similar conditions, watch television they hardly understand, and seldom have access to any form of recreation. Their greatest expenses are their phone calls to Mexico – their link to the outside world – and the remittances they send to Mexico every two weeks. These workers are not at ease while travelling. They have no resemblance to the image of the cosmopolitan elites that preoccupies many writers.

Pico Iyer writes of the type of people who are at home everywhere and nowhere, the citizens of the world.[52] He adds an important point: these citizens of the world speak more than one language. Most Mexican temporary migrants in the Okanagan do not speak English. Indeed, the Mexican temporary workers are hardly at home in Canada and even barely citizens in their own country, where they are peasants, poor, and nonwhite. They have great difficulty communicating with Canadians, including their employers, who, in turn, are sometimes proudly monolingual. The food Mexicans consume in Canada is Mexican, usually cooked by the workers themselves with the cheapest Mexican staples they can find. Supermarkets in the Okanagan have begun to have aisles with food specifically targeting these workers, including flour for tortillas, salsa, mole, and the like. In many ways, despite the travelling and the distance from Mexico, these men (most temporary workers in the Okanagan are men) are more in touch with their Mexican co-workers and their families at home than with Canadians; they are often isolated, anxious, overworked, and bored. The connection with Mexico is thus essential for their wellbeing.

This is an era of instant international communications for the kinetic elites through BlackBerries, iPhones, Skype, e-mail, twitters, chats, and the like. In contrast, Mexican workers in Canada are usually forced to rely on phone cards to call, at great cost, their families' cellular phones at home using pay phones or at times phones provided by their employers. A $5 card, said one of the workers, lasts only twelve minutes; at more than 40 cents a minute, this is a sizable amount of money for them. And for documents, Mexican workers must rely on faxes that are sent to corner stores and other places where they pay to send or receive. This is also more expensive than the use of the electronic devices that the kinetic elites have already normalized in their lives.

Workers' communications with their families are almost as important as remittances. This is the most obvious and steady connection with Mexico and home. Remittances are the central purpose of the workers' trip and one of the key motivations for the Mexican government to participate in the SAWP. These workers are people who make $10 an hour and who in a "good" week work sixty or sixty-five hours, grossing about $600. A biweekly paycheque might reach $1,000 or $1,200. Most often, these temporary workers keep around $150 from their paycheques and send home the rest of the money. Here, transfer is quick,[53] as money is often sent via Western Union, a multinational company that makes profits through transfers that are expensive, costing a minimum of $15 at source, plus profits from the exchange rate charged to the recipient in Mexico. Certainly, Western Union is not the only company that makes profits from the temporary workers in Kelowna. Workers are paid by cheque or direct deposit and thus need to open bank accounts, and banks usually charge them a fee. The workers must keep their accounts year round to be able to receive their tax refunds while they are away. Workers often claim their refunds electronically through their bankcards when in Mexico, paying a fee to the bank in Canada and losing from the exchange in Mexico.

No wonder workers experience a sense of relief when they reinitiate their movement and, loaded with second-hand presents from

Value Village, return to Mexico after a season working the land in the Okanagan Valley, a trip that lasts as many hours as the one that brought them to Canada at the beginning of the season. The workers involved in these yearly trips certainly do not experience a "liquid world"[54] or global citizenship. They are very much aware that their experience has been one of marginalization, exploitation, segregation, and confinement.[55] In pragmatic terms, they force themselves into this restrictive type of mobility, a form of mobility that for many becomes a way of life, as they voluntarily choose to return year after year to Canada in search of means of survival. A globalized world has facilitated this strategy at the cost of their immobility and rights.

CONCLUSION

Influenced by the idea that it is imperative "to rethink the social world by placing movement, flows, and the very evanescence of social life at the forefront of sociology,"[56] we have studied the movement of temporary agricultural workers from Mexico to Canadian farms, more specifically to farms in the Okanagan Valley of British Columbia. We claim that if we are to rethink the social world in these terms, this rethinking must be inclusive of the broad types of mobilities present in the globalized world of today. No doubt, distant locales share functions and meanings on the basis of electronic technologies and fast transportation corridors, but the lives of those "always on the move" may vary drastically. The richness and diversity of the experience of mobility and how the transformations occasioned by this experience effect the social life of different locales need to be closely and carefully investigated.[57] Rethinking ideas of national identity, citizenship, and cosmopolitanism as well as rethinking the notion of travel as a fleeting encounter barely registered by individuals may take very different dimensions depending on who participates in this undertaking and their reasons for doing so. Starting from the premise that the large majority of the world's population is tied to place and nation, and thus to local landscapes, and considering that they seldom participate in the nodes of modernity and corridors of hypermobility in the way that the kinetic elites do, we have focused our attention here on the duality of mobility and immobility experienced by workers of the South in their quest to find employment in the North. From this perspective, notions of borders, place, territory, landscape, citizenship, and rights, to name a few, take on very different meanings in the dynamic world of the twenty-first century. We have tried to demonstrate how, in the globalized world of the twenty-first century's spaces of flows, some individuals are solidified into harsh spaces of immobility.

In fact, since the late 1960s workers from the South have been imported to Canada to fill the positions in agriculture that Canadians refuse to accept under the conditions imposed by employers. The agricultural industry is heavily dependent on these workers, yet they are classified as low-skilled and are denied rights that are taken for granted by Canadian citizens and permanent residents. Under the SAWP, foreign temporary farm workers are not entitled to live in Canada for more than eight months in a year, and employers determine the length of their stay; they must leave the country when their employers decide. Their movement between employers is restricted, and they have to accept the accommodations provided for them by their employers. Thus their willingness to travel when called is a prerequisite for work, and their immobilization in Canada is also a prerequisite for employment. In a contradictory manner, they are expected to embrace the flexibility imposed by post-Fordist capitalism but are subject to the precariousness of neoliberal employment. They must be capable of the hypermobility required for participation in a globalized labour force but must accept being immobilized by the terms of bilateral agreements that grant employers the power to use a postmodern form of indentured labour to run their farms, orchards, and nurseries in Canada. Temporary foreign agricultural workers must be aero-mobile like a cosmopolitan global citizen, but must undergo the surveillance of a suspicious Canadian state and cross unfriendly borders while running the risk of being turned back at any point after their arrival.

4

Debates on Temporary Agricultural Worker Migration in the North American Context

CHRISTINA GABRIEL AND LAURA MACDONALD

INTRODUCTION

Canada, the United States, and Mexico implemented the North American Free Trade Agreement (NAFTA) in 1994, establishing the world's largest free trade area. Economic integration has not been accompanied by the development of significant continental mobility rights. Indeed, migration was largely sidelined in the NAFTA debate. However, migration issues – temporary labour, irregular flows, people smuggling, and the status of migrants – remain on the policy agenda of member countries. In the post-9/11 period, these concerns have been coupled with a greater state preoccupation with security.[1] Nevertheless, proponents of a North American community have argued that labour mobility is critical to deeper integration. For example, a 2005 report advocated that "Canada and the United States should expand programs for temporary labor migration from Mexico. For instance, Canada's successful model for managing seasonal migration in the agricultural sector should be expanded to other sectors where Canadian producers face a shortage of workers and Mexico may have a surplus of workers with appropriate skills."[2]

Canada's Seasonal Agricultural Worker Program (SAWP) figures prominently in official policy discourses at both the regional and global levels. For example, Prime Minister Stephen Harper noted during Mexican President Felipe Calderón's 2010 visit to Canada's Parliament that "Over the last 16 years, the North American Free

Trade Agreement has brought Mexico and Canada closer together
than ever before ... Educational and cultural exchanges are flourish-
ing, and our Seasonal Agricultural Workers Program is widely recognized as a model for international labour mobility arrangements."[3]
In turn, the Calderón administration has characterized the program
as a "pillar" of the Canada-Mexico bilateral relationship.[4] Similarly,
at the global level the program is also characterized as an example of
"good practice."[5] This construction of the SAWP as a model for temporary worker programs stands in stark contrast to its US counter-
part, the H-2A visa program, which is also directed at the recruitment
of migrant farm workers but is often seen as deeply problematic.

The United States and Mexico have attempted for years to fashion, either bilaterally and/or nationally, programs to address Mexican cross-border labour migration (much of which is irregular) to
the United States. To date, these attempts have foundered on the
shores of domestic political debates and the rise in anti-migrant
sentiment in the United States. Canada's seasonal agriculture program is frequently held up by both Canadian and Mexican actors
as a means to address some aspects of the US-Mexican migration
policy impasse.[6]

This chapter examines the workings of two guest worker programs
that govern temporary labour in the agricultural sector: the Seasonal
Agricultural Worker Program in Canada and the H-2A visa program
in the United States.[7] Here, the asymmetries that characterize North
American regional integration are particularly evident. In each case,
it is Mexico that provides farm labour to its more wealthy northern neighbours. The first section of the chapter situates these two
sector-specific programs within global and regional contexts. The
following sections outline and briefly compare the dynamics of the
two programs while underlining the critical importance of national
variations. Despite the fact that, as our discussion shows, the two
programs are substantially similar, it is only the Canadian program
that is held up as a model of best practices, whereas the US system
is commonly perceived as "broken." This chapter interrogates this
paradox and suggests that arguments for using the SAWP as a possible model for US reform and/or as a more comprehensive framework for continental labour mobility are profoundly misplaced.

THE CITIZENSHIP DIVIDE AND TEMPORARY LABOUR: GLOBAL AND REGIONAL SCALES

Temporary labour migration – involving temporary workers, seasonal workers, working holidaymakers, and contract workers – is an important aspect of international migration today. Indeed, the Organisation for Economic Co-operation and Development (OECD) notes that this form of mobility now exceeds the number of permanent labour migrants in OECD countries.[8] This section considers some of the broader issues associated with the phenomenon of temporary migration at the global and regional levels.

Temporary worker programs are designed to recruit workers from across the skills spectrum. However, there is an increasing differentiation within temporary worker flows between highly skilled, skilled, and low-skilled individuals. Programs governing the entry of low-skilled workers are often much more tightly regulated, and participants may have access to fewer rights than those who are admitted under the auspices of a skilled or high-skilled temporary work scheme. Migrants who enter under low-skilled temporary work programs also frequently fill occupations characterized as "3-D jobs – dirty, dangerous and difficult work."[9] Agriculture is an exemplar of a 3-D job sector and relies heavily on migrant labour. According to the International Labour Organization (ILO), "The United States has the most hired farm workers: some 2.5 million persons are employed for wages at some time during a typical year, most of them for less than six months. About 90 per cent of the migrants who work seasonally on farms ... were born abroad. The share of irregular or unauthorized workers among all hired crop workers rose from less than 10 to over 50 per cent during the 1990s."[10]

The ILO further notes that less than 10 per cent of the world's hired farm workers are represented by unions or other types of workers' organizations. Migrant farm work is often characterized by little or no access to collective bargaining rights, inadequate income, and no "social protection from unemployment, sickness, and injury."[11] But additionally, as Peter Stalker observes, these programs are themselves constituted by social forces. In his words, national workers have been "conditioned to reject the 3-D jobs." He points out that

increases in tertiary and postsecondary education and the expansion
of the middle class have had an impact on the number of manual
workers available for these types of jobs. Compared to nationals,
3-D workers generally enjoy lower wages and status. But there are
further differences among migrant workers depending on country of
origin. He argues that "most receiving countries have a hierarchy of
immigrants and give the most unpopular jobs to the least-favored
nations."[12] Here, the complex intersections of race, gender, and citizenship come to the fore.[13] The broader social relations occasioned
by these intersections are coupled with the unequal positionings of
nations within the global political economy, and both underpin the
global asymmetries that frame migration generally and temporary
migration specifically.

These asymmetries have led migration scholars to consider the
ways that citizenship functions as a tool of exclusion.[14] In their discussion of the "north/south citizenship divide," Daiva Stasiulis and
Abigail Bakan note that processes of neoliberalism and globalization have exacerbated unequal relations associated with legacies of
colonialism and imperialism in the global South and have increased
pressures to migrate even as countries in the global North have simultaneously enacted greater migration controls.[15] They write, "The
First World state's ability to deny Third World migrants access to
naturalization becomes a legal and internationally sanctioned means
of discrimination ... Denial of citizenship guarantees also intensi-
fies class exploitation, creating pools of labour cheapened and made
vulnerable to abuse by threats of deportation, and by pitting recent
immigrants against poor and working class citizens."[16] This insight
informs our assessment of the programs that govern the movement
of farm workers within the North American region. More specifically, temporary work programs allow receiving states, such as Canada and the United States, to meet ostensibly short-term labour needs
using labour from Mexico that is in many cases unfree, cheap, and
flexible. This form of migration also does not usually require receiving states to make long-term commitments to social integration and
broader citizenship rights. Migrant temporary workers, while earn-
ing much needed income, are placed in a precarious position by the
temporary nature of their form of employment. But beyond this circumstance, temporary workers' status relegates them to the margins

of a national community insofar as they are systematically excluded from both formal legal and substantive social citizenship rights.[17] In this manner, agricultural temporary work programs in both Canada and the United States are implicated in the North-South citizenship divide, albeit in different ways.

GLOBAL DYNAMICS AND THE MANAGEMENT OF MIGRATION

At the global level, "regulated liberalization of the global labour market" is touted as being the potential remedy for demographic deficits, development challenges, and brain drain.[18] The Global Commission on International Migration, for example, comments that "States and the private sector should consider the option of introducing carefully designed temporary migration programmes as a means of addressing the economic needs of both countries of origin and destination."[19] Similarly, the Global Forum on Migration and Development (GFMD) has identified temporary labour migration as a means to ensure legal access to labour markets and a means to protect the basic rights of migrant workers.[20] The United Nations states that "migrants benefit from having legal status and countries of origin gain from remittances and the eventual return of migrants ... Receiving countries secure workers they may need."[21] And the World Bank argues that low-skilled temporary labour mobility may aid in the fight against poverty reduction.[22]

Gerald Boucher observes that this emerging global policy discourse converges around a number of themes. First, "the structure of the global capitalist system in its neoliberal form is taken for granted, and not portrayed as part of the problem." Second, conservative elements in the nation-states of the global North are identified as the force behind restrictionist immigration policies. And third, the solution to the problems of migration management is legal temporary labour market programs.[23]

The global discourse of managed migration and its proposal for better designed temporary worker programs that are attuned to the human rights of migrants is "seen as liberal and progressive because it intends to achieve co-development goals and triple wins for migrants, countries of origin and destination."[24] Indeed, nation-states are attracted to temporary work programs for a variety of reasons. It is claimed that states' interest in these programs is informed by a number of motivations: "For the sending countries and the migrants such an approach promises access to work opportunities, human capital formation and remittances without long-term brain drain. For receiving countries, it promises to fill certain seasonal, temporary or permanent labour market needs across the skills spectrum at the lowest economic and political costs in terms of integration of new residents."[25] Boucher charges that the temporary migration proposal is in the interests of the global North and capitalist employers. The interests of migrants (who may benefit, especially if they are high-skilled) are of a secondary order. And he points out that temporary migration is only lastly aimed at the interests of countries in the global South since these reports do not demonstrate how they will actually benefit "beyond hypothesised increased levels of remittances, diaspora investment, and real brain gain."[26]

The other noteworthy aspect within the global policy dialogue and its emphasis on temporary migration is that Canada's SAWP is often raised as a model of best practices. For example, a background paper prepared for the GFMD meeting in Athens in 2009 refers to the SAWP as a "highly successful (albeit small scale) circular migration program."[27] The following year, a GFMD study on social protections also referred to the SAWP as an example of "good practice."[28] Civil society groups at GFMD meetings have felt compelled to challenge the construction of the SAWP as a "gold standard" model.[29] Further, the program itself, given the asymmetrical relationship between the states involved, the unequal positioning of employers and workers, and the current political climate, may not provide a viable basis for reform that overcomes the inequalities associated with the North-South citizenship divide.

REGIONAL DYNAMICS OF TEMPORARY LABOUR MIGRATION: NORTH AMERICA

The movement of people is recognized as a key feature of globalization, and specifically within North America, "immigration contributes to growing continental integration."[30] As we have argued elsewhere, migration patterns within the region of North America are considerably differentiated, but in each case the United States is the nodal point of a particular flow.[31]

Mexican migration to the United States has been the subject of extensive scholarly and policy focus. Considerable attention is directed to Mexicans' low-skilled and irregular migration, but it should be noted that Mexicans are also represented on the skilled side of the flow. Moreover, although Mexican labour migration to the United States is not new, recent years have seen dramatic increases in the numbers of Mexicans entering the United States. In 2008 Mexican immigrants in the United States numbered 12.7 million individuals, or about 32 per cent of the total immigrant population.[32] These figures, although striking, still obfuscate two significant tendencies. First, Mexican migration to the United States has been growing dramatically. In the period 1970–2008, the Mexican-born population multiplied seventeen-fold.[33] This movement northward is intimately connected both to the Mexican state's neoliberal-inspired development project initiated in the 1980s and to the growing labour demands of the US economy. Second, a large proportion of cross-border migration is irregular, and it has continued to grow despite US control strategies.[34] It is estimated that the irregular population of Mexicans in the United States stands at 59 per cent of the estimated total irregular population of 11.9 million.[35] Moreover, the undocumented proportion of the population that is Mexican-born is growing more rapidly than the documented proportion. The legal population from Mexico roughly doubled between 1990 and 2002, whereas the undocumented population grew by 165 per cent.[36] This sustained inward flow of undocumented Mexican migrants reflects the failure of US policymakers to address the growing needs of the US economy for low-skilled migration and to open up adequate legal avenues for migration. This complexity of Mexican migration to the United States and the ever-present reality of the irregular population pose considerable challenges for US and Mexican policymakers. In this context, the legal H-2A visa program, discussed below, is entirely inadequate to meet the demand for low-skilled agricultural labour in the United States.

Canadians also move to the United States, but their numbers are much smaller. Canadians account for only 2.2 per cent of the total foreign-born population in the United States. In contrast to the

US–Mexico case, which is characterized by mobility at the lower tiers of the labour market, Canada and the United States are linked more closely at the skilled end of the spectrum. For example, in terms of temporary movement, as Deborah Meyers and Kevin O'Neil emphasize, "Particular nationalities tend to dominate categories, as Mexicans comprise nearly all H-2A agricultural workers and Canadians receive significant numbers of H-1B high-skilled worker visas."[37]

Compared to the US situation, the flow of Mexican migrants to Canada is small. But some trends are particularly noteworthy. Chief among these is the rapid growth of the numbers of Mexicans in Canada, who form "the largest group of immigrants from Spanish speaking Latin America and [are] among the fastest growing from any country."[38] In terms of temporary workers, Mexico placed second to the United States as a source country in the period 1994–2003. The number of temporary migrant workers entering Canada legally from Mexico increased by 112 per cent in the period 1994–2001. However, most of this growth can be traced to the expansion of Mexicans' participation in the SAWP as opposed to their participation via other temporary worker categories, such as those specified in NAFTA's mobility provisions.[39] Finally, Canada has historically maintained a good image within Mexico because of its lack of a visa requirement for Mexican short-term visitors. However, the 2010 imposition of a visa requirement by the Harper government has soured the Mexican view of Canada and may reduce the numbers of Mexicans travelling to Canada.[40] In the next sections, we examine the nature of Mexicans' participation in temporary worker programs in Canada and the United States, highlighting the way that the structural factors shaping migrant flows to both countries reproduce the North-South citizenship divide described by Stasiulis and Bakan.

CANADA'S SEASONAL AGRICULTURAL WORKER PROGRAM

The bilateral relationship between Canada and Mexico within North America precedes NAFTA and spans a sixty-year period. In this section, we briefly review the workings of the SAWP, and given that the program is often touted as a "model," we consider its relevance as a model for labour mobility in North America.

The SAWP is part of a formal bilateral agreement between Canada and Mexico. In 1966 the Canadian state established the Commonwealth Caribbean and Mexican Seasonal Agricultural Worker Program to address domestic labour shortages in the farm sector. Migrant labour was recruited initially from the Caribbean and as of 1974 from Mexico.[41] It is not the intent of this section to offer a detailed overview of this program,[42] yet a few facts should be noted. In 2008 21,328 workers came to Canada. Of these workers, 11,798 were Mexicans, and Mexico was the largest sending country. The majority of workers were employed in Ontario.[43] Women also participate in this program but in small numbers – 4 per cent of all participants. However, their numbers have also risen. In 1989 37 Mexican women entered the program. In 2010 women numbered 609, largely concentrated in the Niagara region and Leamington, Ontario.[44] Gendered assumptions and subjectivities inform men's and women's differing experiences of the SAWP program.[45]

Canadian farm employers apply to local government offices to obtain workers, and they have to hire Canadians first where possible. To qualify to hire Mexican (or other SAWP) migrants, farm employers must guarantee at least 240 hours of work over six weeks and provide board and meals (or kitchen facilities). They must pay the higher of two rates – either the minimum wage or the prevailing piecework rate. The employer pays the cost of the migrant workers' transportation and then deducts wages to cover this cost. Importantly, farmers may name the workers they want. There are fines for hiring unauthorized workers and for lending migrant workers to other farm employers.[46] Under the terms of the program, workers come to Canada for a defined period, anywhere from four to eight months, and work ten to twelve hours a day, six days a week.[47] At the end of the period, migrants must return home; there is no mechanism to change one's status from temporary worker to permanent resident.

As mentioned above, the Mexican Seasonal Agricultural Worker Program is frequently hailed as an example of best practices. Thus former Canadian prime minister Jean Chrétien told Mexicans, "This program, where your farmers can come and work in Canada, has worked extremely well and now we are exploring [ways] to extend that to other sectors. The bilateral seasonal agricultural workers program has been a model for balancing the flow of temporary foreign workers with the needs of Canadian employers."[48] Similarly, Carlos Obrador, Mexico's vice consul in Toronto, characterized the program as a "real model for how migration can work in an ordered legal way."[49] It is commonly argued that the bilateral agreement is an aspect of best practices in the governance of international mobility insofar as (1) the sending state, Mexico, plays an active role in the recruitment of workers and the determination of wages and working conditions; (2) farm employers are involved in program design and implementation; and (3) the Canadian government is involved through Human Resources and Skills Development Canada (HRSDC).[50] Such programs are also attractive to sending states because their citizens can legally enter another country's labour market, which would normally be closed to them, and such agreements "allow sending governments to take back some of the authority from receiving governments. They do so by acknowledging the authority of the sending countries to represent their citizens outside their own borders."[51] Policy think-tanks allude to the fact that many workers would prefer to participate in the Canadian program than risk crossing the dangerous US-Mexico border and joining the ranks of the irregular population in the United States. That workers return at the end of the season to Mexico makes the program particularly attractive to policymakers and politicians.

These constructions of best practices have to be read in terms of governing strategies to manage migration. The program is not necessarily an example of best practices in terms of workers' rights and in fact places them in precarious conditions. As Jenna Hennebry and Kerry Preibisch have argued, there is a considerable disjuncture between the workings of the SAWP and the ideal of a well-designed temporary migration program promoted on a global scale. They note, "The lack of access to permanent migration ... the failure to recognize migrants' skills and work experience, and the mechanisms that constrain workers' labour mobility, not only encourage irregular migration among some workers but heighten all migrants' vulnerability to exploitation and abuse... This, coupled with inadequate rights and protections to enable farm workers to unionize in all provinces, provides migrants with little recourse to challenge mistreatment or improve their under-regulated working and living conditions."[52]

It is evident that the "best practices" moniker attached to the SAWP is hardly straightforward, and arguments to expand the SAWP model to other sectors are problematic. But importantly, it is unlikely that in the current political conjuncture the program will be expanded and deepened, despite lobbying by the Mexican government.

Two recent policy moves by Canada's Conservative government should be noted. First, there has been a rapid expansion of temporary worker programs in Canada, including a Low-Skill Pilot Project (2002). Here, the government has chosen not to expand the SAWP into other sectors nor to use the similar tool of a cooperative bilateral agreement. Rather, the pilot project operates alongside the SAWP. The new temporary work programs offer far fewer protections for workers than does the SAWP. Moreover, within this initiative, Mexico, despite being a NAFTA partner, is not afforded any special status, and Mexicans enter under the same conditions as other workers. Second, the Conservatives now seem to be pursuing actions that are designed to forge a stronger bilateral relationship with the United States while apparently sidelining Mexico. As one analyst has posited, "It appears that the current Canadian government views North American trilateralism as weakening its relationship with the U.S. as opposed to being complementary to solid bilateral ties with Washington and Mexico City."[53] The recent imposition of a visa requirement on Mexican nationals who wish to visit Canada is indicative of this strategy.

TEMPORARY MIGRANT WORKER AGRICULTURAL PROGRAMS IN THE UNITED STATES

Whereas the Canadian SAWP is commonly portrayed as a clear success story and an example of best practices, the US immigration system, including its provisions for temporary agricultural migrant workers, is commonly seen as "broken." There is a long and problematic history of guest worker programs in the United States. It is important to remember that, as in Canada, these programs are not isolated from trends in the broader economy but are deeply embedded in global, regional, national, and subnational labour markets. Thus changes in the legislative framework, supply of labour (both national and international), macroeconomic conditions (again, both national and international), and other factors all play into the nature and impact of temporary migrant worker programs in the United States and into the framing of these programs. In particular, the demand for these programs is shaped by the fact that the miserable working conditions and wages in agriculture mean that individuals who obtain citizenship status regularly leave agricultural work for other jobs, creating a constant demand for easily exploited foreign workers. It is also important to note that the impact of these programs also varies by state and that the legislative framework of programs is often less important than the mechanisms for enforcement of workers' rights, which are usually weak or absent.

Immigration and immigration reform have been hot-button topics in the United States for many years. Emotive and ideological responses to "illegal" immigration have impeded rational discussion of labour market needs or worker rights. Even though NAFTA says little about migration and the United States resisted Mexican wishes to include low-skilled migration within the agreement, the country's migration issues are heavily influenced by the position of the United States within the informal North American labour mobility regime. In contrast to Canada, where the numbers of undocumented workers are still relatively small, the availability of large numbers of unauthorized workers strongly skews the operation of and the discourses surrounding the US temporary seasonal agricultural program (the H-2A visa).

In the early years of US agriculture, labour was sufficiently mobile and the supply of labour was sufficiently plentiful that a formal migrant worker program was not required by farmers. However, workers remained in a highly vulnerable situation, and farmers depended upon various noneconomic forms of coercion to obtain cheap and easily exploitable labour.[54] During the Depression, public outrage about the situation of white American migrant workers (largely stimulated by John Steinbeck's 1939 novel *The Grapes of Wrath*) led to increased pressure on the government to regulate the conditions of workers in agriculture and to adopt standards similar to those used in other industries. A Senate subcommittee recommended that these rights be extended to farm workers.[55] Ultimately, however, the legislation adopted during the New Deal "institutionalized the second-class status of agricultural laborers."[56] For example, farm workers were denied both the right to collective bargaining protected in the National Labor Relations Act and the right to minimum or overtime wages enshrined in the Fair Labor Standards Act.[57] As a result of the failure of the federal government to provide protection to agricultural workers, the gap between the wages of agricultural workers and the industrial wage rate continued to widen: whereas farm workers had earned 70 per cent of industrial workers' wages in the early 1900s, this figure had dropped to 25 per cent by 1940.[58] These structural conditions continue to exercise downward pressure on wages and labour rights among all categories of agricultural workers.

During the Second World War the supply of workers who were white US citizens dried up, and California growers pushed for the development of the first large-scale formal seasonal agricultural program, the so-called "*bracero*" program, which was put in place in 1942. Under this program, which was cancelled in 1964, Mexicans filled some 4.5 million mostly agricultural jobs.[59] The Mexican government pushed for certain conditions: that the US government guarantee the contracts offered to Mexican workers, that farmers pay round-trip transportation for workers from the site of recruitment to the worksite, and that Mexican workers receive the same wages as US farm workers were receiving.[60] Another small guest worker program, the H-2 program, was created in 1943 to import a much smaller number of Caribbean workers to the East Coast.[61]

The establishment of the bracero program contributed to the creation of longstanding migrant social networks, in which migrants from Mexico are easily able to obtain jobs through their ties with other migrants from the same communities. These networks contribute to a continuous flow of workers from rural Mexico to the United States.[62] The failure of the government to enforce safeguards for workers that existed in labour law resulted in the de facto reduction of agricultural workers and displacement of domestic workers with citizenship rights.[63] In 1963 an accident occurred in which thirty-six bracero workers were killed in a bus transporting them from the fields to their labour camp in the Salinas Valley, and the bodies were not immediately claimed. Outrage over this event as well as pressure from labour groups led to the decision of Congress to end the bracero program on 31 December 1964.

Many undocumented seasonal workers were able to gain citizenship rights in the 1986 Congressional amnesty. Many of these workers then switched into other occupations, and those who remained in agriculture are now reaching the end of their fieldwork careers since few farm workers remain in this work after the age of forty-four because of its arduous character. The conditions were thus laid for the massive increase in numbers of undocumented farm workers; today, roughly 40 to 50 per cent of the US seasonal agricultural labour force are undocumented, with numbers as high as about 90 per cent in California. The massive numbers of undocumented workers act as a massive structural force exerting downward pressure on wages and rights for both undocumented and documented workers.

The termination of the bracero program led to the emergence of a new legal framework for temporary agricultural migrant labourers. Growers increasingly turned to the use of the H-2 visa. The H-2 program had originally operated alongside the bracero program and was primarily used to recruit Caribbean workers for fields in Florida and the Northeast, where workers were required for short harvest periods, whereas California growers required Mexican workers for up to eleven months a year. In 1986 the current H-2A visa was created by Congress as part of the Immigration Reform and Control Act; an H-2B category was also created in 1986 to cover nonagricultural jobs. Most of the foreign workers who enter under this category are from Mexico or the Caribbean, but unlike the Canadian SAWP program, the H-2A program is not a bilateral program, and workers may be recruited from any country approved by the Department of Homeland Security. As a result, the sending country plays no formal role in recruiting workers or overseeing their working conditions.

On paper, under the provisions of the H-2A regulations and statutes, H-2A workers have rights superior to those of farm workers with US citizenship rights and some rights superior to those of workers in the Canadian SAWP (see table 4.1). Under the H-2A program, in an effort to ensure that domestic workers are not displaced, the Department of Labor (DOL) requires employers to pay farmers the

Table 4.1
Comparison of provisions of the Canadian SAWP and the US H-2A visa

	SAWP	H-2A[1]
Governance and recruitment	Bilateral agreements (memorandums of understanding) with Mexico and Caribbean governments (Jamaica, Barbados, Trinidad and Tobago, and Organization for Eastern Caribbean States); HRSDC responsible for program; nonprofit organizations, FARMS and FERME,† administer program; sending states carry out recruitment, selection, and facilitation of travel and monitor working conditions	Federal visa program – no involvement of sending states;[2] private recruitment; Department of Labor (DOL) issues H-2 labour certifications and oversees compliance with labour laws; US Citizenship and Immigration Services (USCIS) adjudicates H-2 petitions; Department of State (DOS) issues visas to workers at consulates overseas.[3]
Wages	Best of provincial minimum wage, prevailing wage identified by Government of Canada, or same rate employer pays Canadians for same type of work[4]	Best of minimum wage, prevailing rate, or adverse effect wage rate
Other benefits	Employer provides housing and cooking area with pots and pans, part of round-trip airfare, cost of travel to worksite from airport, and workers' compensation insurance; employer ensures workers are registered with provincial health insurance plan[5]	Employer provides housing
Mobility	Worker must stay with employer who nominates him or her; worker can be repatriated by employer and has no system of appeal	Worker must stay with employer who nominates him or her
Certification of employer	HRSDC certification required; employer must show that no Canadian workers are available	Department of Labor certification required
Number of workers in category (2008)	21,328[6]	64,404[7]
Extension	Farmers may "name" workers for rehiring the following year; no limit on renewals	Up to three years
Adjustment of status?	No	No

† FARMS is the Foreign Agricultural Resource Management Services, and FERME is La Fondation des entreprises en recrutement de la main-d'oeuvre agricole étrangère.

Table 4.1 (continued)

Sources: (1) Papademetriou et al., "Aligning Temporary Immigration Visas with US Labor Market Needs"; (2) as of 18 January 2012, nationals from the following countries are eligible to participate in the H-2A visa program: Argentina, Australia, Barbados, Belize, Brazil, Bulgaria, Canada, Chile, Costa Rica, Croatia, Dominican Republic, Ecuador, El Salvador, Estonia, Ethiopia, Fiji, Guatemala, Haiti, Honduras, Hungary, Iceland, Ireland, Israel, Jamaica, Japan, Kiribati, Latvia, Lithuania, Macedonia, Mexico, Moldova, Montenegro, Nauru, Netherlands, Nicaragua, New Zealand, Norway, Papua New Guinea, Peru, Philippines, Poland, Romania, Samoa, Serbia, Slovakia, Slovenia, Solomon Islands, South Africa, South Korea, Spain, Switzerland, Tonga, Turkey, Tuvalu, Ukraine, United Kingdom, Uruguay, and Vanuatu (see United States Citizenship and Immigration Services, "H2-A Temporary Agricultural Workers"); (3) United States Department of Homeland Security, "H-2A Temporary Agricultural Worker Program"; (4) Human Resources and Skills Development Canada (HRSDC), "Seasonal Agricultural Worker Program"; (5) different provisions apply regarding benefits in British Columbia (see ibid.); (6) United Food and Commercial Workers (UFCW) Canada, *The Status of Migrant Farm Workers in Canada, 2008–2009*; (7) this number reflects the number of visas in this category issued abroad, not the total number of workers, since the same worker may be issued more than one visa in a given year (see United States Department of State, Bureau of Consular Affairs, "Multi-Year Graphs").

higher of three wages: the minimum, the prevailing, or the adverse effect wage rate. Employers are thus required to provide these workers with higher pay than the rates prevailing for undocumented and even citizen workers as well as with free housing and free transportation to their job site. To receive Department of Labor certification, employers also must attest that no domestic workers are available to fill these jobs and must demonstrate that there will be a labour shortage in the upcoming season.[64]

Advocates of the program say that the program is appealing because it encourages labour force stability, with close to 90 per cent of workers hired under the H-2A returning the next year.[65] Employers are dissatisfied with the current program because of the bureaucratic requirements involved in contracting labour as well as the relatively high wages required (compared to prevailing rates). Both workers and employers may thus be less likely to pursue this legal framework for contraction of agricultural labour (as table 4.1 shows, the United States issued only about three times as many visas under the H-2A program as the number of workers contracted under the SAWP in 2008, despite the much larger size of the US agricultural economy and the longer growing season). Both US employers and workers may find undocumented labour a preferable alternative, albeit for different reasons. Michael Holley argues, however, that despite the bureaucratic requirements of the program, H-2A workers are seen as desirable by employers because, "as a practical matter, they cannot hope to enforce their relatively generous substantive rights. Federal statutes, regulations and case law have helped to render H-2A workers vulnerable, inhibiting them from enforcing their employment rights guaranteed by their H-2A contracts."[66] Thus the informal practices of civic stratification and the global North-South citizenship divide severely limit the substantive citizenship rights that visa holders are able to access in practice.

The uncertainties of the seasonal agricultural workforce in the context of the presence of huge numbers of undocumented workers have led to increased pressure by employers for the expansion of the H-2A program. In 1996 about 15,000 H-2A workers were contracted in the United States; this number nearly tripled to 42,000 workers in 1999, largely because of the use of this program by increasing numbers of employers in the southern United States (i.e., North Carolina, Georgia, and Kentucky). By fiscal year 2009, the DOL had granted permission to fill 94,000 jobs with H-2A workers.[67] Employers tend to engage in illegal practices once they have begun to contract H-2A workers: they may refuse domestic applicants, pretend they have no housing for domestic workers, or invent performance tests to disqualify domestic applicants.[68] Like SAWP workers in Canada, H-2A workers are vulnerable because of their physical and linguistic isolation and their lack of knowledge of the social services and legal rights available to them. As well, unlike other US farm workers, and similar to the workers under the Canadian SAWP program, H-2A workers are tied to a single employer. If dissatisfied with the working conditions of their employment, workers have no choice but to tolerate them or quit and return to their home country.[69] This option is distasteful for Mexican workers because new border-control policies have made return to the United States increasingly difficult. Workers also typically have to pay fees or bribes to labour recruiters and government officials, which requires them to go into debt before they gain access to employment and makes the options of leaving their jobs or voicing complaints even more difficult. H-2A workers may be deported if they "violate their visa terms or commit acts determined under the INA [Immigration and Nationality Act] to be grounds for deportation."[70] Workers are generally authorized to stay in the United States for less than a year, and they have a grace period of ten days to leave the country after their visas end, at which point they may be deported.[71]

In addition, despite the relatively generous rights provided on paper, H-2A workers cannot access normal procedural legal rights in order to protect their substantive rights. Employers have lobbied the government to weaken these provisions, with the result that Department of Labor regulations regarding alleged violations of H-2A employment contracts lack specific procedures for initiating or investigating complaints and lack timetables or deadlines for required DOL response, or even for reporting on the status of a complaint. This situation is in contrast with the regulations regarding immediate remedies for growers' complaints against domestic workers.[72] H-2A regulations restrict the right of an H-2A temporary agricultural worker to appeal a DOL decision not to take action on a complaint based on violations of the H-2A program by the employer.[73] In the absence of the federal government assuming responsibility for enforcing the provisions of the H-2A program that protect the rights of both domestic and foreign workers, state courts are the main remedy to which workers can turn; however, "Mexican guest workers run a significant risk of biased treatment in many of the state trial courts in the rural regions where they are likely to work."[74]

During the late 1990s, there was a tremendous increase in the numbers of undocumented workers in the US agricultural labour force, as well as increased pressure from a wide range of forces to tighten up control over the country's borders in order to restrict the entry of undocumented workers.[75] In response, growers have been pushing for expansion of the H-2A program or for its replacement with a less restrictive guest worker program that would remove the restrictions on workers' mobility and permit them to move from farm to farm seeking jobs. As well, they are pushing for programs in which employers are not responsible for housing or transportation. These proposals for a new bracero program have been strongly opposed by unions, churches, and *latino* activists. After Mexican president Vicente Fox came to power in 2000, extended negotiations occurred between Fox and US president George W. Bush, which stalled over demands by Fox not just for an expansion of the existing temporary worker program but also for an "amnesty" or "regularization" of the immigration status for Mexicans already in the United States without documentation (the "whole *enchilada*"), while Bush held out for a guest worker program in which workers would not be granted access to citizenship rights.[76] These negotiations ended after the attacks of 11 September 2001, but in recent years debate has heated up.

In 2004 continued demand by US businesses for Mexican labour and the failure of more intensive US border-control measures to limit Mexican migration prompted President Bush to revive his support for migration reform. To gain the support of conservative Republicans, Bush's speeches placed heavy emphasis on tight border-control policies. However, in contrast to the right wing of his own party, Bush advocated a temporary worker program to alleviate border tensions: "This program would create a legal way to match willing foreign workers with willing American employers to fill jobs that Americans will not do. Workers would be able to register for legal status for a fixed period of time, and then be required to go home."[77]

Bush rejected Fox's proposal for the regularization of immigration status for Mexicans already in the United States on the grounds that such a program would reward those who had broken the law and encourage others to do so. Bush's proposals thus failed to provide a path to citizenship for Mexican migrants and are instead reminiscent of the bracero program. In the Congressional elections of November 2006, the Republicans made illegal immigration a high-profile issue. Given the continued stalling of any comprehensive migration reform legislation, some high-profile Democrats have continued to push for measures to address growers' demands for an expanded agricultural guest worker program.

Before Bush left office in 2008, his administration adopted some limited changes to the regulations of the H-2A program to make the hiring process easier for employers and to ease labour shortages. Under these new rules, employers could petition for multiple unnamed H-2A beneficiaries based on employers' attestations that they are unable to find sufficient US workers to fill their labour needs (rather than requiring a DOL certification that no US workers are available). As well, the rules allowed the use of local prevailing wage surveys to determine wages, increased the penalty for employers who violated various terms of the program, and permitted

H-2A workers to begin working for a new employer provided that employer was enrolled in the E-Verify program.[78]

However, the administration of US president Barack Obama put on hold these changes to the H-2A regulations, apparently under pressure from farm worker advocacy organizations.[79] Subsequently, the Department of Labor issued new regulations requiring employers to undertake more steps to find Americans to fill agricultural jobs, increasing the average pay for temporary farm workers by nearly $1 per hour and requiring state workforce agencies to inspect worker housing.[80] Employers continue to promote reform and expansion of the H-2A program and removal of what they perceive as cumbersome and costly application processes, while immigration advocates continue to push for more comprehensive immigration reform.[81] Under the latest proposal for an Agricultural Job Opportunities, Benefits, and Security Act (AgJOBS), reintroduced into the Senate in May 2009, up to 1.35 million undocumented farm workers would be able to apply for probationary "blue card" status and eventually earn permanent resident status after additional employment in US agriculture over the next three to five years. The proposal also includes employer-friendly changes in the H-2A program, making it easier for employers to employ workers, replacing the requirement for free housing with a housing allowance of $1 to $2 per hour, depending on local costs, and freezing the adverse effect wage rate at 2002 levels, which would result in an average pay reduction of about 10 per cent.[82] Proposals for immigration reform continue to face considerable political obstacles.

CONCLUDING OBSERVATIONS

In this chapter, we have compared the Canadian Seasonal Agricultural Worker Program and the US H-2A temporary agricultural visa program in their global and regional contexts. As we have seen, there has been in recent years an increased demand globally for the creation and expansion of temporary migrant worker programs in order to attempt to provide cheap and vulnerable labour forces and to contain the pressures toward undocumented migration. States, under pressure from employers, have thus strategically deployed migrant worker programs in order to manage and contain unregulated flows of people across state borders in the context of globalization. In the North American region in particular, the geographical proximity of Mexico, a developing country experiencing rising levels of poverty and inequality, to the United States, the regional and global hegemon, creates even greater problems of management and control. Earlier patterns of cyclical migration have created deeply ingrained habits of cross-border labour mobility that are difficult to forestall, and US businesses remain reliant upon the import of Mexican workers. The fall-out from the attacks of 11 September has further compounded the problem, as attempts by US and Mexican elites to politically manage the situation were stalled by the rise of increased pressures from a broad spectrum of groups in the United States to control the US-Mexican (and US-Canadian) border. In this context, the existing legislative and judicial framework for the existing temporary migrant worker program, the H-2A program, has been revealed as sadly inadequate. The program has been regularly associated with high levels of abuse, and it fails to meet the needs of either workers or employers.

It is perhaps understandable, therefore, that many (particularly Mexican government officials) have turned to the Canadian SAWP as a potential alternative to the inadequate H-2A program in the United States. Although serious criticisms of the SAWP have been raised in Canada, the presence of Mexican farm workers has not ignited the type of deep resentment and confrontation that has emerged in the United States, partly because the large majority arrive under regulated conditions. Overall, however, as we have seen above, although there are important differences between the Canadian SAWP and the US H-2A visa for seasonal agricultural workers, the programs are broadly comparable. Both are temporary programs designed to meet the needs of agricultural employers for low-skilled workers. Neither offers a path to citizenship. Workers in both programs are often isolated, vulnerable, and subject to exploitation (although Mexican workers in the United States may be less isolated because of the existence of large Mexican and Mexican American communities in many parts of the country). Program design is geared toward the interests of employers, and there is inadequate supervision to ensure that workers' rights are respected (although in the Canadian program the Mexican and Caribbean governments play a role in representing the interests of their nationals). The main differences between the two programs lie not in their institutional design but in the surrounding political, legal, and social contexts. In particular, the existence of a large population of undocumented Mexican workers in US agriculture distorts the impact of the program, exercising downward pressure on wages and living conditions. As well, the H-2A program has become caught up in the divisive politics of immigration reform in the United States. It is not surprising, therefore, that it is so commonly subjected to criticism by employers, workers' organizations, and pro- and anti-immigration reform spokespersons.

The problem, then, is not just in the design of the H-2A program but also in the lack of sufficient measures for enforcement of the legislated protections for workers. As well, the presence of huge numbers of undocumented workers in the US agricultural labour force inevitably exerts enormous downward pressure on wages and working conditions for all workers, whether citizens, undocumented, or temporary. As a result, it is impossible to solve the crisis of migration policy in the United States without first addressing the presence of a huge undocumented population lacking access to secure citizenship rights.

The portrayal of the Canadian program as a model of best practices is thus largely an artifact of the absence of a regional framework to govern the labour mobility of low-skilled workers in North America and the failure of the US political system to accomplish comprehensive immigration reform. In this dysfunctional context, the Mexican and Canadian governments have collaborated in casting the Canadian program as a superior alternative to the US system, ignoring significant weaknesses in the SAWP and the real similarities between the SAWP and the H-2A visa. Both programs are reflections of, and aggravate, the existing global North-South citizenship divide. In this context, it is important to resist the temptation to portray the SAWP as a good model for the United States to follow in any redesign of its temporary worker program.

A version of this chapter was presented at the 2008 International Studies Association meeting. We thank the Social Sciences and Humanities Research Council of Canada for its support.

5

"The Exception that Proves the Rule": Structural Vulnerability, Health Risks, and Consequences for Temporary Migrant Farm Workers in Canada

JENNA L. HENNEBRY AND JANET MCLAUGHLIN

INTRODUCTION

For nearly fifty years, temporary labour migration in Canada has been an indispensable resource for farmers facing numerous pressures in the agriculture industry. As early as the 1940s, international guest worker programs (including the infamous US-Mexico *"bracero"* program), were spawned in North America during what was then deemed to be "exceptional" circumstances of war. In part to remain competitive with producers in countries invoking such schemes, Canadian farmers began to pressure the government for their own foreign worker program. Demands were ramped up in the 1950s and 1960s in response to what employers claimed to be "exceptional" circumstances of industrialization, urbanization, increased agricultural competition, and demographic change, in which reliable domestic employees could not be sufficiently recruited to work under the difficult, demanding, low-paid conditions in agriculture.[1] In 1966 the Canadian state conceded to employer demands, creating what is now known as the Seasonal Agricultural Worker Program (SAWP), through which Jamaican migrant men could work seasonally in agriculture but would not be permitted to stay beyond their contracts. More than forty years on, and the song remains the same, although today both men and women are employed from a variety of countries of origin, and states and employers can now add contemporary globalization – and concurrent conditions constituting a continual "race to the bottom" for wages and labour standards – to the unique circumstances that necessitate the continued expansion of migrant labour to bolster Canadian agriculture. Indeed, this constant "state of exception"[2] – in which labour desires drive the perception not only that there are labour shortages but also that the national imaginary, built in part on the tradition of Canadian agriculture, is at risk – creates a permanently inscribed liminal space (i.e., a limbo) for temporary labour migration.

These "exceptional" circumstances have been mapped onto migrants while they fill these "temporary" labour demands, rendering migrant farm workers (MFWS) particularly vulnerable to health risks – more so, we argue, than their Canadian counterparts in agriculture. Specifically, migrant farm workers' vulnerability is rooted in the structural frameworks that govern temporary migration in agriculture, which treat these workers as "exceptional" insofar as they are noncitizen, nonresident, nonimmigrant, temporary workers who are thought to be passing through to fill labour shortages in "exceptional economic times." Although governments, policies, and workplaces may treat MFWS as exceptional and temporary, the factors that contribute to their vulnerability are far from exceptional and migrant workers are also far from temporary. Although the rationale for temporary migration has evoked the "exceptional" situation of short-term labour shortages, Canada's SAWP and broader Temporary Foreign Worker Program (TFWP) are really "the exception that proves the rule." We argue this for the following reasons: (1) the SAWP has been in existence for over forty years and has continually expanded over this time (demonstrating that the labour shortages, and the desire for foreign labour in agriculture, are far from unique or unusual); (2) workers typically migrate for multiple years (demonstrating that this is not an exceptional or one-time experience for most migrants); and (3) MFWS' vulnerabilities to health risks and rights violations are widespread and structural (demonstrating that it is not just a case of a few unusually bad employers). Thus these exceptionalities have become the norm and therefore "the rule" for temporary migrants in Canadian agriculture.

Based on a decade of multimethodological and multisited ethnographic study[3] carried out by the authors, including participant observation on farms and with migrant support groups, hundreds of qualitative interviews with migrants, employers, government and public health officials, and healthcare practitioners, as well as standardized questionnaires with nearly 600 temporary migrants working in agriculture across southern Ontario from Mexico and Jamaica,[4] this chapter examines the realities and consequences of being "exceptional" for MFWs' vulnerability to health risks. Adopting a transnational approach to research,[5] the chapter integrates the data gathered from our combined research carried out in Canada, Mexico, and Jamaica with detailed ethnographic data presented through the use of a case study design.[6]

Drawing on an approach to structural relations and the practices of power informed by Anthony Giddens[7] and Dorothy Smith,[8] this chapter focuses on the explication of Giorgio Agamben's concept of the "state of exception" – particularly on how this exceptionality is embedded in the relations of ruling that organize and structure the everyday experiences of migrant agricultural workers in Canada. We begin this chapter by offering a theorization of the state of exception as it relates to MFWs and then provide background on and a brief comparison of the two primary streams of foreign worker programs currently operating in Canadian agriculture. Following this, we explicate the relations of ruling of the SAWP through an analysis of the major consequences of this exceptionality, highlighting some illustrative case studies from our qualitative research that demonstrate the structural factors that heighten MFWs' vulnerability to health risks in their everyday lives.

THE EXCEPTIONALITY OF MIGRANT FARM WORKERS

Agamben's theorization of the state of exception is a useful frame to understand how a "permanently temporary" migration program, which systematically fails to protect the rights of participants, can be rationalized and sustained in a country like Canada – purportedly an ideal of the principles of liberal democracy, human rights, multicultural integration, and social inclusion. A state of exception, according to Agamben, arises in a situation where exceptional measures, including suspending normal rights for certain groups of people, are seen to be necessary and become normalized. He argues that modern state power is defined by such exceptions.[9] The use (and abuse) of migrant workers in Canada has been rationalized by various tropes of exceptionalism: the existence of "exceptional" or short-term labour shortages that warrant migrants' employment; the temporariness of migrants' presence in Canada, which assumes migrants will be in Canada only for a short time and thus should not qualify for the rights and obligations of citizenship; and the unusualness of cases of mistreatment, illness, or injury in an otherwise successful system. In each of these cases, however, our research demonstrates that the opposite holds true: the labour conditions that necessitate the migrants' presence have only continued over time; many migrants return for years or decades to Canada; and the propensity for abuse, illness, and injury is predicted by the program's structure, which inherently disempowers workers. The remainder of this section unpacks the primary ways that the state of exception has emerged around temporary agricultural migration in Canada. Then the second part of the chapter discusses the last point – the issue of systemic vulnerability to health concerns – in more detail.

Temporary migration programs, both in Canada and throughout the world, have historically been framed as stop-gap or emergency measures, in which the state responds to industries facing particular or unusual needs by meeting acute and immediate labour shortages. Clearly, however, these labour shortages have proven to be far from acute or temporary, as agricultural employers have come to depend on – and indeed plan their production around – the use of an unlimited supply of a "just-in-time," super-productive, easily replaceable labour force enabled by managed migration programs. This constant state of exception is invoked by employers as well as the state, whose calls for exceptional labour arrangements in agriculture are only strengthened by rural communities, who feel their way of life may be threatened with extinction, and of course by the growing popularity of "buy local" campaigns, which emphasize the near-sacred importance of "local" agriculture. Simultaneously, a growing migration industry has formed around temporary migration in Canada, serving to prop up demand for foreign workers and the revenue they generate for recruiters, consultants, employment agencies, and money transfer services, to name a few.[10]

Thus the use of temporary migration to do jobs not desired by Canadians has quietly become normalized, during which time temporary migrants have returned to Canada annually in some cases for several decades. In a recent survey of nearly 600 migrant agricultural workers in Ontario, current participants had come to Canada for an average of eight years, although we know that a large number return to Canada for upward of twenty years, and in some cases thirty years.[11] Many MFWs thus live in a state of permanent temporariness, year after year.

Despite their long-term presence and centrality to the Canadian agricultural economy, discourse and policy frameworks combine to relegate migrant agricultural labourers to a position outside of the state (as exceptional), and being temporary and exceptional is about being outside of the system in which rights are conferred and protected (i.e., permanent residency and citizenship). This exceptionality serves to legitimize their precariousness and differential treatment, drawing on the language of difference, which separates "Canadians" from "foreign" farm workers. As Nandita Sharma argues, the use and acceptance of the oppositional categories of citizen worker and migrant worker help to secure the organization of "difference" within Canada, with the notion of citizen being the dominant oppressive half of the binary.[12] This differentiation is embedded in migration policies through processes of separation and categorization, particularly with the distinction between permanent and temporary migrants. Source countries from which MFWs are drawn (in the case of the SAWP, Mexico and the Caribbean) are previously colonized, non-European, and predominantly nonwhite. Immigration policy – and the channelling of individuals into temporary versus permanent categories of entrance – is the forcible isolation of these differences.[13] The outcome leads to a racialized system of movement, whereby those different from the white European point of reference are subject to social control through a migration policy and a labour system that simultaneously devalue credentials of highly skilled migrants from these countries and funnel the unskilled into tightly controlled labour relations and migration regulations that guarantee their isolation and consequent vulnerability.

Not only is this exceptional status the dominant discourse with respect to the TFWP in general, but it is also the common defence when criticisms are lodged against the SAWP or the TFWP, the view being that any instances of abuse must be few and far between within an otherwise successful system. We argue, however, that workers' vulnerability is not an exceptional or rare outcome but is in fact structured into the TFWP itself. Vulnerability to health problems and a lack of power to change circumstances are not unusual or exceptional outcomes of the program; rather, these are predictable and predominant consequences of the way that the TFWP is structured and of the way that the policies and programs are administered.[14] Assigned to work for a specific employer, on whose property they must live, MFWs find themselves integrated into a managed migration system in which they are deeply and structurally vulnerable. Such circumstances are sustained by the argument that the specific demands of labour-intensive agriculture require a "captive, unfree," cheap, and compliant labour force in order for the industry to remain globally competitive.[15] The following sections outline the structures of Canada's TFWP in agriculture and provide an analysis of how these structures heighten the vulnerability of MFWs to health risks. From this analysis, we argue that this vulnerability is largely a consequence of the structures of the TFWP and the state of exception invoked to justify its use in agriculture.

CANADA'S TEMPORARY FOREIGN WORKER PROGRAMS IN AGRICULTURE

Canada's TFWP now operates two primary programs (or program streams) in agriculture: the SAWP since 1966 and the Pilot Project for Occupations Requiring Lower Levels of Formal Training (also known as the Low-Skill Pilot Project, or LSPP) since 2002 (an agricultural stream of the LSPP was added in 2011). Even this later program, framed explicitly as a "pilot," has only continued to expand and has become a permanent fixture in Canada's TFWP over the past decade. Canada has a long history with agricultural labour migration dating back to the Second World War.[16] The SAWP began bringing workers to Canada from Jamaica in 1966, followed by Trinidad and Tobago (1967), Barbados (1967), Mexico (1974), and the

Organization of Eastern Caribbean States (1976) – under the same bilateral agreements that govern the program today. The SAWP has grown steadily since that time, with roughly 25,000 migrants per year now entering Canada. In 2007 there were 26,585 confirmed Labour Market Opinions (LMOs) for hiring foreign workers under the SAWP, and in 2010 there were 27,835, the majority of which (nearly 20,000) were concentrated in Ontario.[17] Starting in 2002, with the introduction of the LSPP, the federal government expanded the temporary labour migration of workers (from any sending country) to Canada in occupations designated as "low-skilled," including agriculture. With the two programs operating in the agricultural sector, there were nearly 35,000 confirmed foreign worker positions in both the SAWP and the LSPP in 2008 and 2009.[18] In 2008 the International Organization for Migration facilitated the migration of 3,313 MFWs from Guatemala to Canada, nearly 80 per cent of whom worked in Quebec.[19]

The structures of both the SAWP and the LSPP create the conditions for vulnerability among MFWS, yet the programs have some distinctions. Table 5.1 outlines some fundamental similarities and differences in the two programs with respect to healthcare, housing, and workplace safety. In order to meet the requirements of the SAWP, employers must pay the prevailing wage rate set by Human Resources and Skills Development Canada (HRSDC), provide transportation, and arrange medical coverage. This means that access to provincial healthcare coverage is mediated by the employer, who must ensure that workers receive health cards and can have time off work and transportation to health facilities when necessary. The employer must also provide "adequate" seasonal housing to the workers, and the housing must be inspected by a licensed municipal housing inspector.[20] At this point, despite the long history of MFW housing in Canada, the federal government has not implemented detailed, standardized housing requirements, mechanisms to monitor changing conditions during the growing season, or a process for workers to lodge complaints about problems. There is great variability in housing inspections and conditions across provinces and municipalities since housing inspections are carried out by local public health officials and since the inspections are done *prior* to the arrival of MFWs, after which conditions may change. Most

Table 5.1
Healthcare access, housing, and workplace safety of TFWPs in agriculture

	SAWP	LSPP
Access to provincial healthcare	Eligible upon arrival in most provinces; health cards obtained via employers	Three-month waiting period; employers are required to provide access to private healthcare insurance
Workers' compensation	Eligible, but specific systems vary by province	Eligible, but specific systems vary by province
Occupational health and safety and labour codes	Eligible, but codes vary by province	Eligible, but codes vary by province
Labour representation	Varies by province, with no collective bargaining rights for all farm workers in Alberta and Ontario	Varies by province, with no collective bargaining rights for all farm workers in Alberta and Ontario
Housing supply and costs	Employers must provide adequate on-farm housing but may recover the cost by deducting up to 7 per cent of workers' pay for a maximum of $550 per year[a]	Employers must demonstrate that affordable accommodation is nearby;[b] workers are required to pay for their off-farm housing; on-farm housing provided through new "agriculture" stream at $30 per week[c]
Housing inspections	Required annually by licensed local housing inspectors to provincial and municipal standards	No required inspections for off-farm housing; on-farm housing inspected by local housing inspectors or private inspection service
Housing location	Typically, on farm in existing buildings, trailers, or portables	Urban or on farm, often in rental units in more urban areas

[a] Human Resources and Skills Development Canada (HRSDC), "Temporary Foreign Workers: Your Rights and the Law"; varies by country of origin.

[b] HRSDC, ibid., describes "affordable" as housing that costs one-third of the workers' gross pay but does not define the term "nearby."

[c] Under the new "agricultural" stream of the LSPP, employers must provide suitable accommodations at $30 per week unless applicable provincial standards specify a lower amount. At any time during their employment, workers may choose to leave their employer-provided housing in favour of private accommodations. For more information, see http://www.hrsdc.gc.ca/eng/workplaceskills/foreign_workers/Agricultural/directives.shtml (accessed 31 January 2011).

workers never meet these inspectors, they are not given information about how to make complaints, and if they do have a concern, they are reluctant to report it anyway since their landlord is also their employer.

In the LSPP, workers are not eligible for provincial healthcare on arrival but instead are subject to a three-month probationary period, during which time employers must provide workers access to a private health insurance plan.[21] Under the agricultural stream of the LSPP, employers must provide suitable accommodations, although workers may choose to live in private accommodations. Similar to the SAWP, this program requires that employers enter into a contract with the employee, pay transportation costs, arrange medical coverage, and pay foreign workers the prevailing wage rate set by HRSDC.

STRUCTURAL VULNERABILITY AND HEALTH RISKS

There is mounting international evidence that migrant groups engaged in temporary, precarious work suffer disproportionately from health problems. The World Health Organization contends that many migrants are vulnerable to health risks during movement and often experience poverty, marginality, and limited access to social benefits and health services, and it notes that temporary and seasonal migrants classified as "low-skilled," in particular, are often concentrated in sectors and occupations with high levels of occupational health risks.[22] A review of recent literature demonstrates strong evidence that precarious employment, particularly temporary work, is linked to poorer occupational health and safety outcomes, with both cause-specific and overall mortality rates being significantly higher for temporary than for permanent workers.[23] An Associated Press investigation found that Mexican workers are approximately 80 per cent more likely to die on the job than their US-born counterparts and twice as likely to die on the job as other immigrants. They are more likely to die even when doing similarly risky work.[24]

Although similar comparative data in Canada are not available, a burgeoning body of Canadian research suggests disturbing and consistent patterns in farm workplaces. These include consecutive

long days of strenuous work without adequate rest; exposure to
dangerous pesticides and other chemicals without adequate (or any)
protective clothing or masks, information, or training; exposure to
intense sunlight and heat, as well as to various airborne dusts and
animalborne diseases; depression, stress, anxiety, and other mental
health concerns; exposure to hazardous conditions causing work-
related injuries; inadequate facilities (e.g., running water) to wash
off chemicals before eating; and a lack of knowledge or understanding of safe work practices, rights, entitlements, and so on. The
problems of poor housing (e.g., crowded, poorly ventilated, and in
proximity to pesticides) have also been documented by researchers. Other challenges to MFW health include barriers to healthcare
access (e.g., language, social exclusion, and poor transportation and
communication access). Research also points to the transnational
health implications of these barriers, indicating that when workers
become ill they are unlikely to receive adequate treatment and thus
return home with the illness unresolved.[25] In addition, researchers
have argued that migrant workers are not given parallel access to
health and social services compared with their permanent counterparts.[26] For example, MFWS' healthcare is mediated by their employers, and they lack access to vaccination programs and routine,
long-term healthcare.

There are high levels of occupational illness and injury facing all
agricultural workers in Canada, but MFWS' vulnerability to such
risks is compounded by their precarious employment and immigration status.[27] Although certainly not a definitive list, table 5.2 provides a brief overview of what we believe are the top ten factors that
heighten MFW vulnerability in Canada. The first two factors also
pertain more generally to agricultural labourers, although migrant
workers face greater vulnerabilities than Canadian workers, for reasons explained below. The third factor – having migration status tied
to employment status – is certainly the most important in terms of
MFW vulnerability. If MFWS lose their employment status, they lose
their access to healthcare and eventually lose their migration status
upon expiration of their visa or earlier. Although these factors can
leave MFWS vulnerable to mistreatment, abuse, exploitation, or harm
of various kinds, the following section concentrates on the heightened vulnerability to health risks.

Table 5.2
Top ten factors that heighten migrant farm worker vulnerability in Canada

1 Concentration in occupation with high rates of accidents/injury and history of poor health and safety standards/protections[a]
2 Inadequate rights and protections to enable fair labour representation[b]
3 Migration status, work permit, and healthcare access are tied to employers/employment contract
4 No job security, no independent and confidential reporting mechanism (for health violations/abuse), and no appeals process (for firings/deportations or future exclusions from the program)
5 Inconsistent/inadequate on-farm housing, insufficient guidelines, and underregulation
6 Social exclusion, racism/discrimination, poorly accessible and unsafe transportation, and language and literacy barriers
7 No mechanism to assist workers to switch employers and no sector-specific work permits
8 No direct path to permanent residency
9 Inadequate incentives for employers to protect workers
10 Economic need, including debts to third-party recruiters/intermediaries, resulting in pressure to continue working under poor conditions

[a] Although both Canadian and migrant farm workers experience these risks, MFWs are often expected to work longer hours, under more difficult conditions, and they are more likely to fear refusing dangerous work for reasons explained below.

[b] All farm workers in Ontario and Alberta are excluded from collective bargaining rights, and in other provinces workers face pressures not to join unions. MFWs in particular may be effectively threatened with the loss of current or future employment for engaging in labour activities because they do not have the freedom to change employers or secure future employment.

Source: Adapted from Hennebry, "Not Just a Few Bad Apples," 76.

The everyday life of MFWs is laden with the consequences of structural vulnerabilities due to their exceptional status. To illustrate how these structural realities converge on and are embedded within the everyday lives of MFWs, what follows is the description of a typical day in the life of a migrant worker on an Ontario farm, as recounted from ethnographic fieldwork carried out between 2002 and 2005:

7:00 AM: Mexican workers wait outside the barn leaning on a van. The Canadian workers punch in at a time clock, and the Mexican workers do not. The farmer arrives and instructs the crew leader: "Take eight Mexicans and go finish the rows there and then move onto the other field." In the back of the pickup truck, workers sit on wooden benches against the sides of the truck. At their feet is a pile of machetes that jostle wildly against their lunch coolers as the truck reaches seventy kilometres an hour on the county road that separates large fields of trees and potatoes. Holding onto the benches and bracing themselves against the truck rails, workers peer out through the narrow windows on the side of the cab at the small towns and farms as they fly by. Upon arrival at the field site, workers are instructed to grab a machete and begin pruning the kilometre-long rows of trees. Emerging from the back of the pickup, they jump down with their small lunch coolers and then reach in and grab for the best machetes. Working nonstop in the heat of the mid-July sun without protection, using machetes with no gloves, no leg guards, and no other protective gear, the workers move up and down the rows, steadily swinging their machetes up and down the trunks of the ten-foot pines.

12:00 PM: The crew head arrives with the truck and calls for lunch. Dropping their machetes, workers grab their coolers, look for a spot of sparse shade, and have a seat on the ground. After eating, a few of the workers step behind the trees to go to the "bathroom." After twenty minutes the crew head tells the workers to get back to work, and the crew head departs in the truck, leaving the group of Mexican workers to finish the work.

Soon after, a worker is stung by a swarm of wasps after disturbing the nest with his machete. The crew head has already left, and no one has a cell phone, transportation, or a first aid kit, so the worker, feeling unwell, sits and rests while the others continue working. In two hours the crew head returns and asks why the worker is "taking a siesta on the job." When the worker shows him the wasp stings, the crew head replies: "Sorry, Tattoo, you will have to wait until we get back to the farm, I don't got any first aid stuff in my truck, man. You're not allergic are ya?" Unable to understand his English, the worker nicknamed "Tattoo" ("you know, after the short brown man from Fantasy Island," says the crew head) shrugs, picks up his machete, and gets back to work until the crew head returns.

9:00 PM: Returning from the long day's work, the workers stiffly spill out of the back of the truck with sore muscles and calloused hands after dark. Once the ten workers are inside their ten-by-fifteen-foot portable, they flop onto the small bunk beds in their shared room to await their turns in the one bathroom and with the one stovetop in the space where they prepare their nightly meals and pack their lunches for the next day. After the day's heat, the temperature in the portable is sweltering, and the portable's lone window is propped wide open, despite the flies that stream in. Sitting around the table, three workers discuss their families, check to see if they have prepaid phone cards, and decide who will get to use the phone in the barn to call home. After dinner some workers wash their clothes in the laundry tub, then hang them outside on the farm equipment stored nearby, while others look at photos from home and fall asleep to the sound of ranchero music playing on the portable radio in the kitchen.[28]

This is a daily routine for many migrant workers across Canada, although the crop and type of work may vary and the music might be reggae instead of ranchero. Still, they typically all start early, end late, and perform strenuous, repetitive tasks in harsh environments with little or no protection. The above account demonstrates the everyday realities of unsafe and unprotected work, social exclusion, racism, unsafe transportation, and poor housing. Despite the long history of migrant farm labour in Canada, poor and unregulated housing is a widespread problem, particularly in the SAWP, where migrants often live in overcrowded, makeshift on-farm housing that was not originally intended to house workers. The trend in Ontario is to house seasonal workers in existing dwellings, mobile homes, or modular buildings on one of the parcels owned by the farm operation. Seasonal farm worker housing tends to be clustered near the principal residence in order to tap into existing water and sewer facilities. On average, between six and fifteen workers are housed in a single building.[29] It is not surprising that among the migrant workers surveyed in Ontario, nearly 30 per cent agreed with the statement "My residence is hazardous to my health."[30] Common

problems identified by workers are overcrowding, lack of venti-
lation, insufficient cooking amenities, and a lack of privacy and
security. However, given the inadequate regulations and the lack of
monitoring and complaint mechanisms mentioned earlier, there are
no incentives for employers to better migrant farm housing. Moreover, ignorance and racism serve to justify poor housing as an exception for MFWS, who are perceived to be accustomed to substandard
housing. As employers often contend, "It is bound to be better than
what they have back home," and they are an exception to the norm
since, as one employer rationalized, "They are Mexicans, for them it
is fine, but for the workers from Newfoundland or Ontario we have
to at least have what they are used to."[31] In addition, migrant workers are also assigned to work on farms and have no control over the
type of work, employer, or farm location, furthering their sense of
powerlessness and difference from Canadian workers, which is even
more pronounced when they experience racism from co-workers
or employers, as seen above. Migrant workers also cannot easily
leave unsafe work environments by choosing to work for another
employer since there is no centralized mechanism to assist them to
find other employers with valid LMOs, and they are unable to work
freely in agriculture without a sectoral work permit – effectively
trapping them with a single employer.

The ethnographic account above also demonstrates the lived
reality of working in dangerous, difficult conditions in an occupation with unusually high rates of accident and injury and in under-
regulated environments with little or no training and protective
equipment. In Ontario lost time claims for injury in manufacturing, services, construction, food services, and agriculture (where
LSPP and SAWP migrants are employed) are particularly high.[32] The
Canadian Agricultural Injury Surveillance Program (CAISP) reports
the following statistics: "In the fifteen years from 1990–2004, 453
people were killed in agricultural injury events in Ontario ... or 13.7
per 100,000 agricultural population, per year ... In the fourteen
fiscal years from April 1, 1990, to March 31, 2004, 3,682 people
were admitted to hospital for at least one day as a result of agricultural injuries in Ontario."[33] Although the CAISP report observes
that most acute deaths and injuries occur among farm owners (who
may be more likely to use farm machinery and/or to be the primary

workers on smaller farms), there are no data provided that distinguish between Canadian and migrant farm workers, nor does the report capture hospital stays of workers who were repatriated to countries of origin immediately after an injury. Nonetheless, for the same reasons cited earlier, combined evidence suggests that migrant workers may be particularly vulnerable to injuries and illnesses.

It is difficult to obtain statistics on migrant worker deaths and injuries in Canada, but some major incidents have been publicized. For example, thirty-nine-year-old Samuel Maurilio Gil-Montesinos of Oaxaca died when a tractor ran over him in 2006, and thirty-eight-year-old Jamaican Ned Peart died in 2002 when a heavy bin fell on him.[34] In 2007 two Thai farm workers died on the same farm, although the cause remains unknown.[35] In 2010 two Jamaican workers died after inhaling toxic fumes on an apple farm in Ontario.[36] Many more workers have died due to unsafe transportation, including substandard work transportation as well as riding bicycles without a helmet, reflector, or lights on rural roads. One crash in 2005 killed two Jamaican workers and seriously injured another near Simcoe, Ontario, as they were biking to town to call home, and a third Mexican worker was killed on a bicycle near Leamington that same year.[37] In a well-known case, in 2007 three farm workers died, and another thirteen were injured, after the crash of an overcrowded van filled with farm workers without seatbelts in British Columbia.[38] Such instances of unsafe transport are not isolated; 46 per cent of MFWs surveyed in Ontario indicated that they are transported to worksites in vehicles with no seatbelts.[39]

Migrant farm labourers also work during the seasonal months that correspond with high rates of enteric, foodborne, and waterborne disease transmission, yet they often work outdoors, in poor sanitary conditions, and without sufficient protection.[40] A lack of federal-level guidelines regarding occupational health and safety (including use of pesticides and fertilizers), food-handling practices, field sanitation, and housing, combined with the absence of meaningful consequences for employers who are found in violation of provincial health and safety regulations, leaves MFWs exposed and more likely to engage in unsafe work practices. As research from the United States indicates, untrained and unprotected use of fertilizers (such as manure) and of pesticides, herbicides, and fungicides to protect crops have been shown to affect the health of farm workers, especially with respect to respiratory and skin health.[41]

Among MFWs surveyed in Ontario, nearly 40 per cent indicated that they worked with machinery, and of these, the majority did so without the necessary training and certifications required to minimize the risk of injuries.[42] As one Mexican worker insisted, "We need more training about safety and working with machinery. We need protection equipment to work safely."[43] Nearly one-quarter of the workers interviewed in Ontario stated they had not been trained to do their jobs. Likewise, nearly half of respondents who worked with chemicals stated they directly applied them without the necessary protection, such as gloves, masks, and goggles. As one worker explained, "We don't have anything to protect ourselves. We have to buy the necessary equipment such as boots and gloves. I have been suffering from constant infection on my skin from fumigations."[44] Another added, "I apply chemicals without protection ... we have to work under extreme heat conditions, sometimes some of us vomit and got headaches, itchy skin and blurred vision."[45] It is not surprising that 55 per cent of migrant workers surveyed agreed with the statement "My work is hazardous to my health."[46]

Nonetheless, many workers are reluctant to seek medical attention. In fact, 45 per cent of those surveyed in Ontario and 48 per cent of Mexican workers surveyed in British Columbia said their co-workers would keep working amid illness or injury because they were afraid to tell their employer.[47] This is a significant number and supports our qualitative findings, which suggest that migrant labourers work under pressure and often face implicit or explicit threats from employers and, more specifically, that many fear repatriation. As one worker recounted, "I fell from a lift truck and broke my ankle. I went to the hospital afraid that I might lose my job. My employer got angry and pressured me to continue working."[48] Fear of reprimand, compounded by the absence of job security, of independent and confidential reporting, and of a grievance system or appeals process for migrants, makes them much less likely to refuse unsafe work or to demand safe work practices, training, or equipment. Additionally, financial dependency, social exclusion, and inadequate rights and protections to enable fair labour representation combine to ensure worker silence. Specifically, since farm workers do not have the right to collectively bargain in Ontario and Alberta, for example, acting as a group to challenge employers to improve workplace safety is not a viable option, keeping individual MFWs exposed to loss of employment and migration status.

Even when MFWs want to seek medical care, other structural problems may prohibit them from doing so. Our survey found that nearly 20 per cent of workers did not have access to their provincial health insurance card. Even once workers are provided with their health cards, however, numerous barriers still inhibit effective, accessible healthcare. One Jamaican worker recalled his experience:

> I was in Canada working for four years before I ever got a health card. During that time I was injured when a tractor ran over my foot. The worker who ran over me begged me not to tell the boss because he didn't want to get in trouble, and I was new here so I didn't know my rights. I just kept working through the injury. Now we have our health card, but we have to ask the boss for them – he doesn't just give them to us. The boss also told us if we go to the doctor with any complaint, not to tell him it's work-related – tell them we got hurt off the job. We don't think this is fair.[49]

This worker articulated the multiple ways that the power dynamics between employers and workers can affect access to healthcare. Workers' dependence on employers for healthcare access creates a unique set of circumstances. At the most fundamental level, awareness of rights and access to the means and knowledge to attain benefits are often mediated by employers. As well, even when workers are aware of their rights, they may be intimidated by external factors that preclude their being able to access them. In this case, the employer may not have wanted the worker to report a workplace injury because this could result in an increase in the employer's dues to the Workers' Compensation Board. Many injured workers in our research had faced similar pressures and thus were not able to receive the compensation they may have needed to assist them with recovery and recuperation of costs for long-term injuries and illness.

Moreover, 93 per cent of the workers surveyed in Ontario indicated that they were unaware of their eligibility for workers' compensation and did not know how to make a claim.[50]

One worker advocate explained, "Many [employers] don't give them [the workers] their health card, RBC [private supplementary insurance from the Royal Bank of Canada], or SIN [social insurance number] cards. They keep them [the cards] and they treat them [the workers] like kids, so if the worker needs something, they have total control over them. The worker has to go to them for any need they have. Then they have to go with someone to the doctor, so they have no privacy whatsoever."[51] Employers' mediation of workers' rights, personal information, and access to benefits and services clearly presents a number of serious problems for workers. This role as intermediary is perceived as justified due to the exceptional nature of the program. Seen as merely temporary workers, migrants do not have access to sustained social support, community integration, language training programs, and all of the other support and integration services offered to immigrants and those considered "members" of a community. The extreme power imbalance between employers and employees is only exacerbated by employers' multiple and compounded roles in determining not only the right of workers to be and work in Canada but also their access to housing, transportation, healthcare, and other services and their ability to secure future employment.

Perhaps the greatest way that employers can exert power over workers is in the structure of the SAWP, which enables them to fire and repatriate workers without any appeals or monitoring process. In this respect, the SAWP agreement states, "Following completion of the trial period of employment by the WORKER, the EMPLOYER, after consultation with the GOVERNMENT AGENT, shall be entitled for non-compliance, refusal to work, or any other sufficient reason, to terminate the WORKER'S employment hereunder and so cause the WORKER to be repatriated."[52] In practice, any perceived violation of a worker's employment contract can result in firing and "pre-mature repatriation." "Breaking the contract" thus refers to a situation where a worker is considered not to have fulfilled the expectations of the contract, including if the worker wishes to return home for personal reasons (e.g., death in the family). If this is the case, the worker must bear the cost of the flight home. If a worker needs to return home for medical reasons (and the condition was not present prior to the worker leaving the country of origin), the employer must cover the travel costs. Yet how a preexisting condition is determined is not specified and is up to the discretion of "government agents."[53]

Without any job security or independent appeals process, workers are well aware that they can be fired and repatriated at their employer's discretion, and this threat exerts effective control. As one worker explained, "We are always afraid of repatriation. The employers try to keep us intimidated, afraid of being sent home."[54] With the expansion of the LSPP to include workers from any country in the world, the increasing levels of competition between different ethnic workforces also enhance the feeling among workers that they are disposable and interchangeable. A Guatemalan worker reflected, "Stop the threats from supervisors – physical and mental. Supervisors threaten to replace us with Cambodians if we don't work hard enough. Employees are repatriated for reporting abusive supervisors."[55]

Employers determine not only if and when a worker is repatriated but also influence whether workers may return to the program the following year. A Jamaican Ministry of Labour official explained that injured workers are often excluded from employers' request lists and hence from future participation in the program:

> You find that especially the employers are afraid that when a worker suffers an injury that "I don't want to take back John because John might do the same thing again next year." You know, and it becomes a hassle between the compensation board and the employer, so they say the best thing is that I don't send for John ... Of course, there are cases where the worker has been injured, and the employer called him back and they just keep working as normal. So it's not really a hard and fast ... so that it's a bit more of a grey area ... [But] if the recommendation comes down that he doesn't go back, then he won't go back.[56]

However, even in cases where employers may wish to keep employing workers, or to assist them in certain situations, they may experience structural barriers related to the program that make this difficult. One employer recalled such a situation:

One year, one of the guys ... his wife had a baby while he was
here. It was hard for him. He wanted to go back. He was worried, and I understand that. Something went wrong with the
birth ... and, you know, they thought she [the wife] would die.
I felt kinda bad, you know. So I asked him if he wanted to go
home. He didn't speak much English, and he said he didn't
want to break his contract. I told him that he could come back.
He was a really good worker and I needed him. The problem
is, though, FARMS [the employer-run agency that manages the
program] doesn't like it. They say we are not supposed to, but I
called FARMS anyway, but it was the weekend. No one was there.
We wanted to get him on a plane ASAP, so I called Air Canada
directly and we got a bereavement flight for 200 bucks and sent
him home. Boy ... did I get an earful from FARMS, and the Consulate [the workers' own government agents] too. They said I
was in breach of contract, etcetera. But what was I supposed to
do, keep the guy here while his wife dies?[57]

Poverty, debt, and a lack of financial resources are further reasons
that many MFWs do not take time off work when sick or injured or
do not report unsafe work practices or workplace accidents, with
55 per cent of those surveyed in Ontario and 62 per cent of those in
British Columbia identifying this as a concern for their co-workers.[58]
These factors are also likely related to the structure of the programs
insofar as migrant workers are in Canada for a set time and send
significant remittances home monthly that may sustain them for the
rest of the year.[59]

All of these structural factors work together to heighten the vulnerability of MFWs to health risks. Furthermore, as outlined in the
evidence above, additional structural factors make them less likely to
seek care, demand changes to unsafe work environments, or receive
compensation for work-related injuries or illness. Sadly, this means
than many workers often return home with illnesses and injuries
untreated, making their access to care and compensation even more
challenging and raising significant transnational health complica-
tions.[60] This is particularly problematic since occupational illness
and injury can frequently be cumulative – with workers developing
symptoms over months or even years. For example, some symptoms

associated with pesticides may manifest themselves after prolonged exposure, or may emerge long after the time of exposure, and can develop into longer-term problems. In numerous cases we have tracked in our research, workers have developed serious long-term conditions such as motor impairment, cancer, and kidney failure after prolonged exposure to pesticides without protection. Yet due in part to the complex etiology of such conditions, it is exceedingly difficult to prove a direct causal association, and thus these former workers have remained without access to any long-term compensation, support, or healthcare. Canada's social safety net does not extend to migrant workers who have returned to their countries of origin, no matter how many years they worked in Canada paying taxes and contributing to benefit programs. There is no long-term system of portable health or employment insurance in place for workers. Partners and widows of workers killed or severely injured have been left without a breadwinner or any support; in some cases, without any reasonable alternatives, they have become migrants themselves to sustain their families.[61]

CONCLUSION

In this chapter, we have demonstrated how agriculture's positioning as a unique industry necessitating "exceptional" labour arrangements has become quietly institutionalized and normalized within Canada. Year after year, decade after decade, increasing numbers of foreign workers are invited to work in Canada on a "temporary" basis. The programs, which legally employ MFWs, do not provide the structures to ensure their health, safety, and wellbeing; to the contrary, workers' vulnerability to health risks is structured into a system that tilts power entirely in favour of employers and that does not allow workers to safely access their rights.

Much combined qualitative and quantitative evidence now demonstrates the negative health outcomes of these circumstances and suggests that workers' health problems are not unfortunate random occurrences but the outcomes of structures that systematically prohibits workers' empowerment and put their health in jeopardy. The employment of migrant workers in such precarious circumstances, initially rationalized as necessary in a unique industry attempting to survive changing socio-demographic circumstances, is now justified by the exceptional needs of the agricultural industry as it attempts to remain viable amid globalized competition. The argument is that increasing MFWs' rights, pay, access to benefits, freedoms, and so on could undermine the viability and sustainability of an endangered and essential industry. Differences in and discrimination based on race, class, and citizenship further underlie these inequities: poor workers of colour from the global South, who do not "belong" in Canada, are deemed to be "lucky" to live and work in virtually any circumstance since these conditions are assumed to be better than they would find "at home."

Yet what is at stake is the creation of a type of internal apartheid within Canada – a system that differentiates between those who belong and are deemed worthy of full and equal access to rights and those who are viewed as unworthy of belonging and thus as unworthy of rights or membership, even though their labour is seen as essential to the economy. Under the radar of many Canadians, this state of exception has become permanently inscribed in the Canadian social order. As temporary foreign worker programs expand beyond agriculture to other industries, this exception will likely continue to prove the rule: for increasing numbers of people living and working temporarily in Canada – a country that prides itself on its reputation for upholding human rights and equality – the state of exception in which foreign workers find themselves represents the chasm between the kind of country that Canada purports to be and the kind of country that it is.

6

Costly Benefits and Gendered Costs: Guatemalans' Experiences of Canada's "Low-Skill Pilot Project"

CHRISTINE HUGHES

INTRODUCTION

Canada's rural landscape is transformed every year by thousands of migrant farm workers who come to seize economic opportunity and fill labour shortages cited by agricultural producers. In the present political economic context, in which the federal government increasingly prefers temporary over permanent types of (im)migration and agricultural producers demonstrate an increased demand for foreign labour,[1] there is a "new kid on the block" among agricultural labour migration streams to Canada. In 2002 the federal government introduced what is officially called the Pilot Project for Occupations Requiring Lower Levels of Formal Training (NOC C and D),[2] hereafter referred to as the Low-Skill Pilot Project (LSPP). The LSPP provides opportunities for low- and medium-skilled temporary foreign workers in several sectors, including construction, manufacturing, services, and agriculture.[3] Compared to the Seasonal Agricultural Worker Program (SAWP), the LSPP has received little critical attention to date,[4] owing largely to the project's short history. This chapter seeks to make a contribution to the nascent dialogue about the LSPP by focusing on the experiences of Guatemalans who participate in this labour migration scheme. It presents reflections centred on workers and their families – garnered through interview-based fieldwork in Guatemala and Canada – on some of the benefits, costs, and gendered impacts of Guatemalans' labour migration to Canada.

Although both migrants and their partners emphasized the financial benefits of working in Canada, migrants raised a number of
concerns about the conditions of this work. Many of these concerns echo those raised in the rich body of literature on migrant
farm work in Canada and on temporary foreign worker programs more generally.[5] Based on poignant antiracist,[6] feminist,[7]
and rights-based perspectives,[8] this growing corpus of research has
delivered migrant workers' experiences from silence and invisibil-
ity and brought them into the consciousness of academics, activists,
and the broader public, raising awareness about the human beings
and employment relations that drive Canada's agricultural industry.
Countering an overriding focus in this body of work on Caribbean
and Mexican workers participating in the SAWP, this chapter makes
important new contributions by focusing on different institutional
arrangements and actors. The LSPP is characterized by less government oversight than the SAWP, and I argue that the nature of Guatemalan migrants' experiences and their reluctance to speak out about
mistreatment stem in large part from the employer-driven nature of
the LSPP.

In addition to a focus on workers' experiences in Canada and
the institutional arrangements configuring them, this chapter also
provides some reflections on the experiences of migrants' female
partners left behind in Guatemala, particularly the gendered socio-
cultural impacts of men's migration. These women are critical
enablers of men's migration, but migration scholarship too often
fails to consider them.[9] With insights from emerging research on the
impacts of migration on family members, as well as from gender and
migration scholarship, this study demonstrates that the migration
of their husbands can impose considerable burdens on Guatemalan
women, often in ways that reinforce gender inequalities.

The chapter argues, in sum, that although one cannot deny the
economic benefits that migration has brought to many Guatemalan
households, these benefits come at a human price in terms of rights,
opportunities, and responsibilities for many migrants and their partners. I preface the analysis with a brief outline of the processes and
institutional actors involved in agricultural employment under the
LSPP, the conditions of work in Canada for Guatemalan migrants,
and the fieldwork informing this study.

THE INSTITUTIONAL AND WORK CONTEXT

Although international labour migration is not a new phenomenon for Guatemalans,[10] this particular phenomenon of agricultural labour migration to Canada dates to 2003, largely facilitated by shifts in Canada's immigration policies. Prior to 2002 the Temporary Foreign Worker Program (TFWP) was primarily focused on the entry into Canada of high-skilled labour, with the Seasonal Agricultural Worker Program and Live-in Caregiver Program being the only streams of the TFWP for lower-skilled workers. The LSPP was established in order to facilitate the entry of temporary foreign workers (TFWs) to fill labour shortages in a broad range of lower-skill occupations and from any source country.[11] With respect to agricultural employment, in addition to not restricting source countries to Mexico and those in the Caribbean region, the LSPP differs from the SAWP in several ways. For instance, it offers longer work permits but no labour market mobility,[12] and it does not involve bilateral governmental agreements[13] and thus permits a lesser role for government involvement and oversight, an issue discussed below.[14]

Guatemalans' participation in the LSPP is facilitated by nonstate actors, namely the International Organization for Migration (IOM)[15] in Guatemala and private producer organizations in Canada that manage foreign agricultural labour (FERME in Quebec, FARMS in Ontario, and WALI in Alberta and British Columbia).[16] In the case of Ontario, Alberta, and British Columbia, the IOM recruits and prepares workers in Guatemala in response to requests from FARMS and WALI, based on memorandums of understanding between the IOM and each producer organization. (Such an arrangement was also in place until recently for FERME in Quebec, but FERME broke off its agreement with the IOM and in early 2011 opened its own operation in Guatemala to recruit workers and facilitate migration to Canada.) Among the other institutional actors involved in Canada, Human Resources and Skills Development Canada (HRSDC) assesses employers' Labour Market Opinions, where a positive evaluation means that a given employer can hire foreign labour;[17] Citizenship and Immigration Canada (CIC) evaluates work permit applications for prospective TFWs; and Guatemalan consular services assist workers in Canada. Meanwhile, the Guatemalan government plays a "support role"[18] in Guatemala, with the Ministry of Labour assisting with recruiting workers and evaluating contract terms.[19]

Guatemalans' migration under the LSPP has grown in leaps and bounds since a small group of 215 (180 men and 35 women) ventured to Canada in 2003.[20] In 2009 3,800 Guatemalans arrived to labour in Canadian fields and greenhouses, followed by 4,300 in 2010.[21] Guatemalans work in Canada in a range of agricultural operations, including field crops, greenhouses, and tree and poultry farms. Among Canadian provinces, Quebec receives the bulk of Guatemalan workers, whereas Alberta, British Columbia, and Ontario host smaller proportions. Workers' contracts tie them to a particular employer for the duration of the work visa, and they labour according to terms of contracts signed between themselves and their employers, which stipulate, among other things, the length of the work term (ranging from three months to two years) and the wage to be paid. Workers are subject to and protected by provincial labour laws, such as those concerning minimum wage, occupational health and safety, and employment relations (i.e., unionization).[22] Workers also pay into plans for employment and health insurance and into pension plans, and they pay income tax.[23] Although employers pay for return airfare, workers must pay for their food and lodging (usually on the farm premises).

CASE STUDY AND FIELDWORK

This chapter draws on interview-based fieldwork undertaken from December 2009 to May 2010 in Canada and Guatemala. The perspectives of Guatemalans informing this discussion were garnered through fieldwork conducted primarily from February to May 2010 in Guatemala. While living in an Indigenous (Kaqchikel) farming village, Vista Hermosa,[24] in the Central Highlands area of Tecpán, I carried out forty-five semistructured interviews of one to two hours with twenty-nine migrants (fourteen men and fifteen women) and sixteen partners (fifteen women and one man). Migrants had worked on farms in Alberta, Quebec, and British Columbia under contracts ranging from three to twelve months. These perspectives at the village level were complemented by those from several government officials, representatives of nongovernmental organizations, and academics in both Canada and Guatemala.

BENEFITS OF MIGRATION TO CANADA

Time and again, study participants in Vista Hermosa stated that they or their migrant partners had travelled to Canada "por necesidad" (out of necessity), citing persistent and worsening economic difficulties caused by poor crop turnout, low prices for their agricultural yields, rising consumer prices, and lack of employment options. "No se puede hacer nada aquí" (one can't do anything here) is a refrain I heard often. Many migrants had gone to Canada with the intention of paying off paralyzing debts, and others aspired to build new or better houses, buy land, or save for their children's future. Overall, unselfish motivations characterized decisions, not taken lightly, to migrate: "one dreams about goals for the family," said one woman, "that's why you go, to help your family."

The IOM's evaluations of the project reveal considerable economic benefits for migrants and their families,[25] and I found that Vista Hermosa migrants were largely successful in meeting their economic goals through migrating to Canada. Workers in Canada generally earn at or above the provincial minimum wage or prevailing wage rate for their particular occupational sector.[26] Even with deductions from their pay factored in, workers usually earn more in an hour in Canada than they would make in a day in waged agricultural work in Guatemala. Respondents were hesitant to disclose in interviews the amount of a season's earnings, and these can vary widely, but IOM sources put the net income figure at approximately $1,500 per month, which would be $18,000 in a twelve-month period.[27] The economic benefits that migration to Canada has brought to families in Vista Hermosa cannot be understated. I found material evidence in the several cement-block homes under construction in the village, which would replace thatch or laminate structures, as well as new practical and "luxury" household items. The results of less tangible benefits, such as education and medical care, will take longer to measure, but on the whole, according to village leaders, the households in Vista Hermosa are now better off than those in other villages that have fewer or no migrants to Canada.

NO BENEFITS WITHOUT COSTS

Although migration often brings significant economic benefits to migrants and their families, "there are consequences that this brings."[28] Several workers raised what they perceived as problematic working or living conditions of varying degrees of severity, including long and exhausting work days, work terms that did not coincide with those stipulated in their contracts, lack of holidays, exorbitant living expenses, lack of freedom to leave farm premises, language barriers preventing communication with employers, poor medical attention, and crowded living quarters.

To elucidate some workers' accounts of problematic conditions, I profile here a farm in Quebec that employs mostly female workers.[29] The four Vista Hermosa women I interviewed who had worked on this farm offered similar accounts of troubling working and living conditions, some of which constituted human rights violations. They had faced long work days, averaging twelve to fourteen hours, and the work of picking and packing fruit demanded a great deal physically from the women. One woman remarked that "if one wants to work, one has to *echar ganas* [put in a real effort], because one feels as though one is going to fall down because of all the crouching and bending over all day." Supervisors are "really demanding," the same woman claimed, and one of her co-workers complained about not getting enough rest breaks during the day and about having only a half-hour for lunch, which she and her co-workers often had to spend in the fields, no matter the weather.

Of particular concern was the level of strict control and surveillance to which the women had been subjected during and outside working hours. The women spoke of being closely watched while working and discouraged from "chatting": "In your work, it's better that you don't talk, because the *señora* sees you from far away ... and it gets her attention," one remarked. All four women referred to the supervisors' and bosses' tendency to *regañar* (to scold or yell at) them. The women seemed to commonly believe that workers who angered or disappointed their supervisors or bosses would not be given the opportunity to return the following year. One woman claimed, "It's better, no matter what one does, that we *aguantamos* [put up with it]. If we don't listen to the señora, she tells us we won't have the opportunity next year."[30]

The women's mobility and ability to associate and communicate also seemed significantly curtailed. They were permitted to call their families in Guatemala only once a week and were not allowed to receive visitors to the farm property. "The señora doesn't allow anyone to enter there with us," said one woman. Nor were the women allowed to freely leave the farm premises – for instance, to go to church or even for a walk. "They hardly let us leave," one woman remarked, and another said they were "*bien encerradas* [really shut in]." The only off-farm time they received was a half-day once a week when they would be transported to a nearby town to do their shopping and banking. During that time, women cited being closely monitored by an accompanying supervisor and told not to speak with local townspeople: "It scares us to talk to them because *la señora nos regaña* [the woman yells at us]." If a supervisor was not with the women during a trip to town, an indirect surveillance prevailed; one woman was told by her boss or supervisor that cameras were on them, such as in the supermarket, and that if she were caught behaving "badly," she would be denied a day of work.

To some extent, the women spoke matter of factly about these working and living conditions, saying, for instance, "work is like that, you have to do it well." They also tended to apply a discourse of caring to these circumstances, interpreting their supervisor as a mother caring for them.[31] One worker said that although treatment was strict and she felt controlled, she also felt well cared for: "Sometimes we say that we're a little mistreated, and sometimes we say, they're taking care of us like that." The no-visitors rule in particular was interpreted as protecting vulnerable women from unwanted intruders and from "problems" that arise when women and men intermingle while working in Canada. However, a couple of the women considered some of their circumstances to amount to mistreatment. One claimed, "what they do to us isn't just." Whether women felt cared for or mistreated, they felt their work was appreciated, and the quality of the experience often came down to earnings. One woman remarked, "The work is really hard. It's hard, but as I say, one earns."

The problems that Guatemalan workers in Quebec have allegedly faced have captured the attention of some institutional bodies, such as the Commission des droits de la personne et des droits de la jeunesse, the province's human rights commission. The commission investigates cases of alleged violations of Quebec's Charter of Human Rights and Freedoms and provides public education and direct advice to employers. One of the commission's officers, Carole Fiset, was familiar with the alleged mobility, communication, and association issues on that particular farm. She contended that employers there were protective of their female workers: "[The farm] wants to protect the women because they think that women are more easily abused than men, because of language, because of lack of knowledge about the customs in Quebec."[32] Having spoken with many of the farm's female workers, she asserted that they knew their rights and that pregnancy, not mobility, was the women's key concern. She voiced concern, however, that the conditions on this and other farms threatened to violate several rights in Quebec's charter, such as those to association, privacy, and nondisclosure of confidential information.

Another key institution involved in the Quebec context is the Guatemalan Consulate in Montreal. This office receives calls for assistance from workers across the country, and a few workers expressed disappointment in their Consulate's seeming unwillingness or inability to assist them. Two officials interviewed there in early 2010 before a change in personnel[33] expressed considerable concern about their compatriots' circumstances in Canada and referred to "abuses, mistreatments, repression, and the violation of fundamental rights."[34] Among the problems that they had encountered among workers and/or for which workers had asked for intervention, they emphasized the issues of mobility and communication, especially among women: "They've been prohibited from leaving the farm outside working hours. They're reprimanded if they talk with anybody who isn't a worker on the farm ... Here, they live in a system of slavery."[35] As for their ability to step in and advocate on behalf of those they represent, the officials claimed that they were overworked, underappreciated, and limited in their ability to assist Guatemalan workers adequately. They stated, "we need to work on these problems, but here it's just the two of us in Canada working on this."[36] They were two men, with one vehicle, responsible for doing monthly visits to each farm in Quebec and for attending to inquiries and complaints from over 4,000 workers. They reported feeling threatened and under considerable pressure, especially from the producer organization FERME, to act in ways that would leave workers' rights violated: ".FERME puts the pressure on, so that the rights of these workers aren't defended ... We are totally limited in what we can do."[37] They reported that, because Guatemalans – both workers and their Consulate – are trying to claim and defend workers' rights, FERME is looking for ways to reduce the number of Guatemalans: "That's not convenient to FERME, so they don't want more Guatemalans."[38] By and large, workers "have to *sufrir y callar* [suffer and shut up] ... If they don't, they're expelled from the program."[39] They wanted FERME and employers to see Guatemalans not just as workers, or economic units, but as "human beings, with dignity, as a complete person."[40]

The intent in discussing here some of the negative experiences of workers is not to demonize the farms' owners or to suggest that generalizations can be extended to all farms that employ Guatemalan labour. Among all study participants, those who were relatively satisfied with their experiences were as numerous as those who cited difficulties. Many said the work experience was "fine" or "normal," with no serious problems. Almost all migrant workers admitted that the work was hard and the hours were long, but such demands were not unexpected. One female field-crops worker remarked, "They treat you well there; you eat well, you have a good house ... For me, there's nothing bad there." She spoke matter of factly about the rules and strictness: "The bosses are strict, but they have to be ... there are rules everywhere one goes, and you have to respect that." She claimed not to have a problem with twelve- or fourteen-hour days because she could earn more.

It should be noted, however, that migrants I spoke with, especially those who were going back to Canada following our interviews, may have presented their experiences in a positive light and not been forthright about problems they had experienced because of concerns about job security. I heard many times that workers had not been called back, as well as variations on assertions that they had been cautioned against speaking with outsiders about their experiences and that workers who complained too much would be expelled from the program. For instance, one worker said, "I realized that there can be a complaint with the employer or the [IOM] office, but they don't give you the opportunity to go again." As much as I assured workers of measures to provide anonymity and clarified my identity, some were nervous about proceeding with the interview and a few refused the invitation. The fear that workers have of speaking out also hampers the IOM in its efforts to garner feedback and improve workers experiences. One IOM official, Delbert Field, spoke of migrants who are "so desperate" for their work that "they don't trust each other even more than they don't trust us," suggesting that some migrants may refuse interviews or not speak ill of employers for fear that other migrants in their community will report negatively about them to employers. It is difficult, therefore, to decide how to judge workers' positive or ambivalent evaluations of their experiences.

EMPLOYER INFLUENCE

The key reason for frequent nondisclosure and for the problems arising and reported by workers with respect to working and living conditions is the employer-driven nature of the LSPP.[41] This concern has been raised by other scholars in reference to the TFWP generally,[42] which has been referred to as "a new style of immigration that is driven by employers rather than the state."[43] This contention aligns with scholarship pointing to the increasing neoliberalization of Canada's immigration policy, evidenced, for instance, by decreasing state interference in the management of labour markets.[44] This argument also falls in line with analyses of labour migration programs generally that indicate their economic biases or orientations.[45] Destination countries, prioritizing their macroeconomic interests over other concerns, design labour migration programs to meet economic objectives and address employers' needs. The extent to which governments involve themselves in issues related to workers rights tends to be overshadowed by employers' influence over employment relations and workers' experiences.[46]

It is apparent that the LSPP is economically oriented and employer-driven. Of course, employer demand drives Canada's whole TFWP,[47] but employers also wield considerable influence over the configuration and operations of the LSPP and thus shape workers' fortunes. Pressure from employers was the major impetus behind the establishment of the LSPP in 2002,[48] and the running of the pilot project has since catered largely to the needs and perspectives of employers. For instance, a review conducted of the LSPP for HRSDC in 2006 overwhelmingly focused on employers' experiences with the project and did not consult with workers,[49] and outcomes of this review have made the project more "employer-friendly."[50] In the Quebec context at least, it seems that the influence of the employer association FERME has been considerable. Guatemalan consular officials were particularly outspoken about FERME and the consequences of its influence on workers: "Their [FERME's] interest is the money that each worker represents," one said. "They don't see the worker as a human being."[51] Once the worker arrives, the other official continued, "FERME forgets that the worker exists. They completely forget."[52] The key problem, they said, is that this labour migration is treated as a business and migrant workers as commodities.

As noted above, there is no bilateral agreement regulating Guatemalans' migration to Canada. Given the dearth of governmental involvement, variations on the term "privatized" came up in some interviewees' descriptions of the LSPP. In referring to the SAWP in comparison to the LSPP, one Guatemalan consular official stated: "That's at the governmental level, that's the key difference. This one isn't, it's private."[53] And Delbert Field of the IOM described Guatemalan migration to Canada as "private-sector-driven." United Food and Commercial Workers Canada, an active institutional player with respect to protecting and extending migrant farm workers' rights in Canada, has also expressed concerns about what one of its national representatives, Andrea Galvez, sees as the "privatization of the policymaking in terms of labour and immigration." Also the coordinator of the Agricultural Workers Alliance, which operates several migrant worker support centres across Canada, Galvez asserted that the LSPP, more so than the SAWP, is passing responsibility for setting the terms of migrants' entry, work, and living conditions "from the government – from HRSDC and CIC – toward the employer."

Countries sending labour for the LSPP have no formal role in the project and therefore have even less ability than do SAWP countries to supervise the treatment of their citizens or intervene on their behalf.[54] Consular officials purportedly represent Guatemalans in Canada, but their role is not formalized, and as described above, they consider their abilities to intervene as often limited. Galvez asked, "who's actually speaking for those workers?" She suggested that government involvement is important; even if Mexico does not have a lot of power in the international labour market to negotiate for and demand the rights of its citizens, it has more power to defend Mexicans abroad than the IOM has to defend Guatemalans and more interest in doing so. The IOM, for its part, admits a considerable employer influence: "everything that happens, you have to show how this improves the business," said IOM official Field.

In this labour migration context, then, because of the employer-oriented nature of the LSPP, economic and labour market considerations have taken priority over migrants' rights and the quality of their experiences in Canada more generally. Most notably, speaking out can result in repatriation, and institutional actors charged with protecting the rights of workers have been unable to sufficiently do so. In Vista Hermosa there was little question about the economic benefits that migrants and their families have enjoyed, but economic necessity has put too many of these workers and their families at the mercy of business interests,[55] and "it's the worker who's going to pay the price at the end of the day."[56]

This discussion turns now to exploring the experiences of the other human side of Vista Hermosa's migratory projects: female partners left behind.

THE ENABLERS OF MIGRATION TO CANADA: WOMEN LEFT BEHIND

This section rests on the contention that migration scholars and policymakers have tended to focus on certain aspects and actors in migration processes at the expense of considering others. A focus on migrants and the economic consequences of their movement has rendered far less studied and visible the social impacts of migration and the experiences of nonmigrating family members, and until fairly recently, the migration analysis lens has been focused primarily on male migrants. Speaking to the economic bias of migration studies, Jean Grugel and Nicola Piper note that the social dimensions of outcomes of these labour migration schemes do not receive enough attention from policymakers.[57] Included among these social dimensions, I would argue, are the wellbeing and quality of life of nonmigrating partners. Although the individuals on the nonmigrating side of transnational family arrangements are central to maintaining the family's emotional connections,[58] wellbeing, and sense of unity, most research about international migration disregards the importance of family members who stay behind and how migration affects them.[59] Adding to scholarship that is gradually attending to this neglect,[60] this chapter examines here the gendered socio-cultural impacts on female partners[61] left behind in Guatemala, particularly as concerns gender roles and relations.

Gender is now acknowledged as a central concept for studying migration.[62] Both the experiences and results of migration are gendered, affecting women and men differently as well as shaping the relations between them.[63] There is a considerable body of scholarship examining the impacts of temporary or circular migration on household gender practices, roles, and relations.[64] Among the possible experiences that female partners may face, owing to men's migration, are roles and responsibilities that they may not have performed before or to the same degree. Indeed, the IOM in its first evaluation maintains that this is the case for Guatemalan women left behind by their migrating partners and that this may contribute to ongoing changes in household gender relations. Scholarship on this issue in the Guatemalan context reveals nuances and complexities. For instance, Cecilia Menjívar and Victor Agadjanian conclude that "the lives of the women who stay after their partners migrate change significantly" but in a bittersweet way that "cannot be easily categorized as gains or losses."[65] These authors found that Guatemalan women's material conditions improve because of remittances but that their lives are both more constrained because their movements and decisions are significantly controlled and more burdened because of having to assume new responsibilities.

With a couple of exceptions, my study confirmed assertions found in this body of scholarship about the limited and temporary nature of changes to gender roles as well as about continued control and surveillance of women left behind. Additionally, I found that men's migration can actually contribute to an intensification of the gender roles of these women both during and after the migratory period.[66] I agree with Deborah Boehm, who argues that it is certainly not the tendency for household gender relations to move "from female subservience to emancipation" as a result of men's migration.[67]

Gender roles and relations between conjugal partners in Vista Hermosa households are characterized, by and large, by patriarchal arrangements and a fairly strict gendered division of labour with respect to household versus extrahousehold work. In short, women are seen as caretakers and men as the primary breadwinners. Women devote themselves to cooking, cleaning, and the bulk of childcare and remain in the house for most of the day, unless they assist their male partners with agricultural work or go to area markets. Men are seen as the primary or proper income earners and spend long days outside the home, working primarily in agriculture. Men's responsibilities at home are limited largely to supplying firewood and water, caring for large animals, and performing some minimal childrearing activities. One male migrant matter of factly remarked, "Here, the one who maintains the husband is the woman – the kids and the husband – [she] takes care of them ... I come back from work, and [there's] nothing more do ... Work here in the home, it's not a lot that the man or husband does." Several women were engaged in income-earning activities, such as through weaving or tending the family store, but these activities were complementary to the male partner's primary responsibility for the household's economic wellbeing. With respect to *quién manda* (who is in charge) in the home as regards financial management and decision making, the study revealed a continuum ranging from near-total male control (derived in part from men's economic contributions) to fairly egalitarian arrangements in which partners would make decisions together.

Men's migration brought varying degrees of change to a "normal" day's activities for their female partners in Vista Hermosa. A few of these women assumed some of the farm work tasks of their male partners, but it was more common that they, through their husband's remittances, paid *mozos* (day labourers) to perform these tasks. This was due in part to limitations imposed on women's time by their household responsibilities but also because of the gendered nature of farm work. Although most women did not perform their male partners' farming duties, paying and overseeing mozos added to their responsibilities. Other responsibilities that some women assumed to a greater degree in men's absence fell largely in the realm of financial management, including handling money, making financial decisions, and purchasing items with remittance money that men would generally buy, such as building materials and agricultural inputs.

Women's degree of freedom in making decisions and purchases, however, was usually significantly limited by the influence of their male partners from afar and of other family members present in the village. Telephone communication between migrants and partners was frequent, and during these conversations, men would often instruct women regarding what to direct remittance monies toward, and women would tell men what they had spent the money on. One male migrant described it this way: "She is like an informant – I need this, I need this – [and she says] I've spent this, [so] I know." Women usually also consulted men on most decisions concerning the household or children, such as where to take them for medical care.

In addition to men's continued influence over the phone, the potential for women to have more financial and decision-making liberty was also sometimes curtailed by the "in-law factor." Vista Hermosa is a village characterized by patrilocal living arrangements; it is not uncommon for a couple to live close to or on the same property as the husband's parents. Judith Adler Hellman has found these arrangements to significantly curtail women's liberties during husbands' migration from Mexico.[68] Although I did not encounter in-law control to the same degree through my interviews, a few women suggested considerable in-law influence. One young woman, for instance, had not received or managed any of her husband's remittances; instead, the money went directly to her father-in-law, who would give her an allowance of sorts under direction from her husband. Another woman cited in-law pressure on her choice of where to take her children for medical care and reported feeling that she had to tell her mother-in-law when she left the house to visit her own mother. A leader in the nearby municipal women's office explained the *suegra* (mother-in-law) interference as a demonstration of mothers "watching out" for their sons by preventing sons' wives from usurping too much of the sons' household power.[69]

Hellman found in the Mexican context that mothers-in-law can be particularly influential in curtailing women's physical mobility based on the threat that mobility is seen to pose to women's faithfulness. One woman in Hellman's research put it this way: "every time you left the house, the family was at risk of scandal because you might stop to talk to a man ... Sometimes your suegra would accuse you directly of plotting an affair."[70] Several women in Vista Hermosa felt that their mobility was restricted by community members' tendency "to talk." The community seems to represent a "shame culture," "in which people – for better or for worse – mind each other's business."[71] In order to "avoid problems" (i.e., gossip and accusations about what women could be doing in their husbands' absence), some women in Vista Hermosa said they hardly left the house, only leaving out of necessity or for church-related activities. Or if they did leave the house, they would advise their husbands by phone. Asked why she did not leave the house much, another woman put the situation clearly: "to avoid problems, because they [the men] go to work, and people here don't think about the fact that they're suffering there, but rather about what they [women] are doing here."

Moreover, if women could avoid the gossip and were presented with reasons to leave the house, many of them would encounter another obstacle: their responsibility for single-handedly caring for children. Although men in Vista Hermosa engaged far less than women in parenting, women missed the assistance men would provide when they were at home, such as by playing with children or watching over children when mothers had to go out. One woman whose mobility was restricted by children during her husband's absence said, "When they [the men] aren't here, one can't go out whenever. In the afternoon [when children are home from school], one can't go out because they're not here. When he's here, and the time comes to go out, one goes." This issue of caring for children on their own came up often when women were asked about the most difficult aspect of their experiences of being without their husbands. In addition to not being able to leave the house as desired, women cited lack of rest, having to worry about and care for children who seemed to fall ill more during their fathers' absence, or having to soothe children who would cry because they missed their fathers. The combination of not being able to leave the house and having to manage childcare and housework on their own left many feeling sad, alone, and stressed.[72]

The overall impression given by women left behind was that they felt at best ambivalent about but more often burdened by their male partners' migration, that migration periods were situations they "got through" and "resigned themselves to." Although some women had assumed greater control over household affairs, this was often not seen in a positive light but instead as a stress-inducing situation. Nelly Salgado de Snyder points out that if the migration of their male partners "empowers" women left behind (i.e., grants them new powers over household management), women may not enjoy or desire this, contrary to what women's advocates might believe.[73] The woman quoted above as having difficulties leaving the house because of her children provided a telling explanation of these circumstances: "I have a bit more control over everything, and I have more to take care of as well. And if it's not enough [the money], I have to figure out what to do. So one has to think more as well [when they're not here] ... that's what's hard for me ... I have to think about how to do everything."

When male migrants returned from Canada, many women cited being happy about having their husbands' help again, and men tended to reassume their own roles and responsibilities, including those that their female partners had taken on during their absence, such as financial management. Some women said they felt less burdened when their husbands returned. One woman put it this way: "I felt less weight because he was a big help. If one [child] was crying and I have my housework to do, he would go get her while she calmed down a bit ... Here alone, if one cries, the other cries, and there's no one to see to them, whereas when he's here, there's help." Women often referred to things as going back to "normal" with the resumption of their *costumbres* (customs).

I argue that in some cases, moreover, men's migration and return had the effect of heightening or intensifying women's "normal" roles as wives who care for their husbands. A couple of women claimed to treat their husbands in extra special ways during their time at home before going back to Canada, noting that their husbands work hard in Canada and have to cook and do housework there and that sometimes husbands return more demanding of their wives. Hellman

describes the situation this way: "he keeps talking about his sacrifices, but doesn't appreciate hers, and he expects to be waited
on like a king to make up for all he's done without."[74] Indeed, one
male migrant in my study claimed to be treated like a king when he
returned, and his wife said that she would really cater to him when
he was at home because it would often be only a few months before
he would set off again, so it was best to treat him "a su gusto" (as
he likes it). Another woman matter of factly remarked, "he takes
advantage of the time that he's here – he doesn't do anything [laugh-
ter]. But when he's there, he does everything."[75]

It is not my contention that all male migrants returned more
demanding of their wives and were unappreciative of their wives'
efforts. Indeed, a few women cited husbands who were more loving
of them and appreciative of their housework – sometimes because
men, having had to cook and clean in Canada, had come to better appreciate how difficult and valuable this work was. The IOM's
evaluations make similar assertions and report that, overall, men's
migration "contributes to improving the situation of women."[76] Such
contentions, however, are contrary to my overall findings of a return
to or intensification of "normal" pre-migration household gender
roles and relations. In the case of Vista Hermosa, I agree with Sandra
Weinstein Bever and with Boehm that, although migration may temporarily alter gender roles, gender ideologies – the "expectations,
values and attitudes attributed to being male or female"[77] – resist
change more strongly and that, more than disrupting gender norms,
migration can reinforce forms of male dominance and privilege.[78]

CONCLUSION

This chapter has explored the experiences of migrants and their families with labour migration to Canada by examining a case study
of Guatemalans participating in the low-skilled stream of Canada's
Temporary Foreign Worker Program. This discussion has focused on
three key points. First, this instance of labour migration to Canada
has generated significant economic benefits for migrants and their
families. Second, these economic benefits have come with a price
tag in the form of the mistreatment of workers and violations of
their rights, which the employer-oriented nature of the project has

largely fostered. Third, this labour migration imposes a considerable practical and emotional burden on migrants' female partners, who respond with a great deal of strength, perseverance, and stoicism. One woman put it poignantly when she said, "he suffers there and I suffer here."

Based on these observations, I offer a few recommendations. First, the IOM should negotiate mechanisms with employer associations and the federal government to enable workers to speak out in circumstances of unjust working or living conditions without fear of being fired or blacklisted. Second, barring the possibility of a bilateral agreement between Canada and Guatemala, the ability of the Government of Guatemala to protect and advocate for its citizens must be enhanced, such as by increasing personnel in consular offices in Canada and enhancing the Consulate's powers vis-à-vis employers in situations of worker mistreatment. Third, women's groups or organizations in Guatemala, possibly with partial funding from Canadian sources, should be more attentive to the needs of migrants' female partners, such as by establishing support groups or communal childcare opportunities.

There is no end in sight to the perceived need among Canada's agricultural producers for foreign labour or to the desire among Guatemalan families to *salir adelante* (get ahead) through labour migration to Canada. However, more safeguards and supports must be put in place to ensure that economic benefits for both parties do not come at the expense of workers' rights or women's quality of life.

7

Provincial/Territorial Nominee Programs: An Avenue to Permanent Residency for Low-Skilled Temporary Foreign Workers?

DELPHINE NAKACHE AND SARAH D'AOUST

INTRODUCTION

Migrant workers of all skill levels have become an important feature of the Canadian labour market. Employers are using both "skilled" and "low-skilled" migrant workers to fill long-term and even permanent vacancies,[1] "low-skilled" workers being referred to here as workers performing jobs categorized as c and d under the National Occupational Classification (NOC).[2] Despite the need for "temporary foreign workers" (TFWs) on an ongoing basis, temporary labour migration remains structured in Canadian immigration law as a "temporary" phenomenon. For example, the rationale behind the restrictive nature of the temporary migrant work permit, which often ties TFWs to one job, one employer, and one location, is that temporary labour migration programs serve as a tool to fill specific shortages in the labour market and are thus designed to respond to current employer needs.[3] In addition, in Canadian immigration legislation, TFWs are expected to leave the country once their work permits expire. Up until recently, there was no limit to the number of renewals of the work permit in the legislation. Yet in April 2011 the federal government implemented regulatory changes aimed at limiting the stay of TFWs for a maximum of four years, followed by a period of six years during which they are not allowed to work in Canada.[4] The government noted that

"This provision would signal clearly to both workers and employers that the purpose of the TFWP is to address temporary labour shortages,"[5] thereby reinforcing the temporary nature of labour migration programs. However, if we move away from the rigid legal framework governing the entry and stay of TFWs in Canada, and if we locate existing labour migration programs in the more general context of the changing face of economic immigration to Canada,[6] we realize that immigration law has in fact been modified in order to enable skilled TFWs to transition to permanent residency from within Canada. In contrast, low-skilled TFWs, with a few rare exceptions, have not been given the same opportunity to immigrate to Canada permanently.

These modifications highlight the tension and contradiction at the heart of Canadian immigration law, as well as the inherently discriminatory nature of immigration law.[7] In 1973 the category of the "temporary foreign worker" was introduced for the first time in the legislation with the underlying assumption that there were certain types of work that unemployed Canadians were unwilling to perform.[8] Today, the same assumption exists, but given that Canada now relies heavily on TFWs to fill jobs on an ongoing basis, this assumption has been reformulated around a "high-skilled"-"low-skilled" TFW dichotomy. Through this legal dichotomy, skilled TFWs, who perform jobs that Canadians are willing to perform, are seen as deserving permanent resident status; in contrast, low-skilled TFWs, who perform the "dirty jobs," are expected to spend years in Canada as workers but not as future citizens.[9] This dichotomy is a clear example of "the incessant adjustment of migration law to meet national need and the use of national need as a device to justify migration statutes."[10]

It is important to note that the exclusionary dimension of Canadian immigration law as regards the low-skilled migrant worker has, until now, been addressed only in relation to *federal* avenues available for TFWs to attain permanent residency from within Canada. This is due to the fact that Canada has traditionally maintained a fairly centralized immigration system, even if the constitutional framework enables the regionalization of immigration regulation (subject to a degree of centralized control). Over the past three decades, however, Canada has shared its federal authority over immigration with Quebec and, more recently, with other provincial and territorial governments.[11] This shift occurred through a series of bilateral agreements between the federal and provincial/territorial governments, which resulted in the formation of Provincial/Territorial Nominee Programs (PTNPs).

Nominee programs are seen as a response to the shortcomings of the traditional federal immigration streams and as a means to address the unique demographic and economic challenges that provinces and territories face as a result.[12] Despite the growing importance of PTNPs and their potential to address the uneven distribution of newcomers in Canada,[13] little is known about the real opportunities for low-skilled TFWs to access permanent residency from within Canada through these programs. More specifically, one often reads about "variations" in PTNPs that affect the "opportunities" for TFWs to make the transition to permanent residency,[14] but what, in fact, are these opportunities? This question is important for two main reasons. First, in a context where federal avenues currently available for transitioning from temporary to permanent status from within Canada are almost exclusively the preserve of skilled TFWs, PTNPs are largely seen – and presented – as low-skilled TFWs' "best bet" to obtain permanent resident status.[15] It is therefore imperative to determine whether this is in fact the case. Second, given the increasing trend toward devolution to provinces and territories in immigration matters in Canada, it has become necessary to assess whether the exclusionary nature of immigration law and policy toward the low-skilled migrant worker has been reinforced or diminished through PTNPs.

In this chapter, we address the following research questions: (1) Do PTNPs offer unique opportunities for TFWs to access permanent residency? (2) Are PTNPs the most likely avenue to permanent residency for low-skilled TFWs? (3) What are some of the limitations of these programs in providing access to permanent residency for low-skilled TFWs? In addition to documentary analysis of PTNP websites across Canada, our study of PTNPs is based on the results of questionnaires that were completed by key governmental actors in the administration of PTNPs from May to August 2010 and represents a compilation of the latest data available on these programs.[16]

As we show, although not all low-skilled TFWs can access permanent residency from within Canada through a PTNP, PTNPs are today the most likely path to permanent residency for low-skilled TFWs. However, PTNPs come with their own sets of limitations. First, in order to be eligible for permanent residency, TFWs must have a permanent job offer with a local employer. This requirement has the potential to create uncertainty for TFWs who find themselves in a position of unemployment or whose work permits may have expired. Second, in many provinces and territories, low-skilled TFWs are eligible to apply for nomination only if they are working in specific occupations or industries.[17] Therefore, because PTNPs are designed to fill labour market shortages unique to each province, these "low-skilled" TFW categories vary considerably across Canada. Finally, although some PTNPs appear on paper to exclude low-skilled workers from applying for nomination, certain provinces make case-by-case determinations on low-skilled applications and even allow low-skilled workers to apply under the skilled worker categories. Although it does not entirely exclude the low-skilled (a positive development), the case-by-case determination process in some provinces is lacking in transparency, which makes it difficult for a potential candidate to navigate through the appropriate channels. Thus we show that the increased authority of provinces and territories over immigration selection ultimately benefits low-skilled TFWs and is likely to reduce – although not entirely – the exclusionary effect of Canadian immigration law.

We begin our analysis by briefly outlining the legal and practical barriers faced by low-skilled TFWs in attaining permanent residency through existing federal immigration streams. We show that these barriers allow Canada to sustain a clear policy goal, which is to have low-skilled TFWs leave the country after a certain period of time and to have skilled TFWs settle permanently. We then evaluate the real opportunities for low-skilled TFWs to make the transition to permanent residency through PTNPs. We conclude that PTNPs primarily target skilled TFWs but that they also offer some opportunities for low-skilled TFWs to access permanent residency from within Canada. However, these opportunities remain very limited (and we show why), except in Manitoba, which is the only province with a category open to TFWs of all skill levels.

A LACK OF IMMIGRATION OPPORTUNITIES FOR
LOW-SKILLED TFWS THROUGH EXISTING FEDERAL
STREAMS

Overall, the number of people entering Canada on a temporary basis is on the rise, and the highest increase is in TFWs.[18] One of the reasons for this is that temporary migrants have discovered that it is "administratively simpler" to apply for and obtain permanent residency if they have already been admitted to Canada as a "temporary" worker than to do so from abroad.[19] Given that the number of low-skilled TFWs entering Canada is on the rise,[20] the discussion regarding the limited avenues available to them to transition from temporary to permanent residency is timely and extremely important.

All TFWs, except seasonal workers admitted under the Seasonal Agricultural Worker Program (SAWP),[21] may apply for permanent residency. Although TFWs are expected to leave Canada after their authorized period of stay, intent to become a permanent resident does not preclude them from being admitted temporarily, as long as the immigration officer "is satisfied that they will leave Canada by the end of the period authorized for their stay."[22] In other words, TFWs are not legally barred from applying for permanent residency.

TFWs have four avenues to change from temporary to permanent resident status from within Canada: (1) the Live-in Caregiver Program (LCP), (2) the Federal Skilled Worker Program (FSWP), (3) the Canadian Experience Class (CEC), and (4) the Provincial/Territorial Nominee Programs. As we have shown elsewhere,[23] the LCP provides the opportunity for low-skilled workers to apply for permanent residency, but this opportunity is applicable only to live-in caregivers hired under this program. The FSWP and the CEC, in contrast, are almost the exclusive preserve of skilled TFWs. This situation shows that the federal government wants only skilled TFWs to stay permanently in Canada, an objective that was emphasized with the April 2011 regulatory changes limiting the stay of TFWs to a maximum of four years, followed by a period of six years during which they are not allowed to work in Canada. The federal government noted that these regulatory changes should "encourage the use of appropriate programs and pathways to permanent residency in order to respond to the long-term labour needs of employers."[24] However, given the limited opportunities for low-skilled workers to transfer from temporary to permanent resident status from within the country, this change reinforces the message that the skilled are welcome to settle here permanently, whereas the low-skilled are expected to leave when their temporary work permits expire.

Family unity rules are another illustration of policy initiatives aimed at discouraging low-skilled workers' long-term integration. Although under immigration legislation there is no regulatory bar to having family members accompany TFWs to Canada, low-skilled workers are less likely than skilled workers to bring their families with them. TFWs have to demonstrate to the immigration officer that they are capable of supporting their dependants while in Canada. A key point that is considered when processing such applications is the employment situation of the applicant's spouse. Whereas the spouse of a skilled worker is entitled to enter Canada with an open work permit – one with no restriction on the employer – the spouse of a low-skilled worker is not eligible for an open work permit and requires a Labour Market Opinion if applying for a work permit.[25] According to Citizenship and Immigration Canada (CIC), this requirement, combined with the fact that workers with lower levels of formal training generally earn less,[26] raises "very legitimate concerns regarding the applicant's bona fides and ability to support their dependents while in Canada." That being said, PTNPs offer more promising work opportunities for the spouses of low-skilled workers since the spouses of low-skilled workers who have been nominated for permanent residency under a PTNP are entitled to apply for an open work permit for the duration of the TFWs' work permit, regardless of their skill level.[27] This is a significant exception to the TFWP's family unity rules, as it renders family accompaniment for provincial nominees more realistic and thus TFWs' possibilities for settling permanently in Canada more likely.

In sum, although low-skilled TFWs are not barred on paper from applying for permanent residency from within Canada, the legal barriers to attaining permanent residency in practice are such that it is impossible for these workers to settle permanently in Canada through the existing federal immigration streams. This situation illustrates the exclusionary role of Canadian immigration law as applied to low-skilled TFWs.

SIMILARITIES AND DIVERGENCES BETWEEN PTNPS IN
THEIR APPROACH TO TEMPORARY FOREIGN WORKERS

For most low-skilled TFWs, the only viable option for accessing
permanent residency is through a Provincial/Territorial Nominee
Program. PTNPs are federal-provincial/territorial agreements that
allow provinces and territories to play a greater role in recruiting,
selecting, and attracting immigrants according to the economic
needs of the region. Under this agreement, a province or territory
obtains sole responsibility for selection of potential immigrants and
their nomination for immigration into the province/territory, yet the
federal government retains partial control over the process (once
the applicant is nominated, federal security, criminality, and health
checks are conducted, and CIC makes a final decision on the permanent resident application). In addition, CIC is also involved in placing limits on the number of approved nominees in certain provinces
and territories. For example, in Saskatchewan and British Columbia, the province, in coordination with CIC, must mutually agree
on the nominee targets for each year.[28] However, some provinces
have greater autonomy in setting nominee targets. For example, in
2003 the Manitoba government negotiated that the limits on the
number of nominees for the province be removed.[29] As a result, the
Manitoba government can, in consultation with CIC, determine its
own nominee program quotas.[30] Similarly, in 2006 the Newfoundland and Labrador Agreement on Provincial Nominees was renewed
with the federal government, and it places no limit on the number of
immigrants who can be nominated through the province (this agreement is of indefinite duration).[31] In 2007 the federal government also
signed framework agreements with Alberta and Nova Scotia that are
of indefinite duration and place no limit on the number of immigrants who can be nominated through these provinces' nominee
programs.[32] CIC does not impose a minimum selection threshold for
these candidates. In addition, PTNP agreements do not require provinces or territories to obtain CIC's approval when they create new
PTNP categories; they are required only to inform CIC.[33]

    To date, all provinces (with the exception of Quebec)[34] and terri-
tories (with the exception of Nunavut) have negotiated PTNP agreements with the federal government. Although they are a relatively

new phenomenon (the first PTNP was introduced in 1998 in Manitoba), admissions under PTNPs have grown quickly, from approximately 500 in 1999 to 36,419 in 2010. To accommodate continuing growth of these programs, CIC anticipates admitting up to 40,000 provincial and territorial nominees annually between 2010 and 2012. These projections indicate that the number of provincial nominees is growing at the expense of the Federal Skilled Worker Program and could become the primary source of economic immigrants to Canada by 2012.[35]

The details of the nominee programs vary across provinces and territories, as each program is developed according to the specific interests of the region. Since the inception of the first PTNP in Manitoba in 1998, the provinces and territories have created more than fifty different immigration categories, each with its own selection criteria.[36] Therefore, a key aspect of PTNPs is their individuality. This means in practice that two TFWs with the same employment history and qualifications have different opportunities to settle permanently in Canada based on the selection criteria unique to each province or territory. In addition to the diversity of eligibility criteria, provincial/territorial application-processing times vary considerably. For example, in Alberta, under the current "employer-driven" stream, the processing time is "at least" twelve months after the application is received at the Alberta Immigrant Nominee Program Office.[37] In Saskatchewan the processing times under all categories of its nominee program are on average 4.4 months,[38] and in Manitoba in 2009 more than 50 per cent of applications in the priority streams ("employer direct," "strategic initiatives," and "international student") were processed within three months.[39] According to CIC, the processing time for a permanent residency application from a provincial nominee, which is always processed outside of Canada, generally takes between twelve and twenty-four months to finalize.[40]

Although PTNPs differ greatly in detail, they do share a few common characteristics, particularly in their approach to TFWs. First, all provinces and territories with PTNPs enable access to permanent residency from within Canada for TFWs. However, this unique commonality between the programs is not immediately apparent when examining the different nominee program websites. Certain provinces and territories (including the Yukon, the Northwest Territories,

British Columbia, Alberta, Saskatchewan, Manitoba, Prince Edward Island, and Ontario) outline specific categories under which TFWs can apply,[41] whereas other provinces (namely New Brunswick,[42] Nova Scotia,[43] and Newfoundland and Labrador) do not outline specific categories for TFWs but do in fact allow TFWs to apply through their programs. For example, New Brunswick and Nova Scotia do not have any specific categories for TFWs, but they are eligible to apply under any of the provinces' categories.[44] Our research participant from New Brunswick, for instance, indicated that nearly all applicants in New Brunswick's "skilled worker with employer support" category are TFWs who are already residing in the province.[45] In a similar way, the Newfoundland and Labrador Nominee Program does not outline a specific category for TFWs; however, TFWs can apply for nomination under the "skilled worker" category.[46]

Second, PTNPs impose obligations on the employer "that are designed to ensure both that the employer is not exploiting the worker and that the worker will be able to integrate into the provincial labor market."[47] In Alberta, for instance, under the "semi-skilled worker" category, the employer must (1) demonstrate that accommodation for the nominee candidate is available at a cost that does not exceed 33 per cent of the candidate's gross salary; (2) ensure that the candidate is competent in understanding, reading, speaking, and writing English prior to nomination; and (3) provide a Foreign Worker Settlement Plan that identifies opportunities for career advancement training, activities undertaken to help the worker integrate into the workplace, and the type of assistance that will be provided to the worker's family members when they arrive in Alberta. Employers must also attach an employer compliance declaration form to their application, responding to questions about the status of their business with respect to employment standards, the Public Health Act, occupational health and safety, workers' compensation, and human rights.[48]

Third, all TFWs applying for permanent residency through a PTNP must have basic proficiency in English prior to nomination. At present, the only province that does not place any formal language requirements on provincial nominee applicants is Ontario; however, the province places the onus on the employer to support an applicant with "sufficient language skills to be able to work in the approved position."[49] In some provinces, if the provincial nominees do not have basic proficiency in English, the employer must cover the costs of language training (Alberta and British Columbia) or make arrangements for language training (Saskatchewan).[50]

Fourth, all PTNPs, in the context of temporary labour migration, are usually employer-driven. Applications from TFWs for permanent residency through a PTNP are quite often tied to a job with a specific employer, so if there is a change in the employment status of the TFW prior to attaining permanent residency, the application for permanent residency may be cancelled. In Alberta, for instance, if employment with an approved employer is terminated while an application is being processed, the Alberta Immigrant Nominee Program "reserves the right to withdraw its nomination."[51] TFWs in Alberta wait two to three years before obtaining permanent residency; if they become unemployed a few months before permanent residency is granted, they must start the process all over again with a new employer – if they can find one.[52] In British Columbia it is unclear what happens to applicants when they lose their job, as the BC Provincial Nominee Program (BC PNP) website presents conflicting information on this subject. The "What If You Lose or Change Your Job?" section of the website indicates, "A change in your employment status does not mean the BC PNP will automatically withdraw your nomination. If a change in employment occurs, the BC PNP will review the circumstances surrounding the change in employment and determine if program requirements continue to be met."[53] This statement appears to indicate that nominations will not automatically be withdrawn if the applicant loses his or her job and that a review process will be initiated. However, "program requirements" are unlikely to continue to be met if the applicant no longer has a full-time offer of employment. In contrast, the "Entry-Level and Semi-Skilled Pilot Project" section of the website provides a completely different answer to the same question: "If an unemployed nominee has not obtained employment in an occupation that is eligible under the program within four weeks, the Provincial Nominee Program will withdraw the individual's nomination, and the original employer will be required to pay the air fare of the nominee back to their country of origin."[54] Although there is a considerable amount of uncertainty regarding the situation of TFWs who become unemployed while their application for permanent residency is being processed, many of the PTNP websites also do not explicitly state the possible consequences of an expired work permit while TFWs are awaiting nomination and approval for permanent residency. However, most of the PTNP websites do emphasize that TFWs applying for nomination must maintain legal status in Canada and must have a valid work permit in order to be eligible for nomination. Our research participants provided further insight on the consequences of an expired work permit prior to nomination, as well as after nomination and prior to permanent residency approval at the federal level. Interestingly, they gave fairly consistent answers on this point. They indicated that if a work permit expires after a TFW has been nominated by the province but while the TFW is waiting for permanent residency approval from the federal government, the nominee programs will provide a "work permit support" letter to enable the TFW to apply for an extension with the federal government.[55] However, if the applicant is waiting to be nominated by the province, he or she will need to obtain another temporary work permit from Service Canada, as letters of support are not issued unless the applicant has already been nominated (Manitoba and Prince Edward Island).[56] In Saskatchewan and British Columbia the onus is on the applicant to apply directly to Service Canada for a work permit extension so as to "maintain legal status in Canada."[57] In New Brunswick applicants whose work permits are going to expire are given priority processing, but these applicants must possess a valid work permit before they can be nominated by the province.[58]

Finally, despite the fact that all PTNPs enable access to permanent residency from within Canada for TFWs, the opportunities for low-skilled TFWs are nonexistent in Ontario and limited elsewhere. Foremost, although all PTNPs have skilled migrant workers categories, only six out of the eleven PTNPs have specific categories for "low-skilled" or so-called "semi-skilled" TFWs (Alberta, British Columbia, Saskatchewan, Prince Edward Island, the Northwest Territories, and the Yukon).[59] The existing categories for low-skilled TFWs all limit eligibility to specific occupations and/or industries.[60] Thus, even though low-skilled workers employed in specific occupations may access permanent residency through certain PTNPs, the growing unskilled portion of TFWs across Canada is still largely excluded. This point is explained in greater detail in the sections that follow. It should be noted, however, that the Manitoba Provincial Nominee Program has some exceptional characteristics in regards to its opportunities for low-skilled TFWs. Although Manitoba does not have a specific category for low-skilled TFWs per se (and thus is not included in the aforementioned list of provinces and territories), its "employer direct" category (which recruits TFWs) does not have a specific NOC designation and is therefore open to low-skilled TFWs.[61] The following section explores the opportunities for low-skilled workers to access permanent residency through the Manitoba Provincial Nominee Program in order to compare these opportunities to those available to the low-skilled in other provinces and territories.

THE MANITOBA PROVINCIAL NOMINEE PROGRAM: SOME REAL OPPORTUNITIES FOR LOW-SKILLED TFWS TO TRANSITION TO PERMANENT RESIDENCY

As the first province to implement a nominee program, Manitoba has successfully promoted its program as an effective mechanism to attract immigrants. In 1998 Manitoba's initial target for provincial nominees was 200.[62] Since that time, the program has expanded rapidly, and in 2006 the Manitoba Provincial Nominee Program (MPNP) announced a new target: to welcome 20,000 immigrants through the program by 2016.[63] The importance of the MPNP in attracting immigrants to the province is demonstrated by the fact that approximately 70 per cent of all immigrants who land in Manitoba do so through its nominee program.[64] Furthermore, some authors believe that increased immigration to the province is attributed entirely to the MPNP.[65] From 1999 to 2009, 48,264 provincial nominees landed in the province.[66]

One of the primary objectives of the MPNP is "to assist the province in meeting immigration targets as specified by the economic growth strategy by *nominating skilled worker[s] and entrepreneurial immigrants* for permanent residence."[67] This objective demonstrates the emphasis placed on attracting immigrants to Manitoba who fall within the skilled worker categories. However, despite the province's stated objective to attract skilled workers, the MPNP also provides real opportunities for low-skilled TFWs to apply for nomination.

All TFWs are eligible to apply for permanent residency through the MPNP after acquiring six months of work experience and with ongoing employment in the province.[68] This is the "employer direct" stream, which has no specific NOC requirement. Interestingly, the majority of migrant worker applicants in this stream fall within NOC C and D categories.[69] To be considered for nomination in Manitoba through the MPNP's "employer direct" category, migrant worker candidates must demonstrate that they have (1) a formal offer of a long-term, full-time job with a Manitoba employer; (2) the training, work experience, and language ability required for the job they have been offered; and (3) the intention and ability to settle permanently in Manitoba.[70] For example, the vast majority of TFWs employed by Maple Leaf Foods' hog-processing facility in Brandon have been approved for provincial nominee status (it is worth noting that access to permanent residency is a provision in Maple Leaf Foods' collective agreements across Canada).[71]

The ability for TFWs of all skill levels to apply for nomination under the MPNP is significant, as other provincial/territorial nominee programs place a lot of emphasis on recruiting low-skilled TFWs within specific occupations. In contrast, according to our research participant from Manitoba, "the MPNP is based on the human capital model and not occupation-based/driven. Consequently, applications are accepted from all occupations."[72] It should be noted, however, that the MPNP was at one point occupation-driven.[73] Up until 2004 the MPNP nominations were guided by a "high demand occupation list."[74] However, upon review of the program, it was discovered that this list did not adequately reflect the changes in the labour market over time.[75] Consequently, the "high demand occupation list" was eliminated, which enabled individuals from a greater variety of occupations to apply for nomination.[76] This is significant since it demonstrates how the longest-standing nominee program has changed over time and has adapted its categories to be more in sync with the labour market needs of the province.[77] In doing so, the MPNP has created opportunities for TFWs of all skill levels to apply for nomination through the program and to eventually access permanent residency.

In summary, given the need to draw large numbers of immigrants to the province, all TFWs in Manitoba are "considered a source of permanent immigrants ... as their temporary status is but the first step along the path to permanent immigrant status."[78] However, Manitoba is an isolated example: as we show below, nowhere else in Canada is it possible to refer to TFWs as "transitional workers," as the Manitoba government and some researchers do.[79]

MORE LIMITED OPPORTUNITIES FOR LOW-SKILLED TFWS TO ACCESS PERMANENT RESIDENCY FROM WITHIN CANADA THROUGH OTHER NOMINEE PROGRAMS

Contrary to Manitoba's "employer direct" stream, which allows employers to recruit both low-skilled and skilled TFWs for full-time job vacancies, several provinces and territories limit eligibility for the category of low-skilled TFWs (NOC C and D occupations) to a narrow list of industries or occupations. Furthermore, many categories specifically designed for low-skilled TFWs are of a very limited duration. Finally, although on paper some provinces don't appear to offer opportunities for low-skilled TFWs to access permanent residency, they do consider applications from low-skilled TFWs on a case-by-case basis if such workers meet current locally defined needs.

Limitations Placed on the Specific PTNP Categories for Low-Skilled TFWs

In Alberta, British Columbia, Saskatchewan, Prince Edward Island, the Northwest Territories, and the Yukon, low-skilled TFWs employed in specific occupations or industries may access permanent residency through a PTNP. It should be noted that the label "semi-skilled" used in Alberta, British Columbia, the Northwest Territories, and the Yukon refers to workers falling within low-skilled occupations (NOC C and D).

In Alberta, for instance, TFWs may be considered for nomination under the "semi-skilled worker" category in the food- and beverage-processing, hotel and lodging, manufacturing, long-haul trucking, and food services industries.[80] In the food- and beverage-processing, hotel and lodging, manufacturing, and long-haul trucking industries, TFWs must have worked in the relevant occupations in Canada for at least six months.[81] In the food services industry, TFWs must have three years of work experience (either in Canada or abroad) in a related occupation and must have nine months of work experience in Alberta before they are eligible to apply for nomination.[82] Furthermore, in the food services industry, a pilot project aimed at addressing labour shortages is limited to 600 nomination allocations for three eligible occupations: food and beverage servers, food counter attendants, and kitchen helpers. Once the target of 600 nominations has been achieved, no further applications will be accepted under this pilot project.[83]

Similarly, British Columbia also has an Entry-Level and Semi-Skilled Pilot Project, which allows TFWs in the tourism/hospitality, long-haul trucking, and food-processing industries to apply for nomination.[84] TFWs applying under this category must have at least nine months of work experience in the position in order to be eligible to apply through the PTNP.[85] This pilot project ended on 31 August 2011.[86]

In Saskatchewan, under the "long-haul truck driver"[87] and the "hospitality sector pilot project"[88] categories, the only TFWs who can be nominated are those who are currently working as food and beverage servers, food counter attendants/kitchen helpers, housekeeping and cleaning staff, or long-haul truck drivers and who have been employed in their position for at least six months.[89] Of interest in the case of Saskatchewan is that between 2005 and 2009, three of the top ten occupations held by provincial nominees (principal applicants) were low-skilled positions (accounting for 10.6 per cent of the total), with truck drivers being ranked third.[90]

In addition, the Yukon and the Northwest Territories have both created "critical impact worker" categories that are geared specifically to low-skilled TFWs (NOC C and D) who have worked in the hospitality and service industries for six months. Despite targeting low-skilled workers, these categories, which are clearly designed to help fill shortages in the territorial labour markets,[91] are of limited duration.[92] For example, the Northwest Territories explicitly states that the "critical impact worker" category "will be closely monitored and will remain in place until the labour market for semi-skilled workers within the NWT economy indicates that this category is no longer required."[93]

Prince Edward Island is an interesting example, as its nominee program has recently changed to include a specific category for low-skilled TFWs. At the time the PEI Nominee Program was consulted for the data collection for this research (summer 2010), a pilot project targeting low-skilled workers was under consideration but had not yet been put in place.[94] As of March 2011, a "critical impact worker" stream was added to the PEI Nominee Program.[95] This newly created stream is designed to assist with "labour shortages" in specific industries.[96] Under this stream, low-skilled TFWs (NOC C and D) in five occupations (truck drivers, customer service representatives, labourers, food and beverage servers, and housekeeping attendants) are able to apply for nomination.[97] The TFW applicant must have at least six months of work experience with the employer in the province.[98] Like the low-skilled categories highlighted in the other provinces and territories, this "critical impact worker" stream is considered a pilot program that will be reviewed each year.[99]

The limited duration of the "critical impact worker" categories/streams in Prince Edward Island, the Yukon, and the Northwest Territories as well as the limited duration of the other low-skill pilot projects mentioned for Alberta, British Columbia, and Saskatchewan demonstrate that although opportunities do exist for low-skilled TFWs to access permanent residency through these nominee programs, there is a clear attempt to limit the numbers of low-skilled workers entering these regions permanently.

The Absence of Explicit Low-Skilled TFW Categories and Case-by-Case Assessments Dependent on Labour Market Needs

Whereas Alberta, British Columbia, Saskatchewan, Prince Edward Island, the Yukon, and the Northwest Territories all outline specific categories for low-skilled workers, not all provinces are as overt in the recruitment of the low-skilled. This is evidenced in the provinces of Newfoundland and Labrador and New Brunswick.

The Newfoundland and Labrador Nominee Program has four categories: (1) "skilled worker," (2) "international graduate," (3) family connection," and (4) "entrepreneur." Although none of these categories is specifically geared toward low-skilled workers, the Newfoundland and Labrador Nominee Program does give low-skilled workers opportunities to access permanent residency.[100] Interestingly, if an employer can demonstrate a "critical need" for a worker in a low-skilled position, low-skilled workers can apply under the "skilled worker" category in Newfoundland and Labrador.[101] In fact, between April 2007 and May 2010, 9 per cent of principal applicants were in NOC C occupations, and 9 per cent were in NOC D occupations.[102]

New Brunswick is another province where low-skilled workers are not overtly targeted by the provincial nominee program yet can still apply under an unlikely category. The categories of the New Brunswick Nominee Program include (1) "business plan/business proposal," (2) "skilled worker with employer support," (3) "skilled worker with family support," (4) "skilled worker with community support," (5) "skilled worker: international student," and (6) "international student entrepreneur pilot program." Although on paper these categories appear to be geared uniquely toward skilled workers, our research participant from New Brunswick indicated that individuals from all NOCs (including the low-skilled C and D) are eligible to apply for nomination under the "skilled worker with employer support" category.[103] Furthermore, our research participant indicated that, outside of the three major cities in New Brunswick (Fredericton, Saint John, and Moncton), the largest concentrations of recent nominees in the "skilled worker with employer support" category are working in low-skilled occupations (mainly as aquaculture and food-processing workers and as truck drivers).[104] This finding is confusing because, on the New Brunswick Nominee Program website, it appears as though the program is geared exclusively toward skilled workers, but in reality workers of all skill levels are eligible to apply under the "skilled worker with employer support" category, as long as they meet New Brunswick's present labour market shortages.

Thus the examples of New Brunswick and Newfoundland and Labrador are encouraging, as they do not exclude low-skilled workers from applying for nomination; however, that low-skilled workers are processed under the skilled worker categories in both provinces raises two questions: (1) Why are these provinces not more transparent regarding the recruitment of low-skilled workers (e.g., by outlining a specific category for the low-skilled)? (2) Given the lack of clarity on the respective nominee program websites, how are low-skilled TFWs made aware that they are eligible to apply through the program? Low-skilled TFWs must therefore overcome a number of practical challenges before they can apply for permanent residency in these provinces.

In sum, PTNPs, which have not replaced the federal immigration program but are instead alternative routes for obtaining permanent resident status, have increased opportunities for skilled TFWs – who are primarily targeted – to settle permanently in Canada. Although these programs also offer some opportunities for low-skilled TFWs to access permanent residency from within the country, these opportunities remain very limited – except in Manitoba, which is the only province with a category open to TFWs of all skill levels. It is important to note that some provinces that do not have specific categories to recruit low-skilled TFWs are considering expanding their nominee programs to include categories for low-skilled TFWs. For example, in Nova Scotia low-skilled applications are currently considered on a case-by-case basis, but the "policy implications" of a separate low- or semi-skilled stream are being considered.[105] That a low-skilled category is under consideration in Nova Scotia and that Prince Edward Island has recently established a new low-skilled category are encouraging developments, as they demonstrate that the nominee programs are continually evolving and are moving toward providing more explicit opportunities for low-skilled TFWs to apply for nomination and to become fully integrated into Canadian society. In this sense, the trend toward devolution to provinces and territories in the area of immigration selection seems to be beneficial to both skilled and low-skilled TFWs.

CONCLUSION

The implementation of Provincial/Territorial Nominee Programs across Canada over the past decade represents a promising development for low-skilled TFWs to access permanent residency from within Canada. PTNPs offer a creative solution to an immigration context where federal avenues available for transitioning from temporary to permanent status are almost the exclusive preserve of skilled TFWs. Although PTNPs can be viewed as a unique avenue for TFWs to transition from temporary to permanent status, these programs come with their own limitations. First, most PTNPs are "employer-driven," which means that TFWs must have a full-time permanent job offer with a local employer in order to be eligible for nomination. This requirement has the potential to create a power imbalance between the employer and the TFW, notably because such workers face uncertainty under this program in many provinces when they lose their job or their temporary work permit expires. Second, although several PTNPs have outlined specific categories for low-skilled TFWs, these categories often limit eligibility to a narrow range of occupations or industries. Consequently, low-skilled TFWs must fit within narrow categories based on occupations or industries that are different in each province or territory dependent on their unique labour market needs. Third, several specific categories geared toward low-skilled TFWs are pilot projects that are of limited duration. This demonstrates that these categories are not "priority categories" but rather are designed to attract the low-skilled to the provinces and territories only until labour shortages are filled. Finally, although some provinces do not have specific categories for low-skilled TFWs per se, certain provinces (namely Newfoundland and Labrador and New Brunswick) enable low-skilled TFWs to apply under the program's skilled worker categories. This means that if low-skilled TFWs meet locally defined needs, their applications will be considered on a case-by-case basis. Although it does not entirely exclude low-skilled TFWs, the case-by-case determination process that exists in some provinces demonstrates a lack of transparency in the recruitment process and reinforces the message that these programs more overtly target skilled TFWs.

Overall, our findings suggest that the new forms of interaction between the federal government and the provinces and territories in the area of immigration selection are working to the benefit of TFWs of all skill levels. In this sense, the new nature of immigration regulation in Canada, which signals a departure from a long-standing tradition of viewing immigration primarily as an area of national interest and federal activity, may act as an important safeguard against the exclusionary mechanisms contained within federal immigration law. However, we should keep in mind that PTNPs are short-sighted, being focused on immediate local labour market needs and on qualifications for specific occupations rather than on human capital characteristics of applicants: these considerations should form the basis of any much needed future analysis of the legal and policy consequences of a more decentralized immigration system for Canada through PTNPs.

8

Provincial Nominee Programs and Temporary Worker Programs: A Comparative Assessment of Advantages and Disadvantages in Addressing Labour Shortages

TOM CARTER

INTRODUCTION

Canada is experiencing a significant demographic shift. The proportion of seniors is increasing at a higher rate than any other age group, and fertility rates have declined below replacement levels.[1] Immigration actually surpassed natural increase as the primary driver of population growth in Canada in the mid-1990s.[2] Canada, because of these trends, is experiencing labour market shortages in both the skilled and less skilled sectors of the economy, which is likely to be an increasing problem in the near future. In 2008 the Canadian Chamber of Commerce predicted a labour shortage of nearly 1 million people by 2020.[3] With the transition into a more knowledge-based economy, there is also a great deal of competition to attract skilled workers. Other industrialized countries are facing the same challenges as Canada.[4] This situation has had a major impact on Canadian immigration policy in recent years: immigration policy has been much more proactive and expansionist. Immigration is crucial to both population growth and labour force vitality.

Circumstances within Canada have also prompted changes to immigration policy. Immigrants to Canada have settled disproportionately in the three largest cities – Toronto, Montreal, and

Vancouver. Recent immigrants (arriving 2001–06) are 2.5 times more likely than the population as a whole to live in Toronto, and 40 per cent of recent immigrants call Toronto home, compared to only 16 per cent of the overall population. Approximately 69 per cent of recent immigrants reside in the three Census Metropolitan Areas (CMAS), compared to only 35 per cent of the total population.[5] Ontario, Quebec, British Columbia, and Alberta have been major provincial destinations over the past couple of decades. Other provinces and second- and third-tier cities like Regina, Winnipeg, and Halifax have received far fewer immigrants, although they are experiencing the same nationwide trends of population aging and labour force shortages.

The nation as a whole, many provinces, second- and third-tier cities, and even smaller centres have worked to increase immigration to address these issues and in the process have modified immigration programs and policies to suit national, provincial, and local needs. This chapter examines two immigration programs that have been instrumental in addressing labour force shortages: the Provincial Nominee Programs (PNPs) and the federal Temporary Foreign Worker Program (TFWP). Employers, governments, and communities who look beyond Canada's borders to address labour force shortages have taken advantage of both initiatives. The chapter compares and contrasts the two programs, looking briefly at their history, policy implications, major issues and challenges, the linkages between the two, the advantages and disadvantages of each for migrants, foreign workers, employers, governments, and communities, and other positive and negative outcomes. To illustrate some of the issues, the chapter draws heavily on the experiences in Manitoba. Manitoba has the most active PNP and the linkages between the PNP and the TFWP in Manitoba are more significant than in most provinces.

The broader theoretical framework for this analysis lies within the discourse on immigration and integration policy. Canada, as noted, has a proactive immigration policy and works to attract immigrants to serve many objectives, particularly labour force needs. The policy also encourages economic, social, and cultural integration of immigrants. Important integration mechanisms include employment, family unity, and permanent residency.[6] However, there is another side to our immigration policy, or at least to our policy to address labour force needs: the extensive use of temporary foreign workers (TFWs). There appears to be a discrepancy between policy and practice when it comes to the employment of temporary foreign workers, relative to similar treatment of immigrants. Often their rights to long-term employment, family unity, and permanent residency are restricted. It is within this broader framework of immigration and integration policy that the chapter compares the TFWP and PNPs and discusses the best instruments to address labour force needs and to provide the environment most suited to the protection of workers' rights.

IMMIGRATION OVERVIEW: PERMANENT AND
TEMPORARY ARRIVALS TO CANADA

A brief overview of immigration to Canada is presented here to provide context for the chapter's specific focus on the program initiatives noted above. International migrants to Canada enter the country under various classifications. Those who came as permanent residents fall into three broad categories: "family class," "economic immigrants," and "refugees." "Family class" arrivals fluctuated between 60,000 and 70,000 over the period 2000–10 (see table 8.1). "Economic immigrant" arrivals fluctuated between 131,000 and 187,000 over the same period. "Refugee" arrivals fluctuated between 22,000 and 36,000, with the numbers showing a downward trend. When other minor categories of immigrant arrivals are added, the total international arrivals ranged from a low of 221,348 in 2002 to a high of 280,636 in 2010; from 2000 to 2010 the ten-year average was 245,000.[7] Generally, arrivals under the "economic immigrants" category have been increasing as Canada competes for greater numbers of skilled workers; arrivals under the "family class" have been relatively constant; and "refugee" arrivals have been trending downward. The biggest shift has been within the "economic immigrant" category. This category includes arrivals under the Federal Skilled Worker Program (FSWP), entrepreneurs, self-employed and investor immigrants, live-in caregivers, and provincial and territorial nominees. The significant shift has been the increasing number of people arriving under the PNPs – from 1,252 in 2000 to 36,419 in 2010 – accompanied by declining numbers of arrivals under the FSWP until

Table 8.1
Immigration facts and figures, 2000–10

	2000	2001	2002	2003	2004	2005	2006	2007	2008	2009	2010
Permanent arrivals to Canada											
Family class	60,616	66,794	62,291	65,117	62,266	63,364	70,515	66,242	65,577	65,200	60,207
Economic immigrants											
Skilled workers	118,588	137,234	122,730	105,224	113,451	130,238	105,944	97,852	103,734	95,962	119,337
Prov./terr. nominees	1,252	1,274	2,127	4,418	6,248	8,047	13,336	17,094	22,418	30,378	36,419
Other	16,447	17,212	13,006	11,404	14,049	18,027	18,971	16,298	22,919	27,158	31,125
Total	136,287	155,720	137,863	121,046	133,748	156,312	138,251	131,244	149,071	153,498	186,881
Refugees	30,092	27,919	25,115	25,984	32,687	35,776	32,499	27,955	21,860	22,846	24,693
Other immigrants	460	206	3,780	9,200	7,124	6,787	10,375	11,312	10,737	10,634	8,848
Total	227,455	250,640	229,049	221,348	235,825	262,241	251,642	236,754	247,247	252,179	280,636
Temporary arrivals to Canada											
Temporary foreign workers											
Entries	116,540	119,688	110,898	103,228	112,543	122,694	139,047	164,792	192,281	178,478	182,322
Existing	89,746	96,463	101,174	109,781	125,230	140,906	161,046	199,457	250,256	282,194	283,096
Foreign students											
Entries	69,092	80,915	76,943	69,708	66,122	67,885	71,792	74,039	79,528	85,140	96,147
Existing	114,046	136,664	150,455	159,602	164,741	167,084	170,035	175,884	177,963	196,138	218,243

Source: Citizenship and Immigration Canada, *Immigration Facts and Figures 2010*.

a surge to 119,300 in 2010. In the four years from 2007 to 2010, arrivals under the FSWP averaged just over 100,000, down from an annual average of nearly 120,000 in the previous seven years.[8] The numbers of arrivals in other subcategories of the "economic immigrant" category have changed very little. The PNP program is a growing force within immigration arrivals and immigration policy.

The above categories represent immigrant arrivals who come as permanent residents. Turning to temporary foreign workers, we see that the numbers have been increasing significantly. The total number of foreign workers entering Canada stood at 116,540 in 2000 (see table 8.1). This figure rose to 192,281 in 2008 before dropping to 178,478 in 2009 as the effects of the recession reduced labour force requirements. It increased again slightly to 182,322 in 2010. When the number of TFWs present in the country as of 1 December each year is considered, the trend is similar, rising from 89,746 in 2000 to 283,096 in 2010.[9] The increases in TFWs have been significantly higher than the increases in immigrants who come as permanent residents.

Foreign students are also a category of temporary resident. Although most attend class full time, they are now allowed to remain and work in Canada for three years after they graduate. The number of foreign students entering Canada increased from 69,092 in 2000 to 96,147 in 2010. The number present on 1 December of each year increased from 114,046 in 2000 to 218,243 in 2010 (see table 8.1).[10]

What these figures illustrate is that Canada is depending to an increasing extent on TFWs to address labour force shortages. In addition, the PNPs are becoming a more important source of labour within the categories of immigrants arriving as permanent residents. Having established the growing importance of PNPs and the TFWP in the context of Canadian immigration policy, the chapter now turns to a comparison and discussion of the two programs.

THE HISTORY OF DEVELOPMENT AND PROGRAM STRUCTURES

The TFWP was introduced in 1973. The program initially targeted people in high-skilled sectors – academics, engineers, scientists, and business executives – people who were not available in sufficient numbers in Canada. Following the introduction, employers pressured the federal government to allow the entry of people with lower skills, particularly to address labour shortages in the construction and resources sectors. The federal government eventually responded in 2002 with a Pilot Project for Occupations Requiring Lower Levels of Formal Training. The requirement for admission was a high school diploma or two years of occupation-specific training. This often became a short period of on-the-job training. In 2007 the program was made even more attractive for employers when work permits became valid for two years, as opposed to one. In the same year the Expedited Labour Market Opinion Pilot Project accelerated applications in twelve occupations in very high demand in Alberta and British Columbia. Applications under this pilot project were expedited and processed within five business days. In 2008 another twenty-one occupations were added to the list of high-demand occupations, or occupations under pressure, as they became known. These occupations included the hospitality industry, food and beverage services, residential cleaning, and construction.[11] The TFWP is not governed by quotas but instead is driven by employer demand. Not surprisingly, entries under the program rose rapidly to 192,281 in 2008, up 65 per cent since 2000. The number of entries fell in 2009 to 178,478, with lower demand in an economy in recession (see table 8.1), but rose again to 182,322 in 2010.

The statistics highlight a number of trends. First, employers are increasingly turning to the TFWP to address labour force shortages. This is particularly the case in resource-based Alberta, as in recent years approximately 64 per cent of TFWs were employed in Alberta.[12] Second, the demand has been increasingly focused on low-skilled jobs – not the original intention of the program. The switch to lower skill levels under the program is also quite significant. In 2002 57 per cent of TFWs were in National Occupational Classifications (NOC) O, A, and B (skilled positions). By 2008 this had fallen to 37 per cent. Lower-skilled positions rose from 26 to 34 per cent. The very low-skilled positions (NOC D) increased from 1 to 9 per cent over the same period.[13] The shift to workers with lower skill levels is particularly strong in Alberta. This is not surprising given that nearly two-thirds of all TFW entries go to Alberta.

The PNPs, as pointed out earlier, were introduced to influence the regional distribution of immigrants so that second- and third-tier cities, smaller rural communities, and provinces with smaller populations could also address labour force shortages and experience some of the other benefits of immigration.[14] PNPs represent a significant departure from federally administered immigration programs such as the FSWP. Provincial governments play a direct role in determining the goals and the application criteria – deciding who gets in. Immigrants wanting to immigrate to a particular province apply directly to that province. The applications are vetted by provincial officials to determine whether they meet program criteria. Acceptable applicants are then nominated by the province for permanent resident status and the nominated applications are sent to the federal government. Citizenship and Immigration Canada (CIC) then determines whether each nominee meets federal health, criminality, and security requirements. Provinces establish criteria that the targeted migrants can more easily meet than the federal selection criteria, particularly under the FSWP. Application processing times are also faster under PNPs. For example, the processing time for a skilled worker applying through the FSWP in Beijing is fifty-seven months. The same application, if approved by a province through the PNP, would take about ten months.[15]

The first nominee agreements were signed in 1998. With the exception of Quebec, which acquired a role in selecting economic immigrants under a separate agreement in 1978 that was expanded in 1991, all provinces now have nominee programs. In addition, the Yukon and Northwest Territories have territorial nominee agreements. Arrivals under these programs have grown rapidly. In 1999 477 immigrants landed in Canada through PNPs. This number grew to 36,419 in 2010. CIC predicts growth in arrivals will continue under PNPs, reaching 40,000 by 2012.[16] If this trend continues, PNPs will eventually surpass the FSWP as the source of economic immigrants to Canada.[17] Manitoba has been a leader in developing and expanding nominee programs. Between 1999 and 2009, 45 per cent of all nominees landing in Canada arrived through the Manitoba PNP.[18]

Provinces have created multiple streams within their respective PNPs. Each stream has its own eligibility criteria. Table 8.2 provides

Table 8.2
Provincial Nominee Programs by stream and province, 2010

	General	Family	Employer direct	Strategic recruit- ment	Business invest- ment	Inter- national student	Farm owners/ operators
Alberta	√	√	√	√			√
Manitoba		√	√	√	√	√	√
Newfoundland and Labrador		√	√	√	√	√	
Ontario			√	√			
Saskatchewan	√	√	√	√	√	√	√
British Columbia		√	√	√			
New Brunswick	√	√	√	√			
Nova Scotia		√	√			√	
Prince Edward Island	√	√	√				

Source: Carter, Pandey, and Townsend, *Manitoba Provincial Nominee Program*; also prepared from provincial websites and key informant interviews.

a list of streams and indicates which provinces have such a stream.[19] The most common is the "employer direct" stream. Eligibility under this stream requires that applicants have a full time job offer from an employer. All provinces also have a "strategic recruitment" stream. Eligibility under this stream is based on skills to work in certain occupations. The occupations are based on labour force shortages in the province, particularly labour force shortages related to strategic initiatives like large hydroelectric and oil sands developments. Such initiatives are usually major long-term development projects. Applicants under both of these programs are often already working in Canada, or a particular province, as TFWs. Most provinces offer a "family support" stream. Applicants have to demonstrate they have family support in the province. Unlike the federal "family class" program, applicants are also vetted to make sure their skills and qualifications match provincial labour force needs and requirements. Most provinces have a "business immigrant" scheme for entrepreneurs who want to invest in or purchase and manage a business in the province. Some provinces have also introduced an "international student" stream for international students who have recently graduated from a university in Canada and who have been working in the province for at least six months under a postgraduation work permit. In some provinces, international students who have recently graduated can also apply under the "employer direct" program if they have been offered a full-time job by an employer.

The various streams are generally designed to be integrated and complementary in nature. Manitoba, the province with the most activity and comprehensive program, provides a case in point. Since the introduction of the program in 1998, streams in Manitoba have included: "employer direct," "international student," "Manitoba young farmer," "business immigrant," "family support," "community support," "strategic recruitment," and a "general" stream. The wide-ranging criteria and guidelines are very flexible. Applicants can be directed to the best route on a case-by-case basis. If a person does not have a job offer but has a family member in the province, the application can be shifted to that category – provided he or she has skills that are required in the province. Foreign students, who now have approval of the federal government to remain up to three years after their studies are complete, can apply under the "employer direct" stream if they have a job offer. In Manitoba TFWs are eligible to apply after they have been in Manitoba for six months. Many are sponsored by their employer (e.g., Maple Leaf Foods in Brandon) under the "employer direct" stream. The streams have been designed to strengthen and support each other.[20]

Nominee programs do not restrict a successful nominee's ability to move within the country. Doing so would violate the mobility rights of new immigrants provided under the Charter of Rights and Freedoms. This encourages provinces to develop streams and selection criteria that are likely to maximize retention in the province. If there is a good match between immigrant skills and labour requirements as well as immigrant relationships to family already in the province, immigrants are much more likely to stay. Family and community connections, which are considered in the application process, are an important determinant of settlement. PNPs in most provinces, particularly Manitoba, examine the "entire package" of characteristics of applicants when assessing applications.

The skill level of nominees is very different from that of people arriving under both the FSWP and the TFWP. In general, nominees have lower levels of education and skills than workers admitted through the FSWP. This can be attributed to the fact that nominees are often selected on the basis of specific types of trades – truck drivers and welders, for example.[21] People with such skill levels would not meet the eligibility criteria of the FSWP. However, the skill levels of PNP arrivals are considerably higher than those arriving under the TFWP. A survey of provincial nominees in Manitoba conducted by myself and colleagues found that 37 per cent of the principal applicants had a bachelor's degree, another 15 per cent had a master's degree, and 3 per cent had a doctoral degree. One-third had a trade certificate or college diploma, and 8 per cent had a high school diploma. Even the spouses of principal applicants were reasonably well educated. Approximately 46 per cent had a university degree. Based on education levels, migrants under PNPs have a much higher level of skills than those under the TFWP but are not as well educated as those under the FSWP.[22]

PROGRAM POLICY OBJECTIVES: DIFFERENT
APPROACHES TO INTEGRATION

The evolution of the two programs and the programs' criteria suggest different policy objectives. PNPs are obviously designed to encourage integration and long-term retention of arrivals, preferably in the province of destination. The TFWP, however, has different objectives. Delphine Nakache and Paula Kinoshita[23] as well as Ryszard Cholewinski[24] consider three possible policy perspectives with respect to Canada's position on TFWs: (1) the country sees temporary labour migration as an opportunity to integrate workers, (2) the country is indifferent to their future position in society, or (3) the country tries to prevent their integration. Canada does not necessarily fall clearly and completely into any of the three policy objectives. Depending on the circumstances, its objective can be any one of the three.

As pointed out previously, some provinces, Manitoba being one of them, blend the PNP and TFWP by allowing those who arrive as TFWs to apply under the PNP. Temporary labour migration is viewed as an opportunity to integrate workers on a long-term basis. In Manitoba, for example, after TFWs have been in the province for six months, they are allowed to apply for permanent immigrant status under the PNP. Often they do this with the support of their employer. Maple Leaf Foods in Brandon sponsors some employees under the PNP "employer direct" program – particularly if it wants to keep and benefit from the skills of a particular employee. However, the TFWs in Manitoba can apply to the PNP under other streams if their skills or perhaps family connections qualify them for a particular stream.[25] Their chances of permanent status and long-term integration in Canada depend a great deal on their employment situation (does their current employer want them on a long-term basis), their skill level, and their family connections.

For those who do not have the skills, family connections, or support of employers, it can be argued that the country is indifferent to their future position in society. They return to their country of origin, perhaps to reenter for another term or never to return. They are a source of short-term labour, but the country has no long-term integration objective. The agricultural workers may be a case in point. Many agricultural workers from Mexico, as well as other countries, return annually for the period March or April through to October in order to work in various agricultural areas. There is no intention or objective to provide them with permanent immigrant status, even if this is their wish. They help to plant, weed, pick, and harvest, and then they leave. They can, of course, apply under other immigrant programs, including the PNP, but are unlikely to get employer support, and few agricultural workers have the skills required for a successful application under the FSWP or PNP. Although it may be a harsh and somewhat crass generalization, the country "uses them and then sends them home."

Does Canada try to prevent TFW integration? This is more difficult to answer. One can argue that TFWs have the opportunity to apply under other immigrant programs, as noted above, with mixed potential for success depending on their characteristics. However, others have suggested that the current policy model and program structure do discourage, even prevent, those with lower skill levels from seeking opportunities for long-term settlement and integration in the country.[26] For example, the spouses of highly skilled TFWs are able to acquire open work permits, and highly skilled TFWs have the opportunity to get permanent residency from within Canada. In contrast, the spouses of lower-skilled TFWs must apply for a restricted work permit, and lower-skilled workers, with few exceptions, have very limited opportunity to migrate permanently. They can renew their temporary status as long as they have work, but they are prevented from achieving longer-term integration.[27]

The foregoing comments on the three possible policy perspectives are probably more applicable to the FSWP, where high skill levels are required for entry. They are less applicable to PNPs. As noted above, earlier PNPs were developed because the FSWP was not meeting regional needs in terms of occupations and skill levels, the number of immigrants required, and processing times.[28] Some provinces required people with a lower-level skill set. As already noted, the majority of people arriving under PNPs have good skill levels, but other people with lower skill sets also enter under the program – the Manitoba situation being a case in point, with Maple Leaf Foods' meat-processing workers (a relatively lower-skilled occupation) applying with employer support. However, even under PNPs, few lower-skilled workers get access to permanent immigrant status and long-term integration.[29] Perhaps the argument that Canada tries to prevent TFW integration is a little too strong, but the "cards" are obviously stacked against TFWs with lower skill levels. PNPs improve their potential, but PNPs in general look for higher skill sets in specific occupations. The occupations sought under the PNP do not necessarily match those occupations that employers need to fill in order to address labour force shortages. Employers want people in the meat-processing industry as well as agricultural workers, but they are generally indifferent to permanent immigrant status and long-term integration for these people.

In the case of the policy on long-term integration under the PNPs, the situation is far less complex and much more straightforward. In terms of integration policy, arrivals under PNPs have definite advantages and much greater long-term potential. The discussion to this point has highlighted the many streams under the PNP that attempt to match immigrants' skills and circumstances of family and lifestyle to occupations in the respective provinces – "family support," "business immigrants," "international students," "strategic recruitment," "employer direct," and so on. All of these streams emphasize skills, long-term potential, or family support – attributes TFWs do not generally have. PNPs, it can be argued, go even further to enhance integration potential than the FSWP. High skill levels are the raison d'être of the FSWP. PNPs focus on skills but also look at other attributes likely to facilitate integration. Integration and retention in the province of destination are the objectives that PNPs strive to achieve.

The limited opportunities of TFWs to achieve permanent immigrant status and long-term integration also have to be viewed within the context of the TFWP's status as a pervasive feature of Canadian labour market policy.[30] It can no longer be considered temporary. Perhaps it is time to reconsider the short-term focus of labour migration policies. Are they realistic? Are they helping to achieve Canada's long-term goals of labour force stability and growth? Some TFWs spend several years in Canada. Others return (reenter) several times. If there is a continued and ongoing need for lower-skilled workers, which appears to be the case, then perhaps it is time to consider a different approach. Would a stream under PNPs for unskilled workers serve the same purpose while providing better integration possibilities for TFWs?

This possibility raises another important question. Are the industries that use TFWs long-term sustainable industries with ongoing job requirements that cannot be filled by local labour? The 2008 recession and the drop in TFWs in Alberta might be an argument against the long-term need for TFWs. However, recessionary times result in permanent immigrants losing their jobs as well. The reduction of TFWs in Alberta in 2009 was attributable largely to falling demand for labour in resource-based industries. Most PNPs have a "strategic recruitment" stream. Such initiatives are not always long-term, but arrivals under such programs have opportunities for permanent residency and long-term integration. Perhaps TFWs should have the same opportunities. Many PNP migrants arrive without a guaranteed job, as they come under streams other than the "employer direct." Not all of them are highly skilled individuals. It could be argued that it is time to level the playing field between PNP migrants and TFWs.

PROGRAM RIGHTS AND REQUIREMENTS

Beyond the aspect of integration, there are significant differences between PNP migrants and TFWs. TFWs are tied to one job, one employer, and generally one location. Those arriving under the PNPs are not tied to a specific job. "Employer direct" arrivals come to take a specific job, but their right to move to another job with another employer is never questioned. PNP migrants are not tied to a specific location. They may apply to a specific province, arrive, and leave – all within the same year. Although retention rates in the province of destination are high,[31] there is secondary migration. The ability to move to different jobs, employers, and locations after arrival is also characteristic of other immigrant programs, such as the FSWP.

The other key argument in favour of the TFWP versus other immigration programs, including the PNP, is processing times. Employers can get TFWP requests processed much faster than PNP requests, which in turn are processed faster than FSWP requests. Employers in Alberta and British Columbia can get completed applications for TFWs for certain occupations processed within five business days of their receipt by Services Canada.[32] With timeframes like this, the program offers a much more rapid and less cumbersome response to labour force needs than the route through regular immigration programs. From an employer's perspective, this is a definite advantage of the TFWP that is not available under the PNP, as it allows rapid response to rapidly changing labour force needs. PNPs also provide relatively rapid processing times. The processing time for "employer direct" applications in Alberta is currently ten months, in Saskatchewan four to eight months, and in Manitoba four to seven months.[33]

In a comparison of the TFWP and PNPs, another area that deserves attention is the issue of the rights of TFWs. A range of rights in several fields can be considered, including health, housing, family unity, employment, vocational training, language and integration courses, trade unions, and secure residence status.[34] Because arrivals under the PNPs have permanent immigrant and resident status, they are generally eligible for any of the services provided to citizens of Canada and have the same rights and responsibilities as Canadians. They are subject to the same criteria and waiting times as permanent residents, but they have the benefit and protection of the same services and rights as Canadians.

In contrast, the rights of TFWs are very complex and confusing. Immigration is a matter of shared federal-provincial responsibility. The federal government makes laws with respect to "aliens," "unemployment insurance," and "crime," but "civil rights" are under the authority of provincial legislation – the provinces govern health-care, education, housing, and employment rights, for example.[35] The federal government regulates entry and stay periods and unemployment insurance, but almost everything else is covered by provincial governments. The jurisdictional quagmire is difficult for lawyers to navigate and is even more difficult for TFWs.

Despite the confusion, there is little doubt that TFWs face greater restrictions and have fewer protections and safety-net alternatives than PNP migrants. First, there is the limited duration of their work permits and the fact that TFWs have no guarantee of an extension. PNP migrants do not face the challenges of limitations on how long they can work or the threat of not being able to renew their labour force access in Canada. Second, as noted elsewhere in this chapter, PNP migrants have every right to change jobs, employers, employment sectors, and workplace location. TFWs have no flexibility or rights in these areas. TFWs are protected by workers' compensation legislation, but research in Alberta has noted that there are few TFWs who report claims to Alberta's Workers' Compensation Board and that those who do report a claim often find the protection offered them is quite different from what other Albertans get because of work permit restrictions and their temporary status.[36] TFWs and their employers make payments into employment insurance (EI), as do all Canadian workers. EI also includes sickness benefits, compassionate care benefits, and maternity or parental benefits. However, there are problems with TFWs claiming EI. Some on short-term jobs may not work long enough to qualify. Others may not be entitled to EI because their "employer specific" work permit restricts them from being available to work for other employers.[37] No one can collect EI unless they are available for work and there are no jobs available.

There is also the question of access to services generally available to immigrants – language training, skills upgrading, job search, interpretation, housing search, and a range of other services. In most provinces, these services are not available to TFWs. Manitoba, however, often on an unofficial basis, does provide many such services to TFWs – principally because the province see TFWs as a source of PNP applicants.[38] That the potential for TFWs to learn about available services and where to access them is even more limited than for immigrants with permanent status also adds to TFWs' difficulty. Often what is written on paper plays out in a very different and difficult manner in reality – particularly under such divided jurisdictional situations.

There are many other examples that could be used to illustrate the limitations TFWs face in terms of their rights and the services they are eligible to receive. However, the few examples briefly noted in this discussion suffice to illustrate that TFWs face many more difficulties around rights and services than PNP migrants. It is not a level playing field.[39]

PROGRAM LINKAGES

Although a general argument could be made that TFWs can use the PNP as an avenue to permanent residency and long-term integration, this avenue does come with limitations. PNPs, as noted, have become increasingly diverse and complex due to provinces uniquely tailoring their selection criteria to individuals who are likely to contribute to economic development and stay in the province. With such variation in program criteria from province to province, "two temporary foreign workers with the same profile could have different opportunities to settle permanently based on the province or territory of their original work permit."[40] It is important to examine the linkages between PNPs and the TFWP and the role of PNPs in enabling permanent occupancy for TFWs, as different PNPs treat TFWs differently. For example, not all PNPs offer permanent residency to TFWs. Alberta, British Columbia, Manitoba, Saskatchewan, Nova Scotia, Newfoundland and Labrador, and Yukon do, whereas New Brunswick, Prince Edward Island, and Ontario do not.[41] All of these jurisdictions, except Manitoba, primarily accept only skilled TFWs. Unskilled TFWs are largely excluded. Applications from TFWs through PNPs are generally tied to a job with a specific employer. If the worker is laid off prior to receiving permanent residency, the application is cancelled. In Alberta, for example, TFWs often have to wait two to three years before obtaining permanent residency. If they become unemployed as they wait for their application to be approved, they have to start over when, or if, they find another job.[42]

In British Columbia, if TFWs who have applied become unemployed and fail to find employment in an occupation eligible under the PNP within four weeks, their application is cancelled. Nominees also have to accept an equivalent offer of employment from another employer if they receive one; otherwise, the application is cancelled. However, Alberta, British Columbia, and Saskatchewan have recently expanded the range of occupations that TFWs may be nominated under – food and beverage processing, food services, hotel and lodging services, and trucking.

In Manitoba all TFWs are eligible to apply for permanent residency through the PNP after six months of work experience and with ongoing employment in the province – through the employer direct stream. To be considered for nomination, TFW applicants in Manitoba must demonstrate they have a formal offer of long-term, full-time employment in the province, the training, language ability, and work experience for the job they have been offered, and plans to settle permanently in Manitoba.[43] The majority of TFWs employed by Maple Leaf Foods in its hog-processing plant in Brandon have applied to the PNP and obtained permanent residency status. In Manitoba TFWs are "considered a source of permanent immigrants ... as their temporary status is but the first step to permanent immigrant status."[44]

Although the positions of PNPs differ with respect to their treatment of TFWs attempting to gain permanent residency, those that offer permanent residency share some eligibility requirements in common: the need for a full-time permanent job offer, competency in reading, speaking, writing, and comprehending English, assurance that the employer is not exploiting the worker, evidence that the worker will integrate into the provincial labour market, and the employer's compliance with all health and safety requirements. The path to permanency through PNPs is not easy and is particularly difficult for lower-skilled workers, perhaps with the exception of TFWs applying in Manitoba. Criticism of the PNPs highlights their lack of common standards,[45] which means TFWs are not treated equally under PNPs across the nation. Despite some positive linkages between the two programs, there is still concern that for most TFWs Canada's objective is to use them to fill low-skilled or unskilled positions, often for several years, and then show them the way out.[46]

PROVINCIAL NOMINEE PROGRAMS: ARE THEY A SUCCESSFUL INTEGRATION VEHICLE?

The preceding discussion suggests PNPs are a much better approach to meeting labour force requirements and long-term integration objectives. This raises two questions: (1) How successful are PNPs in integrating nominee arrivals into Canadian society? (2) Are they meeting their objectives and achieving their expected outcomes? Not a great deal of evaluation work has been undertaken on the PNPs on a national basis,[47] although CIC currently has a national evaluation underway that should be completed in late 2012. In collaboration with colleagues, I have undertaken evaluation work on the Manitoba PNP.[48] This work is based on an analysis of Statistics Canada's Longitudinal Immigration Database, interviews with nominee arrivals (both principal applicants and spouses), key informant interviews, and data from Manitoba Labour and Immigration files. Grant Thornton has completed an evaluation of the British Columbia PNP for the period 2005–10 based on interviews with nominees, employers, and key stakeholder organizations and on analysis of relevant data bases.[49] The findings in both studies reveal relatively high levels of satisfaction among arrivals and other program stakeholders, although areas of concern are also raised.

The findings of the Manitoba study imply that the Manitoba PNP has been an effective initiative in achieving demographic, economic, and labour force immigration objectives. Since the introduction of the PNP in Manitoba, the provincial share of immigration to Canada has increased from 1.9 per cent in 1999 to 5.6 per cent in 2010.[50] The province has been able to attract people away from the larger CMAs and more populous provinces. The program has led to a better regional distribution within the province, as a growing number and proportion of immigrants are settling outside the major city of Winnipeg. Approximately 30 per cent of arrivals now settle in smaller communities, compared to 10 per cent prior to the introduction of the program.[51] Nearly all arrivals destined for the rural areas arrive under the PNP. The program draws from a diverse number of source countries. Close to one-quarter of arrivals come from the Philippines, 20 per cent from Germany, 10 per cent from Latin American countries, 8 to 9 per cent from each of India, Israel, the Middle East, and China, and another 25 per cent from a range of other countries. Attraction is widespread throughout the world. The majority of households are families with an average of four members (the provincial average is 2.5), and most of the principal applicants are in the prime workforce age range of twenty-five to forty-four years. As pointed out elsewhere in this chapter, education levels are relatively high.

The survey of principal applicants in Manitoba discovered that 86 per cent were working. Nearly all of those not working were attending school or had other reasons for not looking for a job – they were voluntarily unemployed. Ninety per cent of those working had permanent jobs. Eighty-four per cent of the principal applicants started their first job within three months of arrival. Two-thirds of spouses were also working at the time of the interview. Interviewees also expressed a reasonably high level of job satisfaction – 58 per cent of principal applicants were satisfied or very satisfied with their position. Almost one-half were also working to upgrade their education and improve their language skills.

Despite what appears to be a positive labour force experience, 80 per cent of those who had looked for work indicated they had difficulty finding a job. Not surprisingly, 28 per cent indicated their job search difficulties were associated with their qualifications and/or credentials from outside of Manitoba not being recognized, another 24 per cent indicated their job experience from outside of Canada was not recognized, 16 per cent did not have the required language skills, 9 per cent did not have enough Canadian job experience, and another 8 per cent were not able to find a job in their field of expertise. Spouses seeking employment identified the same concerns. These problems are not unique to PNPs. Studies of almost all classifications of immigrants reveal the same difficulties.[52] Nominees also expressed concern that they were not working in their field of expertise. Forty-six per cent of those working were not working in the occupation they had indicated on their application. Thirty-six per cent were working in their field, and 12 per cent were in a related field. The average annual household income was approximately $10,000 lower than the provincial average of $60,242.[53] Eighty-five per cent of monthly income came from employment, compared to only 78 per cent for all households in Manitoba, and there were no households on social assistance.

Most applicants in Manitoba chose the PNP because it was faster, easier, and provided more advantages than other programs. The presence of family and friends in the province was also a key factor. Ninety-eight per cent of arrivals received some form of orientation or settlement assistance after they arrived, and the level of satisfaction with the role of settlement services was very high. The province assumed full responsibility for the administration and delivery of settlement services in the province when the PNP was introduced in 1998, although much of the funding for these services is still provided by the federal government. Work by Christopher Leo and Martine August and key informant interviews conducted by myself and colleagues indicate that the delivery of settlement services improved immediately upon the provincial government assuming management of the services.[54] The province does work extensively with employers, communities, settlement organizations, and other stakeholders in the development of program criteria and in the design of the settlement service framework.

In addition to the above points, trajectories in a number of key areas are positive. Labour force, income, and poverty trajectories are positive. By the third year after arrival, principal applicants were much more likely to be working in occupations in which they had training or experience (83 per cent), compared to 57 per cent in the first year. During the first year 60 per cent of nominee households fell below the "low income cut-offs," but by the third year this had dropped to 25 per cent, although this is still higher than the 17 per cent for all Manitoba households.[55] Ninety-four per cent of those living in the province longer than three years indicated they had enough money to exceed their basic needs, compared to 67 per cent of recent arrivals. Homeownership increased from 39 per cent for those most recently arrived (first two years) to 76 per cent at the end of five years. Language skills improved, with 91 per cent of nominees in the province three or more years indicating they could easily communicate in English, compared to 78 per cent of the most recently arrived.

Most newcomers plan to remain in the province. The Longitudinal Immigration Database suggests that retention rates one year after arrival have consistently been above 80 per cent. Two-thirds of principal applicants interviewed indicated they did not expect to move to another province within the next five years. Another 25 per cent said it was unlikely they would move and would do so only if they found better job opportunities. Only 5 per cent indicated they definitely planned to move.

The study also found that cultural and community ties and activities expand with time. As time passes, nominees are less likely to be involved only in activities with their own ethnic or cultural group. Forty per cent of those living in Manitoba longer than three years said they took part in other community activities, compared to 28 per cent of recent arrivals. The proportion who participated in activities with people from the same ethnic or cultural group fell from 73 to 58 per cent. Maintaining ties with others of the same cultural group appears to lose some importance over time. The social network of nominees expands with the time they are involved in a wider range of activities and with the friendships they develop beyond their own ethnic and cultural group. They become more active members of the broader community.

In summary, the Manitoba program has achieved a number of positive outcomes and has been largely successful in achieving the provinces immigration objectives. The program has attracted a larger proportion of national immigrant arrivals, achieved a better regional distribution in the province, reversed population decline in many communities, and illustrated relatively high rates of retention; despite some problems, labour force integration and income trajectories are positive; language competency improves with time; community satisfaction levels are high; there are high levels of satisfaction with program services; a high proportion of arrivals achieves homeownership; and integration into the wider community appears to be positive. Incomes and education levels are not as high as for those arriving under the FSWP, but poverty rates drop significantly over time, and education and skill levels are significant. A high proportion of those surveyed stated their experience in Manitoba had been better than they expected, and they had encouraged and supported other family and friends to apply under the PNP or planned to do so. Arrivals had "taken root" and felt generally positive about their decision to immigrate and make their home in Manitoba. Based on this evidence, the Manitoba PNP appears to be a vehicle that leads to successful integration.

The evidence from the evaluation of the British Columbia PNP yields similar findings. In British Columbia, 25 per cent of the nominees have settled outside of the Metro Vancouver Region. Ninety-four per cent of the nominees surveyed were working full time. Ninety-four per cent of the nominees surveyed continued to live in the province, and 86 per cent remained in the community where they had initially settled. Seventy-five per cent had purchased a home. Nominees and employers are generally satisfied with the program's services and requirements and the program is meeting its annual program targets.

Although research on the PNPs is still limited in geographical scope and volume, there is growing evidence to suggest they represent initiatives that are working successfully to achieve provincial immigration policy objectives. Will they meet the labour force needs that are met by TFWs? Not entirely, as even with significant numbers of arrivals under the PNPs, there is still a need for seasonal and short-term workers in some sectors of the economy. Generally, PNPs attract a higher-skilled immigrant, and many TFWs fill less-skilled positions. However, the Manitoba PNP illustrates that the program can successfully accommodate workers with lower skill levels and can provide TFWs with opportunities for permanent resident status and for long-term settlement and integration. Even though the eligibility requirements are not always easy to meet, as noted in the preceding discussion, the PNP as it operates in Manitoba provides some TFWs with the opportunity to become long-term members of Canadian society, as opposed to facing a situation where they contribute to Canadian economic and labour force demands and then are sent home. Perhaps there is an argument to be made that many TFWs could enter Canada under different program arrangements and criteria that provide permanent residency status and better long-term integration opportunities.

CONCLUSION

In recent years, Canada and its provinces and territories have been depending to a great and growing extent on the TFWP and Provincial/ Territorial Nominee Programs to fill labour force shortages. The

FSWP represents a declining proportion of economic immigrants. The PNPs and TFWP appear to be better vehicles to address regional needs for specific occupations and the need for less-skilled workers that do not qualify under the FSWP. The two programs are also able to respond to changing labour market demands more quickly, particularly the TFWP. Application approvals for TFWs can be very prompt, and immigrants also arrive in less time under the PNP than the FSWP. Timing is important to employers as they try to adapt to rapidly changing labour force requirements. Hence they too are increasingly relying on the two programs to fill labour force needs, particularly those occupations requiring a lower-level skill set.

The treatment of arrivals under the TFWP and the PNP, as this discussion has illustrated, is very different. TFWP arrivals face far more limitations and barriers than do PNP arrivals. There is also much more confusion with the TFWP regarding a range of rights for TFWs and serious questions about their potential to realize these rights and to access local services. Those arriving under the PNP generally have all of the rights available to Canadian citizens and are able to access the related services – subject to specific program criteria and waiting times. It can be argued, however, that the access of PNP arrivals could also be limited by their lack of knowledge of service availability given that they are entering a new and unfamiliar environment and that, for some, discrimination may play a limiting role. In addition, all jurisdictions provide an array of services specifically designed to assist immigrant integration, but few such services are available to TFWs.

In some provinces there are linkages between the PNP and TFWP that allow TFWs to apply for permanent immigrant status if they so wish. However, opportunities are significantly circumscribed by job requirements, skill sets required, and other characteristics PNPs consider important to successful settlement and long-term retention. The potential for TFWP arrivals to cross over to the PNP is limited, except perhaps in the province of Manitoba.

PNPs, in contrast, although a relatively new component of immigration policy and not subject to extensive evaluation, do seem to be achieving their objectives of long-term retention and successful integration. Their emphasis on a package of characteristics (i.e., job potential, applicable skills, and family connections and support) in assessment of applicants may contribute to this success.

From an immigration policy perspective, the treatment of arrivals under the two programs is very different. The objective of the PNPs is long-term integration. Under the TFWP, adherence to this objective is weak at best. There are few efforts made to encourage TFWs to become long-term members of Canadian society. There is an argument to be made that such an objective should not be a priority for the TFWP. The workers, mostly unskilled, are needed to fill rapidly changing short-term needs. However, the growing importance of the TFWP, the increasing number of arrivals under the program, and what appears to be a long-term sustainable demand for these workers raises a counterargument and perhaps support for more and better efforts toward long-term integration. Perhaps moving toward a variation of the PNP model is worth considering.

In conclusion, the two programs are of growing importance, there are important linkages between the programs, but they treat arrivals very differently. Long-term policy objectives on the issue of integration are also very different, although the PNP model appears to be a more effective route for addressing labour force requirements and seems to treat arrivals in a much better fashion. A great deal more research is required, however, before decisions on program changes or moving the TFWP toward the PNP model can be made. Such decisions are crucial to Canada's future efforts to address labour force shortages and population growth in general.

9

The Political Economy of Migrant Live-in Caregivers: A Case of Unfree Labour?

ABIGAIL B. BAKAN AND DAIVA STASIULIS

INTRODUCTION: FRAMING THE POLITICAL ECONOMY OF MIGRANT LIVE-IN CAREGIVING

Migrant household workers in Canada are a highly vulnerable labour sector of the global economy. In comparison with the Persian Gulf States and many Asian and African countries,[1] there are fewer reported incidences of extreme physical torture and abuse of foreign household workers in Canada, the United States, and western Europe. Nonetheless, the difference between the general conditions of migrant household workers in the global North and South is a matter of degree rather than kind.[2] Indeed, we contend that, globally, migrant domestic workers are constituted as "unfree labour." Unlike with juridically free labour, the constrained working and living conditions of migrant domestic workers are established through legal and sometimes physical, rather than merely economic, compulsion.[3] This unfree condition is also buttressed by a host of racialized and gendered ideologies specific to particular countries and regions. The ability of employers, including working female citizens, to be "freed" from many of the burdens of household labour is contingent upon the imposition of state-enforced and highly punitive conditions of unfreedom on their noncitizen migrant employees.

Despite the pervasive oppressive situation of contemporary household workers, feminist political economy has historically theorized their workplace, the "home," as principally a place of unpaid, rather than paid, domestic labour. One result has been to analytically conceal the interplay and complexities of class, citizenship, race, and gender associated with paid domestic labour. Some scholars of Marxist political economy, however, writing primarily in the 1980s, but with some more recent contributions,[4] have acknowledged and investigated unfree labour in contemporary capitalism, a concept readily applicable to live-in domestic labour; but here little attention has been paid to the household as a specific site of exploitation. To ascertain how the conditions of migrant household workers in Canada fit into the global picture, we suggest that it is helpful to revisit and analytically combine these two types of political economy frameworks – feminist and Marxist – in order to consider (1) the household as a site of paid labour and (2) unfree labour as a concept applicable specifically to paid migrant labour in the household.

A critical feminist political economy of the household, building on the foundational work of Margaret Benston, illuminates how relations of inequality within the family household are structured along gender lines. However, with the importation of a nonfamily member, a migrant woman, into the household whose very presence is defined in terms of her labouring potential and availability, rather than familial ties of affection and obligation, these unequal relations also work through a host of intersecting social relations such as class, race, national/ethnic distinctions, and citizenship. When such inequalities are institutionalized through state programs, such as the Canadian state's Live-in Caregiver Program (LCP), the migrant household worker's vulnerability to abuse and exploitation is magnified.

The migrant caregiver is located on the lower rungs of global and household ladders of oppression, a status legitimized and normalized in institutional and ideological structures at both the local and global levels. Thus an incisive analysis of the contemporary conditions of paid household work requires that classical feminist political economy of the household be amended to incorporate issues addressed by a political economy of migrant and unfree labour. The latter framework examines the dynamics of variable forms of unfree labour[5] and suggests that such work is an "anomalous necessity"[6] of the capitalist mode of production, not only historically but continuously, that is extant in twenty-first-century global capitalism. This argument is elaborated below, preceded by a brief review of the LCP

in Canada, which is taken as a case study through which to context-
ualize this analysis.

THE LIVE-IN CAREGIVER PROGRAM

The Live-in Caregiver Program, which came into effect in Canada in
1992, is considered a "special" federal immigration program whose
objective is to bring qualified temporary workers to Canada to provide care for children, the elderly, or persons with disabilities in private family households. An important requirement of the LCP is
that employees must live in the employer's home based on the federal government's assumption that there is a shortage of Canadian
labour to fill the need for live-in (but not live-out) care work.[7] As
discussed below, there is an intrinsic and self-reinforcing relationship
between the "shortage" of live-in caregivers and the unfree wage-
labour condition of migrant live-in workers. In other words, there
exists no shortage per se of Canadian resident workers who could
engage in, or be trained to engage in, child and elder care work in
the homes of employing families. Rather, there is a shortage of "free"
wage labourers in the Canadian labour market who are willing to
work for low wages and submit to the coercive relations of (re)pro-
duction involved in live-in household labour. The LCP fills the void
by institutionalizing two coercive features: vulnerable, temporary
immigration status and a compulsory live-in requirement as a condition of entry of migrant caregivers to Canada.

To qualify for the program, the applicant must have educational
qualifications equivalent to Canadian grade 12, six months of full-
time training or twelve months of experience in paid employment
in a field related to the job sought as a live-in caregiver, and a good
understanding and practical ability in one of Canada's official languages, English or French. The LCP, moreover, includes a carrot as
well as a stick: once admitted into the program, the applicant is
allowed to apply for permanent residence from within Canada after
being employed as a live-in caregiver for at least two years during
the four years immediately following entry to Canada.[8]

Some significant reforms were introduced to the LCP in January
2007 and again in April 2010. Prior to 2007 live-in caregivers were
issued work permits for only one year and were required to renew

these work permits every year. The reforms extended the duration of the work permits to three years and four months in 2007 and to four years and three months for new work permits in 2010; previously issued work permits, since 2010, have been renewable for the remainder of the four-year period following arrival in Canada. This reform has significantly decreased the number of LCP work permit renewals processed by Citizenship and Immigration Canada (CIC) and has reduced the costs of work permit renewals to live-in caregivers. This is an important change. The costs of participating in the LCP and attaining permanent residence in Canada (including the "landing fee," at its peak $975 but reduced to $490 for principal applicants in May 2006) can be burdensome for poor migrant women and their families. Any reduction in compulsory state administration fees can be seen as a welcome amendment.

Also, in January 2007 a second and more significant change was introduced; for the first time, family members of live-in caregivers were permitted to accompany caregivers to Canada. The new regulation is written in a prohibitive manner, stating that live-in caregivers are not permitted to bring their family members unless they can satisfy the immigration officer that they have sufficient funds to support these family members in Canada, that these family members are not otherwise inadmissible, and that they have permission to live in the home of the caregiver's employer.[9] The ability to support family members in Canada – where costs of living are higher than, for example, the Philippines – poses new challenges for low-wage LCP workers. Most middle-class Canadian homes, moreover, do not have separate living quarters for another family, and few Canadian families would likely acquiesce to the accommodation within their homes of the family members of their migrant employees.

Despite its apparent impracticality, however, the program regulation change is symbolically important and also a welcome reform. It indicates recognition of an inhumane feature of the LCP – the enforced transnational separation of live-in caregivers from their families and the denial of close and sustained familial relations for these workers over years. However, the motivation behind both this change and its timing remains unclear. Certainly, a more realistic option for female migrants, one that would facilitate the family migration of live-in caregivers and their cohabitation during the initial period of their employment, would be to abolish the live-in requirement altogether. As explored below, the live-in requirement and the temporary migrant status continue to be at the core of the unfree labour conditions of the government's "special" immigration program for foreign live-in caregivers.

RECONSIDERING THE POLITICAL ECONOMY OF DOMESTIC LABOUR

Canada's Live-in Caregiver Program poses a formidable challenge to theorizing the political economy of domestic labour. The LCP is an instance of state and global accommodation of the needs of families in the global North through the enforcement of extraordinary conditions for migrant household workers, the vast majority of whom are women from the global South. In considering the diverse relationships of paid domestic labour to the private home, it is useful to revisit the groundbreaking theoretical contribution of Margaret Benston's classic work "The Political Economy of Women's Liberation," first published in *Monthly Review* in 1969 and subsequently widely reprinted, translated, and anthologized.[10] In this article, Benston used Marxist analytical tools to demonstrate the central importance of work in the domestic sphere to the capitalist system of production. Specifically, Benston saw women's labour in the home as necessary to the reproduction of "labour power," the human capacity that Karl Marx identified as the central commodity in producing value in capitalist society. Moreover, Benston maintained that women's engagement in unpaid labour in the household produced goods and services for use rather than exchange. She noted that as "real" value in the capitalist market was measured in commodities produced for exchange, "women's work" in the home remained without "value" in capitalist terms: "In a society in which money determines value, women as a group work outside the money economy. Their work is not worth money, is therefore value-less, is therefore not real work. And women themselves, who do this valueless work, can hardly be expected to be worth as much as men, who work for money. In structural terms, the closest thing to the condition of women is the condition of others who are or were outside of commodity production, i.e., serfs and peasants."[11] Thus cultivating greater access to the paid labour force would not liberate women as long as housework remained privatized and the responsibility of women. In a concept that would be developed in much of the subsequent analytical work advanced by socialist and other feminists, Benston highlighted the "double day," or "double ghetto," where women who worked both outside and inside of the home would "simply do two jobs."[12] And more generally, Benston identified limitations in extant Marxist understandings of historical materialism due to a "failure to understand that sex provides a fundamental basis for the organization of work and power in capitalist societies."[13]

Benston's work is commonly cited as the first comprehensive analysis of the role of women's labour in the private home from a political economy perspective.[14] Moreover, its influence continues to resonate in current feminist inquiries.[15] Contemporary discussions of the political economy of women's labour – in the neoliberal phase of capitalist society generally and in the domestic sphere specifically – continue to cite the original contribution of Benston's classic work.[16] The internationally vibrant "domestic labour debate" of the 1970s and 1980s generated an extensive literature, "and theorists from the Canadian left-wing women's movement," not least Benston's pivotal article, were central in these articulations.[17] Benston's contribution broke a wall of silence about and denial or minimalization of the role of gender in debates within the still (re)emergent Marxist political economy of the times. Her analysis applied Marxist categories to consider the relationship between domestic and waged labour, maintaining that women's work in the home was undervalued because of the systemic isolation of the private household from market relations.

At the same time, the work had limitations, some of which have been respectfully addressed and debated.[18] Although pathbreaking at the time, the analysis was marked by many of the assumptions present in the late 1960s, when feminist and socialist debates on women's work were still emergent. Indeed, despite retaining its significance as a classic work, the analysis shows its age when viewed with the hindsight generated over four decades of scholarship. Here, we suggest that the original argument needs to be viewed with a different lens, one that is framed according to three distinct theoretical vantage points: (1) social reproduction and paid domestic labour,

(2) social labour and globalized capitalism, and (3) the lived inter-sections of class not only with gender but also with racialization and citizenship.

The notion of social reproduction was suggested but not integral in Benston's work. It serves, however, as a useful integrative concept in this reassessment. As Meg Luxton suggests in her theoretically rigorous reading of social reproduction, "a class analysis ... shows how the production of goods and services and the production of life are part of one integrated process" and further "allows for an explanation of the structures, relationships, and dynamics" that are part of those activities in reproducing life on a daily and generational basis.[19] Benston's focus was specifically on women's *unpaid* labour in the home; it fell short of a comprehensive framing of domestic labour and of social reproduction generally as involving different combinations of unpaid and paid household labour, such as pro-vided by the LCP. In other words, social reproduction is performed not only by women doing unpaid work in the household they share with their family members but also by migrant women imported and working under highly regulated conditions who engage in a range of household activities.

Benston's article did marginally consider the role of paid domestic labour but only by way of dismissal of the minority of "the very rich, who can hire someone" to perform the necessary labour "involved in the caring for home, husband, and children."[20] This is problematic on two counts. First, it does not interrogate the processes of work in the home in capitalist society from the perspective of the vast num-bers of women paid to perform this work, who are in turn employed and managed by the supervisory "labour" of others, commonly also women. Second, the reality of the demands of the double workday for women who perform unpaid labour in the home as well as paid public labour – a reality addressed by Benston – often compels hired labour for domestic work, which, as noted, Benston's framework neglected. The latter is especially relevant in the provision of child-care but also increasingly in eldercare. This provision of care can vary greatly in quantity and quality, from part-time babysitting to live-in domestic service work. The class dynamics of a household that employs women as paid domestic servants are therefore ana-lytically absented, thus eliding a key component of the process of social reproduction in a global capitalist economy. In fact, women's work in the global South is not theorized as part of "capitalism." As we elaborate below, that workers in the LCP are in effect "unfree labour" widens the social distance and potential for exploitation in the relationship of employer to employee and links these workers to the circuit of social reproduction. To assume that paid labour in the home is the purview only of "the very rich" is to minimize the extent of the demands for public childcare and eldercare experienced by wider layers of working women and men over the varying life cycles of families in social reproduction.

An alternative framing that considers social reproduction and paid domestic labour from a political economy perspective would challenge the dual systems approach that Benston suggested. She posited that women's work in the home was noncapitalist, adopting terms such as "pre-market" and "pre-industrial," and compared this work to that performed by "serfs and peasants."[21] However, this assignment of noncapitalist status to work in the home is problematic, as it fails to explain how domestic labour interacts with the wider capitalist system of which it is a part, including the often contradictory pressures attending to public and private spaces and various forms of capitalist regulation, pressures central to understanding the workings of the LCP. From the perspective of women who work in the private homes of others, this contradictory nature is very clear. The household as a workplace is both a place "away" from work for the employing family, constituted as "private" space, and simultaneously the "public" workplace for the waged employee. Regardless of whether the private home employs a paid domestic labourer at any given time, the household unit in capitalist society remains at all times *potentially* a place of paid employment, depending upon the particularities of work and home life of the resident adult member(s) of the family. This contradictory space of the "home" – as both a place away from work for some and a place of work for others – is significant in framing the relationship of the household to the market in the global capitalist system. The household has the potential to be a place that is itself divided by class, between employer and employee. The specific conditions that compel this division are socially and politically constructed, varying according to position in a hierarchy of global citizenship, including options available for racialized and gendered employment and for public or private support of childcare, eldercare, healthcare, and so on.

Hence we can consider as an example a family in a household in the global North where a female works as a nurse on rotating shifts in a hospital, a male works as a firefighter, and there is one child (or more) in need of adult supervision. The woman's paid work as a nurse is central to reproduction of the society's labour force insofar as injury and disease, unaddressed, inhibit the capacity of workers to sell their labour power to capitalists for a wage. The woman's work in the home is also necessary to ensure the reproduction of the labour power of the next generation. The man's paid work is also necessary to the system, as damage, particularly to invested property but also to productive life, is very costly. This household unit could readily be a site of employment of part-time or full-time paid domestic labour, whose work, in turn, would support the social reproduction of the household unit as a whole.

Another example could be a family where there is one elderly parent and two working adults, which could similarly become a site of part-time or full-time employment for a domestic worker. In such cases, those eligible to perform household domestic service would likely be drawn from a pool of workers who have few other employment options, as paid domestic care is universally precarious work, being undervalued and unrecognized in capitalist economies.[22] Enter the Live-in Caregiver Program. The explanation for this condition of undervalued paid labour in the home is not narrowly reducible to the association with use values produced outside of relations of the capitalist market. However, it is certainly related to one of the key elements in Benston's argument – the apparent removal of work in the private home from the immediately realizable profit nexus of capitalist accumulation. This brings us to a consideration of globalized capitalism.

Benston's analysis suggested that women's domestic labour was performed in homes that were situated in advanced, Western, liberal, capitalist economies, assuming urban settings and a complete separation between labourers (specifically male labourers) and land as a source of subsistence. Household labour was framed as outside of this advanced industrial model, producing purely use values, which were counterposed to the production of exchange values. However,

Marx understood all commodities within the capitalist production cycle to include both use value, suggesting the "need" for a given product, as well as exchange value, which ascribes money value to items on the market. This conceptual limitation inhibits empirical focus on women's work in a globalized context, including paid work outside of the home, unpaid domestic labour within the home that is applied to products purchased on the market, and paid labour or its potential within the home. Moreover, the division of labour between a "breadwinner" male household worker and a "home-maker" female domestic worker excludes many forms and types of families in various forms and types of homes, including combinations of single and married women, same-sex couples, and women workers who perform agricultural labour.

Benston theorized the family in a snapshot mode, assuming one type of family in a static timeframe. In this sense, the totality of the process of social reproduction, particularly considered on a global scale, was obscured. The dynamic and changing process of social reproduction on both a daily and a generational level was not integrated into Benston's essentially dualistic model, which emphasized women as unpaid workers in the home and men as paid workers in the exchange economy. Alternatively, as Jody Heymann summarizes, there are many types of families, and there have been dramatic changes that have affected these varying families internationally: "A labor force transformation has increasingly drawn fathers and mothers worldwide into the formal labor force – simultaneously providing more opportunities and creating new obstacles to caregiving. Urbanization has pulled nuclear families toward new job opportunities and away from extended-family support. And all this has occurred in an era of increased economic globalization, which has brought with it access to lower-cost goods and services but also less ability to bargain for decent wages and benefits. These transformations are affecting every family from Denver to Delhi."[23]

This methodological flaw is not, however, unique to Benston; nor is it uniquely period-specific. Similar reductionist readings have been noted, such as in some contemporary neoclassical readings of Marxism that tend "to shrink problematics of difference to an effect of political economies of spatial differentiation,"[24] thus narrowing our understanding of race, gender, and other forms of oppression in relationship to class exploitation. More dialectical rereadings of Marx and interpretations of Marxism, including those that incorporate the contributions of Antonio Gramsci, Henri Lefebvre, and Raya Dunayevskaya, have helped to adjust this imbalance and could be usefully applied to a contemporary reading of Benston's work.[25]

We suggest an alternative political economy that posits the commodification of labour in a global context, where varying types of labour, performed within and outside of private homes, operate in varying relationships to commodity production in both the global North and South and for both exchange and use. Although Benston made the valid assertion that it was production for exchange value that was treated as "valuable" labour in capitalist society, all commodities must also include some measure of use value in order to find their way to the market, where exchange value is realized. Women's unpaid domestic labour in advanced capitalist economies often involves the transformation of commodities produced for the purpose of exchange – and purchased by the variable capital (i.e., wages) of both male and female workers – into items that can be usefully consumed. This consumption is a necessary part of the realization of the value of the products. Domestic consumption renders the commodity "absent" after its purchase, consumed in the cycle of social reproduction; this absence therefore also generates new demand for future products.

Moreover, there are regions of the global North that might appear less integrated in the capitalist market but nonetheless are part of the cycle of social reproduction. The unpaid domestic labour performed in many households in nonurban settings in the global North, including for example the labour performed on the limited lands retained by Indigenous peoples, may produce commodities for exchange with a use value as well as an exchange value associated with an external market. In the global South, there is relatively more labour performed in conditions combining public wage labour and production associated with the land, where domestic labour also produces commodities directly for private or public consumption, than in the global North overall. In the Philippines, for example, Elizabeth Uy Eviota traces the role of women in the agricultural sector, associated with rice farming, sugar production, and banana export. She notes how women's work both in waged labour and in unwaged production (i.e., small-hold farm and informal sector) increased as demand for male labour in industry intensified. Where women and men shared a household, women's agricultural production served as a means to subsidize male wages. However, "households headed by women are poorer than the average landless worker household."[26] A similar pattern has been identified by Huguette Dagenais regarding women's work in Guadeloupe, where "invisible" labour in rural areas is essential to family income. Here, the work week might include "five or six different small paid jobs" in addition to labour in one's garden and home producing goods to be sold on market days.[27] Considering the global South more generally, Grace Chang notes that when "women take on these extra burdens and are still unable to sustain their families, many have no other viable option but to leave their families and migrate in search of work."[28]

The particular focus of Benston's work was on the unpaid labour of women who were marginally or peripherally employed in the paid, public labour force. In generalizing this type of work to be representative of all women's work, Benston limited the purview of her analysis. She focused on a section of the male working class paid a "family wage," an income considered sufficient to "support the wife and kids." This generalization, however, has been demonstrated to be more ideological than empirically grounded within advanced states, justifying lower pay for women in the paid labour force.[29] Taking Canada as an example, Bonnie Fox and Jessica Yiu note, "In 2006, only 34.6 per cent of all 'census families' (i.e., married or common-law couples or lone parents living with at least one child) consisted of married couples with children 24 years of age or under living at home. Given that 70 per cent of women with children under 16 years of age were employed that year, we can estimate that fewer than 10 per cent of all Canadian families consisted of a married couple, a full-time homemaker, and dependent children at home."[30] On a global scale, however, the applicability of this model diminishes further.[31] This approach also has implications for race and citizenship, to which we now turn.

If domestic labour in the home is perceived at the outset to include, potentially, both paid and unpaid forms, where there is a relationship between employing and employed workers in the home and where both forms of labour are commonly performed by women, new questions are posed regarding the complex relationships among gender, race, and citizenship. These dimensions need to be considered in specific contexts, but collectively they play a role in a capitalist global market and social reproduction. In the case where there is the most concentrated provision of paid domestic care, provided by the live-in domestic worker who is on call over a twenty-four-hour period, for example, the labourers are commonly women of colour from the global South. The options for paid employment and/or achieving a robust form of citizenship that provides access to substantive rights and entitlements in their home countries are often limited.[32] Finding full-time but temporary employment in the homes of families in the global North is usually seen as a means to an end, with the goal being to secure not only better access to economic opportunities but also a citizenship status that offers a larger pool of rights and entitlements (e.g., better and publicly funded healthcare, access to "good" and affordable education, and so on). Such citizenship status, once obtained, in turn serves as a means to leave domestic service as a source of employment or, in the shorter term, to negotiate better wages and less oppressive conditions (e.g., live-out status or caregiving in public institutions such as nursing homes and hospitals).

The employer of a live-in domestic labourer is commonly a member of a family of greater means, often described as "middle class," but this does not necessarily suggest extreme wealth or membership in the capitalist class. More commonly, a portion of wages earned from the labour of members of the employing family – male and female – is transformed into the wages of the domestic worker. In this case, variable capital (wages), having already generated surplus labour and therefore profit in some form, is then taxed by the state where the home/workplace is located in the global North. In turn, a portion (notoriously small relative to standard working-class earnings in these wealthier countries) of these taxed earnings is then transformed into payment for the paid domestic labour performed in the private home. Many live-in care providers are also the principal "breadwinners" who support their own families, the members of which continue to reside in the nations of origin of the paid domestic worker. The earnings that are dedicated to the reproduction of the family in the global North, on a daily and generational basis, are therefore partially transferred to serve as wages for the reproduction of the family of the live-in domestic worker in the global South.

In effect, the labour of the domestic worker supports the reproduction of her employing family, as well as the reproduction of herself and of her own family through remittances. These remittances are also, in turn, taxed as they are transferred to the global South. These funds serve as revenue for the receiving states when foreign earnings are sent as income to members of families who rely on remittances for their survival. The two families are separated yet relationally linked by a nexus of citizenship laws and a host of gatekeepers.[33] Thus the employing family's citizenship entitlements to good quality care are realized through the noncitizenship status of the migrant worker and the sacrifices borne by her family. Notably, immigration authorities and a plethora of private placement agencies in the receiving country work on behalf of the employing family, while establishing barriers to the reunification of the worker with her family. The migrant worker becomes an important member of the household but is not a member of the employer's family, whereas her own family members are rendered invisible in these arrangements and suffer the dire consequences of long-term separation from the migrant worker.[34]

Paid domestic labour is therefore super-exploited labour, producing the complex commodity identified by Marx as "labour power" – the capacity to work that also produces the surplus value that generates profits for capital – as part of social reproduction in the global North and South. This commodity is necessary to the reproduction of capitalist society. Without labourers, human productivity and the production of all surplus value would cease. But divisions among the exploited are another element necessary to the long-term reproduction of the system. The rights of foreign domestic workers in national states and in international law are overwhelmingly neglected, both in the sense of receiving less legislative protection than most other categories of workers and in the sense of receiving some codification, as a result of migrant worker struggles, but not being respected. This political, legislative, and social neglect could at least partly be explained by the fact that the wages of private domestic workers are drawn directly from the earnings of other workers – albeit often salaried, middle-class professionals who strive to distance themselves from identification with working-class life. Notably, however, the source of payment for domestic workers comes from taxed earnings, not from the surplus product and secured profits generated in the first tier of the capitalist productive economy.

This complex relationship is affected not only by gender and class but also by racialization and citizenship status. In the interactions that take place through paid domestic labour, class divisions within the home as a workplace are intensified at the same time as they are hidden, or reified, in the process.[35] Notably, racialized stereotypes, and the related limitations in terms of access to citizenship rights, are reenacted, separating employee from employer within the confines of the private home.[36] Thus overall domestic service has been prone to a racial hierarchy, where often darker-skinned women who suffer from the most demeaning of racial stereotypes are assigned the least desirable and dirtiest forms of domestic labour, whereas lighter-skinned women are assigned the more preferable forms of care work. However, the stereotypes that shape hiring practices are malleable and may result in a previously high-ranking source of domestic workers to be downgraded, and migrant women from a new source may find that their employment becomes the latest fashion. Frequently, when members of a particular community (notably West Indians and Filipinas in Canada) organize to demand their collective worker rights, they find that such activism results in their demotion in the preferential hierarchy. A complex network of gatekeepers who regulate and control access to work, residence, and citizenship in host nations dependent upon migrant women's work continually assesses and reassesses the terms of the hierarchy, linking the interests of employers, professional regulators, and state policymakers as common stakeholders in the process.[37]

This brings us to the third factor relevant to a rethinking of Benston's work: Benston's consideration of the political economy of women's liberation attempted not only to frame the exploitation of women in capitalist society but also to posit an alternative vision of socialist emancipation. This is indeed, as her work suggested, part of the compelling attraction of a political economy analysis. It not only identifies the source of the oppressive practices but also points to the possibility of alteration or elimination of this oppression through conscious human action.

In positing the argument, Benston presented concepts that were universalistic, suggesting categories that included the entire working class in opposition to the entire capitalist system. The framing of women's labour in the home as mainly or exclusively consisting of unpaid housework and childcare presumed a certain modality of the "average" or "normal" working-class woman that was, and is, in fact not universal but contingent and therefore limited. It distorted the conceptualization of the active agent for radical social change. The essential element in advancing a political economy of women's liberation from a level of abstract analysis to strategy is agency, specifically the role of the revolutionary, or radical, subject.[38] However, Benston's framework presumed a constructed heteronormative nuclear family model. She projected "women" as those who lived in heterosexual, married relationships with male breadwinning husbands, and children were associated with heterosexual parental couples. Obviously, this framework was partial rather than universal; it limited the presence and significance of the complex labour performed by lone mothers, single fathers, stepparents, same-sex couples, and transsexual and transgendered people, as well as the role of a wider network of family members and relatives, such as grandparents, aunts, uncles, and cousins. It simultaneously obfuscated the multiple experiences of parenting throughout the course of the lives of the children in the homes considered.

Benston's framework was also a feminist analysis of its time in its analytical omission of the interconnections of gender with race and class. It suggested a universal condition among women that has been repeatedly politically challenged and theoretically critiqued since the 1980s with the recognition of power relations reflected in the racial and ethnic multiplicity of women and women's movements globally.[39] Even in the industrially developed United States and Canada, for example, the "family wage" model was limited to a narrow, higher paid, largely unionized section of white male workers and to a limited period in the post–Second World War era. Wages intended to ensure generational reproduction were not historically available to black or immigrant men, whose labour power was not paid sufficiently to support themselves as well as dependent children and a second adult in the home, namely a wife working only as an unpaid domestic labourer.[40] Benston's approach was therefore, arguably, silent on issues of race and racialization – a characteristic of second-wave feminism that has been amply exposed and debated through an efflorescence in feminist intersectional theorizing that comprehends women's oppressions and identities in the context of multiple and complex webs of social relations and discourses.[41] In the consideration of paid domestic labour, however, the uneven citizenship statuses constructed from the global, class, and racial inequities that define live-in, paid domestic care in particular come into sharp relief. This is a subject that we have extensively explored elsewhere.[42]

Despite these limitations, Benston's approach invited a vision of radical social change that optimistically considers the possibility of a world free of privatized domestic labour, where collective responsibilities for childcare, cooking, and laundry arc imagined. This is an enduring element of her framework, and could well contribute to current discussions of transformation of gender norms in a globalized, borderless world.[43] Benston was refreshingly prepared to challenge the then hegemonic Cold War images of the former Soviet Union and East Bloc states as models of progressive socialism. Instead, she stressed the similar impacts of capitalism in both its Western and Eastern iterations.[44]

Shifting the lens from unpaid to paid domestic labour in the home allows for an identification with women who perform wage labour in private homes as social reproduction for families across national borders. A perspective that imagines an end to the exploitation and oppression endemic in the structures of global capitalism, from the private home to the imperialist world system, promises a wider and more inclusive vision of social transformation. Today, for Benston's work to endure the contested terrain of contemporary debates, a bridge from this classic work in socialist feminism similarly needs to be extended to address issues of social reproduction and paid domestic labour, globalization, and intersectionality in the social relations (including and sometimes moving beyond the trinity of "gender, race, and class") that shape the respective positioning in power relations among women. To further unpack the complex political economy of the family household, with its many contradictory facets (e.g., both as a space of oppression and a refuge from external oppressions), we now turn to addressing the unfree character of migrant household labour in Canada through the prism of the political economy of unfree migrant labour.

LIVE-IN CARE WORKERS IN CANADA AS UNFREE WAGE LABOUR

We began this chapter with the observation that the seeming universality of coerced conditions and the flagrant human rights violations mandated by immigration policies render migrant household workers highly vulnerable due to their temporary or undocumented citizenship status. Countries with liberal-democratic governments are more likely than autocratic ones or states in "emerging economies" to have legislation on the books in relation to work hours, remuneration, vacations, minimal standards for accommodation, and social benefits covering live-in household workers. However, there is typically little or no enforcement of the rights and benefits that are available to foreign domestic workers. The balance between legislative/regulatory measures designed to *control* and *discipline* migrant workers and the measures that exist to *protect* these workers is overwhelmingly in favour of the former in all countries where there are foreign caregivers and household workers. This imbalance, linked to and reinforced by the noncitizen, or alien, status of foreign domestic workers, gives leave for citizen-employers to systematically exploit and abuse live-in care workers, usually without sanctions being applied against offending employers.[45]

For the reasons elaborated above, feminist political economy of the household has provided limited conceptual tools to illuminate the conditions that produce such apparently anomalous labour conditions in liberal capitalist societies. Legally autonomous, formally noncoerced wage labour, or nominally "free" wage labour, as Marx identified, is the form of labour upon which capitalism is quintessentially dependent.[46] Yet in "really existing capitalism," historical sociologists have observed many types of legally unfree and coerced labour. These have ranged from sixteenth- and seventeenth-century slavery, serfdom, and indentured labour to contemporary contract migrant labour. As Nandita Sharma[47] observes, scholars such as Claude Meillassoux[48] have followed Marx in regarding unfree employment relationships as variously precapitalist, a relic of feudalism,[49] and/or peripheral to the capitalist world economy. This misrecognition occurs when several relevant historical phenomena are ignored. First, as Sharma recounts, in the initial period of capitalist development, unfree work conditions were typical for many categories of workers – including "agricultural workers, plantation workers, sailors, those in the handicrafts, whether they were from what came to be known as Europe, Africa, Asia, the Pacific Islands, or the Americas."[50] Second, state regulations, such as attached to immigration policies, have played a critical role in constituting the relative freedom or unfreedom of migrant workers. Similar to how "illegal aliens" are more accurately regarded as an artifact of state regulation and border policies than as embodying "alien" characteristics as migrants, so too is the unfreedom of migrant workers the product of state migration policies rather than "part of the baggage a migrant brings with him or her."[51] Third, ideological practices of racism and nationalism have played a central role in suturing together the idea of unfree migrant labour as distinctly precapitalist and racialized notions of certain peoples as premodern.[52] Rather than constituting part of precapitalist social relations, unfree forms of labour have existed and continue to prevail on a very large scale, permitting the expansion of capitalism.[53]

In two books that both appeared in 1987, Robert Miles, in *Capitalism and Unfree Labour: Anomaly or Necessity?* and Robin Cohen, in *The New Helots: Migrants in the International Division of Labour*, address the problem of the coexistence of unfree labour with the expansion of capitalism. These authors challenge the idea that the capitalist mode of production is based exclusively on the use of free wage labour and address in particular the role of international migration. Both authors rely on a historical materialist analysis to examine a set of historical eras with a view to illustrating the use of slavery and other forms of unfree labour in a number of country and regional case studies, including the United States, the Caribbean, Mexico, South Africa, northern Europe and its labour reservoirs in the Mediterranean countries and former colonies,[54] Australia, South Africa, and western Europe.[55] Thus these authors are filling gaps in Marx's own framework, especially regarding the development of capitalism in non-Western countries.[56] In this sense, they reject the notion common among Marxists of the global North that the development of capitalism in England should be seen as a blueprint for all others. Rather, drawing from Marx's late writings, Miles suggests that Marx rejected the notion of a single "law of capitalist development that can be mechanically applied to a multitude of historically distinct circumstances."[57] Both Miles and Cohen follow this insight to develop a more "systematic analysis of the interrelationship between capitalist development in Europe and extant and newly created modes of production elsewhere in the world (including the colonial system)."[58]

Although both authors examine the persistence of involuntary, or coerced, "unfree labour" under capitalism as resulting from the relationship between capitalist and precapitalist modes (or in Cohen's terms, "forms") of production, their understanding of this relationship diverges. Miles follows an "articulation of modes of production" analysis, developed by Rosa Luxemburg, whereby a noncapitalist mode of production sustained a supply of labour power utilized by an emergent or established capitalist mode of production. He also pays attention to the contradictory dimensions of such articulations, including how the reproduction of unfree labour involves the use of considerable coercive power by the state.[59] In contrast, Cohen contends that "the capitalist mode of production is so determinant that after its initial settlement and conquest in peripheral zones ... we do not have an articulation of modes of production; instead we have a subordination and an encapsulation of the pre-capitalist 'form' of production and reproduction."[60] For Cohen, the unfree labourers who are compelled to migrate, and therefore to work in the core capitalist zones, do so largely as a result of the capitalization of and commoditization in agriculture, such that a region where precapitalist modes predominated becomes "enmeshed" in capitalist social relations. However, Cohen rejects a mechanistic theory of international migration of unfree labour in favour of historically rooted and spatially located analyses of the structural and institutional factors that constrain and guide the opportunities for migrant labour. These factors include rural immiseration; prospects for employment and housing; transport costs; constraints imposed by international law; immigration policies and recruitment policies of employers; and the need to obtain work permits, passports, and other documents.[61] In other words, structural and institutional factors at both ends of the migration process are critical to structuring and regulating the conditions under which migrant labourers live, work, and reproduce.

For Miles, the state is constitutive of unfree relations of production and is also an integral component of unfree production. Miles defines the state "as an institutional complex (government, courts, army, administration, etc.) which organizes social relations within a social formation to ensure the reproduction of a particular mode, or articulation of modes, of production."[62] He further argues that "slave labour, indentured labour, labour tenancy, contractual servitude, and convict labour were never relations of production privately constituted by a relation of domination between producer and nonproducer but were constituted and reproduced by, and were therefore dependent upon the existence of, the state."[63]

One strength of Miles's analysis is that he recognizes the high degree of variation among different forms of unfree labour. He defines unfree labour in terms of direct compulsion, "achieved by physical force and/or legal restrictions," contrasted with free wage labour, where the compulsion is principally economic.[64] This means that diverse forms of labour can represent varying degrees of approximation toward the condition of free labour.[65] In comparison with slave, convict, and indentured labour, contract migrant labour involves a closer approximation to the condition of wage labour. Contract migrants are "formally free wage labourers who are, in reality, substantively unfree"[66] – that is, "there is a formal exchange of labour power for a wage, and so unfreedom of the contract migrant worker is created and reproduced by restrictions on the exercise of the right to dispose of labour power."[67]

In his analysis of the creation and reproduction of unfree contract migrant labour in post-1945 western Europe, which was the type of unfree labour that most closely approximated migrant live-in caregivers in Canada in the LCP, Miles suggests that the legal category of "alien" is doubly determined – by the state within the recruiting nation-state and also by the labour-exporting state that seeks advantage for its own capitalist class through migrant labour export.[68] The recognition that, as Cohen also suggests, both states in the migration process – labour-sending and labour-receiving – reproduce the pressures to migrate and also the specific constellation of political/legal compulsions faced by migrant labour is an important point suggested in this approach. It is one that is not addressed by feminist political economy of domestic labour and that is also notably ignored in much critical legal scholarship on migrant domestic workers. The latter argues for reforming laws and policies in the receiving state on the grounds that restrictive legal conditions can not be considered "demonstrably justified in a free and democratic society."[69] The 2007 and 2010 reforms to the LCP, discussed earlier, whereby LCP applicants have fewer administrative renewals and where family members of LCP participants are legally permitted to accompany and live with the live-in caregiver, serve as a case in point. The constellation of economic, political, and ideological compulsions to migrate and send home remittances, the imposition by the receiving state of a compulsory live-in status, and the interests of both sending and receiving states to control the mobility of this contract labour work against more meaningful reform of the LCP and its attendant construction of a coerced labour force.

Neither Miles nor Cohen, however, examine the type of unfree migrant labour that is specifically recruited to perform domestic or care labour in private households. Cohen does offer some analytical attention to gender issues but in a very limited manner. For instance, he discusses the proletarian family in advanced capitalist countries and the peasant household in developing societies as the unit of reproduction (whereas Miles's unit of social reproduction tends to be the same as the mode of production). For Cohen, female labour is critical for economically subsidizing the costs of labour power as a commodity to the employer and for ideologically reproducing certain "patriarchal" relations of production and reproduction. But Cohen's gendered analysis also indicates the types of social inequalities that have impacted women through the migrant labour systems, where men are the predominant migrant labourers. As we have suggested in our analysis of a feminist political economy of the household, much more attention needs to be paid to the layers of economic, political, and ideological forces that constitute migrant women as unfree labour reproducing the labour of their employers and employing families.

In global capitalism, the spatialization of the contract labour migration of domestic and care workers encompasses more than simply one labour-sending and one labour-receiving country, as suggested in Miles's framework. The conditions of work and life are more coercive in some regions of the world, where the conditions of immiseration are often overwhelming. Many live-in caregivers, for example, have migrated directly from the Gulf States and southeast Asia. In one study of LCP participants in Montreal, a focus group suggested that the low number of incidences of discrimination and abuse reported among the 119 predominantly Filipino respondents who participated in a questionnaire survey was attributable to the relative judgment that the discrimination and abuses in Canada were less severe in comparison to their past work and living conditions in the Middle East and "Asian Tiger" countries.[70] The relative unfreedom imposed by the LCP may be experienced as less coercive for a migrant worker who has spent some years as a domestic slave in a country such as Saudi Arabia or illegally under lock and key in a country such as Lebanon, Singapore, or Hong Kong. That the international labour market in private household work contains a geospatial sliding scale of degrees of unfree work conditions, acknowledged by workers in a very mobile labour force, is also ignored in Sharma's analysis, which focuses specifically on the role of nationalist ideologies and on one national labour market in host countries such as Canada.[71] These other variants and sites of unfree labour exist at the extreme end of the free-unfree continuum. This does not, however, mitigate the structural condition of virtually indentured labour in Canadian households as a form of unfree labour. Countries whose domestic migrant labour schemes are closer to the "free wage" end of the continuum are thus permitted to continue to regulate and impose servile conditions on a separate and segmented labour force specifically assigned to live-in domestic service without international censure.

The presence of large numbers of migrant workers performing care work on a live-in basis is neither negligible nor insignificant, even though, as in Canada, this work constitutes only a fraction of the childcare and eldercare work conducted in a particular country: "Far from being marginal to globalization, the global labour market of care work is essential for the reproduction of the global economy – it is indispensable in maintaining human life and families, and in enabling workers (many of them women) with family responsibilities in developed countries to remain economically active."[72] As we have sought to demonstrate, it is critical to be attentive to the conditions of legal and possibly physical compulsion as well as to ideological practices that define migrant caregivers as a form of unfree labour. Their situation is "anomalous" when judged by the standard of free wage labour, which constitutes the majority of labour in liberal-democratic states. However, for women and their families in the global South, the structural significance of this labour market is grounded not only in the quantity of jobs provided – where such numbers are themselves regulated by a complex network of gatekeepers to citizenship in the global North – but also in the persistent *potential* for a necessary labour market targeted specifically at women's work in unfree conditions. Moreover, this apparently "anomalous" form of work has the potential to expand at any point, evidenced through the accelerated import to Canada of other categories of "unskilled" and unfree labour through temporary work migration.[73] Migrant caregivers are an "anomalous necessity" when viewed through the lens of global capitalism, where states – labour-receiving and labour-sending – place increasing pressures on the household and its most vulnerable members (including nonfamily migrant workers) to provide care labour.

IN CONCLUSION: REPRODUCING GLOBAL CAPITALISM

The perspective presented here suggests that households can be viewed as necessary to the production and reproduction of global capitalism. Households serve as one of the principal shock-absorbers for the vicissitudes of the global economy. These are institutions and sets of social relations that can reorganize to scale back consumption and that can intensify unpaid labour to compensate for a decline in household wages. When paid workers are brought into the family household, crises in the larger economy can lead to an intensification of the exploitation of these nonfamily members. Thus in

Canada there are increasing reports of household employees who
are forced to work for more than one family or for their employers' family business. The elasticity of what constitutes "housework"
also leads employers, who are often themselves harried by over-
work and stress in a neoliberal economy, to strive to decrease their
own domestic labour burdens and costs. Job descriptions of live-
in caregivers are amended without notice or formal recognition to
include tasks such as washing cars, caring for pets, providing volunteer labour at schools on behalf of parents, and so on, resulting
in increased exploitation. In the Canadian context, these are tasks
implicitly prohibited by the Live-in Caregiver Program insofar as
such forms of work are distantly related to caregiving.[74] When such
practices are exposed to be outside the bounds of the LCP, however,
it is the migrant household workers who are penalized.[75] Foreign
domestic workers bear the burden of women's work in the home
and, as we suggest, service the reproduction of capitalist social relations in myriad dimensions. Seeing capitalism from this perspective reminds us that central to the search for a radical alternative is
progressive scholarship that follows in the best tradition of critical
feminist and Marxist political economy.

From Temporary Worker to Resident: The LCP and Its Impact through an Intersectional Lens

SARA TORRES, DENISE L. SPITZER,
KAREN D. HUGHES, JACQUELINE OXMAN-MARTINEZ,
AND JILL HANLEY

INTRODUCTION

Thousands of temporary foreign workers, especially women from the Philippines, come to Canada under the Live-in Caregiver Program (LCP) to work as live-in caregivers (LICs). These workers must complete twenty-four months of full-time work in the house of their employers within forty-eight months, raised in 2009 from thirty-six months as stipulated in 1992 when the LCP was established.[1] LICs participate in the LCP, first, because they have a need for immediate income and, second, to obtain permanent residency (PR), which makes them eligible for family reunification. Whereas Canada receives LCP workers because they are "temporarily" needed to respond to the care deficit, live-in caregivers participate in the LCP because they want to stay permanently in Canada.

In this chapter we (1) explore why these individuals come to Canada and what it is like for these workers to live under the LCP, (2) identify the supports they receive to live in Canada beyond the LCP, and (3) expose the intersections among gender, "racialization," immigration, labour market participation, PR status, and family separation as former live-in caregivers integrate into Canadian society. In so doing, we examine the consequences of interacting inequalities for former LCP workers[2] occupying different social locations while

integrating into Canadian society, and we analyze the ways LCP policies shape these inequalities.[3] We use an "intersectional analysis"[4]
because such an analysis shows how current and former live-in caregivers can be marginalized along multiple dimensions that intersect at the macro level (i.e., global and Canadian policies) and the
micro level (i.e., the employer, employee, and community) in creating these inequalities.

CAREGIVING, THE LCP, AND INTERSECTIONAL ANALYSIS

The literature shows that for over a century socio-economic development and population growth in Canada and other Western countries
have resulted in a care deficit.[5] This care deficit "is a social problem
for which various solutions are sought,"[6] such as bringing temporary
foreign workers (TFWs), especially women, from the global South to
the global North. Michael Fine argues that in most developed economies, care has now "gone public" and that it is no longer solely
a private, familial concern that can be automatically assigned to
women to be undertaken without pay.[7] In Canada many families are
able to purchase the labour of less economically advantaged southern women to take care of their children or family members.[8]

Poor women in Canada and in southern countries bear the
inequalities and inequities of patriarchal systems that undervalue
caregiving. For poor southern women, selling their caregiving
labour in northern markets[9] may be their best option, although it
relegates them to disadvantaged social locations. For live-in caregivers in Canada, selling their labour also means long periods of separation from their families.[10] Their "absence creates a 'care deficit'
back home,"[11] as workers must hire caregivers in their home countries to take care of the children left behind. Northern countries have
an abundant labour pool from which to draw temporary foreign
workers because of the fierce global competition for jobs resulting
from extreme levels of poverty aided by the lack of policies to protect labour rights.[12] Mobilizing women from southern to northern
economies reproduces colonial relations.[13] In modern times, these
relations are perpetuated by the structural adjustment programs
(SAPs) imposed by the World Bank and the International Monetary
Fund,[14] which exacerbate poverty and exclusion through measures

such as privatization of health and social services. In response to its SAPs, especially its debt repayment obligations, the Philippines developed a clear income strategy of labour export in the form of TFWs. As a result, the Philippines is a site of social reproduction for a low-waged global underclass.[15] This global underclass has become a steady source of remittances for the country. These remittances represent a central economic pillar not only for the Philippines but also for other poor countries.[16] For example, in 1994 alone over 300,000 Filipinas[17] left the country to work abroad. As an export labour strategy, the Philippine government named its migrant workers "new national heroes"[18] or "heroines"[19] of the Philippine economy. Philippine labour policies glorify migrant workers' labour flexibility[20] and encourage, through various arrangements with banks, the secure transfer of remittances from TFWs back to the Philippines. Remittances represent "about 10 percent of the country's GNP [which] speaks clearly to the lack of dynamism and opportunities in the domestic economy."[21]

Canada's Live-in Caregiver Program is the most recent iteration of a series of programs that the federal government has maintained for more than a century to fill the care deficit in looking after the elderly, children, and people with disabilities.[22] Federal government policies respond to the care deficit by bringing in TFWs and by establishing a series of policies directed at protecting Canadian employers. Through the LCP, federal government policies instituted restrictions on domestic caregivers' labour mobility by imposing the live-in requirement. The LCP policies binding workers include granting only temporary (precarious) immigration status, obligating workers to reside with their employer for a mandatory period of twenty-four months, and restricting efforts to update their professional degrees. In exchange, workers can apply for PR in Canada after finishing the program, although the granting of this is not guaranteed.[23] The stipulations of the LCP do not protect live-in caregivers from exploitation in the home of employers who take advantage of live-in caregivers' precarious immigration status to violate their labour rights.

A growing critical literature on the LCP has looked at current and former live-in caregivers through various lenses: "race," class, and gender analysis,[24] policy and health intersections,[25] labour market participation and "racialization,"[26] gender,[27] human trafficking,[28] transnational feminism,[29] and intersectionality.[30] Intersectionality is an emerging framework that has its roots in critical race-feminist theory.[31] It takes a critical view of second-wave scholars and feminist organizations for ignoring issues pertaining to nonwhite, poor, lesbian, and non-able-bodied women.[32] Intersectionality theory has been useful in helping scholars and researchers to move away from debating the relative importance of race, gender, and class[33] and instead to embrace an approach that examines how intersecting oppressions work together to keep groups and populations in marginalized social locations.[34] As a method of analysis, intersectionality attempts to empirically examine the consequences of interacting inequalities for people occupying different social locations.[35] Notwithstanding the difficulties in operationalizing such an analysis,[36] it contributes to a better understanding of how current and former LCP workers can be marginalized along multiple dimensions that intersect at the individual, community, and societal levels, creating poverty and exclusion for these workers in their attempt to make Canada their new home.

METHODS

The research project informing this chapter employed both qualitative and quantitative methods to explore the post-LCP experiences of LICs in three major sites of immigrant settlement in Canada: Vancouver, Toronto, and Montreal. We conducted fifty-one face-to-face qualitative interviews with former live-in caregivers and conducted five focus groups with a total of thirty-six participants.[37] The focus groups and interviews were conducted between 2006 and 2007. Interview sessions lasted from forty-five to ninety minutes. All interviews were tape-recorded and transcribed verbatim. The use of qualitative methods allowed for in-depth exploration of participants' reasons for coming to Canada to work under the LCP, of their experiences during the LCP, and of their settlement, employment, educational pursuits, and family reunification experiences after the LCP.[38] We used an inductive analysis of the qualitative data, searching for content and themes using the qualitative analysis software QSR NVivo7. Since the focus group data corroborate findings from interviews and vice versa, the interpretation and analysis presented in this chapter integrate all sources of data throughout. The personal approach secured quantitative data from a survey delivered at the time of the interviews and focus groups. In addition, we administered a survey to a larger sample, from which we received a total of 104 responses, with an approximately equal number being from each of the three research locations. The surveys were analyzed using the SPSS statistics program. Survey data are used to complement various parts of this chapter as necessary. Although the survey results cannot be considered statistically representative of the broader population that has completed the LCP, they do provide a general "snapshot" of the experiences and quality of life of those who participated in this study. In 2008 we also conducted one focus group with representatives from organizations/agencies working on behalf of live-in caregivers and another focus group with policymakers within the federal government to validate our findings.[39]

FINDINGS

Our findings are organized into three sections. The first part highlights how former live-in caregivers came to Canada to work under the LCP, primarily to escape poverty and social exclusion in their countries of origin and, second, in some cases, to be reunited with their families. The second part reveals the living conditions of workers under the LCP, in the post-LCP period, and while they wait for permanent residency in Canada – as these conditions relate to underemployment, employment in caregiving, and the role of employers. It illustrates that participants continue to experience poverty and social exclusion but on Canadian soil. The third part discusses former live-in caregivers' social support networks, which aid them in settling, adapting, and integrating in Canada after the LCP. Furthermore, we address the impact that "interacting inequalities" have on factors such as informal and formal support, labour market participation, and family reunification for these workers.

ESCAPING POVERTY AND EXCLUSION: THE REASONS THAT BRING FORMER LIVE-IN CAREGIVERS TO CANADA

Before coming to Canada, several respondents had migrated to third countries, where it is easier to find employment, even though they knew that in those countries – such as China (Hong Kong), France, the United Arab Emirates, and Singapore – workers are not allowed to settle permanently or to bring their families. Canada's LCP is the only exception. We address this in more detail later.

At the macro level, an intersection of social stratification factors reveals why former live-in caregivers in our study left their country of origin, factors that included being women, who – owing to their gender – are apt to perform caregiving work and to experience poverty and social exclusion.[40] Given the lack of dynamism in the Philippine economy and the Philippine government's export labour strategy, working abroad may be becoming a norm in Filipinos' employment options. Marina[41] decided at an early age to work overseas:

> When I was in high school, I always said to myself that I'm gonna finish my university first, and then I'm gonna go abroad because ... to work in the Philippines there's not much opportunity for me.

At the micro level, some participants seemed to have internalized their roles as heroes and heroines. In this view, workers know that working abroad helps not only them but also the country.[42] Nancy, one of the few participants able to work post-LCP in her profession in Canada, knows that the Philippines is a poor country and that the remittances sent to relatives are very good for her country's economy:

> The business I'm in now, like the bank, we can see that people are really sending money, so it's good for ... not only for our community here, the Filipino, but also for the country.

Participants who were married with children and in a situation where both partners were unemployed also saw going abroad as the best possible option to address their socio-economic hardships. Several participants had full-time jobs in their country of origin, but their incomes were insufficient to meet their financial needs. After addressing their poverty, family reunification offers a strong second reason for workers to participate in the LCP.

Many of the single participants came to Canada for purely economic reasons. A small number of participants who were single had full-time professional jobs in their country of origin that met their individual needs, but they still went overseas because they wanted to help their close relatives. In this case, strong family ties motivated them to leave the stability of their lives in order to work abroad.

A common challenge faced by participants was the significant financial outlay required to migrate overseas. The costs included the LCP application fee, medical screening, remittances to recruitment agencies to find employers, expenses related to predeparture training, and travel fares. Most participants indicated that these expenditures meant that they came to Canada not only cash-strapped but also hugely indebted.

Participants whose friends or relatives in Canada located their employers avoided paying fees to a recruitment agency. Finding employers through relatives, however, might also be disadvantageous, as potential LICs may experience pressure from family members to join the LCP despite their own plans, desires, or misgivings. After Vivian's aunt completed the LCP requirement, she asked her employers whether Vivian could take her place. Vivian explained,

> She [my aunt] get me because my mom told ... she told me
> that she wants to help us because we are not rich family in the
> Philippines ... I gonna get your daughter so that ... you can have
> a better life.

Coming to Canada to escape poverty is a long journey for live-in caregivers regardless of their country of origin. Although they seek improved social status, they typically find that the social location in which they are positioned in Canada is as disadvantaged as the one from which they were trying to escape.

LIVING UNDER THE LCP/WAITING FOR PERMANENT RESIDENCY: POVERTY AND EXCLUSION ON CANADIAN SOIL

Examining the experiences of former LCP workers through an intersectional lens reveals both the interacting inequalities embedded in the employer-employee relations in private homes and the impact of LCP policies on the integration of live-in caregivers in Canada. The findings in this section focus on former live-in caregivers' struggles in three areas: (1) underemployment, (2) employment in caregiving as a career path, and (3) the impact of LCP employers' support or nonsupport on their employees.

Underemployment

One of the biggest factors that impede participants' integration into Canadian society is that Citizenship and Immigration Canada (CIC) policies do not allow LCP workers to pursue academic courses longer than six months while under the auspices of the program. These regulations particularly impacted participants in our study who were well educated; over one-half (56 per cent) possessed a bachelor's degree, and almost three-quarters (71 per cent) had participated in at least some postsecondary education.[43]

Former live-in caregivers who were well educated spoke of seeing their skills eroding during the LCP. Isabel explained,

You cannot use your education that you earn in the Philippines because in Canada it's different. I mean let's face it, even if you finish a certain course in the Philippines, you cannot use it here, like me, I am accounting graduate but I cannot use it.

Within the macro context, most of this study's participants were among the thousands of what are commonly known as "skilled" live-in caregivers who enter Canada annually under the LCP but who are quickly downgraded in terms of skills. CIC statistics show that between 1993 and 2006, 36,640 women and men entered Canada under the auspices of the LCP and that 67 per cent of these workers fell within the skill level C category. Among the occupations and qualifications that CIC defines as skill level C are "clerical occupations; assisting occupations in health services; intermediate occupations in sales and services – Educational or training requirements: one to four years of secondary school education, or up to two years of on-the-job training, training courses or specific work experience."[44] Since the credentials of skilled LICs are not recognized, these LCP applicants are placed in a lesser skill category than would otherwise be the case, which puts them in a subordinate social position that forces them to remain in the field of care work.[45]

Caregiving as a Career Path

Few participants in our study had limited or no formal education: less than 2 per cent possessed a grade 9 education or less, and 3 per cent reported having only a high school diploma. An additional 16 per cent had completed some college or university courses.[46] Most of these respondents saw caregiving as a lifetime career path. Some participants had been working as nannies all their lives. Phoebe had been living in Canada for less than five years after working in the Middle East for more than fifteen years. For Phoebe, working as a nanny had been her life-long career:

> Actually, it's hard for me to decide. I just want to live my life like a normal life. I don't have that much ambition ... first of all, in my early age, my early twenties, I already started working abroad in the Middle East as a nanny.

At a macro level, workers with no or little higher education represent an important asset for Canada's and other northern countries' economies, especially in the field of domestic work. Indeed, the literature indicates that Canada has a permanent need not only for highly skilled foreign workers but also for those who are lower skilled. The aging of the Canadian population guarantees growing labour shortages in a variety of employment sectors, including sectors that do not require postsecondary training.[47]

The Role of Employers

Whether former LCP workers had professional or nonprofessional training, the majority shared a concern about the harsh conditions to which many were exposed, especially because of their inability to challenge their employers.

According to participants' descriptions, employers could facilitate or hinder their efforts to integrate into Canadian society while working under the LCP. Unsupportive employers expected workers to be available twenty-four hours a day to respond to their ongoing needs and those of care recipients. These expectations resulted in an elevated number of overtime hours (many of which were not paid) as well as restrictions on participants' mobility. Some workers were allowed neither to leave the employer's home in the evening or on weekends nor to take time off. When an employer violated the worker's labour rights, respondents indicated that there was no way to complain. Many wanted to leave an abusive employer but remained with the employer because of their desire to complete the program in the shortest time possible with the goal of obtaining PR status and bringing their families to Canada. Even after they complete the LCP, CIC regulations make it burdensome for LCP graduates to seek different employment until they receive their open work permit.[48] As a result, some participants were compelled to remain with abusive employers until after they received their open work permit. Respondents who changed employers during the LCP faced the consequence of taking longer to complete the program, thus extending the separation from their families.

In contrast, employers supportive of live-in caregivers guaranteed routine work hours, which allowed workers to plan free time activities on evenings or weekends. Workers who had supportive employers felt more secure on the job and were less apt to change employers. A few of the participants used their free time to upgrade their skills through part-time nonacademic courses, some attended church or other community activities or spent time establishing friendships and social networks, and several took on volunteer work.

. A small number of respondents indicated that, because they were able to take nonacademic courses during the LCP, they managed to obtain better paying and more professional work upon completion of the program.

Since some participants felt that their employers exploited them, they hoped that the government would at least make changes to the LCP in order to lessen the opportunities for exploitation. Henrietta stated,

We are being exploited and abused, so we are hoping that the Canadian government or the immigration authorities will hear our request for them to listen to our struggles.

While under the LCP, live-in caregivers as temporary workers are excluded from nearly all CIC and provincial settlement services. If they wish to know more about their labour rights or immigration matters, they must connect with domestic workers' organizations. Lack of informational support further entrenches their social disadvantage.

SOCIAL SUPPORTS IN SETTLING, ADAPTING, AND INTEGRATING AFTER THE LCP: INTERACTING INEQUALITIES

According to the literature and to findings from our study, former LICS experience poverty and exclusion in Canada.[49] Yet most respondents, especially those coming from poor backgrounds, saw themselves as doing better in Canada in comparison to their countries of origin.[50] For many, "better" meant the freedom to seek any job they wanted; for others, it meant the ability to go back to school even though the tuition was expensive; and for the majority, it meant the opportunity to live permanently in Canada with their families.

Participants drew on both formal and informal support[51] to aid them as they integrated into their communities and Canadian society.

Informal Support

Informal support refers to the assistance that is regarded as available outside of formal support services.[52] In our study, participants received informal support primarily from friends and from members of co-ethnic church communities. Factual support included guidance on how to navigate the Canadian system and information about possible jobs, especially in the cleaning and caregiving fields, or about unsupportive employers. Participants who relied solely on informal support from other former live-in caregiver friends may have been the most vulnerable in their efforts to integrate and improve their situation in Canada because, like themselves, their friends occupied disadvantaged social locations and had access to few social capital networks. According to the literature, these types of informal networks facilitate the exploitation of immigrant workers, especially in times of economic restructuring and changing political contexts.[53]

Formal Support

Formal, or institutional, support[54] refers to aid offered through government institutions and not-for-profit organizations whose function is to support and facilitate TFWs integration into Canada, including domestic workers' and immigrant settlement organizations.

Most participants who had established formal relationships with domestic workers' organizations appeared to have gained a sense of empowerment by sharing their hardships and also by learning about their rights. In a focus group, Lia remarked,

> During that time, of course, I don't know my rights as a nanny. I don't know how much they have to pay me. I don't know about my benefits. I don't know everything until I became a member of [a domestic workers' organization].

At the macro level, the existence of domestic workers' organizations in the three cities of the study appears to have provided participants with the social capital required for collective action. Domestic workers' organizations develop trust and provide participants with opportunities to do volunteer work where workers can channel their energies into improving the LCP.

The existence of domestic workers' organizations in the three metropolitan cities of our study is part of the development of transnational activist organizations and networks that have arisen to address migrant rights and to lobby regulatory institutions[55] across levels of government. These organizations lobby to protect the human rights of migrant workers and to denounce rights violations experienced by current and former live-in caregivers. For example, in Montreal organizations lobby CIC to remove the restrictive nature of the LCP work permit on the grounds that it violates the Charter of Rights and Freedoms.[56] In the absence of domestic workers' organizations, especially in smaller centres, LCP workers may not be finding the established networks that are necessary for their integration in Canada.[57]

Labour Market Participation

All participants expressed concerns at meeting the social and financial needs of the post-LCP period, such as permanent housing and steady employment (preferably in their fields). Some respondents felt that their contribution through the LCP was important for the Canadian economy and that in exchange they should receive institutional support to settle in Canada.[58] For many, the government's delay in issuing an open work permit right after their completion of the LCP created a significant barrier to continuing the social and economic integration process in Canada.

Nearly three-quarters (74.7 per cent) of study participants who completed the LCP were currently employed. A sizable number (28.3 per cent), however, were working in multiple jobs. Notably, participants with formal professional education felt that they were not supported in their efforts to find employment in their fields. Only 28.1 per cent of participants worked in jobs related to their education, and more than one-half of participants (59.4 per cent) reported that they felt overqualified in their current positions. This figure was much higher than for the Canadian population as a whole, where only 27 per cent of workers report feeling overqualified relative to their experience, education, and training.[59]

With regards to institutional support for training in the post-LCP period, former live-in caregivers were often channeled into low-wage fields through access to loans that enabled them to take up training in occupations that were in high demand but offered modest pay – such as resident care attendant, dental assistant, personal support worker, and early childhood educator.

Slightly over one-quarter (25.3 per cent) of the participants were unemployed at the time they participated in the study. The types of formal support available to unemployed participants varied. One informant received financial support because of a work disability. The few respondents who bore children in Canada could not afford to pay for private or publicly funded childcare services. Ironically, the paucity of childcare spaces in Canada has been a major impetus for the creation and maintenance of the LCP.[60] Currently, the workers who have been brought to this country to resolve this issue find themselves facing similar problems. At the macro level, the inability of these mothers to find employment because of having small children reveals the lack of institutional support in the form of publicly funded, affordable childcare spaces. The inability to enter the labour force also means that these mothers, who had been in Canada for more than two years, were situated in the lowest echelons of the labour market alongside immigrants who were newly arrived.[61]

In essence, the challenges our respondents experienced in securing jobs within their fields can be regarded as deriving from the "racialization" of temporary foreign workers. For example, some employers' attitudes reflected the expectation that workers, especially Filipinos, would stay in the field after completing the LCP or occupy subordinate roles in the labour market and continue to face direct discrimination.[62]

This "racialization" is further evidenced by a lack of institutional support in work settings where individuals are made to feel that as former live-in caregivers they do not belong to the institution. Jasmin explained,

Now I'm working as a [...] counsellor, yet in my job I still experience that with my co-workers when I, like, deliver some of the workshops ... even in the office itself they know that I was under the caregiver. I was [...] before as a live-in caregiver, and the way they see me and the way they, like, they treat me is different, totally different from those two people who's been, like, here [...] a long time.

The role of "racialization" in diminishing LICs' opportunities to secure employment crosses both the informal and formal realms. Some respondents spoke of the lack of support they received from other members of their Filipino community. They felt that some independent Filipino immigrants who were working in their chosen profession were dismissive of former live-in caregivers and were unwilling to support them in gaining access to social networks. This internalized racism can diminish the potential support that independent community members provide their LIC compatriots. This notion might also contribute to what Philip Kelly and colleagues call the "racialized" Filipino identity, wherein individuals appear to accept a culture of self-denigration as well as their defeats in the labour market.[63]

Family Reunification

"What reunification?" asked one informant in response to one of our questions about the topic. At the time of the interviews, she had been unsuccessful in bringing members of her family to Canada.

All participants, whether their family had arrived or not, reported extreme sadness and anxiety at the long separation due to paper work requirements of CIC. A few participants had been reunited with their younger children but had to leave behind children who were twenty-two or older at the time of obtaining permanent residency. Their applications were disallowed, as participants were financially unable to keep their older children enrolled in full-time academic courses, which CIC requires if children older than twenty-two are to be eligible to join their parent in Canada. Tansi questioned the meaning of "family reunification":

What [do] they mean by family reunification? If one of your children [is] left in the Philippines, where is the family reunification there?

By the time her permanent residency application was approved, Tansi had to leave her twenty-five-year-old daughter behind because she was enrolled in short-term nonacademic courses in the Philippines, which did not meet CIC criteria.

Most participants felt that the long separation created by the processing of paper work indicated an implicit lack of support from CIC for family reunification. Women also felt torn over being able to send money to their children but not being home to mother them and having to rely instead on close relatives to perform this role. More broadly, this highlights a gendered division of labour in which the mother is expected to provide her children with emotional support and love, whereas most of the fathers who stay with their children are expected to provide financial, rather than emotional, support.[64]

DISCUSSION: LICS' RESILIENCY, INTERACTING INEQUALITIES, AND SOCIAL EXCLUSION

Whereas Canada receives foreign domestic care workers because they are "temporarily" needed to respond to the care deficit, women and men participate in the LCP because they want to stay permanently in Canada. All participants indicated a desire to live in Canada in order to improve the social and economic status of their families and to provide or take advantage of opportunities for educational and economic advancement in Canada for themselves and family members who would join them. If these migrants manage to transition into long-term settlement in Canada, they do so with only minimal state support. In addition, reunification with their families is often drawn out by CIC policies and bureaucratic processes. Although family reunification along with PR status are promoted in order to attract foreign domestic workers, the LCP policy is designed primarily to meet the care deficit in Canadian society.

An intersectional analysis reveals how LCP policies contribute to discrimination against and subordination of live-in caregivers in Canada. An intersectional analysis depicts the interacting inequalities experienced by former live-in caregivers in their efforts to improve their situation in Canada as "racialized" immigrant women from the South facing social and economic deprivation in a predominantly white and patriarchal society. In contrast to independent immigrants, who, despite barriers, arrive with more resources, plus the freedom to search for more lucrative employment, LICs start their lives in Canada through selling their labour without protection of their rights. The immigration status of these workers has been "racialized" since 1955 when women from the West Indies became the predominant caregiving/domestic labour pool. West Indies workers were granted temporary status only, in contrast to European women who obtained landed immigrant status,[65] along with its rights and privileges. Although currently all LICs obtain temporary status, workers from "racialized" backgrounds are expected to remain in caregiving, cooking, and cleaning work[66] well beyond the LCP. As with many foreign-trained professionals, in the post-LCP era the academic credentials of live-in caregivers are not recognized, and they are constantly reminded – by society at large and by many members of their own communities – that their live-in caregiver work is not valued in Canada. Additionally, the separation from families adds to their social exclusion in Canada.

An intersectional analysis also highlights the need for changes to how the LCP is administered and regulated, as well as making the case for the multilevel provision of appropriate programs and services.[67] For example, Human Resources and Skills Development Canada may change the "private nature" of live-in caregiver work by declaring the home a workplace.[68] Live-in caregivers would then be protected under labour legislation, allowing for systematic monitoring of contracts and removing the onus on workers to file a complaint.

What are the caregivers' abilities and perceptions of integration and resettlement in Canada? Former live-in caregivers are very resilient. Although a number of participants spoke of scrapping the LCP because of the restrictive mobility and exposure to employers' exploitation, most workers called for reforms to the program. In this study and other research by Denise Spitzer and Sara Torres,[69] all workers have indicated that coming to Canada has been worth it. As mentioned earlier, respondents who worked as live-in caregivers in a third country also applied to come to Canada because they valued the opportunity to move permanently and to be reunited with their families in this country – a feature that makes Canada's LCP unique among migrant-receiving countries. Both current and former live-in caregivers have also said that no worker should be exploited in the private home of an employer. However, the social and labour rights of a live-in caregiver are often not protected, perhaps because they do not represent an organized political power and their temporary status as TFWs makes these workers non-"voters" in the view of policymakers.[70] In addition, imposed family separation leads both to emotional hardship and to workers sending money back home instead of investing their earnings in Canada.[71]

CONCLUSION

That live-in caregivers arrive in Canada with very few financial resources, with huge debt, with few social support networks, without their families, and tied by their employer's power and the LCP's restrictive mobility policies leads to former LCP workers being placed in disadvantaged social locations. CIC policies constrain the integration of these workers due to LCP restrictions that lead to workers' downward social mobility during and beyond the LCP. A possible strategy to address poverty and exclusion would be to start the integration process from the moment migrants arrive to work under the LCP rather than after they complete the program. Broader analyses, such as those facilitated by intersectional analytical frameworks, show how interacting inequalities hinder successful integration. Effectively dealing with these inequalities requires addressing unfair working conditions during the LCP and providing institutional support for workers during and after the LCP. Live-in caregivers contribute to meeting Canada's care deficit; as one participant in our study stated, "they need the necessary formal supports to make Canada their new home."

"Good Enough to Work? Good Enough to Stay!" Organizing among Temporary Foreign Workers

JILL HANLEY, ERIC SHRAGGE, ANDRE RIVARD, AND JAHHON KOO

INTRODUCTION

Canadian immigration organizers, advocates, and academics have long been aware of the difficult conditions facing specific categories of workers within the federally legislated Temporary Foreign Worker Program (TFWP).[1] With the Seasonal Agricultural Worker Program (SAWP) and the Live-in Caregiver Program (LCP), documentation of how the racialized and gendered programs of the TFWP have placed migrant workers in situations vulnerable to exploitation and, at best, inequality with other workers is readily available.[2] With the increasing reliance on foreign labour in sectors distinguished by the Low-Skill Pilot Project (LSPP),[3] it is widely felt that there is a new wave of workers from the global South who are simply joining the ranks of their LCP and SAWP predecessors in terms of vulnerability to exploitation and categorization as "less than equal"[4] (see Tomic and Trumper, Preibisch and Hennebry, and Hennebry and McLaughlin in this volume).

The academic literature has done a good job of documenting LCP and SAWP workers' motivations, or push factors, for migration,[5] their work conditions here in Canada, and their access to social rights in the Canadian welfare state. Previous research has dealt with how both LCP and SAWP workers face difficulties in terms of their social, labour, and immigration situations.[6] Newly emerging research is finding the same for LSPP workers.[7] These difficulties are experienced differently according to the social location of the worker (i.e., race, gender, language ability, and class)[8] – but the structure of the TFWP itself gives these experiences a common framework.

Less well-known is how these workers have organized to defend their rights and improve their quality of life.[9] Understanding how migrants have self-organized, how concerned community groups have addressed the situation, and how a wide variety of organizations have come together in coalition to improve the conditions of temporary foreign workers (TFWs) is key if these efforts are to be strengthened and, ultimately, successful.

Drawing on several empirical projects dealing with the experiences of TFWs as well as on our practice experience with the Immigrant Workers Centre (IWC) in Montreal, we· use this chapter to explore the ways that LCP, SAWP, and LSPP workers organize and how allies have helped them to remedy the injustices that they face. We begin with an examination of the different forms of organizing in which the three categories of workers engage – social organizing, labour organizing, and immigration organizing – and show that different types of actors undertake this work, including self-organized workers, activist collectives, ethnic associations, community groups, unions, provincial and federal coalitions, and allies within para-public and government agencies. We then revisit common factors that make organizing very challenging for LCP, SAWP, and LSPP workers yet that also provide ripe material for consciousness-raising. We conclude with a discussion of personal and institutional relationships and leadership both in formal organizations and in nonlinear processes of social, labour, and immigration organizing. Given the relative advances in terms of labour rights for TFWs, we close by suggesting that the time has come to devote organizing resources to sustained and united pressure for a reorientation of Canadian immigration policy – one that demonstrates a shift away from programs conferring precarious immigration status upon foreign workers and toward programs that offer full equality for migrants to Canada.

STUDYING MIGRANT ORGANIZING IN QUEBEC

This chapter draws on a decade of experience working with migrant workers through the Immigrant Workers Centre in Montreal. As co-founders of the organization in 2000 (Hanley and Shragge) and as more recent members (Rivard in 2007 and Koo in 2008), the authors of this chapter have been involved in casework, education, and campaigns around, first, the rights of LCP workers and, more recently, SAWP and LSPP workers. As academics, our research has focused on the rights and resistance of migrant workers in terms of their labour, health, and social rights.

Most of the research reported here is from the IWC Research Group, of which the authors are members.[10] The group recently concluded a study that examined the labour experiences of (im)migrants[11] in terms of their experiences of work and their resistance to labour exploitation. We conducted semistructured, open-ended interviews with more than fifty workers. Included among them were permanent residents, people under programs such as the LCP or the SAWP, refugee claimants, and those without status. Their stories included workplace problems (e.g., the violation of their rights and economic exploitation), problems in accessing social programs, and other miscellaneous personal problems. The research was committed to better understanding both how the problems arose and workers' experiences in contesting these conditions. All of them worked in low-paying and often precarious jobs. In this chapter, we share some of the experiences and organizing lessons garnered from this study that might be applied to incoming groups of temporary migrant workers.

We also draw on a recent action research project in collaboration with PINAY,[12] as well as on two other ongoing projects, one looking at access to Medicare and CSST benefits[13] for all categories of precarious status migrants (including LCP, SAWP, and LSPP workers)[14] and the other studying access to social rights in general for TFWs in particular.[15] All three of these projects include a preoccupation with migrants' strategies to resist exploitation and to deal with problems once they arise, whether through individual or collective action.

There are several factors that make the experience of TFWs in Quebec unique. The first is that Quebec has a higher degree of autonomy when it comes to immigration than other Canadian provinces. The Canada-Quebec Accord, adopted in 1991, has allowed Quebec the provincial jurisdiction to select its permanent and temporary migrants, whereas the federal government deals with health and security clearances. This autonomy has enabled Quebec to vary its criteria from the federal criteria in order to shape the newcomers it desires, but the accord also means that migrants have to deal with two levels of bureaucracy. Also, the province is entirely responsible for all settlement services. A second major difference is the language context. Quebec's public language is French, yet many jobs require French-English bilingualism. The impact is that for migrants who speak only French or only English as a second language, the possibilities for integration into broader society and into the labour market are limited.

In the following section we discuss three interrelated forms of organizing in which people engage to contest and to improve their situations in Quebec. We structure this discussion by looking at each of the three programs (LCP, SAWP, and LSPP) in relation to the forms of organizing (social networks, labour organizing, and immigration organizing).

LIVE-IN CAREGIVERS: A LONG ROAD TRAVELLED[16]

The LCP is "the women's category of the TFWP." It is characterised by the heavy dominance of Filipina women taking up the program. It is as though, in the popular Canadian imagination, "nanny" equals "Filipina." This dominance is due to a combination of factors both in Canada and in the Philippines,[17] but the dominance of a particular ethnic group and the geographic concentration of the non-LCP Filipino community within the Côte-des-Neiges neighbourhood of Montreal create a sort of ethnic "home base" for LCP workers. That Filipinos have a long history of migration to Canada and that there exists in Montreal a well-established community with Canadian citizenship provides a strong basis for each of the forms of organizing with which we are concerned. As we show in this section, self-organized LCP or worker groups have been able to rally the support of Filipino ethnic associations, labour, women's and human rights organizations, provincial- and federal-level immigrant and refugee coalitions, unions, and allies within certain government or para-public agencies.

Social Networking

The structure of the LCP, notably its requirement that women live in their employers' homes for at least two years, effectively isolates women and makes it difficult to build networks of support and solidarity. What was most upsetting to one of the women we interviewed was that the loneliness, isolation, and control were invisible to her employers. She felt they didn't think about how she might be feeling and considered it normal for her to work all the time "since she's at home anyway." At the same time, she didn't feel she could do anything about it:

A lot of Filipinos and others are silent in their jobs ... they don't say anything in their jobs even if they are exploited because they are scared ... they are scared that if they do something for change, they will be deported ... especially those who are in the Live-in Caregiver Program, and even those with immigrant status, they are scared to be terminated. They feel held at the blade between life and death. – Ilga

However, LCP workers do find many ways to build solidarity. First, before arriving in Canada, there are opportunities to build networks. Most of the women are required to have training before they arrive in Canada. The recruitment and training agencies, concentrated in Manila, bring women together. Many women find their way here through the referrals of relatives and friends, people from their village or community, so upon arrival they know others. One woman illustrated this point:

I came to Canada from the Philippines when I was twenty-two. I only had two semesters left of my university psychology degree, but my mother was really encouraging me. She was already in Canada working [under the] LCP and she found me a job with her employer's friend. She said I shouldn't give up the opportunity to come to Canada, so I immigrated as part of the Live-in Caregiver Program. – Rudy

Second, in the day-to-day activities and chores upon arrival, there are opportunities to build relationships with others in the program. Because of the concentration of employers in wealthier neighbourhoods, domestic workers also meet in parks or other public places as they go about their duties. One LCP organizer described her experience in bringing people together. She drove the children of her employer to school and then was able to give other domestics a lift on her way home. Church provides another important meeting place. The transplanted religious traditions of the home countries play a key role in breaking isolation. Days off become an important time to meet and socialize. Seeking some semblance of a private life, women will share apartments for these days. At a formal level, all women in Quebec in the LCP are required to take courses in French as a way to prepare for their integration into Quebec society as eventual permanent residents. The building of networks between women is an important element in challenging workplace conditions.

Linking Social and Labour Organizing

PINAY is the most important association in Montreal that organizes workers in the LCP. It is a nonprofit organization of Filipina migrant and immigrant women workers created in 1991 in response to the need to organize and empower Filipina women, especially Filipina domestic workers and their families living and working in Quebec. For the first years after its founding, PINAY was an informal group. In 1996 it formalized as a nonprofit organization. Since 1991 PINAY has signed up over 500 members, but because of the nature of the life of LCP workers, membership is difficult to sustain, as people often move, return home, or find another type of work.

PINAY has initiated several campaigns. For example, in 1999 it launched the Quebec Purple Rose Campaign to "Stop Sex Trafficking of Filipino Women and Children." In 2003 PINAY worked with the Front de défense des non-syndiqués to win a campaign to include domestic workers under the Quebec Labour Standards Act.

For the LCP workers, this meant they were eligible, for the first time, to receive the same minimum wage as other workers and to receive overtime pay after a forty-hour week. As a result, LCP workers were finally able to file claims to get paid for overtime work and also gained both the option to file a complaint if their rights were violated and entitlement to compensation.

Through the use of media and its relationship with university researchers, PINAY has been able to expand public awareness not only about PINAY itself but also about subjects such as LCP work conditions, different cases of human rights violations, and the lack of health and injury coverage. PINAY continues to participate in campaigns in collaboration with other organizations, pressuring the Quebec government, for example, to extend coverage of workers' compensation to domestic workers. Similarly, PINAY is also working toward the abolition of the three-month delay for Medicare coverage for newly arrived migrants/immigrants.

PINAY is an example of a group resisting workers' temporary status through an informal organizational process to mobilize and support domestic workers in a collective struggle against specific vulnerabilities caused by their temporary immigration status. It does not have an office but has an executive/leadership and members. What started as a social and emotional support group providing assistance for a few members has become a political organization with a clear agenda. Since PINAY was founded, its target audience seems to have been expanded. PINAY today addresses its services not only to Filipino LCP workers but also to domestic workers from other countries, as well as to women who are being trafficked. One member summed up this change as follows:

Today, I feel that we are fighting not only for the Filipino women but also for all the women that are abused. We are fighting against the injustice in society towards the working class. Not only the caregivers are being exploited. – Louise

PINAY uses social, informal processes to bring people together, ostensibly around issues of work and immigration status but also concerning the social and cultural wellbeing of the women in the LCP. The social and cultural element is a way to build a sense of belonging for workers who have left their families back home and are forced to live in their employers' homes. Being physically isolated and understandably nervous, caregivers engaged in PINAY activities such as dinners, dances, and retreats report higher levels of enjoyment of and integration into Quebec society. French-language classes, outings, and activities that allow the women to collectively explore their new province are advantageous, especially when shared with friendly faces united by similar needs. These needs are varied and can arise from concerns over finances and remittances to family back home, loneliness and depression in a foreign land, questions about their labour or social rights, and queries about immigration. Members feel welcomed both culturally and by virtue of their career path. Although there is no paid staff within the organization, the leadership comes from those who have been able to remain in Canada after the LCP and to build a life there. A couple of these people play staff roles, but PINAY makes a sustained and conscious effort to engage in political education and to build new leadership among its members. It brings members to political events and trains them to be spokespeople in the media.

In the fight for the labour rights of domestic workers, there are other organizations that act as allies to PINAY. The Association des aides familiales du Québec is a community organization that works with domestic workers in all situations. It was founded thirty-five years ago to assist domestic workers coming from rural areas in Quebec in order to work as domestics in large cities. It has evolved over time and devotes a lot of its resources to working with women in the LCP, a reflection of how the use of this program has become omnipresent in the sphere of domestic work. Like many community organizations in Quebec, it has received provincial government recognition and corresponding funding. It provides services, advocates for labour and immigration rights, and lobbies for the reform of policies that have an impact on domestic workers.

Part of the role that PINAY has played, along with the IWC, is to bring the issue of the conditions of LCP workers onto the public agenda, arguing that domestic work is work! New allies have emerged over the years to support PINAY and frontline organizations like the IWC in various campaigns. The fight to include domestic workers under the Labour Standards Act is a good example of this, as well as the campaign to have domestic workers covered by the CSST. PINAY and the IWC have influenced the agendas of organizations such as the Fédération des femmes du Québec (FFQ) and unions to include the situation of domestic workers as part of their demands and programs of action.

Quebec's major union federations, the Quebec Federation of Labour (affiliated with the Canadian Labour Congress) and the Confederation of National Trade Unions, often acting through their women's or immigrant caucus, have become strong allies on LCP issues. One of the more creative initiatives was the (ultimately failed) effort to create a homeworkers' section of iWorkers, the Independent Workers' Association. Due to the impossibility of actually having a collective agreement for LCP workers (no collective employer), iWorkers would be a membership organization that offered services to its members. A joint project of MIGRANTE Canada[18] and the United Steelworkers' Union that began in 2008, the Montreal- and Toronto-based pilot project aimed to offer LCP workers representation in situations of labour disputes with their employer. Whereas the Montreal iWorkers never really got off the ground, the Toronto one remains, and due to high demand for the services offered, such as subsidized dental care, supplementary medical insurance, and discounted legal advice, the membership rolls have steadily risen and the organization has been successfully maintained.

Immigration Organizing

Because the LCP is a creation of immigration policy as specified in the Immigration and Refugee Protection Act, groups have organized for its reform. Demands have focused on the injustice of workers coming to Canada and working in very difficult circumstances in order to have the right to apply for permanent status. Critics familiar with the structure of the LCP deplore the requirement that workers live on site with their employer. Workers are inevitably subjected to conditions under which they are casually on call at the best of times or working in subordinate slave-like environments in the worst cases. Should caregivers become injured or sick while on the job, they face exclusion from provincial workplace health and safety insurance benefits. The linking of work and precarious status contributes to fear about contesting their situations at work. The other barrier to exercising full labour rights is the carrot at the end of the LCP stick: permanent residency. The following is an example:

> [F]or a long time, I knew the rules and wanted to go complain to the Normes de travail [Labour Standards Commission], but I was afraid to lose my job. I worked like a buffalo because I wanted permanent residency and I didn't want to risk losing that job. – Rita

Others talked about mutual support as being the way to get through the three years required to achieve permanent residency without taking the risk of challenging the injustices of the workplace. Yet, despite all of the pressures to swallow bad situations, there have been challenges to the policies surrounding the LCP. There have been campaigns ranging from challenging deportations of domestic workers to making wider demands, such as the demand to "Scrap the LCP." The broadest campaign was in 2001, the "Stop the Expulsion of Melca Salvador Campaign." Salvador, a former LCP worker, was at that time the vice chair of PINAY. While under the LCP, Salvador told her employer that she was pregnant and was promptly fired. As a result, she was able to complete only eleven months of live-in work out of the required twenty-four. Therefore, in 2001 she was about to be deported. The success of the campaign was twofold. Not only did the campaign keep Melca and her son in Canada, but it also helped to expose the oppression and exploitation of LCP workers while building relationships between PINAY, the IWC, and older more established organizations such as unions and the FFQ. There has been debate among Filipinos across Canada about the demand to "Scrap the LCP." Because many women have used the program to gain permanent status for themselves, the idea of scrapping it and moving toward a blanket demand such as "Good Enough to Work? Good Enough to Stay!" is seen by some as too idealistic in the current context and rejected by others as a threat to domestic workers in the LCP.

Another dimension of immigrant organizing has come out of activist social movements like No One Is Illegal. These movements have been allies on questions of deportations and on denouncing the injustices associated with the LCP. Because these groups came out of a generation of activists influenced by anticorporate globalization, they have brought some of the younger activists into contact with organizations like PINAY, asking representatives to speak to younger activists and thus recruiting allies in the struggle for justice for domestic and other workers.

PINAY also tries to promote more flexibility in employment for migrant workers, including cancelling the obligation to indicate the name of the specific employer in the work permit. This campaign also includes a demand for accreditation of Filipino nurses and other professionals. Finally, PINAY advocates granting workers an option to live out. In its opinion, the live-in arrangement invites exploitation of the workers and opportunities for abuse.

As these examples are all drawn from PINAY's work within the context of Montreal and Quebec, it is essential to situate PINAY's struggles within the national movement of LCP workers' rights. Every major city in Canada has organizations organizing around domestic workers' rights, around Filipino migrants' rights, and around temporary foreign workers' rights. PINAY's campaigns, such as the "Melca Salvador Campaign," often receive Canada-wide and even international support, and, in turn, PINAY lends its support to the campaigns of its allies. Organizations in other jurisdictions engage in parallel and connected struggles. Ontario's iWorkers, notably through its labour-community collaboration, brought about changes in immigration regulations in December 2009 through its campaigns with respect to the case of Juana Tejada, a Filipina LCP worker who was refused permanent residency and ordered deported because she couldn't pass the second medical exam in Canada due to her development of cancer while she was under the LCP.

AGRICULTURAL WORKERS (SAWP AND LSPP): FINALLY GETTING THE ATTENTION OF THE PUBLIC

In contrast to the LCP, the SAWP – and now the agricultural application of the LSPP – is "the men's category of the TFWP," with over 90 per cent of workers in Quebec being male. Albeit to a lesser degree than Ontario, Quebec has a history of migration of agricultural workers under the SAWP program since the mid-1960s. During the

program's infancy, the majority of workers came from Commonwealth Caribbean countries, particularly Jamaica. But the past two
decades have seen increasing numbers of Mexican workers, to the
point where they have been the overwhelming majority of migrant
farm workers since the early 1990s. With the lower regulation of the
LSPP as a source of migrant farm labour, however, the balance has
shifted toward Guatemalan LSPP workers, who became the majority
for the first time in 2009.[19]

Even though they have a long history in the province, are often
hired in groups, and mostly share a common language, the organizing of migrant farm workers in Quebec goes back less than ten
years.[20] There are major impediments to organizing within this community. There is the seasonal nature of their contract, their being
barred from becoming permanent residents, and their rural location,
which makes connections with established ethnic communities nearly
impossible, although this may be changing. Rather than through a
tradition of self-organized groups, the organizing of SAWP workers
in Quebec has come about mostly via union or church intervention.
Among agricultural TFWs, social organizing and labour organizing
are strongest. Immigration organizing is done nearly exclusively by
allied third parties.

Social Networking

Similar to the LCP, social networking is at the base of the process
of recruitment and work for agricultural TFWs. Workers for a particular farm are usually recruited from the same village, involving
both family and community ties. In addition, because of the restrictive labour mobility that is part of the program, they share housing
and cooking facilities while in Canada. This de facto social network
is both a blessing and a potential constraint for solidarity. In interviews, workers described an appreciation of being with people they
knew and having the potential to refer friends and family for open-
ings in future years. When workers struggle, they can often rely on
support from their fellow workers. At the same time, a worker who
becomes identified as a troublemaker can put his family members
and even his whole village at risk of not being called back. With
the stakes for being recalled to work the following season so high,

workers reported feeling that their colleagues were ready to report them to the employer or turn their backs on them if their own interests were threatened. With the lack of privacy in their living conditions, some workers felt they were under the constant observation of the "employer's spies."

Despite this underside of having an imposed social group, our research uncovered many situations where a worker's colleagues sought help when the worker himself could not, particularly in cases of ill health. In one story, workers on a farm refused to work until the employer brought their sick colleague to the hospital. Up until that action, the sick worker's requests to see a doctor had gone unheeded. In another health-related situation, we heard of colleagues contacting the local church to get support for a colleague who was suffering from depression and was potentially suicidal.

Apart from farm-based social networking, migrant workers on different farms often meet each other if they are working in an area with a high concentration of SAWP or LSPP workers. The most famous municipalities for such congregations of workers are Saint-Rémi, to the south of Montreal, and Saint-Eustache, to the north. In these towns, the workers often gather on one weeknight (usually Thursday) for shopping and an evening off in town and also meet on Sundays. Sunday is often their only day off during the week, and at least in these two towns, it is known that workers have impromptu soccer leagues and patronize the makeshift taco stands that sprout up to serve them during their time off.

Local Catholic churches are another gathering place for workers. With SAWP and LSPP workers ballooning the numbers of churchgoers during the growing season, a rather progressive network of church workers has developed to serve their spiritual, social, and increasingly, advocacy needs.

Finally, recent years – especially since the conflicts that have arisen with the implementation of the North American Free Trade Agreement – have seen a new wave of Mexican refugee claimants coming to Canada. In the past five years or so, Mexicans have been the biggest group both claiming and receiving refugee status, and many of them are settling in Montreal. This has led to a growth of Mexican ethnic associations with a wide range of political stances, including some that are quite interested in making links with their compatriots working in the fields. These associations have been reaching out through the Catholic Church and through personal contacts to develop links with farm workers.

As we now turn our attention to SAWP and agricultural LSPP labour organizing, it is pertinent to note that the introduction of the United Food and Commercial Workers (UFCW) has at its origin a Mexican farm worker in trouble in 2003 who managed to get in touch with Patricia Perez, a Mexican woman who originally came to Montreal as a political refugee. She began visiting SAWP workers after a desperate phone call from a worker who got her number from the cousin of a friend. The man's employer had stopped paying him after a workplace injury left him unable to work, and the employer refused to bring him to see a doctor. The worker was repatriated following Patricia's first visit; the Mexican Consulate refused to answer her questions. The second time she went into the field, there were fifty workers waiting to talk to her, and the farmer sent her out of the field. Patricia was shocked by what she learned about the situation of agricultural workers and made it her life's work to organize for their rights.[21] After having created the volunteer-based Support Coalition for Agricultural Workers, she later left her job in Montreal to become a full-time organizer with the UFCW.

Labour Organizing

Organizing SAWP workers has been complex and difficult because of the nonpermanent status of the workers, the legal difficulties in defining their minimum labour standards in general, and an ongoing court challenge about the right to unionize seasonal farm workers. A combination of strategies has emerged that includes community-based services, union activities, and advocacy for improved conditions by allied organizations. Across Canada there has been a union presence dominated by the UFCW. Its approach is to establish community-based service centres to build relationships with workers before moving on to a process of unionization. There has been very limited success in unionizing and collective bargaining – with a high price paid by workers who initiate the process of unionizing a workplace. In Quebec nearly all farms that have advanced in the process of unionizing have seen leaders either fired outright or simply not "called back." In some cases, employers have replaced their entire workforce of, for example, Mexican SAWP workers with Guatemalan LSPP workers the following season. For this reason, the union has maintained its hybrid model, using a community approach to fight for the rights of workers in the SAWP. The UFCW founded the Centre d'aide aux travailleurs et travailleuses agricoles (CATTAQ). With a minimal paid staff and growing numbers of volunteers, the centre now has a storefront office in each of the two agricultural towns close to Montreal that are in the heart of "SAWP country": St-Rémi and St-Eustache.

Learning labour rights is a starting point in the organizing process, as it gives workers both a set of tools to challenge their bosses and a sense of self-confidence to do so. As one SAWP worker described,

Because of Daniel and Patricia [CATTAQ organizers], Mexican, Guatemalan, and Salvadoran workers know the laws. Before, I didn't know them; our bosses never gave us that information – they totally used us. They would tell us what to do and we would be blind, we would just do anything. We didn't really have rights. They would lock us up, they wouldn't tell you anything, just threaten to put you on a plane to Mexico, and that was fine for them because we didn't know the laws. Now I just thank God that I'm learning about the laws. – Felipe

Another worker told us,

So now I've learned what the laws are. There are laws that protect workers against discrimination. Now when we mention that, the Québécois listen to us. Now I know. I can say to the boss, "Would you do that to a Québécois? Would you treat them that way?" – Antonio

However, even knowing one's rights is no guarantee of action. "Susanna," another organizer at CATTAQ, put it well:

Before, most workers didn't know their rights. Now most of them know their rights, but they don't demand them – not because they don't know them but because they can't. "Yeah, I know I have the right, but what do you want me to do? What? You want me to demand that from my boss? What do you think he'll say?"

Supporting workers so they can defend themselves involves basic rights education, encouraging solidarity, and helping workers to devise strategies for everyday acts of resistance, as this organizer also explained,

> We try to enforce that alone they can't change anything. Keep together – if it's always one person that says something, they'll get targeted, so approach the boss in groups of three, rotate week to week. There are small victories.

The following anecdote, recounted by Susanna, further illustrates the point:

> One employee had put Kool-Aid in the water dispenser. The fore-man came in yelling and insulting them and to stop putting fla-vour crystals in the dispenser – that they would break it. So one of the workers spoke back and said, "If it breaks, I'll fix it – but you can't just come into our house and talk to us like that." So the next day the foreman targeted him and said, "You! Today you don't go out working" – and the entire gang refused to work. So then the farmer came in to find out what was going on. He told them, "You don't scare me. I'll get Agrijobs [day labour-ers] to replace you and send you all back to Mexico!" The work-ers said, "Fine!" Then that night he came back and said, "Okay, what do you want?" They said, "We want an apology." So the farmer came back with pizza for everyone and publicly apolo-gized, but that's one out of ten times.

After several years of support and organizing work, the efforts of CATTAQ are seeing results. Workers aren't as scared about their foreman seeing them come in to the centre. The staff members have noted some improvements in housing and that some employers have mostly stopped confiscating workers' documents.

But actual unionization has proven more difficult. In June 2006 150 workers on three Quebec farms voted to join the UFCW and submitted a request for union accreditation to the Commission des relations du travail du Québec, the provincial Labour Relations Commission (LRC). Their employers and the Fondation des entreprises en recrutement de main-d'oeuvre agricole étrangère (FERME),[22] the employers' association that manages SAWP and LSPP recruitment, challenged the request, arguing that the Quebec Labour Code does not apply to migrant workers because they are not Canadian citizens. The LRC rejected these claims and accredited one of the three unions requested by groups of workers employed on three farms in year-round greenhouse operations. But the LRC denied the requests of the workers at the other two farms, citing a clause in the labour code that prohibits unionizing on farms that employ fewer than three workers year round (according to the terms of the SAWP, migrant workers are allowed in Canada only from 1 January to 15 December). The logic underpinning the legislation is that small "family" farmers exist, in a sense, outside of the standard capitalist economy and that the increased costs associated with improved working conditions would bankrupt growers. That some of the province's largest horticultural producers acted as spokespeople during the media campaign reveals the fallacy involved in making such claims today. The UFCW challenged this denial of their accreditation by challenging the legitimacy of seasonal farm workers' exclusion from the right to unionize. On 16 April 2010 the LRC issued its decision in favour of the farm workers, saying that the rule excluding them was unconstitutional and that, in fact, the social condition of the workers – a condition of structured inequality with their employer – made the right to organize even more important.[23] Of course, FERME and the employer have appealed the decision, so the workers are blocked for the time being.

The unionizing campaign was nevertheless an important breakthrough, bringing the situation of migrant agricultural workers into public debate. This was the result of long years of organizing, and "Hector" was a large part of these efforts. With eight seasons working on farms in Ontario and Quebec, Hector is a kind of veteran of the SAWP – and after five years of contact with CATTAQ, he knows his rights and has played a pivotal role in organizing workers on his farm. "All we ask is that they respect us," he told us in an interview in 2007:

People ask me if I am scared doing this work, and I say no! I didn't kill or rob anyone. All we are asking for is that our rights be respected. If I get fired, if they send me back to Mexico, they will know they have to respect us, as human beings.

Hector's courage is admirable given the battles he has fought. He was fired soon after union accreditation was filed and his boss learned of his organizing work. "He stopped me while I was working, which was around 5:00 PM, and told me we were going to the airport at 1:00 AM next morning," he recalled. With the support of CATTAQ, he successfully challenged the dismissal:

In the hearing, the farmer said that he would pay me for the hours that were stipulated in the contract, that he would give me all my documents back, and that he would pay for my airplane ticket – and that I would return to work for him.

Immigration Organizing

A strong critique of the SAWP and the TFWP has emerged from faith-based groups, human rights organizations like Amnesty International, activist groups such as Justicia for Migrant Workers, as well as large union federations, including the Fédération des femmes du Québec, BC Federation of Labour, Alberta Federation of Labour, and Canadian Labour Congress. Advocating policy changes is also a strategy pursued by the UFCW. Its demands include provisions in the programs for workers to apply for citizenship, tighter enforcement of the safeguards that exist on paper, and an independent third party to mediate disputes. But instead of strengthening and enforcing existing safeguards, these are being undermined by increased use of the newly expanded TFWP, a program used to hire workers not only for agriculture but also for hotels, hospitals, the Alberta tar sands, the fast food industry, construction, meat packing, and other sectors.[24]

"LOW-SKILLED" WORKERS: FEW AND FAR BETWEEN (AT LEAST IN QUEBEC) BUT ALREADY RUNNING INTO PROBLEMS

The LCP and the SAWP, despite their many documented problems, have been extremely effective at ensuring a steady supply of low-cost, compliant workers for jobs that Canadians are unwilling to take.[25] The Low-Skill Pilot Project was born in 2002, incorporating many of the restrictive measures first applied under the LCP and the SAWP. The LSPP represents an accommodation of employer demand for quick recruitment and compliant workers. Rather than supplying workers for jobs that Canadians are unwilling to fill, it is perhaps more accurate to state that the TFWP is being used to create a supply of labour on employers' terms. The LSPP was introduced in a period of rapid economic expansion and was used to fill labour demand in booming economies such as that of Alberta. Following the recession that began in 2008, however, the program experienced only a slight dip and seems to be bouncing back already.[26]

In Quebec, a province with a traditionally high level of unemployment and a large low-wage sector, the LSPP has not been heavily taken up by employers. The Immigrant Workers Centre, with a grant from the Quebec Ministry of Education, Leisure and Sport, has been preparing educational material on worker rights and has been trying to locate LSPP workers. This task has not been easy. It is estimated that there are just over 400 *nonagricultural* LSPP workers in Quebec, spread throughout the province.[27] Given their dispersion, the contact between these workers and the IWC has been limited.

Social Networking

For LCP workers and agricultural TFWs, there is a sort of ready-made basis for affiliation between them: similar workplace, dominant countries of origin, common language, same gender, and geographic concentration. Almost none of these conditions exist for nonagricultural LSPP workers. They can work in any type of workplace, can come from any country, and may not be hired in groups from the same country, meaning that they may not even share a language, and the gender mix, despite still tending to favour men, is a little more balanced. Basically, there is far from any guarantee that these workers are going to meet each other or easily feel that they have anything in common if they do. Add to this that their tiny numbers are scattered all over the province, especially outside of large urban centres, and the prospects for social networking look grim. On top of these difficulties, neither English- nor French-language competency is required, and there are no government-funded language courses. This further isolates these foreign workers from advocates and organizers, who might otherwise be available to help them contest specific injustices.

Nevertheless, LSPP workers do manage to create social networks. We have been able to identify groups of LSPP workers formed through ethnic neighbourhood connections (Filipino), churches, and general outreach and word of mouth, and in one case a worker even randomly became roommates with one of our student interns. Unlike LCP or agricultural workers, LSPP workers are more likely to live in rented private housing in the community and therefore have easier access to people not directly connected to their jobs or the government.

Labour Organizing

Despite the difficulties in identifying them, several groups of LSPP workers have been organized through the Immigrant Workers Centre. Two of the groups are from the Philippines and have connected to the IWC through contacts in the Filipino community. Another group found the centre through a personal contact with a volunteer there. When the groups approached the centre, they had already self-organized to a certain degree. For the groups from the Philippines, this self-organizing was achieved through the process of recruitment to Canada, shared workplaces, living arrangements, and connections with permanent residents in Montreal from their country. For the other group, it was a shared workplace and work-related issues that brought them together.

The latter is a group of younger workers, men and women, from many countries in Europe, recruited for their language and computer skills. They were hired by a video-gaming studio in Montreal that was contracted to translate manuals and to test the translations of major computer and videogame consoles. Unfortunately, the company was not immune to slowing contracts during the recession, and the group of twenty-eight workers faced a collective layoff without just compensation. They were able to organize themselves and approached the IWC for help. The IWC provided legal and technical information in order to file a collective grievance at the Labour Standards Board. As of April 2010, the board had accepted the case and was proceeding to take action against the employer. There are several lessons to be drawn from this situation. The TFWP is used for workers with a variety of skills and backgrounds. These particular videogame testers were highly skilled and computer literate as well as bilingual, speaking both the language of their country and English. Yet despite these skills, they had little recourse against their employer. They were treated as extensions of a computer and dumped when not needed. But because of their skills, they were able to organize themselves. They had a means of communication – e-mail and Facebook – and were able to circulate information and mobilize themselves. However, despite their mobilization and some access to limited recourse, most of them returned home.[28] Finally, even though most of the workers returned to their countries of origin, if their grievance is successful, they will still be eligible to receive compensation. For the IWC, this situation illustrates how a community-based labour rights centre, because of its reputation and on-the-ground presence as well as its ability to respond rapidly, can support workers in the TFWP to fight back in an effective way.

Especially troublesome to the workers in this case was the lack of adequate notice given to the group before the company officially laid them off. As one worker recalled,

I did understand that the economical crisis could affect me. In standard employment arrangements back home, I would get six weeks' notice that I was going to lose my job, which is also a law over there that you have to get six weeks notice. That was fair enough because in six weeks I could find something else, I could manage myself, and think about what my next step was going   /
to be.

On the other hand, at 10:00 in the morning if you call me for a meeting, and if you give me a paper that says give me back

your stuff, and they say that they will escort me back inside the building to retrieve my things, this is like an insult! At 8:00 I was free to enter there because I was working there, and then at 10:00 I was not.
– Silvia

As critics of the program maintain, the structure of the TFWP has the effect of inherently creating a cheap, flexible, and easily disposable workforce of labourers, many of whom come to work on any given day not knowing whether it will be their last.

In addition to the videogame translators' case, the IWC has two ongoing cases of male Filipino TFWs facing employment and immigration problems. The first group works in landscaping. In several cases, workers were initially contracted to an employer in Alberta but were sent by their initial recruitment agency (a major multinational corporation) to work in Quebec when they were laid off in Alberta. They were living in crowded conditions in an apartment building that happened to have an active member of PINAY as one of the tenants. They met as neighbours, but when the PINAY member heard about their difficult work situation, she referred them to the IWC. The issues they faced were multiple. In terms of the nature of the work, the workers found the conditions to be unhealthy, the pay low, and the supervision disrespectful. Access to healthcare was a problem for some of them as well. Of most concern to them, however, was that they ended up working fewer months than promised and were expected to return to the Philippines to sit out the "down" period before returning for the next year's season. The problems with the return to the Philippines were that they had not made enough money yet to be able to reimburse the moneylenders waiting for them in their home communities, they felt unsure that the employer would really call them back, they expected to have to pay new fees to the recruitment agency in order to process their new visas (some reported as much as $15,000), and they resented not being able to collect employment insurance (EI), as would their Québécois colleagues (despite having paid into the EI plan at the same rate). The IWC worked with this group to try to help them decide what to do at the end of the season. Some of the workers returned to the Philippines and were eventually called back (but we are still waiting to hear what happened to them at home), some tried to find new work in Montreal, some returned to Alberta in the hopes of finding more work, and one went to Ottawa to be in the same town as his fiancée, who was working under the LCP, but he has been unable to find new work. As far as we have heard, none of those who remained in Canada were able to find new LSPP positions, a situation that pushes them into undocumented work and takes away any eventual prospects of being permanent in Canada or being joined there by their families. Over the years, the employer has decided to diversify his source of workers, expanding it to other continents and language groups, a sign of how easily "troublesome" workers can be replaced.

The second group from the Philippines was brought to Montreal to work in the telecommunications industry. This company had won a long dispute with its union, leading to the union's disbandment, and was now in a position to find cheaper, short-term workers through subcontracting. These workers came into contact with the IWC through their connection with the Filipino Workers' Support Group (FWSG), a self-organized activist group. One of these workers simply met a member of the FWSG while shopping in Côte-des-Neiges, and they started chatting about their work. When these workers first came to the IWC, their interest was in finding out how they could become permanent residents in Quebec. When we looked at their work permits, however, we saw that, despite the fact that they were all doing the same job, some of the workers had LSPP permits and some had permits with a high National Occupational Classification (NOC) of A or B. This difference in work permit was critical since those with higher classifications would be able to apply for permanent residency in Quebec after twelve months of work (recently increased from six months), whereas those with the LSPP permits would be excluded. This discovery created much consternation within the group, and they began working to see about changing the NOC category for the LSPP workers so that they could also apply after twelve months of work. However, totally unexpectedly, their company told them that they were being transferred to work in Central America! These workers, reliant on the income, had no choice but to leave Canada, even though this turn of events seemed to take away the possibility of accumulating twelve months of Quebec work experience. At the time of writing, they were working to see what options they had in the face of this disempowering situation.

These examples demonstrate the role that the IWC can play in supporting and organizing temporary foreign workers. It is the presence of a centre on the ground able to respond quickly and to mobilize and educate people living under the conditions of the TFWP that can help them to fight back and build alliances with allies in the union movement. At the same time, the extreme precariousness of LSPP workers and their high mobility have posed serious barriers for effective labour organization.

Immigration Organizing

Immigration organizing is by far the weakest domain among LSPP workers. We are unaware of any immigration campaigns being organized by LSPP workers themselves or even with LSPP workers as active participants. Since their permits are limited to short terms and depend on their employers, it seems difficult to involve LSPP workers in such campaigns. Concerned community groups, unions, and provincial and federal coalitions are slowly stepping to the fore as allies in demanding, first, better conditions for LSPP workers and, second, the right for workers to come to Canada fully equal and with permanent status.

At the community level, activist groups were the first to make LSPP workers a central concern, with the national network of No One Is Illegal and/or Justicia for Migrant Workers chapters taking on this issue. National ethnic associations, such as the Filipino MIGRANTE Canada, have also taken up the cause. Later to come to the organizing table were settlement agencies. Current federal and provincial settlement funding excludes LSPP workers, yet many of them have found their way to immigrant and refugee aid organizations. Several provincial and federal settlement agency coalitions, including Quebec's Council of Immigrant and Refugee-Serving Organizations[29] and the influential Canadian Council of Refugees,[30] have spoken out on the topic, defending the rights of LSPP workers.

Unions have also been active on this issue as a principle of solidarity with all workers but also since LSPP workers are sometimes implicated in union-busting efforts. The UFCW has been leading the charge on this nationally in terms of public education and campaigning, but the Alberta Federation of Labour has been innovative in terms of analysis and services for LSPP workers. The Canadian Labour Congress has also been pushing for a more active campaign on the issue and is involved in putting lobbying pressure on the federal government. Although a full campaign to change the LSPP and the structure of the TFWP more generally has yet to be deployed, more and more groups have come to the conclusion that social networking and labour organizing will remain severely limited as long as LSPP workers remain under the constant threat of immediate deportation.

CONCLUSION

In this chapter we have discussed how workers in different programs of the TFWP are able to organize and work for better social and economic conditions. This organizing takes place despite huge barriers. In fact, all of the programs to bring low-skilled temporary workers to Canada have as an underlying assumption that the workers will be compliant and respond to labour needs of employers regardless of the type of work. The specific barriers to organizing include the nature of their work and issues of immigration status.

The nature of their work makes it difficult for low-skilled TFWs to organize. Often the workplace is isolated geographically or is in a private home, and housing is often tied to an employer. The work itself can be dangerous, low-paid, and (even though in theory workers are contracted for a specific length of time) precarious. Farm work, for example, is among the most dangerous occupations in Canada with respect to workplace injury and death;[31] and domestic workers in Quebec are excluded from workers' compensation.[32] Further, because recruitment agencies play a central role in many workers' relationships with the employer, there is an extra layer of control over a worker's situation.

Immigration status issues are central to TFWs' experience of work in Canada and shape their options in defending their rights through collective action. Without permanent status, there is always a risk hanging over them that they can be sent back or not have their contracts renewed for contesting their situations – something reported often in our interviews. These forces clearly discourage TFWs from contesting workplace or immigration injustices.

Although the nature of their work and their immigration status are factors that make it difficult for TFWs to organize, our research has also documented many positive developments in the struggle. Below are some of the lessons that we have learned about successful approaches, processes, and strategies.

Organizing begins with relationship building and support between TFWs themselves. Earlier in the chapter, we discussed different forms of building solidarity and connections. These include connections between people from the same country, who share language, culture, and similar stakes in their work and status. Sharing the process of recruitment and, in the case of SAWP and LSPP workers, sharing a common workplace are key elements. Organizations that provide a bridge between workers and their organizers and allies are also important. These include churches and cultural organizations. The connection to organizing groups is essential as a means to challenge working conditions. For all of the reasons we have outlined, unionization is extremely difficult with TFWs, except for LSPP workers, who may be hired into already unionized workplaces. Community unionism or community-based labour organizing has become an adopted strategy, as it is a means to interact with people outside of work and to build strategies that allow workers both to challenge their employers without unionization and, with allies, to campaign for policy changes that affect work and immigration. The organizations discussed above bring experience, knowledge, and organizing skills to the task of helping workers to improve their situations. They also have a presence that continues even though many of those under the TFWP are in Canada for relatively short stays. Community-based organizations such as PINAY, the UFCW's support centre, and the IWC provide a safe place for workers to discuss their situations, discover their rights, and decide whether or not to take action. In the case of PINAY, the leadership is from those who have lived the experience of the LCP; in addition, they have built cohesion of their group through a variety of social and cultural activities. Finally, beyond organizing with specific groups of TFWs, building alliances to expose and challenge the conditions of both work and migration has been essential. This alliance building has led to a much greater public understanding of these programs and to the identification of allies within public and para-public institutions such as the Labour Standards Board. Due to increased public awareness of the impact of these programs on workers themselves and on the wider society, workers who take action through the organizations we have discussed find wider support encouraging more action. As more people challenge their employers and exercise their rights, employer control is challenged in terms of work hours, language, and lack of long-term status in Canada. Finally, challenging conditions in the workplace is difficult enough, but there is a broader understanding among organizers, advocates, and allied organizations that the main issue is status. Without permanent residency in Canada, there is an underlying injustice regardless of working conditions. The longer-term objective and demand has been shaped by the slogan "Good Enough to Work? Good Enough to Stay!"

How Does Canada Fare? Canadian Temporary Labour Migration in Comparative Perspective

PATTI TAMARA LENARD

Canada is not alone in turning to temporary labour migrants to fill labour shortages. Across continents, states are choosing to do the same in great numbers, and their motivations for increasing the number of temporary labour migration opportunities are more or less uniform: first, acute labour shortages, along with the belief that relying on temporary migration is a flexible and efficient way to fill these shortages, and second, increasing anti-immigrant sentiment, which encourages governments to remedy labour shortages in ways that at least appear to avoid exacerbating domestic anti-immigrant hostility.[1] The global economic environment, characterized as it is by significant wealth disparities across borders, makes temporary labour migration attractive for citizens of poor states as well. As a result of the global increase in temporary labour migration and increased attention to the plight of temporary labour migrants, we are increasingly treated to reports of the violence and exploitation to which temporary migrants are subject. In Japan, Chinese "trainees" have been forced into slave labour conditions, under the guise of transferring technological expertise; in Israel, attempts to deport the children of temporary foreign migrants, who have never even visited the countries to which they may be deported, are attracting worldwide critical attention; in Kuwait, Nepali domestic workers have been seeking shelter at their embassies in order to escape the virtually indentured servitude that is expected of them by their employers.[2] As these incidents highlight, temporary labour migrants are among the most vulnerable of workers.

The purpose of this chapter is to place the Canadian experience with temporary labour migration programs in a wider, global context in order to illustrate that the pressures and challenges facing Canada as it experiments with these programs are not unique. I argue that, although it may appear Canada does well by its temporary labour migrants, we should be disappointed that, unlike in the past with respect to immigration more generally, Canada is refusing to be a leader in this domain. The Canadian government has unfortunately become preoccupied with securing the temporariness of labour migrants rather than focusing on the best ways to ensure that these essential contributors to our economy can transition smoothly and quickly to Canadian citizenship.

I begin with an outline of the global processes that have led to the increasing worldwide reliance on labour migrants. I outline in very broad terms the role of temporary migration in national immigration schemes in the traditional immigrant-receiving states, in western Europe, and in parts of Asia.[3] I then outline an ongoing concern with respect to what Philip Martin claimed many years ago: "there is nothing more permanent than a temporary foreign worker."[4] Assessments of past temporary work programs, particularly the American "*bracero*" program and the German postwar guest worker program, highlight the frequency with which those who were admitted transitioned either to irregular migrant status or to full membership over time. As a result, contemporary guest worker programs are generally designed to exclude labour migrants from membership *and* from long-term illegal residence. Finally, I compare the states' strategies to ensure that temporary migrants remain temporary, particularly with respect to the policies they deploy to encourage migrants to leave at the conclusion of their contracts. As we shall see in this section, the strategies vary in their coerciveness and therefore also with respect to whether they can be relied upon in countries committed to liberal-democratic principles. I conclude by arguing that Canada's commitment to liberal-democratic principles, alongside its historical commitment to immigration, suggests that it ought to radically rethink its recent embrace of temporary labour migration programs, or at least that it should be working harder to mitigate the negative consequences that historical experience with these programs suggests are likely to emerge.

GLOBAL TRENDS IN TEMPORARY LABOUR MIGRATION

As I said, Canada is not alone in embracing temporary labour migration; wealthy nations around the world have turned to temporary labour migration as an efficient way to respond to domestic labour market shortages. The turn to temporary labour migration is facilitated by improvements in communication technologies that put potential labour migrants in touch with employers seeking them, by improvements in transportation technologies that lower the cost of transporting migrants to labour markets where they are needed and returning them home upon completion of their contracts, and by an increasingly coordinated global economic system that allows the easy transfer of funds from migrants to home countries.[5]

It is alleged by a wide range of industries that access to temporary labour migrants is essential to maintaining a competitive position in the global economic market. Temporary labour migrants provide a "just-in-time" workforce that can respond to the needs of a flexible and ever-changing labour market. Industries in Canada, aided by the Canadian government, can hire temporary labour migrants quickly (the issuance of temporary labour market visas is extraordinarily speedy and getting speedier) and can reduce the number of workers they employ in response to changing economic conditions as needed. In this sense, as Kerry Priebisch and Jenna Hennebry describe in chapter 2 of this volume, temporary labour migrants are treated as commodities – as entities to be consumed and discarded as needed.

Yet there is a kind of tension here. As Piyasiri Wickramasekara observes, "while there has been greater integration of global markets for goods, services and capital across borders, its impact on the cross-border movement of people and labour remains much more restricted, regulated by a complex web of immigration laws and policies that uphold the principle of state sovereignty."[6] Thus, as Patricia Tomic and Ricardo Trumper observe in chapter 3, although the expansion of temporary labour migration programs has facilitated the movement of individuals across borders, the conditions of this movement are highly constrained. In particular, the migrants who labour in advanced economies do so with limited prospects of gaining full access to membership in return for their essential contributions to the economy. The economic demands that press governments to provide a flexible workforce to sustain its industries are mediated by the desire to restrict full entry of these migrants into the larger community. As a result, in most cases, central governments maintain strict control of these migrants, often in conjunction with host countries, rendering these migrants effectively a "captive workforce" with little control over the conditions that govern their working lives.[7] As Preibisch has noted, "immigration policy has thus become an increasingly important arena for regulating the labor markets of high income economies and ensuring their position within the global political economy."[8]

That temporary labour migration programs are able to contribute to the competitiveness of wealthy nation-states stems directly from the vast material inequalities that separate wealthy nations from poor nations: citizens of poor nations are often desperate to migrate in pursuit of improved economic opportunities. The fact of the matter is that, even in the face of these restrictive and often exploitative conditions, these opportunities appear to poor migrants to be far better than they can access in their home countries or via illegal channels.[9] Yet, as the title of this book signals, these programs in effect "legislate the inequality" of temporary labour migrants, not just in Canada but also across all states. It is their material desperation, a condition inflicted on them as a result of global power dynamics, that prompts their willingness to participate in programs that institutionalize their vulnerable status and enable their exploitation.

Canada as a Traditional Immigrant State

The so-called immigrant states – Canada, the United States, New Zealand, and Australia – have typically relied on immigration of all kinds as part of their nation-building projects.[10] The mass migration of citizens from Europe, who migrated to escape poverty and religious persecution or just for adventure, has been essential to building the economy and infrastructure of these countries; more recent migration from Asian and African countries continues to support the economies in all of them. As a result, they have typically been relatively comfortable with integrating large numbers of migrants and have sustained national narratives that celebrate tolerance and respect for diversity.[11] Moreover, these narratives have persisted in spite of the adoption of discriminatory immigration policies – policies that have at times limited the admission of Asian migrants, for example, or required them to pay a fee in exchange for the privilege of entry.

In the "traditional" immigrant-receiving states, this comfort with state-controlled permanent migration – migration that has been foundational to them – has translated in complicated ways into the adoption of temporary migration policies. As outlined in the introduction to this volume, the Canadian immigration system has been constructed to privilege high-skilled (or at least wealthy) immigrants, as well as those who are fluent in one of the national languages. This tightly controlled admission of wealthy, or educated, or at least linguistically competent migrants, for whom the costs of integration are relatively low (as they are for the receiving society), is central to Canada's success as an immigrant nation. Canada's migrants statistically do very well economically (they are often wealthier than non-immigrant Canadians), as a result of which they generally do not occupy the bottom rung of society and therefore do not attract the ire of those who might, otherwise, be inclined to criticize immigrants on racist or other grounds. The preference for attracting high-skilled workers, and enabling them to integrate quickly, is not unique to Canada or to traditional immigrant-receiving nations in general – it is a global preference, which fuels worldwide competition for high-skilled migrants.

For the first time in 2008, the number of temporary migrants admitted to Canada exceeded the number of permanent migrants admitted to Canada. Of these temporary migrants, most continue to be high- rather low-skilled; however, the proportion of low-skilled migrants admitted is increasing every year and is likely to continue to do so. As the contributors to this volume observe, Canadian temporary labour migration programs target low-skilled workers in a range of sectors, including agriculture, caregiving, and service. Although the contributors are critical of all low-skilled programs, at least two of them – the Seasonal Agricultural Worker Program and the Live-in Caregiver Program – are sometimes considered to be models of best practices given the twin aims of temporary labour migration programs, namely to provide needed services and to prevent permanent migration. The two newest programs – the Provincial/Territorial Nominee Program and the Low-Skill Pilot Project – are criticized for their complicated bureaucracy and for their ambiguity with respect to the possibilities for accessing permanent residency.

Although the Canadian government has promised to limit temporary work visas to four years (and thus to ensure that migrants do not reside for extended periods of time in Canada), this change has not yet been enacted, and immigration reform is no longer at the forefront of the agenda.[12] The worry is that the government's reluctance to act to formally limit migrants' stays stems at least in part from its desire to support policies that are (allegedly) best for Canadian industry rather than best for the migrant worker or Canadian society more generally. Because ever fearful of deportation or of being refused future work contracts, long-term resident migrants remain highly vulnerable to exploitative practices ranging from unsafe working conditions to abusive labour practices. In particular, they are not likely to complain about low pay and demands to work overtime, and they are thus ideal workers for Canadian industries concerned only with their profit margin. Yet Canadians should feel discomfort with attempting to justify the legitimacy of relying, economically, on migrants who are barred from citizenship. As Olivia Chow has noted, "Canada is a country built by immigrants, not by migrant workers."[13] Temporary migration programs, especially those that target low-skilled workers, fit uncomfortably into the Canadian national narrative, as the introduction to this volume outlines.

Migration in Europe

European countries face immigration pressures that distinguish them in many ways from the immigrant states in general and from Canada in particular. Modern European countries were by and large fully formed without immigration, as a result of which immigration was rather late to emerge as a subject of national consideration and concern.[14] At least since the Second World War, migration within and to Europe – unlike in the immigration states – has been perceived as temporary and driven by labour shortages in European nations. Migration was encouraged in many western European nations after the Second World War; many migrants came to rebuild the western European economies, many from southern or eastern European nations.[15] In most cases, the migration was intended to be temporary – and in most cases, it turned out to be less temporary than intended. Although the German guest worker program (discussed in more detail below) is best known, temporary migrants were invited in across Europe to rebuild economies devastated by war. The programs were terminated in the mid-1970s as unemployment rose, and although the migrants were encouraged to return home, many stayed on in Europe as second-class citizens – that is, as noncitizen residents without the full complement of rights to which citizens are entitled.[16] Over time, many industries had become dependent on migrant labour, and it eventually became clear that "temporary workers were being recruited to meet permanent labour demand."[17] Not only were these migrants often encouraged by their employers to remain, but European courts also enabled their expanded access to rights as the length of their residency increased. This trend has been well observed around the world: entire industries quickly become dependent on the cheap foreign labour that temporary labour programs provide, and they do so in ways that make it tremendously difficult to deny the permanence of migrants admitted in principle on only a temporary basis.[18]

The fear that European nations will again prove unable to control migration – as a result of which European states will again be forced, by virtue of the inevitable expansion of rights that accompanies long-term residency, to admit temporary migrants as full citizens – in large part explains the European reluctance to turn now to temporary labour migration to fill acute labour shortages, especially in "low-skilled" industries. As in Canada, labour markets across Europe face acute shortages, and the "projected demand for labor of all skill levels" is set to increase markedly over the coming years. For now, however, the number of temporary migration programs that target low-skilled workers remains low; the fear that it will ultimately prove impossible, as it has done in the past, to secure the "temporariness" of labour migrants has stymied governments, which, although aware that there are labour shortages in need of filling, have shied away from the political challenges associated with proposing temporary labour migration programs.[19] Instead, proposals focus on ways that low-skilled labour shortages can be met via inter-European migration; in an assessment of temporary migration programs in the United Kingdom, for example, Stephen Castles observes the United Kingdom's stated intention to eliminate low-skilled migration from outside of Europe, even in the face of demographic changes that suggest doing so will be impossible. The apparent unwillingness of European states to consider legal channels for low-skilled migration (such channels for high-skilled migration are already widely in effect since high-skilled migrants are not thought to pose integration challenges) will, says Castles, only encourage "undocumented migration, and the high risk and exploitation that such migration brings for the workers concerned."[20]

Debates about immigration and integration in Europe are additionally confused by an increase in migrants crossing borders from Africa into southern Europe to request asylum. Europe is now struggling to develop an integrated asylum policy that will treat these migrants, and the states who admit them, fairly, but it is doing so in a political environment characterized by loud, and sizable, xenophobic voices represented in the proliferation of right-wing political parties. These migrants are suspected by many of making spurious refugee claims, of being "merely" economic migrants, and of seeking access to labour markets in Europe or, worse, access to the generous welfare policies to which legitimate refugees are entitled.[21] The belief that these migrants intend to take advantage of generous welfare-state policies is exacerbated by the apparent ease with which refugee claimants can access these services, even as they are banned from (or are claimed to be uninterested in) accessing the labour market. In response to this outside pressure to be let in, European states have witnessed the growth of political parties that are capitalizing on the fear that these migrants will take jobs from "real" Europeans. These migrants are accused additionally of threatening the cultural unity and social cohesion of European societies, which in turn allegedly weakens the welfare state that so many European countries are concerned to protect. European publics (facilitated by sensationalizing media) have been quick to conflate the dilemmas posed by temporary labour migrants and by poor asylum claimants.

The Gulf States, South Asia, and South East Asia

Migration policy in the Asian countries differs considerably from migration policy in Europe and the traditional immigrant-receiving nations. In general, Asian countries have not encouraged permanent migration; instead, although the region is characterized by extensive migration, nearly all of it is (or is considered to be) temporary.[22] Ranging from Japan to Singapore to Malaysia to the Persian Gulf States, the Asian nations protect against permanent migration, largely by treating labour migrants (especially low-skilled migrants) as expendable – that is, as disposable "when convenient."[23] The harsh policies pursued by Asian immigrant-receiving states typically "do not allow settlement of what is commonly defined as 'unskilled' labour."[24] Asian nations are less concerned to respect the "rights" to which the people who perform the necessary labour may be entitled and are aggressive in asserting their sovereign right to control membership.[25]

Many Asian economies rely heavily on temporary foreign labour both as senders and as receivers of foreign labour migrants.[26] On the one hand, the Philippines and, to a lesser extent, Indonesia are actively promoting the migration of their citizens as development policy. The Philippines in particular is well known for aggressively encouraging the temporary out-migration of its citizens to optimize the development benefits that can be reaped from the remittances they send home. One important consequence is the extensive involvement of the Filipino state in the life of its migrants and thus the existence of Filipino-dominated nongovernmental organizations around the world that lobby to have the rights of migrants respected and that offer support to those whose rights have been violated.[27]

On the other hand, the rapid economic development of the Gulf States – Saudi Arabia, Oman, Qatar, Bahrain, Kuwait, and the United Arab Emirates – has relied extensively on temporary migrants willing to labour in a host of industries, including homecare, manufacturing, plantation work, and construction.[28] The number of temporary foreign migrants residing in the Gulf States, many on a long-term basis, reveals the depth of these states' dependence on foreign labour. In 2004 it was estimated that 12 million foreign migrants lived in the Gulf States (37 per cent of the Gulf States' total population). Oman has the lowest proportion of migrants, with only a 23 per cent foreign population, and the others range from this low to 76 per cent in the United Arab Emirates. When considered as a proportion of the workforce population, the numbers are even more astonishing: in Saudi Arabia, for example, it has been estimated that foreign migrants comprise 70 per cent of the total workforce and 95 per cent of the workforce in the private sector and that in the United Arab Emirates foreign migrants make up 98 per cent of private-sector jobs (in many of the Gulf States, the public sector is closed to foreign migrant workers, and nationals look down on private-sector employment).[29]

However, the region has consistently expressed discomfort with the scale of temporary migration, largely for "cultural reasons." At first, the Gulf States encouraged migration from nearby Arab nations, with whom they felt cultural affinity.[30] The initial thought had been that Arab, Muslim migrants, although temporary, would provide the least culturally disruptive form of labour. Yet, over time, the Gulf States worried that the pan-Arabic, and often secular, views of the migrants would instead dilute the rather strict Muslim cultural commitments that characterized them. In response, the governments actively pursued migrants from southeast Asian and south Asian nations, who are now the dominant participants in the Gulf States' temporary migration programs.[31] However, the states continue to fear the negative cultural influences of these migrants, and several of them have begun to aggressively pursue "indigenizing" polices (described in more detail below) that are intended to reduce the dependence of certain industries on foreign labour migrants. Similarly, both Singapore (with a foreign population of 30 per cent)[32] and Malaysia are actively concerned with discouraging temporary migrants from integrating permanently into society. In Singapore, it is frequently noted, domestic care workers are not permitted to marry Singaporean citizens and are forced to submit to twice yearly pregnancy tests; a positive test results in immediate deportation.

The "cultural" concern also dominates the immigration debates in two other Asian countries – Japan and to a lesser extent Korea – and in Israel. At least historically, permanent migration to Israel has been, by law, exclusively Jewish. The Israeli Law of Return has granted Jews living outside of Israel preferential immigration status so that

they can gain near-immediate Israeli citizenship if they choose to
reside there. The role that is now played by temporary foreign workers (providing low-skilled, poorly remunerated labour) had historically been played by Palestinians; as migration from the West Bank
and Gaza into Israel became more difficult, Israeli employers began
looking elsewhere to fill their labour shortages. From 1993 Israel
began relying on temporary foreign labour migration; this relatively
recent increase in temporary migrants, who are not Jewish by ancestry (or conversion), has challenged the national narrative in Israel
in ways that have placed the status of temporary foreign migrants
in Israel at the centre of political debate.[33] Recently, the Israeli government chose to grant permanent status to the children of foreign
migrants, which means they can apply for citizenship once they have
carried out mandatory military training. In the interim, their parents have been granted leave to remain and have been promised formal status in Israel once their children have become citizens. At the
same time, however, the Israeli government announced its intention
to deport the children of irregular migrants at the end of the 2011
school year. For some, the recent changes in Israel illustrate a movement toward accepting newcomers as at least partial members and
are thus a victory for migrant rights advocates, who have worked to
press the Israeli government into loosening its control over membership.[34] For others, the partial status – and the indignities suffered as
a result of this partial status, including the ongoing risk of deportation and the exclusion from political life – is a source of worry;
without citizenship status, these migrants remain vulnerable to the
whims of Israeli political decisions.[35]

   Although (unlike Israel) Japan doesn't consider itself to be an
immigration state, it is facing similar pressures as a result of having
invited in "guest workers" of Japanese ancestry from Latin America
to labour in low-skilled jobs. Formally, Japan does not have a guest
worker program. Rather, it has exploited a visa issued to enable
"family reunification": this visa enables the Nikkejin population –
Latin American citizens of Japanese ancestry – to return to Japan,
and those who took advantage of this visa were quickly employed
in low-skilled occupations with the status of de facto guest workers. These migrants can, with considerable difficulty, transition to
Japanese citizenship, but they are being aggressively encouraged to

return to Latin America now that the economy is doing less well (these return strategies are outlined below).[36]

WHEN TEMPORARY LABOUR MIGRATION ISN'T SO TEMPORARY AFTER ALL

The contemporary response to temporary labour migration is shaped most by two programs: (1) the German guest worker program, which ran from 1955 to 1973 and which invited citizens from southern Europe, the majority of whom were Turkish, to contribute to the rebuilding of postwar Germany; and (2) the American bracero program, which ran from 1942 to 1964 and which, at first, responded to the labour shortages caused by the increasing number of American men serving in the Second World War and, subsequently, supported the American agricultural industry after the war came to an end.[37] During the lifetimes of these programs, the governments of both Germany and the United States expressed satisfaction with their contributions to the national economy. Many of the challenges posed by these programs emerged in full force only *after* they came to an end.[38] In both cases, the employers who had worked with temporary migrants were only too happy to oblige when their workers turned irregular; they had become dependent on the cheap labour that temporary labour migrants had provided, and even though the programs themselves had stopped, the disincentives associated with hiring irregular migrants were low (especially in the United States). Thus one lesson about the historical experience of guest work programs has been this: the closure of long-run and highly successful (in terms of providing much desired access to a labour market) guest work programs tends to produce irregular migrants. As a result, both Germany and the United States were ultimately faced with a long-term migrant population that chose to remain, in some capacity, in the host countries,[39] and in both cases, many of those admitted as temporary were ultimately granted citizenship. The granting of German citizenship to long-term resident Turks was part of moving away from an emphasis on shared ethnicity as the sole legitimate indicator of Germanness and toward accepting the multi-ethnicity of the German nation.[40] Although there is ongoing controversy – manifested most recently in tough new immigration laws under contestation in Arizona – about the role of Hispanic Americans in the United States, the granting of American citizenship to irregular workers did not demand a similar reimagining of the foundation of American citizenship.[41]

States have also noted that one way to control irregular migrants may be by implementing a well-managed guest worker program and permitting migrants to transition from irregular to legal guest worker status without penalty: "a basic principle is that undocumented migration can best be avoided by providing the mechanisms and incentives for legal entry."[42] For example, Taiwan's decision to legalize already resident irregular care workers in the 1990s arose from the belief that "the existent illegal migrant worker population could be better managed and more effectively monitored if they were legalized,"[43] and the same motivation has produced the legalization of many irregular migrants in Italy and Spain.[44] Likewise, a concern about the hiring of irregular migrants prompted a shift in the regulations of Canada's Seasonal Agricultural Worker Program. The program, initially open only to citizens of Caribbean countries (from 1966), was tremendously popular with both employers and migrant workers and initially insufficient to provide for the labour needs of the Canadian agricultural industry. As a result, Canadian farmers chose to hire Mexican citizens working illegally in Canada. In response, "to dry up the pool of unauthorized workers and insure respect for labor standards, the government extended the program in 1974 to include Mexican workers."[45] Similarly, President George W. Bush's attempt at immigration overhaul in the United States was based partly on the idea that expanded guest worker opportunities might serve to stem the tide of illegal migrants from Mexico and, moreover, partly on the idea that it would be in the American interest to enable some of the presently residing irregular migrants to transition to legal guest worker status so that they could participate in these new programs. The Bush immigration proposals were not ultimately passed; among many political hurdles that they failed to overcome was the impression that the proposals were nothing more than "amnesty," which in effect would reward individuals for breaking American immigration laws and thus would encourage others to do the same in the hopes that they too would ultimately be deemed worthy of inclusion.[46]

At issue, then, is whether contemporary guest worker programs can be designed in such a way as to produce the alleged benefit of filling labour shortages without producing the alleged burden of temporary migrants transitioning to permanent status, either legally or through irregular means.

POLICIES TO ENSURE THE TEMPORARINESS OF TEMPORARY WORKERS

Among the lessons from these two experiments with guest workers is that states must manage the "temporariness" of their migrant workers carefully: the claim that the residency of migrants entitles them to citizenship gains force, and significantly so, over time.[47] In response, as the comparative analysis below reveals, states deploy a range of strategies to ensure that migrants remain temporary. For one thing, states issue temporary visas, which are intended to expire and thus to force their holders to return home. The following analysis also reveals that the importance of securing this temporary status can vary by state. It is not surprising that the importance that a state places on securing the temporary status of migrant workers correlates with more aggressive attempts to do so. In general, to the extent that states are liberal and democratic, they choose against pursuing the harshest of tactics to ensure temporariness; that said, even liberal-democratic states are not immune to political pressures to appear to be doing something about migration and thus occasionally resort to the harshest of tactics – that is, the forceful detainment and deportation of irregular migrants. Although the right to deport temporary labour migrants whose visas have lapsed, and who have therefore transitioned to irregular status, is acknowledged as a right of sovereign states, it is generally perceived to be the most coercive, and objectionable, mechanism by which to ensure the removal of migrants from one's territory. Those who oppose forceful deportation point to how frequently it breaks up families, destroys the livelihoods of otherwise law-abiding citizens, and so on. Despite the tendency of liberal-democratic states to respect migrant rights (although the contributors to this volume are clear that rights violations transpire even in liberal-democratic countries), they too often feel forced to exert their state sovereignty rights with respect to controlling membership, even when doing so violates migrant rights.

Types of Temporary Labour Migration Visas/Contracts

What unites all temporary migrant labour programs is, as Martin Ruhs has observed, that whether workers who enter as temporary migrants can attain permanent status in the host country is at the host country's discretion.[48] Technically, this feature does not distinguish temporary visas from permanent ones – since the granting of permanent residency leading to naturalization is at the discretion of the granting government as well. Visas issued to migrants to labour temporarily in a given state typically do not permit them to apply for the right to stay permanently. There are myriad formally temporary visas, with too many specific conditions to enumerate helpfully here.[49] However, we can usefully distinguish among types.

One reason the Canadian Live-in Caregiver Program is thought to be exceptional, and therefore a model for emulation, is that although formally temporary, it allows women who have completed their work requirements to attain permanent residency, and eventually citizenship, in Canada. As Abigail Bakan and Daiva Stasiulis outline in chapter 9, as do Sara Torres and her co-authors in chapter 10, the conditions of this program require women to carry out domestic labour as a resident in the home of an employer; once they have done so for a sufficient amount of time, they are entitled to apply for permanent residency and are no longer required to work in the domestic care industry.[50] The transition from temporary to permanent visa is however marred by bureaucratic hurdles that are to the detriment of the caregivers. As Torres and her co-authors observe, for example, Canadian immigration authorities are often unnecessarily slow in issuing work visas to those women who have completed the terms of their service, thereby posing obstacles to their pursuit of employment outside of the caregiving industry and to their overall social and economic integration.

More generally, in many western European states (e.g., the United Kingdom, France, Switzerland, Spain, and so on), there exists a kind of renewable visa, extended to temporary labour migrants in specific industries. Once migrants have been residing in the country for an extended period, they are often permitted to apply for the right to join the polity in question. The Canadian Provincial/Territorial Nominee Program allows provinces to create programs structured in this way. Whether temporary migrants can transition to permanent status is for now largely at the discretion of the provincial governments; whereas Manitoba has created a program with clear rules that enable the relatively smooth transition to permanent status, as Tom Carter outlines in chapter 8, nominees in all other provinces are struggling to understand the possibilities available to them, if at all, for joining Canada permanently. As Delphine Nakache and Sarah D'Aoust observe in chapter 7, the laws governing the process by which temporary labour migrants can attain permanent residence are often hidden and thus difficult to access. The result is that whether permanent residency can be attained is partly a matter of the province in which a migrant has been hired (if not Manitoba, a migrant is most likely to be successful in New Brunswick and Newfoundland and Labrador) and partly a matter of luck in discovering the routes through which this transition is possible. The result is a haphazard set of rules that appears to treat migrants arbitrarily, based on the location of their labour in Canada.

Seasonal agricultural programs are in operation in many countries, and they typically extend visas, which are expressly limited to the duration of the agricultural season and require that migrants return home during the off-season. These programs vary, particularly with respect to whether they permit and encourage migrants who have participated in the program to return. In the most "successful" cases – from the perspective of states trying to ensure that migrants return home – it was observed early that there are two benefits of permitting and encouraging the return of migrant workers:[51] first, the employers appreciate the opportunity to employ the same migrants year after year since the costs associated with teaching the relevant skills decrease; and second, the risk of migrants overstaying visas is considerably lower when they feel confident that they will not be denied an opportunity to return.[52] The security of future employment in the host country, in other words, appears to positively correlate with the willingness of migrants to return home after completing their temporary labour. To some extent, then, these programs might be defended for the agency that they appear to offer migrants since they can be rewarded for competent work with additional contracts in the future. Yet this agency is highly constrained since even if migrants work hard and return home willingly at the completion of their contract, the opportunity to return is ultimately not guaranteed but is instead at the discretion of the employer and of both the sending and receiving states' governments. As a result, migrants remain highly vulnerable to the whims of their employers and immigration officials in the host country. In some cases, migrants can rely on their own state representatives to lobby on their behalf. Yet, as Christine Hughes illustrates in chapter 6 in the case of Guatemalan agricultural workers in Quebec, state representatives are often underequipped or inadequately motivated to do so. On the contrary, sending states are often motivated to ensure the compliance of their own migrants in order to protect the more general capacity of the state to place their citizens in lucrative overseas work opportunities.

The Persian Gulf States are motivated differently, as described above, as a result of which the "temporary" aspect of the temporary programs is monitored carefully. Even though many guest workers reside in Gulf States for extended periods of time on temporary visas, which are renewable, they appear to have no interest in considering the incorporation of these migrants as full citizens. Contracts are often granted in two-year increments and thus require constant renewal. Recent research indicates that migrants are often resident in Gulf countries for over twenty years. As Nasra Shah writes, "migrant workers are typically not entitled to citizenship by virtue of length of stay in the [Gulf] states. Also, children born in the country are not entitled to citizenship."[53] Similarly, many south and southeast Asian states are reluctant to offer migrants, especially low-skilled workers, opportunities to transition to permanent status.[54] Unlike European states and the traditional immigrant-receiving states, the Gulf States are not moved by the suggestion that residency can, over time, generate a morally weighty claim to full membership. For them, it is clear that state sovereignty rights take absolute precedence over whatever human rights migrants may be said to have or to acquire over time.

Policies to Encourage Temporary Migrants to Return Home
(Rather than Transition to Irregularity)

The freedom either to implement harsh and rights-violating strategies in order to secure the temporariness of migrants or to remove them forcefully is a "luxury" that is limited to nondemocratic countries. In liberal-democratic states, the commitment to the protection of rights has extended, sometimes only in limited ways, to protecting migrants (at least in theory if not always in practice). Migrants, even when temporary, are acknowledged to have a wide range of human rights that require protection.[55] As Ruhs has observed, "the political system may impose certain limits on the range of available" strategies for managing temporary labour migrants: "one may, for example, expect liberal democracies to find it more difficult to restrict the rights of temporary foreign workers (and especially to forcefully deport foreign workers) than countries that do not readily qualify as liberal democracies."[56] In liberal-democratic states, the courts have often required that many rights be extended to migrants, and moreover, liberal-democratic states frequently feel pressure to expand the rights to which these migrants become entitled over time – for example, the right to family reunification, which has been protected by the German courts for temporary migrants labouring in Germany.[57] Historically, as Stephen Castles notes, "in liberal democratic societies, governments could not simply expel legally resident foreigners: the courts protected their rights to secure residence status and to live with their families."[58] These pressures have often led not simply to the extension of greater numbers of rights but also eventually to the full inclusion of those migrants admitted as temporary. As a result, it is sometimes suggested that temporary work programs can "succeed [only] in less democratic states, which deny rights to foreign workers, restrict access to the legal system, and make draconian use of deportation."[59] James Hollifield notes, for example, that "summary deportations and mass expulsions are viable options for controlling immigration in nonliberal states."[60] That said, there are many coercive strategies, beyond visa provisions, that states use in their attempts to control who can legitimately claim membership and thereby to ensure the "temporariness" of migrant workers – from the relatively light coercion associated with the implementation of program features that encourage the return of migrants through to the forceful deportation of migrants who refuse to leave voluntarily.

The most frequently deployed strategy to secure temporariness is to constrain the lives of temporary workers in ways that ensure that they do not get too comfortable in the host society – that is, to remind them that their lives are ultimately lived elsewhere. The most common of these strategies is the refusal to allow guest workers to travel with their family members.[61] If family members are required to stay home, migrant workers are considerably more likely to return to be with them. As many observers of past guest worker programs have noted, temporary migrants will nevertheless go through a great deal of trouble to be with their family members – in some cases, both spouses will take temporary migrant jobs, and in others, workers will arrange to have their family members enter the territory illegally.[62] The objection to this strategy is that the right to be with one's family is a human right to which we are all entitled simply by virtue of our humanity. One response has been to ensure that migrant labour contracts are ultimately very brief – as they are in most agricultural programs, including Canada's – so that the time apart cannot be fairly described as violating a human right. The attention paid to separation of family members has increased of late, largely as a result of what is termed the "feminization" of migration; women are migrating in increasingly large numbers and now make up nearly half of the world's migrants.[63] So many women are travelling as long-term domestic caregivers that increasing numbers of children are being raised without the constant presence of their mothers, and recent research has focused on the possible negative effects of children being raised in single-parent homes.[64] In the Canadian case, live-in caregivers ultimately apply for permanent status, based upon which they can and frequently do apply to have their families join them. Even in this best-case scenario, however, the separation time is extensive, and opportunities to travel back and forth between Canada and the home country during this long-term separation are frequently poorly understood and complicated by bureaucratic hassle.

The purpose of preventing labouring migrants from travelling with their families is to ensure that migrants do not become too comfortable in the host environment; they shouldn't come to think of the host country as "home" in any significant way. Additional strategies to deter "comfort" intend to make life in the host country difficult, and since 2001 these strategies have been pursued by the Gulf States in an attempt to reduce dependence on foreign labour. For example, across the Gulf States, employers are decreasingly required by law to pay for the healthcare of their employees, and the fees associated with purchasing healthcare for temporary migrants are increasing. The fees associated with having foreign credentials recognized in the first place are increasing as well. In Saudi Arabia foreign workers are required to pay regularly into a fund that is explicitly devoted to funding the training of Saudi citizens in various skills and professions.[65]

A second broad strategy to ensure the temporariness of labourers requires that some of the wages owed to the migrant be made available to the migrant only upon exiting the country. In addition to providing migrants with strong incentives to leave, this policy is defended for its alleged additional contribution to development in sending countries. Yet the well-known danger of programs in which wages are held back until the migrant exits the country has been learned from the utter failure of this practice in the case of the Mexican *braceros*, who upon return did not manage to get access to the money that had allegedly been held on their behalves.[66] Alternative proposals suggest that taxes paid to social security programs could be paid upon departure.[67]

These strategies find support from sending nations, which likewise implement policies to encourage their migrants to return home. For example, the Philippines offers returning migrants the opportunity to spend money earned abroad in tax-free stores for two weeks after their return.[68] Sending countries also construct programs to enable returning migrants to invest their additional income not simply in conspicuous consumption but also in programs that enable and encourage broader development in home communities. In this way, sending countries can participate in encouraging migrants to return so that they can contribute income and skills to the development of their countries. Mexico is the leader in establishing these kinds of programs, and the Philippines has followed suit.[69] Some receiving countries explicitly recognize the ways that temporary labour migration programs do, and should, encourage development in sending countries. An explicit goal of New Zealand's Recognised Seasonal Employer Program, which invites low-skilled migrants to labour in agriculture, is to encourage the development of sending societies, and this commitment appears to require the return migration of temporary migrants.[70]

In some cases, the above strategies to secure return migration are complemented by incentives to encourage employers to hire domestically wherever possible. One frequently stated anxiety about guest worker programs is that guest workers (and irregular migrants) depress wages because they are willing to work for less – in some cases, significantly less – than are local workers.[71] To address this problem, some governments create a disincentive to hire guest workers when local workers are indeed available, even if at a somewhat higher wage, by issuing "levies" on employers who rely on guest workers. Singapore has been running a levy system since 1982, and Thailand and Malaysia have followed suit.[72] The Gulf States – motivated both to protect local workers and by a concern for the dilution of their national culture – have pursued even more aggressive "indigenization" policies, undertaking concerted efforts not only to encourage employers to hire domestic workers but also to reduce the number of foreign migrants as a proportion of the workforce. In Saudi Arabia, for example, the government will contribute to the salaries of domestic, but not foreign, employees. These practices contrast with recent Canadian policy changes that make hiring migrant workers considerably easier; as this chapter's introduction has outlined, the Canadian government is consistently expanding the total number of opportunities available to migrant workers in Canada and is steadily reducing the number of bureaucratic hurdles employers must pass in order to hire temporary foreign workers.

The requirement that employers equally remunerate foreign and domestic labourers is likewise intended to protect local workers from "cheaper" guest workers; guest workers are thus required to be paid at least minimum wage, and in some cases employers must guarantee that they will remunerate temporary labourers at competitive wages. For example, in the United States employers wishing to hire "skilled professionals" (under the HI-B scheme) must commit to offering temporary workers "the higher of the actual wages paid to other workers similarly employed or the prevailing wage for the occupation in the vicinity."[73] Additionally, most employers who desire to hire guest workers must pass a "labour market test" to prove that they have been unable to find local workers to carry out the jobs they have available.[74] The government then ascertains whether this condition has been met and issues guest work permits to employers accordingly. The well-known problem with this structure is simply that the system is rigged in such a way that the offered wage for a given position is insufficient to encourage local workers to take up the job. Employers, in this case, simply allege that workers are not available at the offered wage, knowing that raised wages would in many cases motivate local workers to take the jobs available.[75] Frequently, employers allege that being forced to raise wages to attract local workers would make their companies unviable, and they contend that this outcome is adequate to secure the right to employ guest workers, for whom the offered wage is usually more than they can earn in their home country. Yet, as many scholars observe, the unviability claim is often spurious, and in many cases, the inability to procure guest workers has led to mechanization that in the end has made companies more efficient and more profitable.[76]

A third broad strategy is one mentioned earlier in the context of illegal migration, namely ensuring that contracts are renewable over many years. Short-term, one-off contracts increase the incidence of migrants' disappearance into the underground economy as the contract nears its conclusion; when these contracts are known by all parties to be renewable, the incentive to overstay decreases considerably. This kind of strategy can be "well managed," as it has been in the Canadian case in general; employers are required to facilitate the transportation of migrants to and from the workplace at the beginning and conclusion of the contracts, and they are given the power to invite hard-working and compliant migrants to return in subsequent years. These policies are effective in preventing the transition to irregular status, and to that extent they are praised. Yet the vulnerability of migrant workers who participate in these programs is heightened by the extensive control over this process exercised by their employers. As Priebisch and Hennebry document in chapter 2, when employers are the sole arbiter of who can return to labour, migrants are tremendously vulnerable to the whims and preferences of the employers. For many migrants, the risk of being "rejected" as unfit for future contracts is so high that they will often be willing to put up with considerable abuse at the hands of unscrupulous employers.[77] Alternative strategies involve the sending country – often in the form of bilateral agreements of various kinds between specific sending and receiving states – in making decisions with respect to when contracts can be renewed, and these policies may treat migrant workers more fairly. New Zealand is frequently celebrated as having perfected the "bilateral" arrangement strategy for managing temporary labour migration from developing nations.[78]

A fourth strategy is connected to the rate at which guest workers transition to irregular status. In attempting to encourage irregular migrants to exit the country, Gulf States have enacted "amnesties," where those who have become irregular are permitted to exit the country without incurring the penalties that are generally applied to irregular migrants in such a circumstance.[79] Absent the right to reapply, and if the incentives for employers to hire irregular migrants do not shift, there is no particular reason, however, for those irregular migrants who are in lucrative employment to agree to leave simply as a result of being exempt from penalties. Japan has recently deployed a version of this strategy in relation to its Nikkejin population. As the Japanese economy has continued to suffer, the government has been encouraging the Nikkejin to return "home" – that is, to their country of citizenship (an irony given that they were initially encouraged to join Japan's labour market by virtue of shared ancestry). To encourage their return, the Japanese government has extended financial incentives to this population to exit Japan and return to Latin America.[80]

Finally, aggressive deportation techniques are sometimes deployed to return temporary and irregular migrants to their home country. Again, here, the Gulf States are the most likely to engage in regular deportation of migrants who have overstayed their visas, but democratic nations increasingly resort to deportation as well. In these cases, police forces aggressively enter work environments that are known to hire irregular migrants and forcibly detain and deport those who are labouring there. These brutal tactics and their negative consequences are often well publicized; a recent case in the United States highlighted how frequently these detentions separate mothers from their children, sometimes for extended periods.[81] In Israel the use of deportation to return migrants to home countries is not uncommon, and the government has recently threatened to return the children of migrants – often migrants who are present in Israel legally – to their "home" country, even when these children were born in Israel. The status of children of both temporary and irregular migrants living in receiving countries is a subject of tremendous debate, especially in cases where it is clear that the children are socialized in ways that will make integration into their "home" countries difficult.[82]

CONCLUSION

The global reliance on temporary migration is the result of both political and economic trends that are in evidence not simply in Canada. Economically, temporary migrants appear to provide a flexible labour market, and politically, they appear more palatable for culturally and economically anxious domestic populations. This comparative analysis suggests that however significant the benefits that temporary labour migration brings, the widespread reliance on migrant labour poses difficult practical and moral problems around the world. In most countries, there is an anxiety that temporary migrants will become permanent and that in doing so they will negatively affect the economy or the culture of the host country. As the contributors to this volume warn, we may be witnessing a process that itself generates this problem: the granting of permanent status to temporary migrants after many years may itself be the "integration" problem. Temporary migrants are not entitled to the integrating services available to acknowledged permanent residents; they cannot easily access the services that would certainly enable integration beyond entry into the labour market. The challenges temporary migrants face in integrating result from their initial admission as temporary; evidence suggests, as the chapters outline, that the conditions of their admission shape the trajectory of their lives over time. One option might be to offer "integration" services to temporary as well as permanent migrants; the danger is that, in doing so, governments will create the impression among temporary migrants that they are entitled to stay. Yet the benefit appears to be that if these services are provided to temporary migrants, those who are finally admitted to permanent residency will be better integrated and thus less likely to remain at the margins of society, economically and culturally, over time. Certainly, the consequences of admitting low-skilled migrants in increasing numbers have not yet been given adequate consideration by the Canadian government. The danger is that we are in the midst of creating a problem that permanent migration schemes are focused on preventing: we are creating an environment in which temporary migrants, who eventually transition to permanent status, fail to integrate effectively.

To some extent, the way that migrants are treated – including the ease with which they can become permanent – is influenced both by the historical relationship that the state has with migration and by the extent to which the political system is defined by a commitment to liberal-democratic norms. Historically, Canada has been an immigration state – that is, a state that has welcomed hundreds of thousands of migrants from around the world as permanent residents and then citizens; it is, in a true sense, a nation of immigrants. Moreover, Canadians are traditionally proud of the welcome they offer to migrants and of the tolerance they display toward the cultural and ethnic diversity that often accompanies them. Most Canadians are proud of, and celebrate, their nation's "multicultural heritage." As members of the present government would surely be quick to point out, the number of permanent migrants admitted per year continues apace; what has shifted in Canadian immigration policy is the admission of temporary migrants. Yet, as this volume explores, temporary migrants operate at the margins of Canadian society, the victims of multiple forms of discrimination. Moreover, the rights restrictions to which they are often subject legislate their vulnerability to exploitation and indeed often legislate exploitation itself. The purpose of this chapter has been to compare the Canadian and global experiences of temporary labour migration. A sober assessment suggests that, although in some ways temporary migrants to Canada are treated better than they are elsewhere, Canada has much work to do to ensure the fair and just treatment of its migrant workers and that the urgency of this work increases as the Canadian economy becomes ever more reliant on them.

Notes

INTRODUCTION

1 See, for instance, Editorial, "Helping Nannies Live In," which discusses protections for live-in caregivers.

2 Bourette, "Welcome to Canada"; Economist, "Not Such a Warm Welcome"; Preibisch and Binford, "Interrogating"; Preibisch, "Migrant Agricultural Workers"; Sharma, "On Being Not Canadian."

3 Li, *Destination Canada*, 15.

4 Ibid., 24.

5 Independent immigration is distinct from other immigration programs Canada has in place, like family sponsorship programs that allow Canadian citizens and permanent residents to sponsor their family members' immigration to Canada.

6 Labour market integration is of course not the only indicator. Others include the sense of belonging expressed by second-generation migrants, linguistic facility, levels of education, and so on.

7 Of course, the political motivations behind the implementation of the Multicultural Act are disputed; however, it seems undeniable that the act recognizes the merits and rights of immigrants in Canada.

8 This number refers to independent immigration applications based on the points system and does not include sponsorship applications.

9 World Bank, *At Home and Away*, 118.

10 Nakache and Kinoshita, *Canadian Temporary*, 5.

11 World Bank, *At Home and Away*.

12 Depatie-Pelletier, "Under Legal Practices."

13 Citizenship and Immigration Canada (CIC), *Facts and Figures 2009*.

14 CIC, "Regulations Amending."

15 Nakache and Kinoshita, *Canadian Temporary*, 4.
16 Ibid., 5.
17 Ibid., 11.
18 This is not to say that the federal government is not involved: "the federal government ... maintains control over PNP admissions by stipulating that all nominated applications must meet federal security, criminality, and health requirements." Ibid.
19 Ibid.
20 Siemiatycki, "Marginalizing Migrants," 62. See also Lowe, "Rearranging the Deck Chairs?"
21 This expectation is borne out by the evidence that suggests a very high naturalization rate among Canadian immigrants. See Bloemraad, *Becoming a Citizen*, ch. 1.
22 Siemiatycki, "Marginalizing Migrants," 63.
23 To be clear, the claim is not that we should avoid selecting migrants who will join the rank of visible minorities in Canada. Rather, the claim is that we would do well to avoid, and we have historically avoided, the perception that poverty has a "colour." In the United States, for example, it is widely believed that poverty has a colour, particularly that those who draw on welfare are black Americans, and this perception fuels ongoing racial tension.
24 World Bank, *At Home and Away*; Basok, "Canada's Temporary Migration."
25 One of the most powerful accounts of the "membership" problem as it pertains to guest workers can be found in Walzer, *Spheres of Justice*, ch. 3.
26 As Carter explains in his account of the connections between the TFWP and the PTNPs, migrants admitted to provinces or territories as part of the TFWP can apply, from within a province or territory, for permission to transition to participation in a PTNP and therefore can gain access to the permanent residency that the PTNPs often enable.
27 For more on this program and its operation, see Carens, "Live-in Domestics."
28 Pratt, "Is This Canada?"; Stasiulis and Bakan, "Negotiating Citizenship: The Case"; Loveband, "Nationality Matters."
29 For an elaboration of the kind of philosophical methodology we apply, see Carens, "Contextual Approach."
30 Hankivsky et al., "Exploring the Promises."
31 Young, *Justice and the Politics*.

32 Denzin and Lincoln, "Discipline and Practice," 4; Van Maanen, "Fact of Fiction," 539.
33 Vipond, "Introduction," 3.

CHAPTER ONE

1 I use the somewhat awkward terms "(im)migration and "(im)migrant" to signal that immigration (and being an immigrant) is a distinct, legal category referring to those admitted with the rights associated with permanent residency. "Migrants," in contrast, are those who are denied such rights and are, instead, placed in a number of subordinated legal status categories. In short, not all migrants are immigrants. Acknowledging this is an important first step in understanding the work that national statuses accomplish.
2 Anderson, *Imagined Communities*, 3.
3 Balibar, "Racism and Nationalism."
4 Isin, *Being Political*.
5 Sharma, *Home Economics*.
6 Ibid., 121.
7 Ibid., 119.
8 Ibid., 121.
9 Ibid.
10 House of Commons Canada, *Temporary Foreign Workers*.
11 Hage, *White Nation*, 121.
12 Global Commission on International Migration, "Migration in an Interconnected World," 1.
13 Richmond, *Global Apartheid*; Deleuze and Guatarri, *Thousand Plateaus*.
14 Sharma, *Home Economics*.
15 There is a large body of work on this, much of it written between the mid-1980s and the late 1990s. For a selection of some of the more influential articles, see Abele and Stasiulis, "Canada as a 'White Settler Colony,'"; Bannerji, *Dark Side*; Bannerji, ed., *Returning the Gaze*; Bolaria and Li, *Racial Oppression*; Brand, "Working Paper"; Ng, "Restructuring Gender"; and Silvera, *Silenced*.
16 Preibisch, "Pick-Your-Own Labor."
17 United Food and Commercial Workers (UFCW) Canada, "Homepage," http://www.ufcw.ca/Default.aspx?SectionID=8d1foa66-oeoa-45cb-89cd-2568fe57e9c9&LanguageId=1 (accessed 27 July 2010).

18 House of Commons Debates, *Official Report: First Session*, 5836.
19 Arat-Koc, "Immigration Policies."
20 House of Commons Debates, *Official Report: Third Session*, 4508.
21 Sharma, "On Being Not Canadian," 4; Sharma, *Home Economics*.
22 Preibisch, "Migrant Agricultural Workers."
23 Anderson, *Imagined Communities*.
24 Arendt, *Origins of Totalitarianism*.
25 Holloway, "Global Capital"; Urry, *Sociology beyond Societies*.
26 Marx, "Secret of Primitive Accumulation," 875.
27 See Linebaugh and Rediker, *Many-Headed Hydra*, for an account of such efforts in the "revolutionary Atlantic" from the seventeenth to nineteenth centuries.
28 Federici, *Caliban and the Witch*, 63–4.
29 Hardt and Negri, *Empire*.
30 Federici, *Caliban and the Witch*, 49.
31 Sharma, *Home Economics*.
32 Balibar, "What We Owe," 42.
33 Billig, *Banal Nationalism*.
34 Linebaugh, *Magna Carta Manifesto*.
35 Ibid., 45.
36 Dye, *Maka'ainana Transformation*.

CHAPTER TWO

1 Giese, "Home Cooking"; Crawford, "Buy-Local Push."
2 Government of Ontario, "Ontario Government to Encourage."
3 Lanthier and Wong, "Ethnic Agricultural Labour"; Mann, "Kelowna's Chinatown."
4 Satzewich, "Business or Bureaucratic Dominance"; Lanthier and Wong, "Ethnic Agricultural Labour."
5 Ibid.; Good Gingrich and Preibisch, "Migration as Preservation."
6 Lanthier and Wong, "Ethnic Agricultural Labour."
7 In British Columbia, employers pay for workers' entire airfare and are allowed to deduct up to $550 for accommodation.
8 Castles, "Guestworkers in Europe"; Plewa, "Rise and Fall."
9 See Basok, *Tortillas and Tomatoes*; Basok, "Migration of Mexican"; Basok, "Mexican Seasonal Migration"; Binford, "Contract Labor"; Binford, "From Fields"; McLaughlin, "Trouble in Our Fields"; Trumper

and Wong, "Racialization and Genderization"; Verduzco and Lozano, *Mexican Workers' Participation*; Verma, *Mexican and Caribbean*; Verma, *Regulatory and Policy Framework*; and Weston and Scarpa de Masellis, *Hemispheric Integration.*

10 Basok, "Canada's Temporary Migration."

11 Griffith, *Canadian and United States Migrant.*

12 Verduzco, "Impact of Canadian Labour"; Greenhill, "Managed Migration"; Greenhill, "Workshop Report"; Basok, "Canada's Temporary Migration."

13 HRSDC, personal communication with author, 25 September 2010.

14 Carvajal, *Farm-Level Impacts.*

15 Basok, "He Came, He Saw," 224.

16 Newland, "Circular Migration"; Bustamante and Aléman, "Perpetuating Split–Household."

17 Fudge and McPhail, "Temporary Foreign Worker."

18 Preibisch and Binford, "Interrogating."

19 Binford, "Contract Labor"; Preibisch, "Tierra De Los (No)Libres."

20 Hennebry and Preibisch, "Model for Managed Migration."

21 Binford, "Contract Labor."

22 Verma, *Mexican and Caribbean.*

23 Verma, *Regulatory and Policy Framework.*

24 McLaughlin, "Trouble in Our Fields."

25 Silvey, "Transnational Domestication"; Hugo, "Labour Export"; Leitner, "Political Economy."

26 Preibisch, "Pick-Your-Own Labor."

27 Preibisch and Binford, "Interrogating."

28 Ibid.

29 Binford, "Contract Labor"; Verduzco and Lozano, *Mexican Workers' Participation.*

30 Binford, "Seasonal Agricultural Workers."

31 Human Resources and Skills Development Canada (HRSDC), "Table 10 (Annual)."

32 Otero and Preibisch, *Farmworker Health.*

33 HRSDC, "Table 8 (Annual)."

34 Fudge and McPhail, "Temporary Foreign Worker."

35 Preibisch, "Migrant Workers."

36 HRSDC, "Table 8 (Annual)."

37 Government of Canada, "Temporary Foreign Worker."

38 House of Commons Canada, *Temporary Foreign Workers*.

39 HRSDC, "Table 10 (Annual)"; HRSDC, "Number of Confirmed."

40 Preibisch, "Pick-Your-Own Labor."

41 International Organization for Migration (IOM), "Migrants and the Host."

42 IOM, "Temporary Labour Migration."

43 IOM, "About IOM."

44 Ashutosh and Mountz, "Migration Management."

45 Ibid., 4.

46 Government of Manitoba, "Worker Recruitment."

47 Hennebry and Preibisch, "Model for Managed Migration."

48 Hennebry, "Bienvenidos a Canadá?"

49 Employers are legally permitted to recruit workers without these services, but many purchase the services of these organizations, which have networks within migrant-sending countries and can easily navigate Canadian immigration procedures.

50 Valarezo, "Pushed to the Edge"; Key informant, interview with author, May 2011.

51 Martin, *Merchants of Labor*.

52 AgCall Human Resources, "Homepage," http://www.agcallhr.com (accessed 4 February 2012).

53 Able Recruiters, "Services," http://www.able-recruiters.com/services.htm (accessed 4 February 2012).

54 HRSDC, "Temporary Foreign Worker Program: Minimum Advertising."

55 Ibid.

56 Office of the Auditor General of Canada, *Report*, ch. 2.

57 Ibid.

58 House of Commons Canada, *Temporary Foreign Workers*.

59 Sharma, "Manitoba's Worker Recruitment."

60 House of Commons Canada, *Temporary Foreign Workers*.

61 Ibid.

62 Hennebry and Preibisch, "Deconstructing Managed."

63 Office of the Auditor General of Canada, *Report*, ch. 2.

64 House of Commons Canada, *Temporary Foreign Workers*; Canadian Broadcasting Corporation (CBC), "Workers Killed"; Chen, "Thai Migrant Workers"; Contenta and Monsebraaten, "How We're Creating."

65 Sharma, "Manitoba's Worker Recruitment."

66 Hennebry, Preibisch, and McLaughlin, "Health across Borders."

67 Canadian Nanny, "Now Offering AIR MILES®."

68 Hennebry, "Bienvenidos a Canadá?"
69 Ibid.; Colby, "From Oaxaca to Ontario."
70 Basok, "Migration of Mexican"; Binford, "Migrant Remittances";
    Colby, *From Oaxaca*; Hennebry, "Bienvenidos a Canadá?"; Hennebry,
    Globalization.
71 Mountz, "Embodying the Nation-State."
72 Ojeda, *Transnational Migration.*
73 Rai, *Gender and the Political.*
74 Martin, *Merchants of Labor.*
75 Ibid., 1.

CHAPTER THREE

We extend our gratitude to all of this study's research participants for generously taking time to share with us their experiences and their expertise on issues related to temporary migrant labour. We also thank our research assistants, Laura Mandelbaum and Rebecca Tromsness, for their excellent work, insights, and dedication to the project. Lastly, we express our appreciation to our community partners, Erika Del Carmen Fuchs from Justicia for Migrant Workers BC and Reasha Wolf from the Safe Harvest Coalition, for their valuable contribution. This collaborative research was supported by a grant from Metropolis BC. The research team consisted of Luis Aguiar (principal investigator) and Patricia Tomic and Ricardo Trumper (co-investigators).

 1 Izcara Palacios and Andrade Rubio, "Guest Workers"; Izcara Palacios,
    "Abusos y condiciones"; Melo, "Coming to America."
 2 Barr, Jefferys, and Monger, "Nonimmigrant Admissions."
 3 Adey, *Mobility*; Blunt, "Cultural Geographies"; Cresswell, "Constellation
    of Mobility."
 4 Cresswell, "Constellation of Mobility."
 5 Tomic, Trumper, and Aguiar, "Housing Regulations."
 6 Aguiar, Tomic, and Trumper, "Mexican Migrant."
 7 Esterberg, *Qualitative Methods.*
 8 Smith, "Problematizing Power Relations."
 9 Trumper and Wong, "Temporary Workers"; Trumper and Wong, "Canada's Guest Workers."
10 Tomic, Trumper, and Aguiar, "Housing Regulations."

11 Ferentzy, "Book Review," 188.
12 Castells, *Informational City*; Castells, *Rise of the Network*, vol. 1, *Information Age*.
13 Castells, "Informationalism," 171.
14 See respectively Bauman, *Liquid Modernity*; and Augé, *Non-Places*.
15 Canada Border Services Agency, "About NEXUS."
16 See Molz, "Cosmopolitan Bodies."
17 Cresswell, "Constellation of Mobility."
18 Orozco, "International Financial Flows"; Harris, *Thinking the Unthinkable.*
19 Lanthier and Wong, "Ethnic Agricultural Labour."
20 Ibid.; Cawston, "John Chinaman"; Mann, "Kelowna's Chinatown"; Oram, "Vernon Celebrates"; Huyskamp, *Report on Kelowna's.*
21 Huyskamp, *Report on Kelowna's.*
22 Ibid.
23 Adilman, "Preliminary Sketch"; Trumper and Wong, "Racialization and Genderization"; Satzewich and Liodakis, *'Race' and Ethnicity.*
24 Choy, *Jade Peony*; Choy, *Paper Shadows*; Anderson, *Vancouver's Chinatown*; Ward, *White Canada Forever.*
25 Trumper and Wong, "Temporary Workers"; Trumper and Wong, "Canada's Guest Workers."
26 Adey, *Mobility*; Blunt, "Cultural Geographies"; Cresswell, "Constellation of Mobility."
27 Virilio, *Speed and Politics.*
28 Just-in-time (JIT) is today the norm in most industries around the world, including agriculture. The online article "Just-in-Time Manufacturing" states that JIT "is based on the total elimination of waste ... It requires that equipment, resources and labor are made available only in the amount required and at the time required to do the job. It is based on producing only the necessary units in the necessary quantities at the necessary time by bringing production rates exactly in line with market demand. In short, JIT means making what the market wants, when it wants it. JIT has been found to be so effective that it increases productivity, work performance and product quality, while saving costs."
29 Sharma, *Home Economics*; Sharma, "On Being Not Canadian."
30 Izcara Palacios, "Abusos y condiciones."
31 See Hellman, *World of Mexican*; and Fitting, "Importing Corn."
32 See Gonzalez, *Guest Workers?*; and Hellman, *World of Mexican.*

33 Miller, "Arizona."
34 HRSDC, "Temporary Foreign Worker Program: Hiring."
35 Tomic, Trumper, and Aguiar, "Housing Regulations"; HRSDC, "Temporary Foreign Worker Program: Hiring."
36 See Barr, Jefferys, and Monger, "Nonimmigrant Admissions."
37 See, for example, Nendick, "Immigrant Workers."
38 Sharma, *Home Economics*; Sharma, "On Being Not Canadian."
39 Castells, "Informationalism."
40 See Adey, "Surveillance."
41 Mendis, *Greenhouse Tomato Industry*, 139.
42 See Cypher, "Mexico's Economic Collapse"; Orozco, *Remittances*; and Orozco, "International Financial Flows." Remittances are crucial for the Mexican economy, with some arguing that these have been central in boosting Mexico's income. Mexico is at the top of the list of countries receiving remittances worldwide, having received about US$20 billion in 2005.
43 Squire, "Labour Shortage Bruising."
44 Workers may receive a subsidy from the Mexican government toward their travel costs in Mexico, depending on how far they have to travel. A Mexican official interviewed for this study said that 50 per cent of the cost of the passport is also subsidized by the Mexican government for SAWP workers.
45 See Lassen, "Life in Corridors."
46 Even after fulfilling all of the requirements and checks in Mexican territory and flying to Canada, workers may still see their visas denied by Canadian immigration officers at the port of entry. Mexican diplomatic personnel whom we interviewed acknowledged that workers have been returned but remained vague about the numbers and about the reasons for Canadian immigration officers refusing to grant them entry rights. In one case, a Mexican official told us that sometimes the name of a worker may appear similar to the name of someone caught entering the United States illegally, which is reason enough to send the worker back.
47 See Martin, "Society of Flows."
48 Fresh Plaza, "Growers Turn to Mexico."
49 HRSDC, "Temporary Foreign Worker Program: Hiring."
50 Tomic, Trumper, and Aguiar, "Housing Regulations."
51 Ibid.
52 Iyer, *Global Soul*.

53 Money transfers are electronic and form part of the data that circulate between Canada and Mexico.

54 Bauman, *Liquid Modernity*.

55 On 15 June 2010 more than 300 Mexican temporary workers, veterans, and active workers marched to the Canadian Embassy in Mexico City to protest against the discriminatory conditions of their contracts in Canada.

56 Ferentzy, "Book Review," 188.

57 Castells, "Informationalism."

CHAPTER FOUR

1 O'Neil, Hamilton, and Papademetriou, *Migration in the Americas*, 4.

2 Council on Foreign Relations et al., *Building a North American*, 27.

3 Harper, "Statement."

4 Paterson, "Troubled Waters."

5 See Holzmann and Pouget, *Social Protection*, 7.

6 "Mexico: Guest Workers," 4. In 1999 former Mexican labour secretary José Antonio Gonzalez singled out the SAWP as a model that could also be used in the United States.

7 Global Workers Justice Alliance, "Migration Data." It should be noted that Mexico also is the host of migrant temporary workers from Guatemala – "*visitantes agrícolas*." These migrant workers are limited to farms in the Mexican state of Chiapas.

8 Organisation for Economic Co-operation and Development (OECD), *International Migration Outlook*, 30.

9 Stalker, *No-Nonsense Guide*, 67.

10 International Labour Organization (ILO), *Towards a Fair Deal*, 49–50.

11 Ibid., 52.

12 Stalker, *No-Nonsense Guide*, 67–8.

13 See, for example, Preibisch and Binford, "Interrogating"; and Stasiulis and Bakan, *Negotiating Citizenship*.

14 See, for example, Abu-Laban, "Reconstructing"; Castles, "Hierarchies of Citizenship"; and Stasiulis and Bakan, *Negotiating Citizenship*.

15 Stasiulis and Bakan, *Negotiating Citizenship*, 25–6.

16 Ibid., 14.

17 See, for example, ibid.; and Sharma, *Home Economics*.

18 Global Commission on International Migration, "Migration," 17.

19 Ibid., 16.

20 Global Forum on Migration and Development (GFMD), "Report of the First Meeting of the GFMD," 65, quoted in International Organization for Migration (IOM), *World Migration 2008*, 93.

21 UN Secretary General, *International Migration and Development* (2006), 18, quoted in International Organization for Migration (IOM), *World Migration 2008*, 93.

22 World Bank, *Global Economic Prospects*, xi, quoted in International Organization for Migration (IOM), *World Migration 2008*, 93.

23 Boucher, "Critique," 1462.

24 Ibid., 1469.

25 Holzmann and Pouget, *Social Protection*, 5.

26 Boucher, "Critique," 1469.

27 Lowell and Lezell, "Background Paper," 7.

28 Holzmann and Pouget, *Social Protection*, 7.

29 Avendano, "Reintegration," 4.

30 Meyers and O'Neil, *Immigration*, 45.

31 Gabriel and Macdonald, "Hypermobile."

32 Pew Hispanic Center, "Mexican Immigrants."

33 Ibid.

34 Cornelius, "Controlling 'Unwanted' Immigration," 777. However, flows have declined significantly, at least temporarily, as a result of the recession that began in 2008. See Papademetriou and Terrazas, "Immigrants in the United States."

35 Pew Hispanic Center, "Mexican Immigrants."

36 Passel, "Mexican Immigration."

37 Meyers and O'Neil, *Immigration*, 45.

38 Mueller, "Mexican Immigrants," 33.

39 Ibid., 33–44.

40 See Valpy, "Visa Controls."

41 For an excellent account of why Mexico was added in to the Seasonal Agricultural Worker Program, see Satzewich, "Business or Bureaucratic Dominance."

42 See Basok, *Tortillas and Tomatoes*; and Preibisch, "Pick-Your-Own Labor."

43 United Food and Commercial Workers (UFCW) Canada, *Status of Migrant*, 8.

44 Becerril Quintana, "New Era."

45 Preibish and Encalada Grez, "Other Side."

46 Martin, Abella, and Kuptsch, *Managing Labor Migration*, 112.

47 Mueller, "Mexican Immigrants," 44

48 Martin, Abella, and Kuptsch, *Managing Labour Migration*, 110.
49 Ibid.
50 FOCAL, *Dialogue on Labour*, 13.
51 Reed, "Canada's Experience," 482.
52 Hennebry and Preibisch, "Model for Managed Migration?" 33–4.
53 Peschard-Sverdrup, "Canada-Mexico Relationship," 6–7.
54 Holley, "Disadvantaged by Design," 573; Basok, "Free to Be Unfree."
55 Martin, "Guest Worker Policies," 46.
56 Ibid.
57 Holley, "Disadvantaged by Design," 580.
58 Ibid., 581.
59 Hendricks, "Ex-Braceros Leery."
60 Martin, *Promise Unfulfilled*, 46–7.
61 Holley, "Disadvantaged by Design," 581.
62 Zabin, "U.S.-Mexico Economic," 344.
63 Holley, "Disadvantaged by Design," 573.
64 Commission for Labor Cooperation (CLC), *Protection of Migrant*, 38.
65 Souza, "H-2A?"
66 Holley, "Disadvantaged by Design," 575.
67 Martin, "Immigration Reform," 1.
68 Holley, "Disadvantaged by Design," 590.
69 Ibid., 593.
70 CLC, *Protection of Migrant*, 50.
71 Ibid., 39.
72 Holley, "Disadvantaged by Design," 595–605.
73 CLC, *Protection of Migrant*, 50.
74 Holley, "Disadvantaged by Design," 606.
75 See Gabriel and Macdonald, "Migration and Citizenship."
76 Martin, *Promise Unfulfilled*, 69.
77 Cable News Network (CNN), "Bush Calls."
78 Muzzaffar and Bergeron, "Obama's Homeland Security." For the proposed rules, see United States Department of Homeland Security, "H-2A Temporary."
79 Souza, "Labor Department."
80 Huffstutter, "Hiring Foreign Farmworkers."
81 See Felix-Romero, "AgJOBS Update."
82 Martin, "Immigration Reform," 5; Farmworker Justice, "Summary."

CHAPTER FIVE

1 McLaughlin, "Trouble in Our Fields"; Satzewich, *Racism and the Incorporation.*
2 Agamben, *Homo Sacer*; Agamben, *State of Exception.*
3 Van Maanen, "Fact of Fiction."
4 This study was funded by the CERIS Ontario Metropolis Research Centre and the Public Health Agency of Canada (PHAC) and was carried out in collaboration with K. Preibisch and J. McLaughlin with the generous assistance of the United Food and Commercial Workers Union, Enlace Community Link, Justicia for Migrant Workers, and numerous research assistants and volunteers, most notably J. Restrepo. The survey employed a standardized questionnaire administered to a purposive nonrandom sample identified using snowball sampling intended to reach workers from both Mexico and Jamaica in areas with high numbers of agricultural migrant workers (i.e., Leamington, Niagara, Simcoe, and Bradford).
5 Appadurai, *Modernity at Large*; Buroway et al., *Global Ethnography*; Urry, "Mobile Sociology."
6 Berg, *Qualitative Research Methods.*
7 Giddens, *Constitution of Society.*
8 Smith, *Texts, Facts and Femininity.*
9 Agamben, "Camp as the Nomos"; Agamben, *Homo Sacer*; Agamben, *State of Exception.*
10 Hennebry, "Bienvenidos a Canadá?"
11 Hennebry, Preibisch, and McLaughlin, "Health across Borders."
12 Sharma, "On Being Not Canadian," 417; Sharma, *Home Economics.*
13 Richmond, *Global Apartheid.*
14 McLaughlin, "Trouble in Our Fields."
15 Basok, *Tortillas and Tomatoes.*
16 Satzewich, *Racism and the Incorporation.*
17 Human Resources and Skills Development Canada (HRSDC), "Temporary Foreign Worker Program: Labour Market Opinion (LMO) Statistics," in *Annual Statistics 2006–2009.*
18 Ibid.
19 International Organization for Migration (IOM), "Seasonal Agricultural Workers."
20 HRSDC, "Temporary Foreign Worker Program: Hiring."

21 The "three-month rule" is consistent with other (im)migration streams, in which new arrivals to Canada must wait three months before they can access provincial coverage (supposedly to weed out people coming to Canada to seek immediate healthcare).

22 World Health Organization (WHO), "Closing the Gap."

23 Kivimäki et al., "Temporary Employment."

24 Pritchard, "Mexican-Born Workers."

25 For more detailed findings and reviews of this literature, see McLaughlin, "Trouble in Our Fields"; Hennebry, Preibisch, and McLaughlin, "Health across Borders"; and Otero and Preibisch, *Farmworker Health*.

26 Basok, *Tortillas and Tomatoes*; Basok, "Human Rights."

27 McLaughlin and Hennebry, "Pathways to Precarity."

28 Compiled from Hennebry's field notes, 22 July 2002.

29 Government of British Columbia, Ministry of Agriculture and Lands, *Regulating Temporary*.

30 Hennebry, Preibisch, and McLaughlin, "Health across Borders."

31 Employer, Alliston Ontario, 2005; Employer, Ivy Ontario, 2005.

32 Workplace Safety and Insurance Board (WSIB), "Workplace Safety."

33 Canadian Agriculture Injury Surveillance Program (CAISP), "Agricultural Fatalities."

34 Osprey-Obituaries, "Obituary for Samuel Maurilio Gil-Montesinos," 2006; "Farm Worker's Body."

35 Bajer, "Here for a Better Life."

36 Jankowski, "Two Farm Workers."

37 McLaughlin, "Trouble in Our Fields."

38 Canadian Broadcasting Corporation (CBC), "3 Dead, 13 Injured."

39 Hennebry, Preibisch, and McLaughlin, "Health across Borders."

40 Ibid.

41 Shipp et al., "Pesticide Safety Training."

42 Hennebry, Preibisch, and McLaughlin, "Health across Borders."

43 Mexican worker, Leamington, 2008.

44 Mexican worker, Bradford, 2008.

45 Mexican worker, Leamington, 2008.

46 Hennebry, Preibisch, and McLaughlin, "Health across Borders."

47 Otero and Preibisch, *Farmworker Health*; Hennebry, Preibisch, and McLaughlin, "Health across Borders."

48 Mexican worker, Simcoe, 2008.

49 Jamaican worker, Niagara, 2007.

50 Hennebry, Preibisch, and McLaughlin, "Health across Borders."
51 Worker advocate, Niagara, 2006.
52 HRSDC, "Agreement for the Employment."
53 Foreign Agricultural Resource Management Services (FARMS), "Employer Information Booklet."
54 Mexican worker, Simcoe, 2008.
55 Guatemalan worker, St Thomas, 2008.
56 Jamaican official, Kingston, Jamaica, 2007.
57 Employer, Bradford, 2005.
58 Hennebry, Preibisch, and McLaughlin, "Health across Borders"; Otero and Preibisch, *Farmworker Health.*
59 Basok, *Tortillas and Tomatoes*; McLaughlin, "Trouble in Our Fields"; Hennebry, "Bienvenidos a Canadá?"
60 McLaughlin, "Falling through the Cracks"; McLaughlin, *Migration and Health*; McLaughlin, "Trouble in Our Fields"; Hennebry, "Mobile Vulnerabilities."
61 McLaughlin, *Migration and Health*; McLaughlin, "Trouble in Our Fields."

CHAPTER SIX

1 Trumper and Wong, "Temporary Workers."
2 NOC refers to the National Occupational Classification system. At the time of writing, the LSPP is still a pilot project, but Human Resources and Skills Development Canada (HRSDC) is in the final stages of evaluating it before deciding whether to make it an official policy stream of the Temporary Foreign Worker Program (TFWP). Valérie Turbide, senior analyst, TFWP, HRSDC, Ottawa, written communication with author, 11 March 2010.
3 Brem, *Migrant Workers.*
4 But see Fudge and MacPhail, "Temporary Foreign Worker"; Valarezo, "Out of Necessity"; Brem, *Migrant Workers*; Vargas-Foronda, "El Programa."
5 For example, see Valarezo, "Out of Necessity"; Binford, "From Fields"; McLaughlin, "Trouble in Our Fields"; Preibisch, "Migrant Agricultural Workers."
6 Preibisch and Binford, "Interrogating"; Abu-Laban and Gabriel, *Selling Diversity*; Sharma, "Race, Class, Gender"; Sharma, "Immigrant and Migrant."

7 Preibisch and Encalada Grez, "Other Side"; Encalada Grez, "Vulner-abilities"; Becerril Quintana, "Transnational Work"; Gálvez Gonzalez and Ramos Rodrígez, "Patriarchy and Exploitation"; Barrón, "Mexican Women."

8 United Food and Commercial Workers (UFCW) Canada, Status of Migrant; Flecker, "Canada's Temporary."

9 Salgado de Snyder, "Family Life."

10 Little, "Introduction"; Montes, "Transformaciones."

11 Turbide, written communication.

12 For instance, the bilateral agreement founding the Canada-Mexico SAWP offers workers some degree of labour mobility, such as the opportunity to change employers, whereas the LSPP limits workers to one employer and stipulates that workers must be automatically repatriated if they lose their job or when the contract expires. See Valarezo, "Out of Necessity."

13 See Reed, "Canada's Experience." The reason for this absence of bilat-eral governmental agreements lies in the principle of nondiscrimination in the General Agreement on Trade in Services that applies to trading part-ners who are members of the World Trade Organization (WTO), whereby "no WTO member country is allowed to give preferential treatment in terms of trade in goods or services to another country"; Turbide, written communication. In 1995 Canada exempted Mexico and the SAWP Carib-bean countries from this rule, but no further exemptions are allowed. As a result, Canada cannot establish a bilateral agreement on migration with Guatemala.

14 A detailed comparison, for employers, of the SAWP and the LSPP in the Ontario context can be found on the Foreign Agricultural Resource Man-agement Services (FARMS) website: http://www.farmsontario.ca (accessed 24 November 2011).

15 The IOM is an intergovernmental organization that provides migration-related services to governments and individuals.

16 FERME is La Fondation des entreprises en recrutement de la main-d'oeuvre agricole étrangère, FARMS is the Foreign Agricultural Resource Manage-ment Services, and WALI is the Western Agricultural Labour Initiative.

17 In Quebec the Ministère de l'immigration et communautés culturelles is also involved in reviewing employers' requests for workers. Turbide, writ-ten communication.

18 Delbert Field, chief of mission, IOM-Guatemala, interview with author, Guatemala City, 26 April 2010.

19 Stefan Mantsch, program manager, IOM-Guatemala, interview with author, Guatemala City, 26 April 2010.

20 Vargas-Foronda, "El Programa."

21 Citizenship and Immigration Canada (CIC), *Canada – Total Entries*.

22 Andrea Galvez, national representative, UFCW Canada, interview with author, Montreal, 7 July 2010. Workers do not fall under the same sets of labour laws in all provinces. For example, agricultural workers are covered under occupational health and safety legislation in Ontario and Quebec but not in Alberta. See also UFCW Canada, "Alberta Continues."

23 International Organization for Migration (IOM), "Second Evaluation."

24 I use a pseudonym for the village name in order to protect the identities of study participants.

25 See IOM, "Second Evaluation"; and IOM, "Project Evaluation."

26 See IOM, "Second Evaluation."

27 IOM, "Project Evaluation."

28 Guatemalan consular official no. 1, interview with author, Montreal, 20 January 2010.

29 Kerry Preibisch and Evelyn Encalada Grez suggest that agricultural employers may prefer women on the gendered assumption that they have a "finer, lighter touch and are more patient, responsible, and productive than men." See Preibisch and Encalada Grez, "Other Side," 302.

30 This labour migration program operates according to a "naming" system whereby employers can request former workers for subsequent seasons. These circumstances encourage workers to work hard but also not to voice complaints.

31 Maternalism on the part of female employers toward female employees has been found by scholars researching domestic workers. Judith Rollins refers to maternalism, which relates to women's supportive family roles, as "the motivation for and the belief system behind such apparently benevolent gestures that make them [workers] highly beneficial to the employer at the psychological expense of the domestic." See Rollins, *Between Women*, 157.

32 Carole Fiset, *agent d'éducation et de coopération*, Commission des droits de la personne et des droits de la jeunesse, interview with author, Montreal, 21 January 2010.

33 It has been reported that one was dismissed and the other resigned after they denounced the working conditions and rights violations of Guatemalans working in Quebec. See Noël, "Des loyers illégaux."

34 Guatemalan consular official no. 2, interview with author, Montreal, 20 January 2010.

35 Guatemalan consular official no. 1, interview with author; Guatemalan consular official no. 2, interview with author.

36 Guatemalan consular official no. 1, interview with author.

37 Guatemalan consular official no. 2, interview with author.

38 Guatemalan consular official no. 1, interview with author. Of note, FERME has recently started contracting Hondurans to work in Quebec.

39 Ibid.

40 Guatemalan consular official no. 2, interview with author.

41 Given that I have profiled the experiences of female workers, it should be said that gender and migration scholarship could be looked to here for explanations of certain troublesome aspects of women's migration experiences and how they differ from those of men; for instance, see Encalada Grez, "Vulnerabilities." Although I include such considerations in my forthcoming dissertation, I wish to focus here on the institutional and political-economic contexts that contribute to workers' vulnerability in general.

42 Fudge and MacPhail, "Temporary Foreign Worker"; Nakache and Kinoshita, Canadian Temporary.

43 Trumper and Wong, "Temporary Workers," 88.

44 Abu-Laban and Gabriel, Selling Diversity.

45 Reed, "Canada's Experience"; Grugel and Piper, Critical Perspectives.

46 Grugel and Piper, Critical Perspectives.

47 Nakache and Kinoshita, Canadian Temporary.

48 Canadian Bar Association, "Low Skilled Worker."

49 Delta Partners, "Review."

50 Fudge and MacPhail, "Temporary Foreign Worker," 7.

51 Guatemalan consular official no. 2, interview with author.

52 Guatemalan consular official no. 1, interview with author.

53 Guatemalan consular official no. 2, interview with author.

54 See Brem, Migrant Workers; and Valarezo, "Out of Necessity."

55 Both the Guatemalan consular officials and the IOM told me that some migrants' families had been victims of extortion.

56 Galvez, interview with author.

57 Grugel and Piper, Critical Perspectives.

58 See Montes, "Transformaciones."

59 Salgado de Snyder, "Family Life."

60 Hadi, "International Migration"; Hadi, "Overseas Migration"; Nguyen et al., "Migration and the Well-Being"; Hellman, *World of Mexican*; Dunn and Gibb, "Gender, Migration."

61 I use the term "partners" to encompass both married women and those in *uniones libres* (free or common-law unions), which are relatively common in Guatemala.

62 Pessar and Mahler, "Transnational Migration."

63 Piper, "Gender and Migration"; Becerril Quintana, "Transnational Work"; Boehm, "Now I Am."

64 See, for instance, Boehm, "Now I Am"; Menjívar and Agadjanian, "Men's Migration"; Resurreccion and Van Khanh, "Able to Come"; Weinstein Bever, "Migration and the Transformation."

65 Menjívar and Agadjanian, "Men's Migration," 1249.

66 My study also examined the impacts on gender roles and relations of women's migration. This is discussed in my forthcoming dissertation but is not the focus here.

67 Boehm, "Now I Am," 28.

68 See Hellman, *World of Mexican*, 47.

69 Claudia Samayoa, Municipal de la Mujer, interview with author, Tecpán, Guatemala, 6 May 2010.

70 Hellman, *World of Mexican*, 48.

71 Ibid., 199.

72 These types of emotional strains have been noted in other research. See, for instance, Nguyen et al., "Migration and the Well-Being"; Salgado de Snyder, "Family Life."

73 Salgado de Snyder, "Family Life."

74 Hellman, *World of Mexican*.

75 One could interpret more demanding husbands as men trying to reassert their masculinity, which, Boehm argues, migration may rob from men due to the exploitation and low-prestige of their work in countries of destination. See Boehm, "Now I Am."

76 IOM, "Project Evaluation," 11.

77 Weinstein Bever, "Migration and the Transformation," 203.

78 Boehm, "Now I Am," 27.

CHAPTER SEVEN

1 Nakache and Kinoshita, *Canadian Temporary*, 26.

2 The National Occupational Classification (NOC) is a standard that classi-
fies and describes all occupations in the Canadian labour market according to skill types O, A, B, C, and D. Senior and middle-management occupations are coded O; professional occupations are A; technical and
skilled-trade occupations are B; and occupations requiring lower levels of
formal training are C and D.

3 See Finance Canada, *Advantage Canada*, 217; Finance Canada, *Budget
2007*, 50; Citizenship and Immigration Canada (CIC), *Annual Report to
Parliament on Immigration 2008*, 9. For more on this topic, see Nakache
and Kinoshita, *Canadian Temporary*.

4 CIC, "Regulatory Changes."

5 CIC, "Regulations Amending."

6 This point is addressed in Nakache and Kinoshita, *Canadian Temporary*.

7 For more on the exclusionary dimension of immigration law, see
Fitzpatrick, *Nationalism, Racism*; Fitzpatrick, *Modernism*; Kyambi,
"National Identity," 20; Bhabha, *Location of Culture*.

8 Sharma, *Home Economics*, 97.

9 See Nakache and Kinoshita, *Canadian Temporary*; Satzewich, *Racism and
the Incorporation*.

10 Dauvergne, "Making People Illegal," 87.

11 Seidle, "Intergovernmental Immigration; Nakache and Kinoshita, *Canadian Temporary*.

12 For more on this topic, see Carter, Morrish, and Amoyaw, "Attracting
Immigrants," 167; Leo and August, "Multi-Level Governance," 496;
Alboim, *Adjusting the Balance*, 5.

13 See Carter, Morrish, and Amoyaw, "Attracting Immigrants"; Pandey and
Townsend, "Quantifying the Effects."

14 House of Commons Canada, *Temporary Foreign Workers*, 10.

15 For more on this topic, see Nakache and Kinoshita, *Canadian Temporary*.

16 Research questionnaires were completed by nine provinces (Nova Scotia, Prince Edward Island, New Brunswick, Newfoundland and Labrador,
Ontario, Manitoba, Saskatchewan, Alberta, and British Columbia) as well
as the Northwest Territories. Although the Yukon has a nominee program,
the territory declined our invitation to participate in this research project.

17 Of the provinces and territories that outline specific categories for low-
skilled workers to obtain nomination through their PTNPs (British Columbia, Alberta, Saskatchewan, Prince Edward Island, the Yukon, and
the Northwest Territories), all restrict low-skilled applicants to specific

occupations or industries. Manitoba is a unique exception, as its "employer direct" category, geared toward attracting TFWs, does not restrict by NOC. This point is discussed in more detail later in the chapter.

18 See Tom Carter's chapter in this volume.

19 Nakache and Kinoshita, *Canadian Temporary*.

20 See Tom Carter's chapter in this volume.

21 It is technically impossible for seasonal workers admitted to Canada under this program to access permanent residency from within Canada: the work permit is valid for one period of eight months and is nonrenewable, and workers must leave the country after the expiration of this period.

22 Immigration and Refugee Protection Act, sec. 22(2); Immigration and Refugee Protection Regulations, sec. 183.

23 Nakache and Kinoshita, *Canadian Temporary*.

24 CIC, "Regulations Amending."

25 For more on this topic, see Nakache and Kinoshita, *Canadian Temporary*, 33–4.

26 House of Commons Canada, *Temporary Foreign Workers*, 14.

27 CIC, "FW 1: Temporary Foreign Worker," 67.

28 Benton Mischuk, manager, Strategic Initiatives, British Columbia Provincial Nominee Program, questionnaire response, 29 June 2010; Dave Boczulak, senior policy analyst, Advanced Education, Employment and Labour, Government of Saskatchewan, questionnaire response, 28 June 2010.

29 Manitoba government official, questionnaire response, 3 June 2010.

30 Ibid.

31 Newfoundland and Labrador government official, questionnaire response, 25 June 2010.

32 CIC, *Annual Report to Parliament on Immigration 2008*, 10–13, 18.

33 CIC, *Facts and Figures 2008*, 21.

34 Canada and Quebec have had immigration agreements since 1971, and Quebec has had the power to select Quebec-destined economic immigrants since 1978. Therefore, Quebec has no need of a PTNP agreement.

35 See Nakache and Kinoshita, *Canadian Temporary*. See also Carter, Morrish, and Amoyaw, "Attracting Immigrants."

36 Office of the Auditor General of Canada, *Report*.

37 Governement of Alberta, "AINP Processing Times."

38 Boczulak, questionnaire response.

39 Manitoba government official, questionnaire response.

40 CIC, "Application Processing Times."

41 Boczulak, questionnaire response; Mischuk, questionnaire response. It is
    important to note here that although the nominee programs in Saskatch-
    ewan and British Columbia do have specific categories under which TFWs
    can apply, our research participant from British Columbia indicated that
    TFWs could potentially apply through any of the nominee categories.
    In addition, our research participant from Saskatchewan indicated that
    skilled TFWs can apply for nomination following six months of employ-
    ment under any category.

42 Although the New Brunswick Nominee Program website does not spe-
    cifically state that TFWs can apply for nomination through the program,
    its "Guide for Skilled Worker Applicants" does mention TFWs under the
    "Skilled Worker with Employer Support" section. See Government of New
    Brunswick, "Guide for Skilled Worker Applicants"; Government of New
    Brunswick, "New Brunswick Provincial Nominee Program."

43 Nova Scotia has since updated its nominee website and does state that
    semi-skilled and low-skilled workers with six months of work experi-
    ence can apply for nomination; however, this possibility is listed under
    the "skilled worker" stream. See Governement of Nova Scotia, "Skilled
    Worker Stream."

44 Michael Theriault, program officer, Population Growth Secretariat –
    Immigration Division, Government of New Brunswick, questionnaire
    response, 15 June 2010; Nova Scotia government official, questionnaire
    response, 28 June 2010.

45 Theriault, questionnaire response.

46 Newfoundland and Labrador government official, questionnaire response.

47 Fudge and MacPhail, "Temporary Foreign Worker," 13.

48 Government of Alberta, "Semi-Skilled Worker."

49 See Government of Ontario, "Opportunities Ontario."

50 Government of Alberta, "Semi-Skilled Worker"; Government of British
    Columbia, "Entry-Level"; Government of Saskatchewan, "Information for
    Saskatchewan."

51 Government of Alberta, "Foodservices Industry."

52 Byl, "Entrenching Exploitation."

53 Government of British Columbia, "What If You Lose."

54 In this case, the BC website notes that some industry associations, such
    as the BC Food Processors Association and the BC Trucking Association,
    work with nominating employers to place any "nominees terminated with-

out cause in an equivalent job with an eligible employer." Nominees must accept an equivalent offer of employment, or else the nomination is withdrawn. See Government of British Columbia, "Entry-Level."

55 Boczulak, questionnaire response; Manitoba government official, questionnaire response; Grant Sweet, senior policy analyst, Immigration Services IIDI, Government of Prince Edward Island, questionnaire response, 7 June 2010; Theriault, questionnaire response. In British Columbia support letters can be issued if applicants' work permits expire after nomination but while they are waiting for permanent residency approval if "the Nominee has a genuine job offer and is urgently required by the employer"; as per Mischuk, questionnaire response.

56 Manitoba government official, questionnaire response; Sweet, questionnaire response.

57 Government of Saskatchewan, "Temporary Work Permits"; Boczulak, questionnaire response; Mischuk, questionnaire response.

58 Theriault, questionnaire response.

59 Alberta, British Columbia, the Northwest Territories, and the Yukon use the term "semi-skilled workers" to describe workers falling within the NOC C and D categories but do not use this term in an attempt to differentiate between the two categories – for example, NOC C being semi-skilled and NOC D being low-skilled. The use of the term "semi-skilled workers" by certain provinces and territories but not others to describe NOC C and D categories is confusing given that the NOC does not make this distinction and refers to them only as low-skilled workers. See Government of British Columbia, "Entry-Level"; Government of Alberta, "Semi-Skilled Worker"; Government of Yukon, "Critical Impact Worker"; Government of Northwest Territories, "NWT Nominee Program"; Government of Prince Edward Island, "Critical Worker Stream."

60 See Government of British Columbia, "Entry-Level"; Government of Alberta, "Semi-Skilled Worker"; Yukon, "Critical Impact Worker"; Government of Northwest Territories, "NWT Nominee Program"; Government of Saskatchewan, "Hospitality Sector"; Government of Saskatchewan, "Long-Haul Truck Drivers"; Government of Prince Edward Island, "Critical Worker Stream."

61 Manitoba government official, questionnaire response.

62 Ibid.

63 Ibid.

64 Bucklaschuk, Moss, and Annis, "Temporary May Not," 65.

65 Pandey and Townsend, "Quantifying the Effects"; Pandey and Townsend, "Provincial Nominee Programs."

66 Manitoba government official, questionnaire response.

67 Ibid., emphasis added.

68 Ibid.

69 Ibid.

70 Ibid.

71 Maple Leaf Foods Collective Agreement, "Agreement between Maple Leaf Foods Inc. and United Food and Commercial Workers Union, Local No. 832" (expires 31 December 2014); and Springhill Farms Collective Agreement, "Agreement between Springhill Farms and Freezerco and United Food and Commercial Workers Union, Local No. 832" (expires 31 December 2015) (both on file with Delphine Nakache).

72 Manitoba government official, questionnaire response.

73 Leo and August, "Multi-Level Governance," 501–2; Carter, Pandey, and Townsend, *Manitoba Provincial*, 10.

74 Carter, Pandey, and Townsend, *Manitoba Provincial*, 10.

75 Ibid.

76 Ibid.

77 For more information on the changes made to the MPNP in 2004, see Leo and August, "Multi-Level Governance," 501–4.

78 Bucklaschuk, Moss, and Annis, "Temporary May Not," 65–6.

79 Ibid.

80 Government of Alberta, "Semi-Skilled Worker."

81 Ibid.

82 Ibid.

83 Ibid.

84 Mischuk, questionnaire response.

85 Ibid.

86 Ibid.

87 Boczulak, questionnaire response.

88 The Saskatchewan Immigrant Nominee Program (SINP) notes the following on its website: "As of April 30, 2010, employers must receive approval from the SINP to participate in the project before their employees arrive in Canada. The SINP will not accept applications from hospitality sector employees who arrive in Canada prior to their employer receiving SINP approval." See Government of Saskatchewan, "Hospitality Sector."

89 Ibid.; Government of Saskatchewan, "Long-Haul Truck Drivers."

90 Boczulak, questionnaire response.
91 Government of Yukon, "Skilled Worker/Critical Impact"; Government of Northwest Territories, "NWT Nominee Program."
92 It should be noted that the Northwest Territories Nominee Program is, in its entirety, a pilot program designed for a three-year period (it was established on 1 June 2009); as per Karen Willy, coordinator, Career and Employment, Department of Education, Culture and Employment, Government of the Northwest Territories, questionnaire response, 30 June 2010.
93 Government of Yukon, "Critical Impact Worker"; Northwest Territories, "NWT Nominee Program," 4.
94 Sweet, questionnaire response.
95 Government of Prince Edward Island, "New Immigration Streams."
96 Ibid.
97 Government of Prince Edward Island, "Critical Worker Stream."
98 Ibid.
99 Ibid.
100 Newfoundland and Labrador government official, questionnaire response.
101 Newfoundland and Labrador government official, follow-up e-mail communication with authors, 26 July 2010.
102 Newfoundland and Labrador government official, questionnaire response and accompanying document, "Provincial Nominees by National Occupational Classification (April 2007–May 2010)."
103 Theriault, questionnaire response.
104 Ibid.
105 Nova Scotia governmental official, questionnaire response, 28 June 2010.

CHAPTER EIGHT

1 Green and Green, "Goals of Canada's."
2 Statistics Canada, *Canadian Demographics.*
3 Cited in Nakache and Kinoshita, *Canadian Temporary.*
4 Abella, "Global Competition"; Citizenship and Immigration Canada (CIC), *Annual Report to Parliament on Immigration 2008.*
5 Carter, Pandey, and Townsend, *Manitoba Provincial*; Statistics Canada, Income and Earnings, *2006 Census.*
6 Nakache and Kinoshita, *Canadian Temporary.*
7 CIC, *Facts and Figures 2010.*

8 Ibid.
9 Ibid.
10 Ibid.
11 Human Resources and Skills Development Canada (HRSDC), "Temporary Foreign Worker Program," in *Annual Statistics 2005–2008*.
12 Ibid.
13 CIC, *Annual Report to Parliament on Immigration 2009*.
14 Carter, Morrish, and Amoyaw, "Attracting Immigrants."
15 CANVISA Immigration, "Immigrate to Canada."
16 Office of the Auditor General of Canada, *Report*.
17 Ibid.
18 CIC, *Annual Report to Parliament on Immigration 2009*.
19 Carter, Pandey, and Townsend, *Manitoba Provincial*.
20 Clement, "Benefits of Immigration."
21 Carter et al., *Evaluation*.
22 Ibid.
23 Nakache and Kinoshita, *Canadian Temporary*.
24 Cholewinski, *Legal Status*.
25 Carter et al., *Evaluation*.
26 Nakache and Kinoshita, *Canadian Temporary*; Cholewinski, *Legal Status*; Kitagawa, Krywulak, and Watt, *Renewing Immigration*.
27 Nakache and Kinoshita, *Canadian Temporary*.
28 Alboim, *Adjusting the Balance*.
29 Carter, Pandey, and Townsend, *Manitoba Provincial*.
30 Sharma, *Home Economics*; Preibisch, "Local Produce."
31 Carter, Pandey, and Townsend, *Manitoba Provincial*.
32 HRSDC, "Temporary Foreign Worker Program," in *Annual Statistics 2005–2008*.
33 Government of Alberta, "AINP Processing Times"; Government of Saskatchewan, "Saskatchewan Immigrant"; Government of Manitoba, "Manitoba Provincial Nominee Program: Common Questions."
34 Cholewinski, *Legal Status*.
35 United Kingdom, *Constitution Act*.
36 Nakache and Kinoshita, *Canadian Temporary*.
37 Ibid.
38 Silvius and Annis, "Reflections."
39 For a much more complete discussion of the rights of TFWs, see Nakache and Kinoshita, *Canadian Temporary*.

40 House of Commons Canada, *Temporary Foreign Workers*, 10.
41 Nakache and Kinoshita, *Canadian Temporary*.
42 Byl, "Entrenching Exploitation."
43 Government of Manitoba, "Manitoba Provincial Nominee Program: Common Questions."
44 Bucklaschuk, Moss, and Annis, "Temporary May Not," 66.
45 Alboim, *Adjusting the Balance*.
46 Nakache and Kinoshita, *Canadian Temporary*.
47 Office of the Auditor General of Canada, "Selecting Foreign Workers," 7.
48 Carter, Morrish and Amoyaw, "Attracting Immigrants"; Carter et al., *Evaluation*; Carter, Pandey, and Townsend, *Manitoba Provincial*.
49 Thornton, BC *Provincial*.
50 CIC, *Facts and Figures 2010*.
51 Carter, Pandey, and Townsend, *Manitoba Provincial*.
52 Picot, Hou, and Coulombe, "Poverty Dynamics."
53 Statistics Canada, *Community Profile*.
54 Leo and August, "Multi-level Governance"; Carter et al., *Evaluation*.
55 Statistics Canada, *Community Profile*.

CHAPTER NINE

1 Human Rights Watch, *Slow Reform*.
2 Anderson, *Doing the Dirty Work?*; Stasiulis and Bakan, "Negotiating the Citizenship Divide"; Stasiulis and Bakan, *Negotiating Citizenship*.
3 Miles, *Capitalism*.
4 Sharma, *Home Economics*.
5 Cohen, *New Helots*.
6 Miles, *Capitalism*.
7 For a recent review of the literature on the LCP, see Spitzer and Torres, *Gender-Based Barriers*.
8 Citizenship and Immigration Canada (CIC), "Operational Bulletin 192." Beginning April 2010, LCP regulations increased the number of years from three to four in which to accumulate two years (or 3,900 hours) of work as a live-in caregiver to be eligible for permanent residence.
9 CIC, "Operational Bulletin 025."
10 Benston, "Political Economy."
11 Ibid., 19.
12 Ibid., 21.

13 Balka, "Obituary," 11.

14 Ibid.; Luxton and Armstrong, "Margaret Lowe Benston"; Luxton and Vosko, "Where Women's Efforts"; Hennessy and Ingraham, eds, *Materialist Feminism*.

15 Brooks, "Valuing Women's Work," 178.

16 Bezanson and Luxton, eds, *Social Reproduction*.

17 Luxton, "Feminist Political Economy," 32.

18 Miles et al., "Margaret Benston's"; Hennessy and Ingraham, *Materialist Feminism*.

19 Luxton, "Feminist Political Economy," 36–7.

20 Benston, "Political Economy," 23.

21 Ibid., 6–7.

22 Bakan and Stasiulis, eds, *Not One*; Vosko, ed., *Precarious Employment*.

23 Heymann, *Forgotten Families*, 6.

24 Kipfer et al., "On the Reproduction," 8.

25 Bakan, "Marxism and Anti-Racism"; Goonewardena et al., eds, *Space, Difference*.

26 Eviota, *Political Economy*, 100–1.

27 Dagenais, "Women in Guadeloupe," 95.

28 Chang, *Disposable Domestics*, 124.

29 Bezanson and Luxton, eds, *Social Reproduction*.

30 Fox and Yiu, "As Times Change," 197–8.

31 Stasiulis and Bakan, *Negotiating Citizenship*.

32 Macklin, "Who Is?"

33 Stasiulis and Bakan, *Negotiating Citizenship*.

34 Bakan and Stasiulis, eds, *Not One*.

35 Lukacs, *History and Class*.

36 Stasiulis and Bakan, *Negotiating Citizenship*.

37 Ibid.

38 Dunayevskaya, *Marxism and Freedom*.

39 Stasiulis, "Relational Positionalities," 183.

40 Mullings, *On Our Own*; Fernando, *Race and the City*; Davis, *Women, Race*.

41 Mohanty, *Feminism without Borders*.

42 Stasiulis and Bakan, *Negotiating Citizenship*; Bakan and Stasiulis, eds, *Not One*.

43 Abu-Laban, *Gendering the Nation-State*.

44 Benston, "Political Economy," 5. When positing more inspirational models, however, Benston presented a curious association, where "cooperatives, the kibbutz, etc." were parenthetically listed. This is problematic, indicating neglect of the occupied land in Israel/Palestine. See Abu-Laban and Bakan, "Racial Contract"; and Pappe, *Ethnic Cleansing.*

45 Depatie-Pelletier, "Under Legal Practices"; Stasiulis and Bakan, "Negotiating the Citizenship Divide."

46 Glickstein, "Is It Capitalism?" 276.

47 Sharma, *Home Economics,* 65.

48 Meillassoux, *Maidens, Meal.*

49 Pentland, *Labour and Capital.*

50 Sharma, *Home Economics,* 61.

51 Ibid., 66.

52 Ibid.

53 Ibid., 65–7; Corrigan, "Feudal Relics?"

54 Cohen, *New Helots.*

55 Miles, *Capitalism.*

56 Anderson, *Marx at the Margins.*

57 Miles, *Capitalism,* 47.

58 Ibid.

59 Ibid., 219–20.

60 Currie, "Review," 191.

61 Cohen, *New Helots,* 35–6.

62 Miles, *Capitalism,* 182.

63 Ibid.

64 Ibid., 33.

65 Ibid., 177.

66 Ibid.

67 Ibid.

68 Ibid., 185–6.

69 Depatie-Pelletier, "Under Legal Practices," 1.

70 Oxman-Martinez, Hanley, and Cheung, "Another Look," 16.

71 Sharma, *Home Economics.*

72 Dejardin, "Gender Dimensions," 3.

73 Stasiulis, "Revisiting the Permanent-Temporary."

74 Oxman-Martinez, Hanley, and Cheung, "Another Look," 11.

75 Diocson, "Filipino Women."

CHAPTER TEN

First of all, I am grateful to the participants in our study for sharing their stories with us. They hoped that many others would learn from their experiences and would feel motivated to improve the LCP. Second, I am thankful to my co-authors for their insights, knowledge sharing, and commitment to making known former live-in caregivers' contributions to Canadian society. It has been a wonderful experience to write this chapter with them. – Sara Torres

1 Citizenship and Immigration Canada (CIC), "Operational Bulletin 192." Throughout the fieldwork of our study, however, all the LCP participants were under the thirty-six-month rule.
2 This chapter draws on the findings of a multisite project called "The Land of Milk and Honey? After the Live-in Caregiver Program," funded by the Social Sciences and Humanities Research Council of Canada through a grant awarded to Denise Spitzer and colleagues. For details on this project, see Spitzer et al., "Land of Milk and Honey?"
3 R. Bishwakarma, V. Hunt, and A. Zajicek, *Intersectionality and Informed Policy* (2007), cited in Olena Hankivsky, Renée Cormier, and Diego de Mirech, *Intersectionality*, 18.
4 Hill Collins, *Black Feminist Thought*; Yuval-Davis, "Intersectionality and Feminist."
5 Ehrenreich and Russell Hochschild, eds, *Global Woman*.
6 Fine, "Social Division," 137.
7 Ibid.
8 Stasiulis and Bakan, *Negotiating Citizenship*.
9 Spitzer and Torres, *Gender-Based Barriers*.
10 Pratt, "Stereotypes and Ambivalence," 159.
11 Ehrenreich and Russell Hochschild, eds, *Global Woman*, 6.
12 San Juan, "Overseas Filipino Workers."
13 Canadian Research Institute for the Advancement of Women (CRIAW), "Intersectional Feminist Frameworks."
14 San Juan, "Overseas Filipino Workers."
15 Kelly et al., "Explaining the Deprofessionalized," 14.
16 Rodriguez, "Migrant Heroes."
17 Fernandez, "Commodified Women."
18 Rodriguez, "Migrant Heroes," 342.

19 Fernandez, "Commodified Women."
20 Rodriguez, "Migrant Heroes," 342.
21 Kelly et al., "Explaining the Deprofessionalized," 14.
22 Spitzer et al., "Land of Milk and Honey?"
23 CIC, "Live-in Caregiver Program." PR applications are rejected if the caregiver, the spouse or common-law partner, or any family members have a criminal record or a serious medical problem or if the LCP worker did not provide truthful information about education, training, or experience to the visa officer when first applying under the LCP.
24 Stasiulis and Bakan, *Negotiating Citizenship*.
25 Oxman-Martinez et al., "Intersection of Canadian."
26 Kelly et al., "Explaining the Deprofessionalized."
27 Spitzer, "Live-in Caregivers."
28 Oxman-Martinez and Hanley, "Border Control."
29 Salazar Parrenas, "Care Crisis."
30 CRIAW, "Intersectional Feminist Frameworks."
31 McCall, "Complexity of Intersectionality"; Nash, "Re-thinking Intersectionality."
32 CRIAW, "Intersectional Feminist Frameworks"; Hankivsky et al., "Exploring the Promises."
33 Manuel, "Envisioning the Possibilities."
34 Hankivsky et al., "Exploring the Promises," 9.
35 Yuval-Davis, "Intersectionality and Feminist"; McCall, "Complexity of Intersectionality."
36 Hankivsky et al., "Exploring the Promises," 9.
37 See Andressen and Hughes, "Summary Report." At the time of the study, the vast majority of participants were between thirty-five and fifty-four years of age. Fewer than one-quarter were in their late twenties and early thirties. Just under 10 per cent of the participants were fifty-five years of age or older. All but one of the study participants were women. This correlates with Canadian statistics that indicate the vast majority of live-in caregivers are women. With respect to countries of origin, the majority of participants come from the Philippines, and others come from the Caribbean, the Middle East, and eastern Europe. Most study participants immigrated to Canada sometime between 2000 and 2007. About one-quarter arrived during the 1990s, and a much smaller number arrived in the 1980s. Fewer than one-quarter had obtained Canadian citizenship. Almost one-half were permanent residents, and about one-third had either

a temporary work permit or an open work permit. Most participants had completed the LCP sometime in the past seven years.

38 Spitzer et al., "Land of Milk and Honey?"
39 Andressen and Hughes, *Summary Report.*
40 Jarman, "Explaining Social Exclusion."
41 The names of all study participants have been changed to protect their confidentiality.
42 San Juan, "Overseas Filipino Workers."
43 Andressen and Hughes, *Summary Report.*
44 Spitzer and Torres, *Gender-Based Barriers.*
45 Spitzer, "Live-in Caregivers."
46 Spitzer and Torres, *Gender-Based Barriers.*
47 Immigrant Workers Centre (IWC) et al., *Reform of the Temporary,* 5.
48 CIC call centre representative, interview, 2010. A CIC call centre representative explained that it takes approximately nine months for live-in caregivers to receive their open work permit, during which time they must stay with their current employer. This means that before the LCP ends, the worker must renegotiate the contract with the employer to ensure that the contract is valid until the open work permit arrives. LCP workers are allowed to change employers only if the potential employer completes a Labour Market Opinion (LMO) through the Department of Human Resources and Skills Development Canada and only if the LMO is approved; they are not allowed work anywhere else.
49 Bonifacio, *From Caregiver.*
50 Spitzer et al., "Land of Milk and Honey?"
51 Neufeld et al., "Immigrant Women."
52 Ibid.
53 Cynthia Cranford, cited in Duffy, "Doing the Dirty Work," 333.
54 Neufeld et al., "Immigrant Women."
55 Piper, "Gender and Migration."
56 IWC et al., *Reform of the Temporary.*
57 Spitzer, "Live-in Caregivers."
58 Spitzer et al., "Land of Milk and Honey?"
59 Canadian Public Research Network (CPRN), "Job Quality Indicators."
60 Stasiulis and Bakan, *Negotiating Citizenship.*
61 Statistics Canada, "Study: Low-Income."
62 Pratt, "Stereotypes and Ambivalence," 159.
63 Kelly et al., "Explaining the Deprofessionalized," 32.

64 Parreñas, "Mothering from a Distance."
65 Macklin, "On the Inside."
66 Duffy, "Doing the Dirty Work."
67 Bonifacio, *From Caregiver*, 41.
68 Spitzer and Torres, *Gender-Based Barriers*.
69 Ibid.; Spitzer, "Live-in Caregivers." In addition, a current study on family
    reunification by Spitzer also corroborates these findings.
70 Manuel, "Envisioning the Possibilities."
71 Kelly et al., "Explaining the Deprofessionalized."

CHAPTER 11

1 Satzewich, *Racism and the Incorporation*, 467; Sharma, "True North";
   Vosko, "Fabric Friends," 45; Bakan and Stasiulis, "Foreign Domestic."
2 Verma, *Mexican and Caribbean*; Zaman, "Transnational Migration";
   Oxman-Martinez, Hanley, and Cheung, "Another Look."
3 The Low-Skill Pilot Project, as it is commonly known, was recently
   renamed the Pilot Project for Occupations Requiring Lower Levels of
   Formal Training (PPORLLFT). Activists amuse themselves by asking, "Do
   policymakers think this program will LLFT the PPOR?"
4 Byl, "Temporary Foreign Workers"; Byl, "Entrenching Exploitation";
   Fudge and McPhail, "Temporary Foreign Worker"; Fuller and Vosko,
   "Temporary Employment."
5 Cook, "Workers of Colour"; Basok, "He Came, He Saw."
6 Arat-Koc, "From 'Mothers of the Nation.'"
7 Byl, "Temporary Foreign Workers"; Byl, "Entrenching Exploitation."
8 Cook, "Workers of Colour."
9 Choudry et al., *"Fight Back."*
10 The Immigrant Workers Centre is a grassroots community group in Mont-
    real that engages in individual advocacy, education, and collective action
    around the labour and immigration rights of migrants. Our Learning to Be
    an Immigrant Worker project, funded by the Social Sciences and Human-
    ities Research Council of Canada through its support of the "Work and
    Lifelong Learning" initiative, included semistructured interviews with
    more than fifty migrant workers and participant observation of the inter-
    ventions of community groups and unions working with this population.
    One of the key goals of this project was to develop organizing tools in
    order to encourage migrants' defence of their rights. Other members of

the IWC Research Group include Aziz Choudry, Steve Jordan, and Martha Steigman.

11 The IWC Research Group conducted interviews with "temporary" (in the eyes of the legislation) migrant workers in the Montreal community and with Canadian immigrants, defined as those newcomers to Canada who have been granted at a minimum either permanent resident status or landed immigrant status, some of whom have gone on to obtain citizenship.

12 This project consisted of a community-based survey of 150 domestic workers to document their employment conditions and their health and safety experiences in the workplace. See PINAY, *Danger!*

13 CSST is the Commission de la santé et de la sécurité du travail, a public provider of workers' compensation.

14 Conducted by Jill Hanley, Sylvie Gravel, Katherine Lippel, Stephanie Premji, and Eric Shragge, this project is titled "The Right to Health and Social Services" and involves a survey of 200 precarious status migrants on their experiences accessing healthcare services and related benefits, interviews with a subset of 40 migrants on their individual, family, and collective strategies to access Medicare and CSST, and a case study of an emerging free clinic for uninsured migrants. Sigalit Gal, Jahhon Koo, Valérie Lavigne, and Anette Sikka have all been involved as student researchers on this project.

15 Conducted by Jill Hanley, this project is titled "L'Accès aux services sociaux" and involves interviews with thirty TFWs and ten policymakers on the subject. Jahhon Koo and Andre Rivard have been student researchers on this project.

16 We would like to thank Sigalit Gal for some of her background work on the PINAY material in this section. She is a doctoral candidate in the McGill School of Social Work.

17 See, for example, Valiani, "Temporary Foreign Worker"; Velasco, "Filipino Migrant Workers"; Chan, "Nanny Trap."

18 For more information, please consult MIGRANTE, "Homepage," http:// www.migrante.ca (accessed 25 January 2012). MIGRANTE is a Filipino rights organization with chapters around the world.

19 For more information, see FERME, "Statistiques," http://www.fermequebec. com/4-Realisations-et-temoignages.html#10 (accessed 25 January 2012).

20 We have heard of a United Farm Workers (UFW) office existing in Montreal in the 1970s, but our understanding is that it was to promote support for American-based UFW campaigns, particularly the Grape Boycott. It

does not seem that they were organizing the migrant farm workers present in Quebec (former UFW employee, personal communication). Although we have not done an in-depth historical search, we have not been able to find any detailed reference to this office in the usual academic literature or in a Google search. One brief reference can be found at http://www.pbs.org/itvs/fightfields/cesarchavez1.html (accessed 25 January 2012).

21 For a synopsis of her work, see United Food and Commercial Workers (UFCW) Canada, "Patricia Perez." Patricia Perez died of cancer in 2007, only a few years after beginning her organizing with farm workers. She was so well respected and so well loved by the workers and their allies, however, that people continue to refer to her all the time.

22 For more information, see FERME, "Page d'Accueil," http://www. fermequebec.com/accueil.html (accessed 25 January 2012).

23 Quebec Labor Relations Commission decision in the case of UFCW Local 501 vs Ferme L'Écuyer and the Attorney General of Quebec, 2010 QCCRT 0191.

24 Byl, "Temporary Foreign Workers."

25 It would appear Canada does not have a problem with "labour shortages" but rather a problem finding enough workers who will accept the degrading working conditions being offered in sectors taking advantage of the TFWP. In the analysis of the Alberta Federation of Labour (AFL), "At least some employers are using the program as part of a deliberate effort to drive down wages and working conditions and to bypass unionized Canadian workers." The union notes that, "in a sense, the program is being used as a union busting tool. And, by allowing the program to be used in this way, our provincial and federal governments are allowing themselves to become partners in union busting." See Alberta Federation of Labour, "2006 May Policy Statement."

26 Citizenship and Immigration Canada (CIC), *Facts and Figures 2010*; Hanlon, "Temporary Foreign Worker"; Derrick, "Foreign Nationals." Some workers brought into Canada under the LSPP face unemployment, a situation that puts into question their right to remain in Canada. In addition, some have been moved by the recruitment agency to other cities or regions to work for new employers. These situations have raised questions for the workers themselves and issues about whether these kinds of situations violate the LSPP.

27 CIC, *Canada – Total Entries*. See also CIC, *Facts and Figures 2010*. Approximately, 3,500 LSPP workers are engaged in agricultural work, providing stiff competition to the SAWP workers. In terms of their organizing

experiences, agricultural LSPP workers have more in common with SAWP workers than with LSPP workers in other sectors, so we deal with their experiences in the chapter's section on the SAWP.

28 The TFWP links workers to one employer for a limited period, but the actual period that they can stay in Canada is longer. Thus, in theory, these laid-off workers could have stayed for a longer period, but securing another job would have been complex. If employers had wanted these workers, they would have been required to apply for a permit and to demonstrate that there were no Canadian workers who could do the work. This is a lengthy process and acts as a deterrent for employment.

29 For more information, see Table de concertation des organismes au service des personnes réfugiées et immigrantes (TCRI), http://www.tcri.qc.ca (accessed 25 January 2012). The TCRI has existed since 1979 and has over 100 members across Quebec.

30 For more information, see Canadian Council for Refugees (CCR), "Homepage," http://www.ccrweb.ca (accessed 25 January 2012). The CCR has existed since 1978 and has over 180 members across the country.

31 Hartling, Pickett, and Brison, "Canadian Agricultural Injury."

32 After a seven-year campaign demanding that Quebec domestic workers be made eligible for workers' compensation, the Ministry of Labour has proposed legislation that takes important steps in this direction. We are waiting to see whether this will come to pass.

CHAPTER TWELVE

1 For a list of reasons why states support temporary migration policies, see Abella, "Policies and Best Practices," 1–2.

2 See respectively, Tabuchi, "Japan Training Program"; Kershner, "Israelis Divided"; and Fahim, "Immigrant Maids Flee."

3 This is evidently not a comprehensive analysis of all states' experiences with temporary labour migration programs.

4 Martin, "There Is Nothing," 1.

5 Hennebry, "Bienvenidos a Canadá?"

6 Wickramasekara, "Globalisation," 1249.

7 For example, see Hennebry, "Bienvenidos a Canadá?"

8 Preibisch, "Local Produce," 421.

9 For an evaluation of the mechanisms by which temporary labour migrants are exploited, see Lenard and Straehle, "Temporary Labour Migration."

10 Freeman, "Modes of Immigration," 887.

11 Kymlicka, *Finding Our Way*.

12 Friesen, "Leap in Temporary."

13 Quoted in ibid.

14 Freeman, "Modes of Immigration," 889.

15 Castles, "Guest-Worker in Western Europe."

16 Castles, "Guestworkers in Europe," 742.

17 Ibid., 743.

18 Freeman, "Modes of Immigration," 890; Martin and Teitelbaum, "Mirage of Mexican," 118; Ruhs, "Temporary Foreign Worker."

19 Freeman, "Modes of Immigration," 890.

20 Castles, "Guestworkers in Europe," 758.

21 For an outline of these anxieties in Europe, see Gibney, "A Thousand Little Guantanamos."

22 Piper, "Rights of Foreign," 75.

23 Ibid.

24 Ibid., 79. See also Hugo, "Best Practice," 24.

25 Nicola Piper points out, for example, that Asian nations have not implemented a regional human rights regime, unlike most other regions. See Piper, "Rights of Foreign," 75.

26 For a list of labour-sending and labour-receiving countries in Asia (and countries that are both senders and receivers), see Wickramasekera, "Asian Labour Migration."

27 Piper, "Temporary Economic Migration."

28 Wickramasekera, "Asian Labour Migration."

29 These statistics are drawn from Shah, *Restrictive Labour*.

30 Kapiszewski, "Arab versus Asian," 6; Louër, "Political Impact," 33.

31 Kapiszewski, "Arab versus Asian."

32 Piper, "Migrant Labor."

33 Bartram, "Foreign Workers in Israel"; Bartram, "Migration, Ethno-nationalist Destinations." For more in general on the status of temporary migrant workers in Israel, see Kemp, "Reforming Policies."

34 Bartram, "Migration, Ethno-nationalist Destinations."

35 Harper and Zubida, "Making Room."

36 Sharpe, "When Ethnic Returnees."

37 Martin and Teitelbaum, "Mirage of Mexican"; Massey and Lang, "Long-Term Consequences"; O'Rourke, "Embracing Reality"; Chin, *Guest Worker Question*; Barbieri, *Ethics of Citizenship*.

38 Nonetheless, as Philip Martin and Michael Teitelbaum have noted, during the program itself, "the number of unauthorized Mexicans slipping across the borders actually expanded in parallel with the number of authorized temporary workers; the illegal flows then continued to accelerate after the program's termination." See Martin and Teitelbaum, "Mirage of Mexican," 122.

39 Ibid., 122–5.

40 For an account of the role that German ethnicity has played in defining the German nation, see Barbieri, *Ethics of Citizenship*; and Canefe, "Citizens versus Permanent." For an account of the way that the presence of Turkish migrants forced the reimagining of the German nation, see Martin, "Germany"; Chin, *Guest Worker Question*; and Rubio-Marin, *Immigration*.

41 There are exceptions, of course, and Samuel Huntington's newest book is among them. See Huntington, *Who Are We?*

42 Castles, "Factors That Make," 875. As James Hollifield has noted, "closing off avenues for legal immigration in Western Europe led to a surge in illegal migration." See Hollifield, "Emerging Migration State," 899.

43 Loveband, "Nationality Matters," 125.

44 Ruhs, "Temporary Foreign Worker."

45 Basok, "Canada's Temporary Migration," 2.

46 Lichtenstein, "Examination of Guest Worker," 704–7.

47 Carens, "On Belonging."

48 Ruhs, "Potential of Temporary," 9.

49 What follows should not be taken as a full list of temporary visas. It is instead a list of temporary visas that target low-skilled workers in developing countries.

50 For general evaluations of this program, see Bakan and Stasiulis, "Foreign Domestic"; and Stasiulis and Bakan, "Negotiating Citizenship."

51 Global Commission on International Migration, "Report of the Global Commission."

52 Basok, "Canada's Temporary Migration"; Abella, "Policies and Best Practices," 22, 45.

53 Shah, *Restrictive Labour*, 5.

54 Piper, "Rights of Foreign," 79; Hugo, "Best Practice," 24.

55 Hollifield, "Emerging Migration State," 892.

56 Ruhs, "Temporary Foreign Worker," 4.

57 Ibid.

58 Castles, "Guestworkers in Europe," 743.

59 Ibid. As Castles notes, however, whether nonliberal states will ultimately be successful in preventing permanent migration is not clear since we are now seeing "trends towards labor market dependency on migrants and increased family reunion in some Asian countries. Moreover, the strikes and demonstrations by migrant workers in Dubai in early 2006 showed the difficulty of permanently suppressing worker rights."

60 Hollifield, "Emerging Migration State," 893.

61 Piper, "Rights of Foreign," 77; Kemp, "Reforming Policies," 23.

62 Martin and Teitelbaum, "Mirage of Mexican."

63 Piper, "Rights of Foreign," 76.

64 Elrick, "Influence of Migration"; Moran-Taylor, "When Mothers."

65 Shah, *Restrictive Labour*, 5–6.

66 Abella, "Policies and Best Practices," 17.

67 In the mid-1980s, Germany offered to return welfare-state contributions to migrants who left; on the whole, however, very few migrants took advantage of this opportunity; see Martin, "Recession and Migration," 686. One known problem with these schemes, at least historically, has been that migrants have shifted from legal access to temporary work to irregular work in order to *avoid* participating in such schemes; see Abella, "Policies and Best Practices."

68 Hugo, "Best Practice," 57.

69 Orozco and Lapointe, "Mexican Hometown Associations"; Binford, "Migrant Remittances." The programs are also criticized by some for the way that they let the government avoid responsibility for providing essential services.

70 For a discussion of temporary labour migration programs in New Zealand, see Lovelock and Leopold, "Labour Force Shortages."

71 Ruhs, "Economic Research," 414.

72 Kaur, "Labour Migration Trends." For more information about the levies applied to employers hiring foreign labour, see Kapiszewski, "Arab versus Asian," 5.

73 Ruhs, "Potential of Temporary," 20n28.

74 Ruhs, "Temporary Foreign Worker."

75 Carens, "Live-in Domestics."

76 Martin and Teitelbaum, "Mirage of Mexican."

77 For one expression of worry about this risk, see Basok, "Canada's Temporary Migration."

78 Hugo, "Best Practice," 35, 58.
79 Shah, *Restrictive Labour.*
80 For an assessment of recent Japanese policy with respect to the Nikkejin population, see Sharpe, "When Ethnic Returnees."
81 Shulman, "Immigration Raid."
82 Harper and Zubida, "Making Room."

Bibliography

Abele, Frances, and Daiva Stasiulis. "Canada as a 'White Settler Colony': What about Indigenous and Immigrants?" In *The New Canadian Political Economy*, ed. W. Clement and G. Williams, 240–77. Montreal and Kingston: McGill-Queen's University Press, 1989.

Abella, Manolo. "Global Competition for Skilled Workers and Consequences." In *Competing for Global Talent*, ed. Christiane Kuptsch and Eng Fong Pang, 11–32. Geneva: International Labour Office/Institute for Labour Studies, 2006.

– "Policies and Best Practices for Management of Temporary Migration." In *International Symposium on International Migration and Development, Population Division, Department of Economic and Social Affairs*, 1–59. Turin, Italy: United Nations Secretariat, 2006.

Abu-Laban, Yasmeen. *Gendering the Nation-State: Canadian and Comparative Perspectives*. Vancouver: UBC Press, 2008.

– "Reconstructing an Inclusive Citizenship for a New Millennium." *International Politics* 37, no. 4 (December 2000): 509–26.

Abu-Laban, Yasmeen, and Abigail B. Bakan. "The Racial Contract: Israel/Palestine and Canada." *Social Identities: Journal for the Study of Race, Nation and Culture* 14, no. 5 (September 2008): 637–60.

Abu-Laban, Yasmeen, and Christina Gabriel. *Selling Diversity: Integration, Multiculturalism, Employment Equity, and Globalization*. Peterborough, ON: Broadview, 2002.

Adey, Peter. *Mobility*. New York: Routledge, 2009.

– "Surveillance at the Airport: Surveilling Mobility/Mobilising Surveillance." *Environment and Planning A* 36, no. 8 (2004): 1365–80.

Adilman, Tamara. "A Preliminary Sketch of Chinese Women and Work in British Columbia, 1858–1950." In *Not Just Pin Money: Selected Essays on the History of Women's Work in British Columbia*, ed. Barbara K. Latham and Roberta J. Pazdro, 53–78. Victoria, BC: Camosun College, 1984.

Agamben, Giorgio. "The Camp as the Nomos of the Modern." In *Violence, Identity, and Self-Determination*, ed. H. deVries and S. Weber, 106–18. Stanford, CA: Stanford University Press, 1997.

– *Homo Sacer: Sovereign Power and Bare Life*. Stanford, CA: Stanford University Press, 1998.

– *State of Exception*. Chicago: University of Chicago Press, 2005.

Aguiar, Luis L.M., Patricia Tomic, and Ricardo Trumper. "Mexican Migrant Agricultural Workers and Accommodations on Farms in the Okanagan Valley, B.C." April 2011. http://mbc.metropolis.net/wp_2011. html (accessed 27 January 2012).

Alberta Federation of Labour. "2006 May Policy Statement on Temporary Foreign Workers." http://www.afl.org/index.php/docman (accessed 25 January 2012).

Alboim, Naomi. *Adjusting the Balance: Fixing Canada's Economic Immigration Policies*. Toronto: Maytree Foundation, 2010.

Anderson, Benedict. *Imagined Communities: Reflections on the Origin and Spread of Nationalism*. London: Verso, 1991.

Anderson, Bridget. *Doing the Dirty Work? The Global Politics of Domestic Labour*. London: Zed Books, 2000.

Anderson, Kay J. *Vancouver's Chinatown: Racial Discourse in Canada, 1875–1980*. Montreal and Kingston: McGill-Queen's University Press, 1991.

Anderson, Kevin. *Marx at the Margins: On Nationalism, Ethnicity, and Non-Western Societies*. Chicago: University of Chicago Press, 2010.

Andressen, Bryna, and Karen D. Hughes. *Summary Report: The Land of Milk and Honey? After the Live-in Caregiver Program in Canada, Results from Survey and Personal Information Forms (PIFs)*. Edmonton: University of Alberta, 2007.

Appadurai, Arjun. *Modernity at Large: Cultural Dimensions of Globalization*. Minneapolis: University of Minnesota Press, 1996.

Arat-Koc, Sedef. "From 'Mothers of the Nation' to Migrant Workers: Immigration Policies and Domestic Workers in Canadian History." In *Not One of the Family: Foreign Domestic Workers in Canada*, ed. Abigail Bakan and Daiva Stasiulis, 53–79. Toronto: University of Toronto Press, 1997.

– "Immigration Policies, Migrant Domestic Workers and the Definition of Citizenship in Canada." In *Deconstructing a Nation: Immigration, Multiculturalism and Racism in 90's Canada*, ed. Vic Satzewich, 229–42. Halifax: Fernwood, 1992.

Arendt, Hannah. *The Origins of Totalitarianism*. Cleveland, OH: World Publishing Company, 1958.

Ashutosh, Ishan, and Alison Mountz. "Migration Management for the Benefit of Whom? Interrogating the Work of the International Organization for Migration." *Citizenship Studies* 15, no. 1 (February 2011): 21–38.

Augé, Marc. *Non-Places: Introduction to an Anthropology of Supermodernity*. London: Verso, 1995.

Avendano, Ana. "Reintegration and Circular Migration – Effective for Development?" Paper presented in Roundtable 2: Migrant Integration, Reintegration and Circulation for Development, at Global Forum on Migration and Development, Athens, 4–5 November 2009.

Bajer, E. "Here for a Better Life: Thai Workers Remembered as Kind." *Chatham Daily News*, 27 April 2007.

Bakan, Abigail B. "Marxism and Anti-Racism: Rethinking the Politics of Difference." *Rethinking Marxism: A Journal of Economics, Culture and Society* 20, no. 2 (April 2008): 238–56.

Bakan, Abigail B., and Daiva Stasiulis. "Foreign Domestic Worker Policy in Canada and the Social Boundaries of Modern Citizenship." *Science and Society* 58, no. 1 (1994): 7–33.

– eds. *Not One of the Family: Foreign Domestic Workers in Canada*. Toronto: University of Toronto Press, 1997.

Balibar, Étienne. "Racism and Nationalism." In *Race, Nation, Class: Ambiguous Identities*, ed. Étienne Balibar and Immanuel Wallerstein, 37–68. London: Verso, 1991.

– "What We Owe to the Sans-Papiers." In *Social Insecurity*, ed. Len Guenther and Cornelius Heesters, 40–55. Toronto: Anansi, 2000.

Balka, Ellen. "Obituary: Margaret Lowe Benston, 1937–1991." *Labour/Le Travail* 28 (Fall 1991): 11–13.

Bannerji, Himani. *The Dark Side of the Nation: Essays on Multiculturalism, Nationalism and Gender*. Toronto: Canadian Scholars' Press, 2000.

– ed. *Returning the Gaze: Essays on Racism, Feminism and Politics*.
Toronto: Sister Vision, 1993.

Barbieri, William A. *Ethics of Citizenship: Immigration and Group Rights
in Germany*. Durham, NC: Duke University Press, 1998.

Barr, Macreadie, Kelly Jefferys, and Randall Monger, for US Department
of Homeland Security. "Nonimmigrant Admissions to the United States:
2007." In *Annual Flow Report* (2008). http://www.dhs.gov/xlibrary/
assets/statistics/publications/ois_ni_fr_2007.pdf (accessed 12 January
2012).

Barrón, Antonieta. "Mexican Women on the Move: Migrant Workers
in Mexico and Canada." In *Women Working the NAFTA Food Chain:
Women, Food and Globalization*, ed. Beth McAuley, 113–26. Toronto:
Second Story Books, 1999.

Bartram, David. "Foreign Workers in Israel: History and Theory." *International Migration Review* 32, no. 2 (1998): 303–25.

– "Migration, Ethno-nationalist Destinations, and Social Divisions:
Non-Jewish Immigrants in Israel." *Ethnopolitics* 10, no. 2 (2010):
235–52.

Basok, Tanya. "Canada's Temporary Migration Program: A Model Despite
Flaws." November 2007. http://www.migrationinformation.org/Feature/
display.cfm?ID=650 (accessed 13 January 2012).

– "Free to Be Unfree: Mexican Guest Workers in Canada." *Labour, Capital and Society/Travail, capital et societé* 32, no. 2 (1999): 192–221.

– "He Came, He Saw, He … Stayed: Guest Worker Programmes and
the Issue of Non-Return." *International Migration* 38, no. 2 (2000):
215–38.

– "Human Rights and Citizenship: The Case of Mexican Migrants in
Canada." Working paper 72, the Center for Comparative Immigration
Studies, University of California, San Diego, 2003.

– "Mexican Seasonal Migration to Canada and Development: A Community-Based Comparison." *International Migration* 41, no. 2 (2003):
3–26.

– "Migration of Mexican Seasonal Farm Workers to Canada and
Development: Obstacles to Productive Investment." *International
Migration Review* 34, no. 1 (Spring 2000): 79–97.

– *Tortillas and Tomatoes: Transmigrant Mexican Harvesters in Canada*.
Montreal and Kingston: McGill-Queen's University Press, 2002.

Bauman, Zygmunt. *Liquid Modernity*. Cambridge, UK: Polity Press,
2000.

Becerril Quintana, Ofelia. "A New Era of Seasonal Mexican Migration to Canada." 2011. http://www.focal.ca/en/publications/focalpoint/ 467-june-2011-ofelia-becerril-quintana-en (accessed 13 January 2012).
– "Transnational Work and the Gendered Politics of Labour: A Study of Male and Female Mexican Migrant Farm Workers in Canada." In *Organizing the Transnational: Labour, Politics, and Social Change*, ed. Luin Goldring and Sailaja Krishnamurti, 156–72. Vancouver: UBC Press, 2007.
Benston, Margaret. "The Political Economy of Women's Liberation," *Monthly Review* 21, no. 7 (December 1969). Reprinted in *Academic OneFile*, 1–6. http://o-go.galegroup.com.aupac.lib.athabascau.ca/ps/i. do? id=GALE%7CA82257991&v=2.1&u=atha49011&it=r&p=AONE &sw=w (accessed 14 January 2012).
Berg, Bruce L. *Qualitative Research Methods for the Social Sciences*. 4th ed. Boston: Allyn and Bacon, 2001.
Bezanson, Kate, and Meg Luxton, eds. *Social Reproduction: Feminist Political Economy Challenges Neo-Liberalism*. Montreal and Kingston: McGill-Queen's University Press, 2006.
Bhabha, Homi K. *The Location of Culture*. London and New York: Routledge, 1994.
Billig, Michael. *Banal Nationalism*. London: Sage, 1995.
Binford, Leigh. "Contract Labor in Canada and the United States: A Critical Appreciation of Tanya Basok's *Tortillas and Tomatoes: Transmigrant Mexican Harvesters in Canada*." *Canadian Journal of Latin American and Caribbean Studies* 29, nos 57–8 (2004): 289–308.
– "From Fields of Power to Fields of Sweat: The Dual Process of Constructing Temporary Migrant Labour in Mexico and Canada." *Third World Quarterly* 30, no. 3 (2009): 503–17.
– "Migrant Remittances and (Under)Development in Mexico." *Critique of Anthropology* 23, no. 3 (2003): 305–36.
– "The Seasonal Agricultural Workers Program and Mexican Development." Policy paper, Canadian Foundation for the Americas, Ottawa, August 2006.
Bloemraad, Irene. *Becoming a Citizen: Incorporating Immigrants and Refugees in the United States and Canada*. Los Angeles: University of California Press, 2006.
Blunt, Alison. "Cultural Geographies of Migration: Mobility, Transnationality and Diaspora." *Progress in Human Geography* (September 2007): 1–11.

Boehm, Deborah A. "'Now I Am a Man and a Woman!' Gendered Moves and Migrations in a Transnational Mexican Community." *Latin American Perspectives* 35, no. 1 (2008): 16–30.

Bolaria, B. Singh, and Peter S. Li. *Racial Oppression in Canada*. 2nd ed. Toronto: Garamond, 1988.

Bonifacio, Glenda. *From Caregiver to Citizen: Transitional Services of Filipino Women in Southern Alberta, Final Report*. Lethbridge, AB: Women's Studies Program, University of Lethbridge, 2007.

Boucher, Gerard. "A Critique of Global Policy Discourses on Managing International Migration." *Third World Quarterly* 29, no. 7 (2008): 1461–71.

Bourette, Susan. "Welcome to Canada, Hope You Weren't Planning on Staying." *Report on Business*, 26 September 2007.

Brand, Dionne. "A Working Paper on Black Women in Toronto: Gender, Race and Class." In *Returning the Gaze: Essays on Racism, Feminism and Politics*, ed. Himani Bannerji, 220–42. Toronto: Sister Vision, 1993.

Brem, Maxwell. *Migrant Workers in Canada: A Review of the Seasonal Agricultural Workers Program*. Ottawa: North-South Institute, 2006.

Brooks, Kim. "Valuing Women's Work in the Home: A Defining Moment." *Canadian Journal of Women and the Law* 17 (2005): 177–95.

Bucklaschuk, Jill, Allison Moss, and Robert C. Annis. "Temporary May Not Always Be Temporary. The Impact of 'Transitional' Foreign Workers and Increasing Diversity in Brandon, Manitoba." *Our Diverse Cities* 6 (Spring 2009): 64–70.

Buroway, Michael, Joseph A. Blum, Sheba George, Zsuzsa Gille, and Millie Thayer. *Global Ethnography: Forces, Connections, and Imaginations in a Postmodern World*. Los Angeles: University of California Press, 2000.

Bustamante, Juan José, and Carlos Aléman. "Perpetuating Split–Household Families: The Case of Mexican Sojourners in Mid-Michigan and Their Transnational Fatherhood Practices." *Migraciones Internacionales* 4, no. 1 (2007): 65–86.

Byl, Yessy. "Entrenching Exploitation." Special report, Alberta Federation of Labour, Edmonton, 2009. http://www.afl.org/index.php/Reports/ entrenching-exploitation-second-rept-of-afl-temporary-foreign-worker-advocate.html (accessed 13 January 2012).

– "Temporary Foreign Workers: Alberta's Disposable Workforce." Special report, Alberta Federation of Labour, Edmonton, 2007.

http://www.afl.org/index.php/View-document/19-Temporary-Foreign-Workers-Alberta-s-Disposable-Workforce.html (accessed 13 January 2012).

Cable News Network (CNN). "Bush Calls for 6,000 Troops along Border." 16 May 2006.

Canada Border Services Agency. "About NEXUS." http://www.cbsa-asfc. gc.ca/prog/nexus/about-sujet-eng.html (accessed 23 January 2012).

Canadian Agriculture Injury Surveillance Program (CAISP). "Agricultural Fatalities and Hospitalizations in Ontario, 1990–2004." 2007. http:// www.caisp.ca (accessed 13 January 2012).

Canadian Bar Association. "Low Skilled Worker Pilot Project." National Citizenship and Immigration Law Section, Canadian Bar Association, Ottawa, 2006.

Canadian Broadcasting Corporation (CBC). "3 Dead, 13 Injured after Crash of Van Packed with Farm Workers." CBC News, 7 March 2007.
– "Workers Killed in Roof Collapse Likely Didn't Speak English." CBC News, 26 April 2007.

Canadian Labour Congress. Canada – Entries of Temporary Foreign Workers by Province and NOC, 2004–2008. Ottawa: Canadian Labour Congress, 2008.

Canadian Nanny. "Now Offering AIR MILES® Reward Miles!" 16 March 2010. http://www.canadiannanny.ca/index.php?p=3_6&nid=56 (accessed 14 January 2012).

Canadian Public Research Network (CPRN). "Job Quality Indicators." 2006. http://www.jobquality.ca/indicator_e/default.stm (accessed 6 July 2007).

Canadian Research Institute for the Advancement of Women (CRIAW). "Intersectional Feminist Frameworks: An Emerging Vision." 2006. http://www.oaith.ca/assets/files/Publications/Intersectional%20Feminist %20Frameworks_CRIAW_e.pdf (accessed 13 January 2012).

Canefe, Nergis. "Citizens versus Permanent Guests: Cultural Memory and Citizenship Laws in a Reunified Germany." Citizenship Studies 2, no. 3 (1998): 519–44.

CANVISA Immigration. "Immigrate to Canada." http:// www.lcvimmigration.com/fastimmigration.html (accessed 10 October 2010).

Carens, Joseph. "A Contextual Approach to Political Theory." Ethical Theory and Moral Practice 7, no. 2 (2004): 117–32.

– "Live-in Domestics, Seasonal Workers, and Others Hard to Locate on the Map of Democracy." *Journal of Political Philosophy* 16, no. 4 (2008): 419–45.

– "On Belonging: What We Owe to People Who Stay." *Boston Review* 30, nos 3–4 (Summer 2005): 16–19.

Carter, Tom, Margot Morrish, and Benjamin Amoyaw. "Attracting Immigrants to Smaller Urban and Rural Communities: Lessons Learned from the Manitoba Provincial Nominee Program." *Journal of International Migration and Integration* 9, no. 2 (2008): 161–83.

Carter, Tom, Manish Pandey, and James Townsend. *The Manitoba Provincial Nominee Program: Attraction, Integration and Retention of Immigrants.* Ottawa: Institute for Research on Public Policy, 2010.

Carter, Tom, Chesya Polevychok, John Osborne, Monica Adeler, and Anita Friesen. *An Evaluation of the Manitoba Provincial Nominee Program.* Winnipeg: Manitoba Labour and Immigration, Immigration Division, 2009.

Carvajal, Lidia. *The Farm-Level Impacts in Mexico of the Participation in Canada's Seasonal Agricultural Workers Program (CSAWP).* Guelph: University of Guelph, 2008.

Castells, Manuel. *The Informational City: Information Technology, Economic Restructuring, and the Urban Regional Process.* Cambridge, UK: Blackwell, 1989.

– "Informationalism and the Network Society." Epilogue to Pekka Hineman, *The Hacker Ethic and the Spirit of the Information Age,* 155–78. New York: Random House, 2001.

– *The Rise of the Network Society.* Vol. 1, *The Information Age: Economy, Society and Culture.* Cambridge, UK: Blackwell, 1996.

Castles, Stephen. "The Factors That Make and Unmake Migration Policies." *International Migration Review* 38, no. 3 (2004): 852–84.

– "The Guest-Worker in Western Europe – an Obituary." *International Migration Review* 20, no. 4 (1986): 761–78.

– "Guestworkers in Europe: A Resurrection?" *International Migration Review* 40, no. 4 (2006): 741–66.

– "Hierarchies of Citizenship in the New Global Order." *International Politics* 42, no. 2 (2005): 203–24.

Cawston, Alfred H. "John Chinaman." *Okanagan Historical Society* 31 (1967): 109–17.

Chan, Cheryl. "The Nanny Trap." *Vancouver Courier*, 26 June 2005.

Chang, Grace. *Disposable Domestics: Immigrant Women Workers in the Global Economy*. Cambridge, UK: South End Press, 2000.

Chen, Dalson. "Thai Migrant Workers Petition for Changes in Foreign Workers Laws." *Windsor Star*, 23 April 2010.

Chin, Rita. *The Guest Worker Question in Postwar Germany*. Cambridge, UK: Cambridge University Press, 2007.

Cholewinski, Ryszard. *The Legal Status of Migrants Admitted for Employment*. Strasbourg, France: Council of Europe, 2004.

Choudry, Aziz, et al. *"Fight Back" – Workplace Justice for Immigrants*. New York: Fernwood, 2009.

Choy, Wayson. *The Jade Peony*. Vancouver: Douglas and McIntyre, 1995.

– *Paper Shadow: A Chinatown Childhood*. Toronto: Penguin, 1999.

Citizenship and Immigration Canada (CIC). *Annual Report to Parliament on Immigration 2008*. Ottawa: CIC, 2008.

– *Annual Report to Parliament on Immigration 2009*. Ottawa: CIC, 2009.

– "Application Processing Times." Updated 15 February 2011. http://www.cic.gc.ca/English/information/times/international/04-provincial. asp (accessed 2 July 2011).

– *Canada – Total Entries of Temporary Foreign Workers from Guatemala as Country of Citizenship by Sex and NOC Codes, 2003–2010*. Ottawa: CIC, 2011.

– *Facts and Figures 2006 – Immigration Overview of Permanent and Temporary Workers*. Ottawa: CIC, 2008.

– *Facts and Figures 2007 – Permanent Residents by Category*. Ottawa: CIC, 2009.

– *Facts and Figures 2007 – Temporary Residents by Yearly Status, 1983 to 2007*. Ottawa: CIC, 2009.

– *Facts and Figures 2008 – Immigration Overview: Permanent and Temporary Residents, Canada, Temporary Residents by Yearly Status, 1984 to 2008*. Ottawa: CIC, 2009.

– *Facts and Figures 2009 – Immigration Overview: Permanent and Temporary Residents*. Ottawa: CIC, 2010. http://www.cic.gc.ca/english/resources/statistics/facts2009/permanent/01.asp (accessed 13 January 2012).

– *Facts and Figures 2010 – Immigration Overview*. Ottawa: CIC, 2011.

– "FW 1: Temporary Foreign Worker Guidelines." Ottawa: CIC, 2010.

- "The Live-in Caregiver Program: Extending Your Stay." http://www.
  cic.gc.ca/english/work/caregiver/extend-stay.asp#resident (accessed 31
  August 2010).
- "Operational Bulletin 025 – January 3, 2007: Instructions to CIC Officers Concerning the Validity Period of Live-in Caregiver Work Permits
  as Well as Family Members of Live-in Caregivers." 2010. http://www.
  cic.gc.ca/english/resources/manuals/bulletins/2007/ob025.asp (accessed
  13 January 2012).
- "Operational Bulletin 192 – Regulatory and Administrative Changes to
  the Live-in Caregiver Program." 2010. http://www.cic.gc.ca/english/
  resources/manuals/bulletins/2010/ob192.asp (accessed 13 January 2012).
- "Regulations Amending the Immigration and Refugee Protection Regulations (Temporary Foreign Workers)." *Canada Gazette* 143, no. 41 (10
  October 2009): n.p. http://www.gazette.gc.ca/rp-pr/p1/2009/
  2009-10-10/html/reg1-eng.html (accessed 13 January 2012).
- "Regulatory Changes to the Temporary Foreign Worker Program Take
  Effect April 1st, 2011." Updated 31 March 2011. http://www.cic.gc.ca/
  english/work/changes.asp (accessed 13 January 2012).
Clement, Gerald. "The Benefits of Immigration: The Manitoba Experi-
  ence." Speech to the Agricultural Manufacturers of Canada, Edmonton,
  5 June 2005.
Cohen, Robin. *The New Helots: Migrants in the International Division of
  Labour.* Aldershot, UK: Avebury/Gower, 1987.
Colby, Catherine. *From Oaxaca to Ontario: Mexican Contract Labor
  in Canada and the Impact at Home.* Davis, CA: California Institute of
  Rural Studies, 1997.
Commission for Labor Cooperation (CLC). *Protection of Migrant Agricul-
  tural Workers in Canada, Mexico and the United States.* Washington,
  DC: Secretariat of the Commission for Labor Cooperation, 2002. http://
  www.naalc.org/english/pdf/study4.pdf (accessed 9 December 2011).
Contenta, Sandro, and Laurie Monsebraaten, "How We're Creating an
  Illegal Workforce: Controversial Federal Program Brings in Foreigners
  for Temporary Jobs, but Leaves Them Ripe for Abuse." *Toronto Star*, 1
  November 2009.
Cook, Verda. "Workers of Colour within a Global Economy." Research
  paper, Canadian Labour Congress, Toronto, 2004.
Cornelius, Wayne. "Controlling 'Unwanted' Immigration: Lessons from
  the United States, 1993–2004." *Journal of Ethnic and Migration Studies*
  31, no. 4 (2005): 775–94.

Corrigan, Philip. "Feudal Relics of Capitalist Monuments? Notes on the Sociology of Unfree Labour." *Sociology* 11, no. 3 (1977): 453–63.

Cortes, Patricia. "The Feminization of International Migration and Its Effects on the Families Left Behind: Evidence from the Philippines." Powerpoint presentation at the "Research Conference on Remittances and Immigration," Federal Reserve Bank of Atlanta, 2010, http://www.frbatlanta.org/documents/news/conferences/10AC_remittances_Paper_Slides_cortes.pdf (accessed 13 January 2012).

Council on Foreign Relations, with the Canadian Council of Chief Executives and Consejo Mexicano de Asuntos Internacionales. *Building a North American Community: Report of an Independent Task Force.* Washington, DC: Council on Foreign Relations, 2007.

Crawford, Alison. "Buy-Local Push Prompts Ontario Grocers to Go Independent." *CBC News*, 15 July 2009. http://www.cbc.ca/news/story/2009/07/14/f-grocery-stores-independent-buy-local-meat-produce.html (accessed 4 February 2012).

Cresswell, Tim. "Constellation of Mobility: Towards Cultural Kinetics." 2006. http://es.sas.ac.uk/events/seminars/19C/Cresswell.pdf (accessed 16 June 2010).

Currie, Bob. "Review: Unfree Labour and Its Persistence into the Capitalist Era: A Critical Review of Recent Books by Robert Miles and Robin Cohen." *Review of African Political Economy*, nos 45–6 (1989): 190–6.

Cypher, James M. "Mexico's Economic Collapse." *NACLA Report on the Americas*, July–August 2010, 51–2.

Dagenais, Huguette. "Women in Guadeloupe: The Paradoxes of Reality." In *Women and Change in the Caribbean*, ed. Janet H. Momsen, 83–108. London: James Currey, 1993.

Dauvergne, Catherine. "Making People Illegal." In *Critical Beings: Law, Nation and the Global Subject*, ed. Peter Fitzpatrick and Patricia Tuitt, 83–100. Burlington, VT: Ashgate, 2004.

Davis, Angela. *Women, Race and Class*. New York: Random House, 1981.

Dejardin, Amelita King. "Gender Dimensions of Globalization." Discussion paper presented at the meeting on "Globalisation: Decent Work and Gender," a side-event to "The Oslo Conference on Decent Work: A Key to Social Justice for a Fair Globalization," September 2008.

Deleuze Gilles, and Felix Guatarri. *A Thousand Plateaus: Capitalism and Schizophrenia*. Trans. B. Massumi. Minneapolis: University of Minnesota Press, 1987.

Delta Partners. "Review of the Foreign Worker Program Pilot Project for Workers Requiring Lower Levels of Formal Training." March 2007.

Denzin, Norman K., and Yvonna S. Lincoln. "The Discipline and Practice of Qualitative Research." In *Strategies of Qualitative Inquiry*, 2nd ed., ed. Norman K. Denzin and Yvonna S. Lincoln, 1–43. Thousand Oaks, CA: Sage, 2003.

Depatie-Pelletier, Eugenie. "Under Legal Practices Similar to Slavery According to the U.N. Convention: Canada's 'Non White' 'Temporary' Foreign Workers in 'Low-Skilled' Occupations." Paper presented at the 10th National Metropolis Conference, Halifax, 2008.

Derrick, Thomas. "Foreign Nationals Working Temporarily in Canada." In Statistics Canada, *Canadian Social Trends*, 1–17. Ottawa: Statistics Canada, 8 June 2010.

Diocson, Cecilia. "Filipino Women in Canada's Live-in Caregiver Program." *Philippine Reporter*, 1 April 2005.

Duffy, Mignon. "Doing the Dirty Work: Gender, Race, and Reproductive Labor in Historical Perspective." *Gender and Society* 21, no. 3 (2007): 313–36.

Dunayevskaya, Raya. *Marxism and Freedom: From 1776 until Today*. Amherst, MA: Humanity Books, 2000.

Dunn, Leith, and Heather Gibb. "Gender, Migration and Crisis: Jamaican Female Migrants in Canada." In *A Global Crisis of Development: Responses and Responsibilities*, ed. Pablo Heidrich, 53–70. Ottawa: North-South Institute, 2010.

Dye, Thomas. *The Maka'ainana Transformation in Hawaii: Archaeological Expectations Based on the Social Effects of Parliamentary Enclosure in England*. Honolulu: T.S. Dye and Colleagues, Archaeologists, 2009.

Economist. "Not Such a Warm Welcome: Canada's Guest Workers." *Economist*, 27 November 2007, http://www.economist.com/node/10177080 (accessed 13 January 2012).

Editorial. "Helping Nannies Live In." *Globe and Mail*, 23 August 2010.

Ehrenreich, Barbara, and Arlie Russell Hochschild, eds. *Global Woman: Nannies, Maids, and Sex Workers in the New Economy*. New York: Metropolitan Books, 2003.

Elrick, Tim. "The Influence of Migration on Origin Communities: Insights from Polish Migrations to the West." *Europe-Asia Studies* 60, no. 9 (2008): 1503–17.

Encalada Grez, Evelyn. "Vulnerabilities of Female Migrant Farm Workers from Latin America and the Caribbean in Canada." In *FOCAL Policy Brief*. Ottawa: Canadian Foundation for the Americas, 2011.

Esterberg, Kristin G. *Qualitative Methods in Social Research*. Burr Ridge, IL: McGraw-Hill, 2001.

Eviota, Elizabeth Uy. *The Political Economy of Gender: Women and the Sexual Division of Labour in the Philippines*. London: Zed Books, 1992.

Fahim, Kareem. "Immigrant Maids Flee Lives of Abuse in Kuwait." *New York Times*, 1 August 2010.

Farmworker Justice. "Summary of the Agricultural Job Opportunities, Benefits, and Security Act of 2007 ('AgJOBS')." http://www. immigrationpolicy.org/just-facts/summary-agjobs-agricultural-job-opportunities-benefits-and-security-act-2007 (accessed 13 January 2012).

"Farm Worker's Body Returns Home." *Jamaica Gleaner* (Kingston), 31 August 2002, http://jamaica-gleaner.com/gleaner/20020831/news/news5.html (accessed 13 January 2012).

Federici, Sylvia. *Caliban and the Witch: Women, the Body and Primitive Accumulation*. Brooklyn, NY: Autonomedia, 2004.

Felix-Romero, Jessica. "AgJOBS Update May 11, 2011." 11 May 2011. http://www.harvestingjustice.org/index.php?option=com_content&view=article&id=641:agjobs-update-may-11-2011&catid=40:immigration-labor-rights&Itemid=68 (accessed 27 December 2011).

Fellman, Clair, ed. *Rethinking Canada: The Promise of Women's History*. 3rd ed. Toronto: Oxford University Press, 1997.

Ferentzy, Alex. "Book Review." *Canadian Journal of Sociology/Cahiers Canadiens de sociologie* 34, no. 1 (2009): 188–90.

Fernandez, Mary Rose. "Commodified Women." *Peace Review* 9, no. 3 (1997): 411–16.

Fernando, Shati. *Race and the City: Chinese Canadian and Chinese American Political Mobilization*. Vancouver: UBC Press, 2006.

Finance Canada. *Advantage Canada – Building a Strong Economy for Canadians*. Ottawa: Public Works, 2006

– *Budget 2007*. Ottawa: Public Works, 2007.

Fine, Michael. "The Social Division of Care." *Australian Journal of Social Issues* 42, no. 2 (2007): 137–49.

Fitting, Elizabeth. "Importing Corn, Exporting Labor: The Neoliberal Corn Regime, GMOs, and the Erosion of Mexican Biodiversity." In *Food for the Few: Neoliberal Globalism and Biotechnology in Latin America,* ed. Gerardo Otero, 135–58. Austin: University of Texas Press, 2010.

Fitzpatrick, Peter. *Modernism and the Grounds of Law.* Cambridge, UK: Cambridge University Press, 2001.

– *Nationalism, Racism, and the Rule of Law.* Aldershot, UK: Dartmouth, 1995.

Flecker, Karl. "Canada's Temporary Foreign Worker Program (TFWP): Model Program – or Mistake?" Ottawa: Canadian Labour Congress, 2010.

FOCAL. *Dialogue on Labour Mobility in North America.* Ottawa: Canadian Foundation for the Americas, 2008.

Foreign Agricultural Resource Management Services (FARMS). "Employer Information Booklet." Mississauga, ON: FARMS, 2005.

Fox, Bonnie, and Jessica Yiu. "As Times Change: A Review of Trends in Family Life." In *Family Patterns: Gender Relations*, 3rd ed., ed. Bonnie Fox, 180–208. Don Mills, ON: Oxford University Press, 2009.

Freeman, Gary P. "Modes of Immigration Politics in Liberal Democratic States." *International Migration Review* 29, no. 4 (1995): 881–902.

Fresh Plaza. "Growers Turn to Mexico for Help." http://www.freshplaza.com/2007/0301/2_mx_growersturntomexico.html (accessed 1 February 2012).

Friesen, Joe. "Leap in Temporary Foreign Workers Will Hurt Canada Long-Term, Critics Say." *Globe and Mail*, 13 May 2010.

Fudge, Judy, and Fiona MacPhail. "The Temporary Foreign Worker Programs in Canada: Workers as an Extreme Form of Flexible Labour." *Comparative Labor Law and Policy Journal* 31, no. 5 (2009): 5–45.

Fuller, Sylvia, and Leah Vosko. "Temporary Employment and Social Inequality in Canada: Exploring Intersections of Gender, Race and Immigration Status." *Social Indicators Research* 88, no. 1 (2008): 31–50.

Gabriel, Christina, and Laura Macdonald. "The Hypermobile, the Mobile and the Rest: Patterns of Inclusion and Exclusion in an Emerging North American Migration Regime." *Canadian Journal of Latin American and Caribbean Studies* 29, nos 57–8 (2004): 67–91.

– "Migration and Citizenship Rights in a New North American Space." In *Requiem or Revival: The Promise of North American Integration*, ed. Isabel Studer and Carol Wise, 267–88. Washington, DC: Brookings Press, 2007.

Gálvez Gonzalez, Andrea, and Osiris Ramos Rodríguez. "Patriarchy and Exploitation in the Context of Globalization." *Labour, Capital and Society/Travail, capital et societé* 39, no. 2 (2006): 126–9.

Gibney, Matthew. "A Thousand Little Guantanamos: Western States and Measures to Prevent the Arrival of Refugees." In *Migration, Displacement, Asylum: The Oxford Amnesty Lectures 2004*, ed. K. Tunstall, 139–69. Oxford: Oxford University Press, 2006.

Giddens, A. *The Constitution of Society: Outline of the Theory of Structuration*. Cambridge, UK: Polity Press, 1984.

Giese, Rachel. "Home Cooking: Alisa Smith and J.B. Mackinnon Talk about the 100-Mile Diet." *CBC News*, 11 April 2007.

Glickstein, Jonathan. "Is It Capitalism?" *Reviews in American History* 25, no. 2 (1997): 276–81.

Global Commission on International Migration. "Migration in an Interconnected World: New Directions for Action." 5 October 2005. http://www.unhcr.org/refworld/docid/435f81814.html (accessed 8 February 2012).

– "Report of the Global Commission on International Migration." *Population and Development Review* 31, no. 4 (2005): 787–98.

Global Workers Justice Alliance. "Migration Data and Labor Rights." http://www.globalworkers.org/migrationdata_MX.html (accessed 13 January 2012).

Gonzalez, Gilbert. *Guest Workers or Colonized Labor? Mexican Labor Migration to the United States*. Boulder, CO: Paradigm, 2007.

Good Gingrich, Luann, and Kerry Preibisch. "Migration as Preservation and Loss: The Paradox of Transnational Living for Low German Mennonite Women." *Journal of Ethnic and Migration Studies* 36, no. 9 (2010): 1499–518.

Goonewardena, Kanishka, Stefan Kipfer, Richard Milgrom, and Christian Schmid, eds. *Space, Difference, Everyday Life: Reading Henry Lefebvre*. New York: Routledge, 2008.

Government of Alberta. "Semi-Skilled Worker Criteria: Industry-Specific Criteria – Foodservices Industry (Pilot Project)." Updated 22 December 2011. http://www.albertacanada.com/immigration/immigrating/ainp-eds-semi-skilled-criteria.aspx#foodservice (accessed 14 January 2012).

– "AINP Processing Times." Updated 20 September 2011. http://www.albertacanada.com/immigration/immigrate/processingtimes.html (accessed 22 June 2011).

– "Semi-Skilled Worker Criteria." Updated 23 July 2010. http://www.albertacanada.com/immigration/immigrating/ainp-eds-semi-skilled-criteria.html (accessed 20 August 2010).

Government of British Columbia. "Entry-Level and Semi-Skilled Pilot Project." N.d. http://www.welcomebc.ca/wbc/immigration/come/work/

about/strategic_occupations/entry_level/who.page? (accessed 17 June
2010).

– "What If You Lose or Change Your Job." N.d. http://www.welcomebc.
ca/en/immigration/come/work/about/strategic_occupations/information/
lose_job.html (accessed 17 June 2010).

Government of British Columbia, Ministry of Agriculture and Lands.
Regulating Temporary Farm Worker Housing in the ALR. Victoria, BC:
Sustainable Agriculture Management Branch, 2009.

Government of Canada. "Temporary Foreign Worker Program Improved
for Employers in B.C. And Alberta." *Marketwire*, 24 September 2007.
http://www.marketwire.com/press-release/temporary-foreign-worker-
program-improved-for-employers-in-bc-and-alberta-773065.htm
(accessed 27 December 2011).

Government of Manitoba. "Manitoba Provincial Nominee Program: Common Questions." Winnipeg: Manitoba Immigration, 2011. http://www.
immigratemanitoba.com/how-to-immigrate/mpnp-resources/
common-questions (accessed 31 January 2012).

– "Manitoba Provincial Nominee Program – Employer Direct." Winnipeg:
Manitoba Immigration, 2009.

– "Manitoba Provincial Nominee Program: Most Popular Questions."
Winnipeg: Manitoba Immigration, 2009.

– "The Worker Recruitment and Protection Act C.C.S.M. C.W197: Valid
License Holders." Updated 6 January 2012. http://www.gov.mb.ca/
labour/standards/asset_library/pdf/wrapa_valid_licensees.pdf (accessed
13 January 2012).

Government of New Brunswick. "Guide for Skilled Worker Applicants."
Updated April 2011. http://www2.gnb.ca/content/dam/gnb/Depart-
ments/petl-epft/PDF/PopGrowth/GuideforSkilledWorkerApplicants-e.
pdf (accessed 14 May 2011).

– "New Brunswick Provincial Nominee Program – Skilled Worker Applicants with Employer Support." http://www2.gnb.ca/content/gnb/en/ser-
vices/services_renderer.201043.html (accessed 14 May 2011).

Government of Nova Scotia. "Skilled Worker Stream." http://novascoti-
aimmigration.ca/immigrants/immigrating-to-ns/skilled-worker (accessed
14 May 2011).

Government of Northwest Territories. "NWT Nominee Program Guidelines." 2009. http://www.nominee.ece.gov.nt.ca/_live/documents/
document ManagerUpload/NTNP_Guidelines-Final.pdf (accessed 22
June 2010).

Government of Ontario. "Ontario Government to Encourage Consumers to 'Buy Ontario.'" May 2007. http://www.omafra.gov.on.ca/english/
infores/releases/2007/051107-1.htm (accessed 13 January 2012).
– "Opportunities Ontario: Questions and Answers." Updated 19 April
2010. http://www.ontarioimmigration.ca/en/pnp/OI_PNPQUESTIONS.
html (accessed 22 June 2010).
Government of Prince Edward Island. "Critical Worker Stream."
Updated 28 April 2011. http://www.gov.pe.ca/immigration/index.
php3?number=1037607&lang=E (accessed 11 May 2010).
– "New Immigration Streams Added to the Provincial Nominee Program." 2011. http://www.gov.pe.ca/immigration/index.php3?number=
news&dept=&newsnumber=7636&lang=E (accessed 11 May 2010).
Government of Saskatchewan. "Hospitality Sector Pilot Project." 2010.
http://www.saskimmigrationcanada.ca/hospitality (accessed 20 August
2010).
– "Information for Saskatchewan Businesses." 2010. http://www.
saskimmigrationcanada.ca/hospitality-information-business (accessed
21 August 2010).
– "Long-Haul Truck Drivers Project." 2010. http://www.
saskimmigrationcanada.ca/trucker (accessed 20 August 2010).
– "Saskatchewan Immigrant Nominee Program: Hospitality Sector Project." 2009. http://www.saskimmigrationcanada.ca/hospitality (accessed
12 October 2010).
– "Temporary Work Permits." 2010. http://www.saskimmigrationcanada.
ca/sinp-work-permits-questions (accessed 18 June 2010).
Government of Yukon. "Critical Impact Worker." 2009. http://www.
immigration.gov.yk.ca/critical_impact_worker_criteria.html (accessed
20 August 2010).
– "Skilled Worker/Critical Impact Worker Program." Updated 19 April
2010. http://www.immigration.gov.yk.ca/ynp_skilled_critical_program.
html (accessed 19 May 2010).
Green, Alan G., and David A. Green. "The Goals of Canada's Immigration
Policy: A Historical Perspective." *Canadian Journal of Urban Research*
13, no. 1 (2004): 102–39.
Greenhill, David. "Managed Migration, Best Practices and Public Policy:
The Canadian Experience." Paper presented at the International
Organization for Migration (IOM) workshop on best practices concerning migrant workers and their families, Santiago, Chile, 19–20 June
2000.

– "Workshop Report." Paper presented at the International Organization for Migration (IOM) workshop on best practices concerning migrant workers and their families, Santiago, Chile, 19–20 June 2000.

Griffith, David. *The Canadian and United States Migrant Agricultural Workers Programs: Parallels and Divergences between Two North American Seasonal Agricultural Labour Markets with Respect to 'Best Practices.'* Ottawa: North–South Institute, 2003.

Grugel, Jean, and Nicola Piper. *Critical Perspectives on Global Governance: Rights and Regulation in Governing Regimes.* New York: Routledge, 2007.

Hadi, Abdullahel. "International Migration and the Change of Women's Position among the Left-Behind in Rural Bangladesh." *Population, Space and Place* 7, no. 1 (2001): 53–61.

– "Overseas Migration and the Well-Being of Those Left behind in Rural Communities of Bangladesh." *Asia-Pacific Population Journal* 14, no. 1 (1999): 43–58.

Hage, Ghassan. *White Nation: Fantasies of White Supremacy in a Multicultural Society.* New York: Routledge and Pluto Press, 2000.

Hankivsky, Olena, and Renée Cormier, with Diego de Mirech. *Intersectionality: Moving Women's Health Research and Policy Forward.* Vancouver: Women's Health Research Network, 2009.

Hankivsky, Olena, Renée Cormier, and Diego de Mirech. *Intersectionality: Moving Women's Health Research and Policy Forward.* Vancouver: Women's Health Research Network, 2009.

Hankivsky, Olena, Colleen Reid, Renée Cormier, Colleen Varcoe, Natalie Clark, Cecilia Benoit, and Shari Brotman. "Exploring the Promises of Intersectionality for Advancing Women's Health Research." *International Journal for Equity in Health* 9, no. 5 (February 2010): n.p. http://www.equityhealthj.com/content/9/1/5 (accessed 13 January 2012).

Hanlon, Andrew. "Temporary Foreign Worker Numbers Soar." *Edmonton Sun*, 15 June 2010.

Hardt, Michael, and Antonio Negri. *Empire.* Cambridge, MA: Harvard University Press, 2000.

Harper, Robin, and Hani Zubida. "Making Room at the Table: Incorporation of Foreign Workers in Israel." *Policy and Society* 29, no. 4 (2010): 371–83.

Harper, Stephen. "Statement by the Prime Minister of Canada on the Occasion of Felipe Calderon, President of the United Mexican States,

Addressing Parliament." 27 May 2010. http://pm.gc.ca/eng/media.
asp?id=3391 (accessed 13 January 2012).
Harris, Nigel. *Thinking the Unthinkable: The Immigration Myth Exposed.*
New York: I.B. Tauris, 2002.
Hartling, Lisa, William Pickett, and Robert J. Brison. "The Canadian Agri-
cultural Injury Surveillance Program: A New Injury Control Initiative."
Chronic Diseases in Canada 19, no. 3 (1998): 108–11.
Hellman, Judith Adler. *The World of Mexican Migrants: The Rock and the
Hard Place.* New York: New Press, 2008.
Hendricks, Tuche. "Ex-braceros Leery of Guest Worker Plan." *San Fran-
cisco Chronicle*, 30 May 2006, A1.
Hennebry, Jenna L. "Bienvenidos a Canadá? Globalization and the Migra-
tion Industry Surrounding Temporary Agricultural Migration in Can-
ada." *Canadian Studies in Population* 35, no. 2 (2008): 339–56.
– *Globalization and the Mexican-Canadian Seasonal Agricultural Worker
Program: Power, Racialization and Transnationalism in Temporary
Migration.* London, ON: University of Western Ontario, 2006.
– "Mobile Vulnerabilities, Transnational Risks: Temporary Agricul-
tural Migrants in Ontario." *International Settlement Canada* 23, no. 1
(2009): 10–15.
– "Not Just a Few Bad Apples: Vulnerability, Health and Temporary
Migration in Canada." *Canadian Issues* (Spring 2010): 74–7.
Hennebry, Jenna L., and Kerry Preibisch. "Deconstructing Managed
Migration's Model: A Critical Look at Canada's Seasonal Agricultural
Workers Program." Paper presented at the Annual Meeting of the Can-
adian Sociological Association (CSA), Vancouver, 3–6 June 2008.
– "A Model for Managed Migration? Re-examining Best Practices in
Canada's Seasonal Agricultural Worker Program." *International Migra-
tion* (forthcoming).
Hennebry, Jenna L., Kerry Preibisch, and Janet McLaughlin. "Health
across Borders – Health Status, Risks and Care among Transnational
Migrant Farm Workers in Ontario." Toronto: CERIS – Ontario Metrop-
olis Centre, 2010.
Hennessy, Rosemary, and Chrys Ingraham, eds. *Materialist Feminism: A
Reader in Class, Difference, and Women's Lives.* New York: Routledge,
1997.
Heymann, Jodi. *Forgotten Families: Ending the Growing Crisis Con-
fronting Children and Working Parents in the Global Economy.* Oxford:
Oxford University Press, 2006.

Hill Collins, Patricia. *Black Feminist Thought: Knowledge, Consciousness, and the Politics of Empowerment.* 2nd ed. New York: Routledge, 2000.

Holley, M. "Disadvantaged by Design: How the Law Inhibits Agricultural Guest Workers from Enforcing Their Rights." *Hofstra Labor and Employment Law Journal* 18 (2001): 573–621.

Hollifield, James. "The Emerging Migration State." *International Migration Review* 38, no. 3 (2004): 885–912.

Holloway, John. "Global Capital and the National State." *Capital and Class* 18, no. 1 (1994): 23–49.

Holzmann, Robert, and Yann Pouget. *Social Protection for Temporary Migrant Workers: Conceptual Framework, Country Inventory, Assessment and Guidance.* Study prepared for the Global Forum on Migration and Development (GFMD), 2010.

House of Commons Canada. *Temporary Foreign Workers and Non-Status Workers: Report of the Standing Committee on Citizenship and Immigration,* 40th Parliament, 2nd Session. Ottawa: Parliament of Canada, 2009.

House of Commons Debates. *Official Report: First Session – Twenty Ninth Parliament.* Vol. 6 (19 July to 21 September 1973). Ottawa: Queen's Printer for Canada, 1973.

– *Official Report: Third Session – Twenty Eighth Parliament.* Vol. 5 (22 March to 5 May 1971). Ottawa: Queen's Printer for Canada, 1971.

Huffstutter, P.J. "Hiring Foreign Farmworkers to Get Tougher under New Rule." *Los Angeles Times,* 11 February 2010.

Hugo, Graeme. "Best Practice in Temporary Labour Migration for Development: A Perspective from Asia and the Pacific." *International Migration* 47, no. 5 (2009): 23–74.

– "Labour Export from Indonesia: An Overview." *ASEAN Economic Bulletin* 12, no. 2 (1995): 275–98.

Human Resources and Skills Development Canada (HRSDC). "Agreement for the Employment in Canada of Seasonal Agricultural Workers from Mexico." 2008. http://www.hrsdc.gc.ca/eng/workplaceskills/foreign_workers/forms/sawpmc2012.pdf (accessed 13 January 2012).

– "Number of Confirmed Temporary Foreign Worker (TFW) Positions under the Seasonal Agricultural Workers Program (SAWP) and NOC C and D, by Specific Employer Industry Sectors and Province/Territory." Gatineau, QC: Government of Canada, n.d.

- "Seasonal Agricultural Worker Program." N.d. http://www.hrsdc.gc.ca/
  eng/workplaceskills/foreign_workers/ei_tfw/sawp_tfw.shtml (accessed
  10 February 2012).
- "Table 8 (Annual): Number of Temporary Foreign Worker Positions
  on Labour Market Opinion Confirmations Issued under the Pilot Project for Occupations Requiring Lower Levels of Formal Training (NOC
  C and D), by Province/Territory." In "Temporary Foreign Worker Program: Labour Market Opinion (LMO) Statistics," in *Annual Statistics
  2006–2009*. Gatineau, QC: Government of Canada, 31 March 2010.
- "Table 10 (Annual): Number of Temporary Foreign Worker Positions
  on Labour Market Opinion Confirmations under the Seasonal Agricul-
  tural Worker Program, by Location of Employment." In "Temporary
  Foreign Worker Program: Labour Market Opinion (LMO) Statistics," in
  Annual Statistics 2006–2009. Gatineau, QC: Government of Canada, 31
  March 2010.
- "Temporary Foreign Worker Program: Hiring Foreign Agricultural
  Workers in Canada." N.d. http://www.hrsdc.gc.ca/eng/workplaceskills/
  foreign_workers/sawp.shtml (accessed 14 May 2011).
- "Temporary Foreign Worker Program: Labour Market Opinion (LMO)
  Statistics." In *Annual Statistics 2005–2008*. Ottawa: Government of
  Canada, 2009. Updated 1 October 2009. http://www.hrsdc.gc.ca/eng/
  workplaceskills/foreign_workers/stats/annual/annual_stats_list.shtml
  (accessed 13 January 2012).
- "Temporary Foreign Worker Program: Labour Market Opinion (LMO)
  Statistics." In *Annual Statistics 2006–2009*. Gatineau, QC: Government
  of Canada, 31 March 2010.
- "Temporary Foreign Worker Program: Minimum Advertising Requirements." Updated 28 February 2011. http://www.hrsdc.gc.ca/eng/
  workplaceskills/foreign_workers/communications/advertrecrutment.
  shtml (accessed 13 January 2012).
- "Temporary Foreign Workers: Your Rights and the Law." Updated
  14 January 2011. http://www.cic.gc.ca/english/work/tfw-rights.asp
  (accessed 25 August 2010).
Human Rights Watch. *Slow Reform: Protection of Migrant Domestic Workers in Asia and the Middle East*. New York: Human Rights
  Watch, 2010. http://www.hrw.org/en/reports/2010/04/28/slow-reform-0
  (accessed 21 June 2011).

Huntington, Samuel. *Who Are We? Challenges to America's National Identity.* New York: Simon and Schuster, 2004.

Huyskamp, Ross. *Report on Kelowna's Historic Chinatown Site.* Prepared for the City of Kelowna's Community Heritage Commission, 2010.

Immigrant Workers Centre (IWC), Montreal Filipino Women's Association (MFWA), and Droits des travailleuses et travailleurs (im)migrantes (DTTI). *Reform of the Temporary Foreign Worker Program: Fundamental Changes Required.* Montreal: IWC, 2008.

International Labour Organization (ILO). *Towards a Fair Deal for Migrant Workers in the Global Economy.* Geneva: ILO, 2004.

International Organization for Migration (IOM). "About IOM." N.d. http://www.iom.int/jahia/Jahia/about-iom/lang/e (accessed 13 January 2012).

– "Migrants and the Host Society: Partnerships for Success." In *International Dialogue on Migration 11.* 2008. http://www.iom.int/jahia/webdav/site/myjahiasite/shared/shared/mainsite/published_docs/serial_publications/RB11_ENG.pdf (accessed 13 January 2012).

– "Project Evaluation: Temporary Agricultural Workers to Canada." In *Working Notebooks on Migration 22.* Guatemala City: IOM, 2006.

– "Seasonal Agricultural Workers Program: Guatemala and Canada." 2008. http://www.iom.int/jahia/webdav/site/myjahiasite/shared/shared/mainsite/activities/countries/docs/guatemalan_seasonal_workers_summaryo8.pdf (accessed 13 January 2012).

– "Second Evaluation: Program Temporary Agricultural Workers to Canada." In *Working Notebooks on Migration 25.* Guatemala City: IOM, 2008.

– "Temporary Labour Migration Programme to Canada from Guatemala Reaches Milestone." 2009. http://www.iom.int/jahia/Jahia/media/press-briefing-notes/pbnAM/cache/offonce?entryId=25318 (accessed 13 January 2012).

– *World Migration 2008: Managing Labour Mobility in the Evolving Global Economy.* Geneva: IOM, 2009.

Iocovetta, Franca, and Marianna Valverde, eds. *Gender Conflicts: New Essays in Women's History.* Toronto: University of Toronto Press, 1992.

Isin, Engin F. *Being Political: Genealogies of Citizenship.* Minneapolis: University of Minnesota Press, 2002.

Iyer, Pico. *The Global Soul: Jet Lag, Shopping Malls, and the Search for Home.* New York: Vintage Departures, 2001.

Izcara Palacios, Simón Pedro. "Abusos y condiciones de servidumbre relacionados con la implementación de los programas de trabajadores huéspedes (el caso tamaulipeco)." *Frontera Norte* 22, no. 44 (July–December 2010): 237–64.

Izcara Palacios, Simón Pedro, and Karla Lorena Andrade Rubio. "Guest Workers in Agriculture: Working Conditions of Tamaulipa's Farm Workers Employed in the United States." Paper presented at the 17th International Sociology Association (ISA) World Congress of Sociology, Gothenburg, Sweden, 11–17 July 2010.

Jankowski, P. "Two Farm Workers at Filsinger's Die from Fumes." *Hanover Post*, 2010. Article ID# 2759304. http://www.thepost.on.ca/ArticleDisplay.aspx?e=2759304. (accessed 13 January 2012).

Jarman, Jennifer. "Explaining Social Exclusion." *International Journal of Sociology and Social Policy* 21, nos 4–6 (2001): 3–9.

"Just-in-Time Manufacturing." Computer Aided Engineering Assignment, Department of Computer Engineering, Curtin University of Technology, Perth, Western Australia. http://kernow.curtin.edu.au/www/jit/jit.htm (accessed 10 May 2011).

Kapiszewski, Andrzej. "Arab versus Asian Migrant Workers in the GCC Countries." Presented at the "United Nations Expert Group Meeting on International Migration and Development in the Arab Region," Population Division, United Nations Secretariat, Beirut, 2006.

Kaur, Amarjit. "Labour Migration Trends and Policy Challenges in Southeast Asia." *Policy and Society* 29, no. 4 (2010): 385–97.

Kelly, Philip F., Mila Astorga-Garcia, Enrico F. Esguerra, and Community Alliance for Social Justice, Toronto. "Explaining the Deprofessionalized Filipino: Why Filipino Immigrants Get Low-Paying Jobs in Toronto." Toronto: CERIS – Ontario Metropolis Centre, October 2009.

Kemp, Adriana. "Reforming Policies on Foreign Workers in Israel." In *OECD Social, Employment and Migration Working Papers, No. 103.* Paris: OECD Publishing, 2010. http://www.oecd-ilibrary.org/docserver/download/fulltext/5kmjnr8pbp6f.pdf?expires=1326483418&id=id&accname=guest&checksum=29B53D25E7DAF8B35EA05CF7960280F3 (accessed 13 January 2012).

Kershner, Isabel. "Israelis Divided on Deporting Children." *New York Times*, 2 August 2010.

Kipfer, Stefan, Kanishka Goonewardena, Christian Schmid, and Richard Milgrom. "On the Reproduction of Henry Lefebvre." In *Space,*

Difference, Everyday Life: Reading Henry Lefebvre, ed. Kanishka
    Goonewardena et al. 1–23. New York and London: Routledge, 2008.
Kitagawa, Kurtis, Tim Krywulak, and Douglas Watt. *Renewing Immigra-
    tion: Towards a Convergence and Consolidation of Canada's Immigra-
    tion Policies and Systems*. Ottawa: Conference Board of Canada,
    2008.
Kivimäki, Mikka, Jussi Vahtera, Marianna Virtanen, Marko Elovainio,
    Jaana Pentti, and Jane E. Ferrie. "Temporary Employment and Risk of
    Overall and Cause-Specific Mortality." *American Journal of Epidemiol-
    ogy* 158, no. 7 (2003): 663–8.
Kyambi, Sarah. "National Identity and Refugee Law." In *Critical Beings:
    Law, Nation and the Global Subject*, ed. Peter Fitzpatrick and Patricia
    Tuitt, 19–36. Burlington, VT: Ashgate, 2004.
Kymlicka, Will. *Finding Our Way: Rethinking Ethnocultural Relations in
    Canada*. Oxford: Oxford University Press, 1998.
Lanthier, Mario, and Lloyd L. Wong. "Ethnic Agricultural Labour in the
    Okanagan Valley: 1880s to 1960s." Victoria, BC: Royal BC Museum,
    2002. http://www.livinglandscapes.bc.ca (accessed 2 September 2010).
Lassen, Claus. "A Life in Corridors: Social Perspectives on Aeromobility
    and Work in Knowledge Organizations." In *Aeromobilities*, ed. Saulo
    Cwerner, Sven Kesselring, and John Urry, 177–94. New York: Rout-
    ledge, 2009.
Leitner, Helga. "The Political Economy of International Labour Migra-
    tion." In *A Companion to Economic Geography*, ed. Eric Sheppard and
    Trevor J. Barne, 450–67. Oxford and Malden, MA: Blackwell, 2000.
Lenard, Patti Tamara, and Christine Straehle. "Temporary Labour Migra-
    tion: Exploitation, Tool of Development, or Both?" *Policy and Society*
    29, no. 4 (2010): 283–94.
Leo, Christopher, and Martine August. "The Multi-level Governance of
    Immigration and Settlement: Making Deep Federalism Work." *Can-
    adian Journal of Political Science* 42, no. 2 (2009): 491–510.
Li, Peter S. *Destination Canada: Immigration Debates and Issues*. Oxford:
    Oxford University Press, 2003.
Lichtenstein, Merav. "An Examination of Guest Worker Immigration
    Reform Policies in the United States." *Cardozo Public Law, Policy and
    Ethics Journal* 5 (2006–07): 689–727.
Linebaugh, Peter. *The Magna Carta Manifesto: Liberties and Commons
    for All*. Berkeley: University of California Press, 2007.

Linebaugh, Peter, and Marcus Rediker. *The Many-Headed Hydra: Sailors, Slaves, Commoners, and the Hidden History of the Revolutionary Atlantic.* Boston: Beacon, 2000.

Little, Walter. "Introduction: Globalization and Guatemala's Maya Workers." *Latin American Perspectives* 32, no. 3 (2005): 3–11.

Louër, Laurence. "The Political Impact of Labor Migration in Bahrain." *City and Society* 20, no. 1 (2008): 32–53.

Loveband, Anne. "Nationality Matters: SARS and Foreign Domestic Workers' Rights in Taiwan Province of China." *International Migration* 42, no. 5 (2004): 121–45.

Lovelock, Kirsten, and Teresa Leopold. "Labour Force Shortages in Rural New Zealand: Temporary Migration and the Recognised Seasonal Employer (RSE) Work Policy." *New Zealand Population Review* 33–4 (2008): 213–34.

Lowe, Sophia J. "Rearranging the Deck Chairs? A Critical Examination of Canada's Shift in (Im)Migration Policies." *Canadian Issues* (Spring 2010): 25–8.

Lowell, Lindsay, and Stephanie Lezell. "Background Paper." Prepared for "Roundtable 2: Migrant Integration, Reintegration and Circulation for Development," "Session 2.1: Inclusion, Protection and Acceptance of Migrants in Society – Linking Human Rights and Migrant Empowerment for Development," Global Forum on Migration and Development, Athens, 4–5 November 2009.

Lukacs, George. *History and Class Consciousness: Studies in Marxist Dialectics.* Intro. and trans. Rodney Livingstone. Cambridge, MA: MIT Press, 1971.

Luxton, Meg. "Feminist Political Economy in Canada and the Politics of Social Reproduction." In *Social Reproduction: Feminist Political Economy Challenges Neo-Liberalism*, ed. Kate Benzanson and Meg Luxton, 11–43. Montreal and Kingston: McGill-Queen's University Press, 2006.

Luxton, Meg, and Pat Armstrong. "Margaret Lowe Benston, 1937–1991." *Studies in Political Economy*, no. 35 (1991): 7–11.

Luxton, Meg, and Leah Vosko. "Where Women's Efforts Count: The 1996 Census Campaign and Family Politics in Canada." *Studies in Political Economy*, no. 56 (1998): 49–82.

Macklin, Audrey. "On the Inside Looking In: Foreign Domestic Workers in Canada." In *Maid in the Market: Women's Paid Domestic Labour*, ed. Wenona Giles and Sedef Arat-Koc, 19–39. Halifax: Fernwood, 1994.

- "Who Is the Citizen's Other? Considering the Heft of Citizenship." *Theoretical Inquiries in Law* 8 (2007): 333–66.

Mann, Albert H. "Kelowna's Chinatown." *Okanagan Historical Society* 46 (1982): 20–8.

Manuel, Tiffany. "Envisioning the Possibilities for a Good Life: Exploring the Public Policy Implications of Intersectionality Theory." *Journal of Women and Politics* 28, nos 3–4 (2006): 173–203.

Martin, Emily. "The Society of Flows and the Flows of Culture: Reading Castells in the Light of Cultural Accounts of the Body, Health and Complex Systems." *Critique of Anthropology* 16 (1996): 49–56.

Martin, Philip L. "Germany: Reluctant Land of Immigration." In *Controlling Immigration: A Global Perspective*, ed. Philip L. Martin, Wayne A. Cornelius, and James Frank Hollifield, 189–226. Palo Alto, CA: Stanford University Press, 1994.

- "Guest Worker Policies: An International Survey." In *Migration and Refugee Policies: An Overview*, ed. Ann Bernstein and Myron Weiner, 45–83. New York: Continuum, 1999.

- "Immigration Reform: What Does It Mean for Agriculture?" *Policy Issues* 5 (September 2009): 1–6.

- *Merchants of Labor: Agents of the Evolving Migration Infrastructure*. Geneva: International Institute for Labour Studies, 2005.

- *Promise Unfulfilled: Unions, Immigration, and the Farm Workers*. Ithaca, NY, and London: Cornell University Press, 2003.

- "Recession and Migration: A New Era for Labor Migration?" *International Migration Review* 43, no. 3 (2009): 671–91.

- "There Is Nothing More Permanent Than Temporary Foreign Workers." *Center for Immigration Studies* 5, no. 1 (2001): 1–5.

Martin, Philip L., Manola Abella, and Christiane Kuptsch. *Managing Labor Migration in the Twenty-First Century*. New Haven: Yale University Press, 2006.

Martin, Philip L., and Michael S. Teitelbaum. "The Mirage of Mexican Guest Workers." *Foreign Affairs* 80, no. 6 (2001): 117–31.

Marx, Karl. "The Secret of Primitive Accumulation." In *Capital*, vol. 1. 1867. Reprint, Harmondsworth, UK: Penguin, 1976.

Massey, Douglas S., and Zai Lang. "The Long-Term Consequences of a Temporary Worker Program: The U.S. Bracero Experience." *Population Research and Policy Review* 8, no. 3 (1989): 199–226.

McCall, Leslie. "The Complexity of Intersectionality." *Journal of Women in Culture and Society* 30, no. 3 (2005): 1771–800.

McLaughlin, Janet. "Falling through the Cracks: Seasonal Foreign Farm Workers' Health and Compensation across Borders." *IAVGO Reporting Service* 21, no. 1, (2007): n.p. http://www.injuredworkersonline.org/ Documents/ONIWGconfMcLaughlin.pdf (accessed 13 January 2012).

– *Migration and Health: Implications for Development.* Ottawa: Canadian Foundation for the Americas, 2009.

– "Trouble in Our Fields: Health and Human Rights among Mexican and Caribbean Migrant Farm Workers in Canada." PhD diss., University of Toronto, 2009.

McLaughlin, Janet, and Jenna Hennebry. "Pathways to Precarity: Structural Vulnerabilities and Lived Consequences in the Everyday Lives of Migrant Farmworkers in Canada." Paper presented at the workshop on "Producing and Negotiating Precarious Migratory Status in Canada." York University, Research Alliance on Precarious Status, Toronto, 16 September 2010. http://www.yorku.ca/raps1/events/pdf/McLaughlin_ Hennebry.pdf (accessed 13 January 2012).

Meillassoux, Claude. *Maidens, Meal, and Money: Capitalism and the Domestic Economy.* New York: Cambridge University Press, 1981.

Melo, Felicia. "Coming to America." *The Nation* 284 (25 June 2007): 14–24.

Mendis, Asoka Charles Nissanka. *The Greenhouse Tomato Industry in Delta, British Columbia.* Vancouver: UBC Press, 2007.

Menjívar, Cecilia, and Victor Agadjanian. "Men's Migration and Women's Lives: Views from Rural Armenia and Guatemala." *Social Science Quarterly* 88, no. 5 (2007): 1243–62.

"Mexico: Guest Workers." *Migration News*, April 1999, http://migration. ucdavis.edu/mn/more.php?id=1769_0_2_0 (accessed 13 January 2012).

Meyers, Deborah, and Kevin O'Neil. *Immigration: Mapping the New North American Reality Policy Options.* Montreal: Institute for Research on Public Policy, 2004.

Miles, Angela, Betsy Warrior, Maria Mies, Margaret Randall, and Collette Guillaumin. "Margaret Benston's 'Political Economy of Women's Liberation': International Impact." *Canadian Woman Studies* 13, no. 2 (1993): 31–3.

Miles, Robert. *Capitalism and Unfree Labour: Anomaly or Necessity?* London and New York: Tavistock, 1987.

Miller, Todd. "Arizona, the Anti-immigrant Laboratory." *NACLA Report on the Americas* 43 (July 2010): 3–4.

Mohanty, Chandra Talpade. *Feminism without Borders: Decolonizing Theory, Practicing Solidarity.* Durham, NC, and London: Duke University Press, 2003.

Molz, Jennie Germann. "Cosmopolitan Bodies: Fit to Travel and Travelling to Fit." *Body and Society* 12 (2006): 1–21.

Montes, Verónica. "Transformaciones de las Relaciones Familiares en el Contexto Migratorio Transnacional: Pueblo Nuevo, Guatemala Como Caso de Estudio Ethnográfico." In *V Congreso International Sobre Migración,* ed. Miguel Ugalde, 276–93. Guatemala City: Instituto de Investigaciones Económicas y Sociales, 2009.

Moran-Taylor, Michelle J. "When Mothers and Fathers Migrate North: Caretakers, Children, and Child Rearing in Guatemala." *Latin American Perspectives* 35, no. 4 (2008): 79–95.

Mountz, Allison. "Embodying the Nation-State: Canada's Response to Human Smuggling." *Political Geography* 23, no. 3 (2004): 323–45.

Mueller, Richard E. "Mexican Immigrants and Temporary Residents in Canada: Current Knowledge and Future Research." *Migraciones Internacionales* 3, no. 1 (2005): 32–56.

Mullings, Leith. *On Our Own Terms: Race, Class and Gender in the Lives of African American Women.* New York: Routledge, 1997.

Muzzaffar, Chishti, and Claire Bergeron. "Obama's Homeland Security Selection Viewed as Focused on Immigration." *Migration Information Source,* 15 December 2008. http://www.migrationinformation.org/USfocus/display.cfm?id=715 (accessed 5 August 2010).

Nakache, Delphine, and Paula J. Kinoshita. *The Canadian Temporary Foreign Worker Program: Do Short-Term Economic Needs Prevail over Human Rights Concerns?* Montreal: Institute for Research on Public Policy, 2010.

Nash, Jennifer. "Re-thinking Intersectionality." *Feminist Review* 89 (2008): 1–15.

Nendick, Karen. "Immigrant Workers Do the Jobs Locals Won't Touch." Letter to the editor. *Kelowna Capital News,* 19 March 2008.

Neufeld, Anne, Margaret Harrison, Miriam Stewart, Karen Hughes, and Denise Spitzer. "Immigrant Women: Making Connections to Community Resources for Support in Family Caregiving." *Qualitative Health Research* 12, no. 6 (2002): 751–68.

Newland, Kathleen. "Circular Migration and Human Development." In *Human Development Research Paper.* New York: United Nations

Development Programme, 2009. http://hdr.undp.org/en/reports/global/
hdr2009/papers/HDRP_2009_42.pdf (accessed 13 January 2012).

Ng, Roxana. "Restructuring Gender, Race, and Class Relations: The Case of Garment Workers and Labour Adjustment." In *Restructuring Caring Labour: Discourse, State Practice, and Everyday Life*, ed. Sheila Neysmith, 226–45. Toronto. Oxford University Press, 2000.

Noël, André. "Des loyers illégaux." *La Presse* (Montreal), 3 July 2010.

Nguyen, Liem, Brenda Yeoh, and Mika Toyota. "Migration and the Well-Being of the 'Left Behind' in Asia." *Asian Population Studies* 2, no. 1 (2006): 37–44.

Office of the Auditor General of Canada. *Report of the Auditor General of Canada to the House of Commons*. Ottawa: Office of the Auditor General of Canada, 2009.

– "Selecting Foreign Workers under the Immigration Program." In *Fall 2009 Report of the Auditor General of Canada*. Ottawa: Office of the Auditor General of Canada, 2009.

Ojeda, Hinojosa. *Transnational Migration, Remittances and Development in North America: Globalization Lessons from the Oaxaca–California Transnational Village/Community Modeling Project*. Mexico City: World Bank, 2003.

O'Neil, Kevin, Kimberley Hamilton, and Demetrios Papademetriou. *Migration in the Americas*. Geneva: Global Commission on International Migration, 2005.

Oram, Edna. "Vernon Celebrates Ninety Years of Incorporation." *Okanagan Historical Society Report* 47 (1983): 29–30.

Organisation for Economic Co-operation and Development (OECD). *International Migration Outlook*. Paris: OECD, 2010.

O'Rourke, Alexandra Villarreal. "Embracing Reality: The Guest Worker Program Revisited." *Harvard Latino Law Review* 9 (2006): 179–94.

Orozco, Manuel. "International Financial Flows and Worker Remittances: Best Practices." 2005. http://www.remesasydesarrollo.org/uploads/media/Orozco2_UNPD.pdf (accessed 3 September 2010).

– *Remittances in Latin America and the Caribbean*. Washington, DC: Organization of American States, 2004.

Orozco, Manuel, and Michelle Lapointe. "Mexican Hometown Associations and Development Opportunities." *Journal of International Affairs* 57, no. 2 (2004): 31–49.

Otero, Gerardo, and Kerry Preibisch. *Farmworker Health and Safety: Challenges for British Columbia.* Vancouver: WorkSafe BC, 2009.

Oxman-Martinez, Jacqueline, and Jill Hanley. "Border Control as an Approach to Countering Human Trafficking." Paper presented at Metropolis Conference, Ottawa, October 2001.

Oxman-Martinez, Jacqueline, Jill Hanley, and Leslie Cheung. "Another Look at the Live-in-Caregivers Program: An Analysis of an Action Research Survey Conducted by PINAY, the Quebec Filipino Women's Association, with the Centre for Applied Family Studies." Centre de recherché interuniversitaire de Montréal sur l'immigration, l'intégration et al dynamique urbaine, September, 2004.

Oxman-Martinez, Jacqueline, Jill Hanley, Lucyna Lach, Nazilla Khanlou, Swarna Weerasinghe, and Vijay Agnew. "Intersection of Canadian Policy Parameters Affecting Women with Precarious Immigration Status: A Baseline for Understanding Barriers to Health." *Journal of Immigrant Health* 7, no. 4 (2005): 241–58.

Pandey, Manish, and James Townsend. "Provincial Nominee Programs: An Evaluation of the Earnings and Retention Rates of Nominees." 2010. http://economics.uwinnipeg.ca/RePEc/winwop/prov_nominee_progs.pdf (accessed 20 August 2010).

– "Quantifying the Effects of the Provincial Nominee Programs." University of Winnipeg Working Paper, Manitoba, 2009.

Papademetriou, Demetrios G., Doris Meissner, Marc R. Rosenblum, and Madeleine Sumption. "Aligning Temporary Immigration Visas with US Labor Market Needs: The Case for a New System of Provisional Visas." Migration Policy Institute, July 2009. www.migrationpolicy.org/pubs/Provisional_visas.pdf (accessed 8 February 2012).

Papademetriou, Demetrios G., and Aaron Terrazas. "Immigrants in the United States and the Current Economic Crisis." *Migration Information Source,* April 2009. http://www.migrationinformation.org (accessed 13 January 2012).

Pappe, Ilan. *The Ethnic Cleansing of Palestine.* Oxford: Oneworld, 2006.

Parreñas, Rhacel Salazar. "Mothering from a Distance: Emotions, Gender, and Intergenerational Relations in Filipino Transnational Families." *Feminist Studies* 27, no. 2 (2001): 361–90.

Passel, Jeffrey. "Mexican Immigration to the US: The Latest Estimates." *Migration Information Source,* March 2004. http://www.migration

information.org/Feature/display.cfm?ID=208 (accessed 8 February 2012).

Paterson, Kent. "Troubled Waters in the Mexico–Canada Relationship." 2009. http://www.cipamericas.org/archives/1812 (accessed 13 January 2012); http://www.pbs.org/itvs/fightfields/cesarchavez1.html (accessed 13 January 2012).

Pentland, H. Clare. *Labour and Capital in Canada, 1650–1860*. Toronto: Lorimer, 1981.

Peschard-Sverdrup, Armand. "The Canada-Mexico Relationship: A View from Inside the Beltway." *Focal Point* 9, no. 4 (2010): n.p. http://www.focal.ca/publications/focalpoint/251-may-2010-armand-peschard-sverdrup (accessed 13 January 2012).

Pessar, Patricia R., and Sarah J. Mahler. "Transnational Migration: Bringing Gender In." *International Migration Review* 37, no. 3 (2003): 812–46.

Pew Hispanic Center. "Mexican Immigrants in the United States, 2008." 15 April 2009. http://www.pewhispanic.org (accessed 8 August 2010).

Picot, G., F. Hou, and S. Coulombe. "Poverty Dynamics among Recent Immigrants to Canada." *International Migration Review* 42, no. 2 (2008): 393–424.

PINAY. *Danger! Domestic Work Can Be Harmful!* Montreal: PINAY, 2008.

Piper, Nicola. "Gender and Migration Policies in Southeast and East Asia: Legal Protection and Sociocultural Empowerment of Unskilled Migrant Women." *Singapore Journal of Tropical Geography*, 25, no. 2 (2004): 216–31.

– "Migrant Labor in Southeast Asia – Country Study: Singapore." N.d. http://www.fes.de/aktuell/focus_interkulturelles/focus_1/documents/8_000.pdf (accessed 10 December 2011).

– "Rights of Foreign Workers and the Politics of Migration in South-East and East Asia." *International Migration* 42, no. 5 (2004): 71–97.

– "Temporary Economic Migration and Rights Activism: An Organizational Perspective." *Ethnic and Racial Studies* 33, no. 1 (2009): 108–25.

Plewa, Piotr. "The Rise and Fall of Temporary Foreign Worker Policies: Lessons for Poland." *International Migration* 45, no. 2 (2007): 3–36.

Poulsen, Chuck. "Valley to Import More Farm Labour: Twice as Many Mexican Workers Expected This Year." *Kelowna Daily Courier*, 28 February 2007.

Pratt, Geraldine. "Is This Canada? Domestic Workers' Experiences in Van-
    couver, B.C." In *Gender, Migration and Domestic Service*, ed. Janet
    Henshall Momsen, 23–42. New York: Routledge, 1999.
– "Stereotypes and Ambivalence: The Construction of Domestic Workers
    in Vancouver, British Columbia." *Gender, Place and Culture: A Journal
    of Feminist Geography* 4, no. 2 (1997): 159–78.
Preibisch, Kerry. "Local Produce, Foreign Labor: Labor Mobility Programs
    and Global Trade Competitiveness in Canada." *Rural Sociology* 72, no.
    3 (2007): 418–49.
– "Migrant Agricultural Workers and Processes of Social Inclusion in
    Rural Canada: Encuentros and Desencuentros." *Canadian Journal of
    Latin American and Caribbean Studies* 29, nos 57–8 (2004): 203–39.
– "Migrant Workers and the Social Relations of Contemporary Agricul-
    tural Production in Canada." Paper presented at the 29th International
    Congress of the Latin American Studies Association, Toronto, 8 October
    2010.
– "Pick-Your-Own Labor: Migrant Workers and Flexibility in Canadian
    Agriculture." *International Migration Review* 44, no. 2 (2010):
    404–41.
– "Tierra de los (No)Libres: Migración Estacional México–Canadá y
    dos Campos de Reestructuración Económica." In *Conflictos Migra-
    torios Transnacionales y Respuestas Comunitarias*, ed. María Eugenia
    D'Aubeterre and Leigh Binford, 45–66. Puebla, Mexico: Benemérita
    Universidad Autónoma de Puebla, 2000.
Preibisch, Kerry, and Leigh Binford. "Interrogating Racialized Global
    Labour Supply: An Exploration of the Racial/National Replacement of
    Foreign Agricultural Workers in Canada." *Canadian Review of Sociol-
    ogy* 44, no. 1 (2007): 5–36.
Preibisch, Kerry, and Evelyn Encalada Grez. "The Other Side of El Otro
    Lado: Mexican Migrant Women and Labor Flexibility in Canadian
    Agriculture." *Signs* 35, no. 2 (2010): 289–316.
Pritchard, Justin, "Mexican-Born Workers More Likely to Die on Job."
    Los Angeles Times, 14 March 2004.
Rai, Shirin. *Gender and the Political Economy of Development*. Malden,
    MA: Polity Press, 2002.
Reed, Austina. "Canada's Experience with Managed Migration: The Stra-
    tegic Use of Temporary Foreign Worker Programs." *International Jour-
    nal* (Spring 2008): 469–84.

Reitz, Jeffrey. "Selecting Immigrants for the Short-Term: Is It Smart in the Long-Run?" *Policy Options* (July–August 2010): 12–16.

Resurreccion, Bernadette P., and Ha Thi Van Khanh. "Able to Come and Go: Reproducing Gender in Female Rural-Urban Migration in the Red River Delta." *Population, Space and Place* 13, no. 3 (2007): 211–24.

Richmond, Anthony H. *Global Apartheid: Refugees, Racism, and the New World Order.* Toronto: Oxford University Press, 1994.

Rodriguez, Robyn M. "Migrant Heroes: Nationalism, Citizenship and the Politics of Filipino Migrant Labor." *Citizenship Studies* 6, no. 3 (2002): 341–56.

Rollins, Judith. *Between Women: Domestics and Their Employers.* Philadelphia: Temple University Press, 1987.

Rubio-Marin, Ruth. *Immigration as a Democratic Challenge: Citizenship and Inclusion in Germany and the United States.* Cambridge, UK: Cambridge University Press, 2000.

Ruhs, Martin. "Economic Research and Labour Immigration Policy." *Oxford Review of Economic Policy* 24, no. 3 (2008): 403–26.

– "The Potential of Temporary Migration Programmes in Future International Migration Policy." *International Labour Review* 145, nos 1–2 (2006): 7–36.

– "Temporary Foreign Worker Programmes: Policies, Adverse Consequences, and the Need to Make Them Work." June 2002. http://www. ccis-ucsd.org/PUBLICATIONS/wrkg56.PDF (accessed 14 January 2012).

Salazar Parrenas, Rhacel. "The Care Crisis in the Philippines: Children and Transnational Families in the New Global Economy." In *Gender Relations in Global Perspectives*, ed. Nancy Cook, 229–40. Toronto: Canadian Scholars' Press, 2007.

Salgado de Snyder, Nelly. "Family Life across the Border: Mexican Wives Left Behind." *Hispanic Journal of Behavioral Sciences* 15, no. 3 (1993): 391–401.

San Juan, Epifanio Jr. "Overseas Filipino Workers: The Making of an Asian-Pacific Diaspora." *Global South* 4, no. 1 (2010): 99–129.

Satzewich, Vic. "Business or Bureaucratic Dominance in Immigration Policymaking in Canada: Why Was Mexico Included in the Caribbean Seasonal Agricultural Workers Program in 1974?" *International Migration and Integration* 8, no. 3 (2007): 255–75.

– *Racism and the Incorporation of Foreign Labour: Farm Labour Migration to Canada since 1945.* New York: Routledge, 1991.

Satzewich, Vic, and Nikolaos Liodakis. *'Race' and Ethnicity in Canada: A Critical Introduction.* Toronto: Oxford University Press, 2010.

Seidle, Frank L. "Intergovernmental Immigration Agreements and Public Accountability." *Options politiques* 30, no.7 (2010): 49–53.

Shah, Nasra M. *Restrictive Labour Immigration Policies in the Oil-Rich Gulf: Effectiveness and Implications for Sending Asian Countries.* Beirut: United Nations Secretariat, 2006.

Sharma, Karen. "Manitoba's Worker Recruitment and Protection Act." Paper presented at the Meeting of the Canadian Labour Congress's Temporary Worker Advocacy Group, Toronto, 25 January 2010.

Sharma, Nandita. *Home Economics: Nationalism and the Making of 'Migrant Workers' in Canada.* Toronto: University of Toronto Press, 2006.

– "Immigrant and Migrant Workers in Canada: Labour Movements, Racism and the Expansion of Globalization." *Canadian Woman Studies* 21/2, nos 4/1 (2002): 18–25.

– "On Being Not Canadian: The Social Organization Of 'Migrant Workers' in Canada." *Canadian Review of Sociology* 38, no. 4 (2001): 415–39.

– "Race, Class, Gender and the Making of Difference: The Social Organization of 'Migrant Workers' in Canada." *Atlantis: A Women's Studies Journal* 24, no. 2 (2000): 5–15.

– "The True North Strong and Free: Capitalist Restructuring and Nonimmigrant Employment in Canada, 1973–1993." MA thesis, Simon Fraser University, 1995.

Sharpe, Michael. "When Ethnic Returnees Are De Facto Guestworkers: What Does the Introduction of Japanese Nikkeijin (Japanese Descendants) Mean for Japan's Definition of Nationality, Citizenship, and Immigration Policy?" *Policy and Society* 29, no. 4 (2010): 357–69.

Shipp, Eva M., Sharon P. Cooper, Keith D. Burau, and Jane N. Bolin. "Pesticide Safety Training and Access to Field Sanitation among Migrant Farmworker Mothers from Starr County, Texas." *Journal of Agricultural Safety and Health* 11, no. 1 (2005): 51–60.

Shulman, Robin. "Immigration Raid Rips Families: Illegal Workers in Massachusetts Separated from Children." *Washington Post*, 18 March 2007.

Siemiatycki, Myer. "Marginalizing Migrants: Canada's Rising Reliance on Temporary Foreign Workers." *Canadian Issues* (Spring 2010): 60–3.

Silvera, Makeda. *Silenced.* Toronto: Sister Vision, 1983.

Silvey, Rachel. "Transnational Domestication: State Power and Indonesian Migrant Women in Saudi Arabia." *Political Geography* 23, no. 3 (2004): 245–64.

Silvius, Ray, and Robert C. Annis. "Reflections on the Rural Immigration Experience in Manitoba's Diverse Rural Communities." *Our Diverse Cities* 3 (2007): 126–33.

Smith, Dorothy E. *Texts, Facts and Femininity: Exploring the Relations of Ruling.* London: Routledge, 1990.

Smith, Katherine E. "Problematizing Power Relations in 'Elite' Interviews." *Geoforum* 37 (July 2006): 643–53.

Souza, Christine. "H-2A: Is This the Future of Ag Work Force?" *Ag Alert,* 8 August 2007. http://www.datatechag.com/news/h2a.htm (accessed 10 August 2010).

– "Labor Department Reverses Changes to H-2A Program." *Ag Alert,* 3 June 2009. http://cfbf.com/alert (accessed 9 August 2010).

Spitzer, Denise. "Live-in Caregivers in Rural and Small City Alberta." Edmonton: Prairie Centre of Excellence for Research on Immigration and Integration, 2009.

Spitzer, Denise, Karen Hughes, Jacqueline Oxman-Martinez, Jill Hanley, and Sara Torres. "The Land of Milk and Honey? After the Live-in Caregiver Program: Discussion Paper for Focus Group with Policy Makers." Ottawa: University of Ottawa, 2008.

Spitzer, Denise, and Sara Torres. *Gender-Based Barriers to Settlement and Integration for Live-in Caregivers: A Review of the Literature.* Ottawa: Citizenship and Immigration Canada and the Metropolis Project, 2008.

Squire, J.P. "Labour Shortage Bruising Industry." *Kelowna Daily Courier,* 26 January 2008.

Stalker, Peter. *The No-Nonsense Guide to International Migration.* Toronto: New Internationalist Publications and Between the Lines, 2001.

Standing Committee on Citizenship and Immigration. "Temporary Foreign Workers and Nonstatus Workers: Seventh Report of the Standing Committee on Citizenship and Immigration." Ottawa: House of Commons Canada, 2009.

Stasiulis, Daiva. "Relational Positionalities of Nationalisms, Racisms, and Feminisms." In *Between Woman and Nation,* ed. Caren Kaplan, Noma Alcaron, and Minoo Moallem, 182–218. Durham, NC: Duke University Press, 1999.

– "Revisiting the Permanent-Temporary Labour Migration Dichotomy." In *Governing International Labour Migration: Current Issues, Challenges and Dilemmas*, ed. Christina Gabriel and Helene Pellerin, 95–111. London: Routledge, 2008.

Stasiulis, Daiva, and Abigail B. Bakan. "Negotiating Citizenship: The Case of Foreign Domestic Workers in Canada." *Feminist Review* 57, no. 1 (1997): 112–39.

– *Negotiating Citizenship: Migrant Women in Canada and the Global System*. Basingstoke, UK: Palgrave, 2003.

– "Negotiating the Citizenship Divide: Foreign Domestic Worker Policy and Legal Jurisprudence." In *Women's Legal Strategies in Canada*, ed. Radha Jhappan, 237–94. Toronto: University of Toronto Press, 2002.

Statistics Canada. *Canadian Demographics at a Glance*. Ottawa: Statistics Canada, 2008.

– *Community Profile: Winnipeg CMA and Manitoba*. Ottawa: Statistics Canada, 2008.

– "Study: Low-Income Rates among Immigrants Entering Canada, 1992 to 2004." 30 January 2007. http://www.statcan.ca/Daily/English/070130/d070130b.htm (accessed 3 February 2007).

Statistics Canada, Income and Earnings. *2006 Census*. Ottawa: Statistics Canada, 2007.

Tabuchi, Hiroko. "Japan Training Program Is Said to Exploit Workers." *New York Times*, 20 July 2010.

Thornton, Grant. *BC Provincial Nominee Program Evaluation Report*. Victoria, BC: Ministry of Jobs, Tourism and Innovation, 2011.

Tomic, Patricia, Ricardo Trumper, and Luis Aguiar. "Housing Regulations and Living Conditions of Mexican Migrant Workers in the Okanagan Valley, B.C." *Canadian Issues* (Spring 2010): 78–82.

Trumper, Ricardo, and Lloyd Wong. "Racialization and Genderization: The Canadian State, Immigration, and Temporary Workers." In *International Labour Migrations*, ed. B. Singh Bolaria and Rosemary Bolaria, 153–91. Delhi: Oxford University Press, 1997.

– "Canada's Guest Workers: Racialized, Gendered, and Flexible." In *Race and Racism in 21st Century Canada*, ed. Sean Hier and B. Singh Bolaria, 151–70. Peterborough, ON: Broadview, 2007.

– "Temporary Workers in Canada: A National Perspective." *Canadian Issues* (Spring 2010): 83–9.

United Food and Commercial Workers (UFCW) Canada. "Alberta Continues to Stall on Farm Safety Recommendations." 2010. http://www.

ufcw.ca/index.php?option=com_content&view=article&id=686&catid=
5&Itemid=99&lang=en (accessed 13 January 2012).
– "Patricia Perez." N.d. http://www.ufcw.ca/Default.aspx?SectionId=
37b8c54f-c1a1-42f2-8ead-1f5acb019100&LanguageId=1&ItemId=
f5913934-7b7b-4c24-aadf-d8ca5d5e7156 (accessed 13 January 2012).
– The Status of Migrant Farm Workers in Canada, 2008–2009. Rexdale,
ON: UFCW Canada and Agricultural Workers Alliance, 2009.
– The Status of Migrant Farm Workers in Canada, 2010–2011. Rexdale,
ON: UFCW Canada and Agricultural Workers Alliance, 2011.
United Kingdom. The Constitution Act, 30 and 31 Victoria, c. 3, secs 91,
92, and 95, 1867.
United States Citizenship and Immigration Services. "H2-A Temporary
Agricultural Workers." Updated 17 January 2012. http://www.uscis.gov/
portal/site/uscis/menuitem.eb1d4c2a3e5b9ac89243c6a7543f6d1a/
?vgnextoid=889fob89284a3210vgnVCM100000b92ca60aRCRD&
vgnextchannel=889fob89284a3210vgnVCM100000b92ca60aRCRD
(accessed 8 February 2012).
United States Department of Homeland Security. "H-2A Temporary Agricultural Worker, Notice of Proposed Rulemaking." Updated 14 September 2011. http://www.dhs.gov/files/laws/gc_1208188057025.shtm
(accessed 13 January 2012).
– "H-2A Temporary Agricultural Worker Program." Updated 9 February 2009. http://www.dhs.gov/files/programs/gc_1234207302139.shtm
(accessed 11 February 2012).
United States Department of State, Bureau of Consular Affairs. "Multi-
Year Graphs." N.d. http://travel.state.gov/visa/statistics/graphs/
graphs_4399.html (accessed 10 February 2012).
Urry, John. "Mobile Sociology." British Journal of Sociology 51, no. 1
(2000): 185–203.
– Sociology beyond Societies: Mobilities for the Twenty-First Century.
London and New York. Routledge, 2000.
Valarezo, Giselle. "Out of Necessity and into the Fields: Migrant Farm-
workers in St Rémi, Quebec." MA thesis, Queen's University, 2007.
– "Pushed to the Edge: The Politics of Seasonally Migrating to Canada."
Paper presented at the National Metropolis Conference, Vancouver, 25
March 2011.
Valiani, Salimah. "The Temporary Foreign Worker Program and Its Inter-
section with Canadian Immigration Policy." Ottawa: Canadian Labour
Congress, 2008.

Valpy, Michael. "Visa Controls on Mexico 'Humiliating,' Senator Says." *Globe and Mail*, 26 October 2009, A13.

Van Maanen, John. "The Fact of Fiction in Organizational Ethnography." *Administrative Science Quarterly* 24, no. 4 (1979): 539–50.

Vargas-Foronda, Jacobo. "El Programa de Trabajo Agrícola Temporal en Canadá (PTAT-C): Mano de Obra Barata de Exportación." *Diálogo*, no. 16 (2010): n.p. http://www.flacso.edu.gt/site/wp-content/uploads/2010/08/dialogo16agosto.pdf (accessed 14 January 2012).

Velasco, Pura. "Filipino Migrant Workers amidst Globalization." *Canadian Woman Studies* 21, no. 4 (2002): 131–5.

Verduzco, Gustavo. "The Impact of Canadian Labour Experience on the Households of Mexicans: A Seminal View on Best Practices." Policy paper, Canadian Foundation for the Americas (FOCAL), Ottawa, September 2007.

Verduzco, Gustavo, and María Isabel Lozano. *Mexican Workers' Participation in CSAWP and Development Consequences in the Workers' Rural Home Communities*. Ottawa: North-South Institute, 2003.

Verma, Veena. *The Mexican and Caribbean Seasonal Agricultural Workers Program: Regulatory and Policy Framework, Farm Industry–Level Employment Practices and the Future of the Program under Unionization*. Ottawa: North-South Institute, 2003.

– *The Regulatory and Policy Framework of the Caribbean Seasonal Agricultural Workers Program*. Ottawa: North-South Institute, 2007.

Vipond, Robert. "Introduction: The Comparative Turn in Canadian Political Science." In *The Comparative Turn in Canadian Political Science*, ed. Linda A. White, Richard Simeon, Robert Vipond, and Jennifer Wallner, 3–16. Vancouver: UBC Press, 2008.

Virilio, Paul. *Speed and Politics: An Essay on Dromology*. New York: Semiotexte, 1986.

Vosko, Leah F. "Fabric Friends and Clothing Foes: A Comparative Analysis of Textile and Apparel Industries under the NAFTA." *Review of Radical Political Economics* 25, 4 (1993): 45–58.

Vosko, Leah, ed. *Precarious Employment: Understanding Labour Market Insecurity in Canada*. Montreal and Kingston: McGill-Queen's University Press, 2006.

Walzer, Michael. *Spheres of Justice: A Defense of Pluralism and Equality*. New York: Basic Books, 1983.

Ward, W. Peter. *White Canada Forever: Popular Attitudes and Public Policy toward Orientals in British Columbia.* Montreal and Kingston: McGill-Queen's University Press, 1990.

Weinstein Bever, Sandra. "Migration and the Transformation of Gender Roles and Hierarchies in Yucatan." *Urban Anthropology* 31, no. 2 (2002): 199–230.

Weston, Ann, and Luigi Scarpa de Masellis. *Hemispheric Integration and Trade Relations: Implications for Canada's Seasonal Agricultural Workers Program.* Ottawa: North-South Institute, 2003.

Wickramasekara, Piyasiri. "Asian Labour Migration: Issues and Challenges in an Era of Globalization." 2002. http://www.ilo.int/public/english/protection/migrant/download/imp/imp57e.pdf (accessed 13 January 2012).

– "Globalisation, International Labour Migration and the Rights of Migrant Workers." *Third World Quarterly* 297 (2008): 1247–64.

Workplace Safety and Insurance Board (WSIB). "Workplace Safety and Insurance Board Annual Report 2007, Statistical Supplement." Toronto: WSIB, 2007.

World Bank. *At Home and Away: Expanding Job Opportunities for Pacific Islanders through Labour Mobility.* Washington, DC: World Bank, 2006.

World Health Organization (WHO). *Closing the Gap in a Generation: Health Equity through Action on the Social Determinants of Health – Commission on Social Determinants of Health Final Report.* Geneva: WHO, 2008.

Young, Iris Marion. *Justice and the Politics of Difference.* Princeton, NJ: Princeton University Press, 1989.

Yuval-Davis, Nira. "Intersectionality and Feminist Politics." *European Journal of Women's Studies* 13, no. 3 (2006): 193–209.

Zabin, Carol. "U.S.-Mexico Economic Integration: Labor Relations and the Organization of Work in California and Baja California Agriculture." *Economic Geography* 73, no. 3 (1997): 337–55.

Zaman, Habiba. "Transnational Migration and Commodification of Im/migrant Female Laborers in Canada." *International Journal of Canadian Studies* 29 (2004): 41–62

Contributors

ABIGAIL B. BAKAN is the head of the Department of Gender Studies and a professor of political studies at Queen's University. Her publications address issues of citizenship, anti-oppression politics, comparative development, and political economy. These include *Negotiating Citizenship: Migrant Women in Canada and the Global System* (with Daiva Stasiulis, 2003), winner of the 2007 Canadian Women's Studies Association book award; *Critical Political Studies: Debates and Dialogues from the Left* (co-edited with Eleanor MacDonald, 2002); *Employment Equity Policy in Canada: An Interprovincial Comparison* (with Audrey Kobayashi, 2000); and *Not One of the Family: Foreign Domestic Workers in Canada* (co-edited with Daiva Stasiulis, 1997).

TOM CARTER recently retired as a professor of geography at the University of Winnipeg. He continues to work as a senior scholar at the university. Tom is also president of Carter Research Associates Inc. His research experience covers housing, neighbourhood revitalization, urban development, immigration policy, and social policy issues.

SARAH D'AOUST is currently finishing her master's degree in globalization and international development at the University of Ottawa.

CHRISTINA GABRIEL is an associate professor in the Department of Political Science at Carleton University. Her research interests focus on gender and migration, citizenship, and regional integration. She is a co-author of *Selling Diversity: Immigration, Multiculturalism, Employment Equity, and Globalization* (2002) and is a co-editor of *Governing International Labour Migration: Current Issues, Challenges and Dilemmas* (2008). She has contributed chapters to various edited collections on issues such as migration, border control, transnational care labour, and North American regional integration.

JILL HANLEY is an assistant professor at the McGill School of Social Work, where she teaches community practice, applied research, and social policy. She studies access to social rights for precarious-status migrants, including organizing to defend these rights. She is a co-founder and an active member of Montreal's Immigrant Workers Centre.

JENNA L. HENNEBRY, is an associate professor in the Department of Communication Studies and with the Balsillie School of International Affairs at Wilfrid Laurier University, where she also serves as the associate director of the International Migration Research Centre (IMRC). Hennebry's research focuses on international migration and mobility, with a specialization in labour migration in Canada and Spain. Her research portfolio includes comparative studies of migration policy and foreign worker programs, migrant rights and health, the formation of migration industries, nonstate migration mediation, the racialization and representation of migrants, and the role of remittances in development.

CHRISTINE HUGHES holds a bachelor of arts in political science from the University of Western Ontario and a master's degree in international development studies from Dalhousie University, and she is currently a doctoral candidate in sociology at Carleton University. Her main research interests include gender and transnationalism, migration and development, and temporary labour migration. Her dissertation research, supported by a doctoral fellowship from the Social Sciences and Humanities Research Council of Canada, examines the gendered impacts of Guatemalan temporary agricultural migration to Canada.

KAREN D. HUGHES is a professor of sociology in the Faculty of Arts and a professor of strategic management and organization in the

School of Business at the University of Alberta. She has published widely on work, caregiving, and entrepreneurship. Her recent books include *Global Women's Entrepreneurship* (co-edited with Jennifer Jennings, 2012) and *Work, Industry and Canadian Society* (with Harvey Krahn and Graham Lowe, 2010).

JAHHON KOO is a doctoral candidate at the McGill School of Social Work, where he is engaged in research related to the health, labour rights, and organizing of temporary foreign workers. Prior to his doctoral studies, he was an organizer at a migrant workers' centre in South Korea.

PATTI TAMARA LENARD is an assistant professor of ethics in the Graduate School of Public and International Affairs at the University of Ottawa. She is the author of *Trust, Democracy and Multicultural Challenges* (2012), and her work has been published in a range of journals, including *Political Studies, Journal of Moral Philosophy,* and *Review of Politics.* Her current research is focused on the moral questions raised by migration across borders, as well as on multiculturalism, trust and social cohesion, and democratic theory more generally.

LAURA MACDONALD is a professor in the Department of Political Science and the Institute of Political Economy at Carleton University. She is the author of *Supporting Civil Society: The Political Impact of* NGO *Assistance to Central America* (1997), a co-author of *Women, Democracy, and Globalization in North America: A Comparative Study* (2006), and a co-editor of *Post-Neoliberalism in the Americas* (with Arne Ruckert, 2009) and of *Contentious Politics in North America* (with Jeffrey Ayres, 2009).

JANET MCLAUGHLIN is an assistant professor of health studies at Wilfrid Laurier University and a research associate with the International Migration Research Centre (IMRC), housed in the Balsillie School of International Affairs. A social-cultural and medical anthropologist, she explores issues of health, human rights, development, food systems, labour, citizenship, and transnational migration, with a particular focus on Latin American and Caribbean migrant farm workers in Canada.

DELPHINE NAKACHE is an assistant professor of law in the School of International Development and Global Studies at the University of Ottawa. Her expertise lies in the areas of Canadian immigration and refugee law, international migration law, international human rights law, and the cultural theory of law. Her research has covered the protection of migrant workers admitted to Canada under the general Temporary Foreign Worker Program (TFWP) and the impact of Provincial/Territorial Nominee Programs (PTNPs) on noncitizens' rights and protections. She is also involved in several research projects that look at the human rights aspects of the detention of asylum seekers in Canada.

JACQUELINE OXMAN-MARTINEZ has a doctorate in sociology and is an established scholar with an expertise in vulnerable women and children and immigration issues. Her most recent publications have been in high-impact journals and demonstrate her depth of knowledge of immigration policies and their effects on women's and children's wellbeing.

KERRY PREIBISCH is an associate professor at the University of Guelph. A sociologist specializing in international migration, she focuses on temporary migration programs, migrant rights, and development; labour and globalized agro-food systems; gender, migration, and rural livelihoods in Latin America; and im/migration and social change in rural Canada. She has published in *International Migration Review*, *Signs*, and *International Migration*, among other journals. Her favourite books are not academic but culinary, and she is most happy when cooking and *conviviendo* with friends and family.

ANDRE RIVARD is a community organizer concerned with issues of human rights and issues of social and political justice. He has been actively involved with the Immigrant Workers Centre and with other support networks struggling for migrant workers' rights. He has a master's degree in social work from McGill University and is now pursuing a doctorate in law at the University of Windsor.

NANDITA SHARMA is an associate professor of sociology at the University of Hawaii at Mānoa. She is an activist scholar whose research is shaped by the social movements in which she is active, including "no borders" movements and those struggling for the commons. Her publications include *Home Economics: Nationalism and the Making of 'Migrant Workers' in Canada* (2006). She is also a co-editor (with Bridget Anderson and Cynthia Wright) of a special issue of *Refuge* (Fall 2009) on "No Borders as a Practical Political Project."

ERIC SHRAGGE is the principal of Concordia University's School of Community and Public Affairs and the president (and a co-founder) of the Immigrant Workers Centre. He has published extensively on community organizing and community economic development.

DENISE L. SPITZER is the Canada Research Chair in Gender, Migration and Health, an associate professor in the Institute of Women's Studies, and a principal scientist in the Institute of Population Health at the University of Ottawa. She has conducted research with live-in caregivers in Canada for more than a decade and is the editor of *Engendering Migrant Health: Canadian Perspectives* (2011).

DAIVA STASIULIS is a professor of sociology at Carleton University. She has published extensively on issues of migration, race and citizenship, intersectional feminist theory, and social movements. She is a co-author (with Abigail B. Bakan) of *Negotiating Citizenship: Migrant Women in Canada and the Global System* (2003), winner of the 2007 Canadian Women's Studies Association book award. She has worked with migrant advocacy and community groups, has served as the chair of the United Nations Expert Group Meeting on Violence against Migrant Workers, and has been a consultant to the federal government on employment equity, ethnocultural political participation, multiculturalism policies, and gender and equity analysis of immigration policy.

CHRISTINE STRAEHLE is an assistant professor of ethics in the Graduate School of Public and International Affairs at the University of Ottawa. Her research investigates questions of justice in migration regimes, health equity, global solidarity, and questions of individual autonomy and vulnerability. Her work has appeared in such venues as *European Journal of Philosophy*, *Contemporary Political Theory*, and *Journal of International Political Theory*. She is also a co-editor (with Patti Tamara Lenard) of *Health Inequality and Global Justice* (2012).

PATRICIA TOMIC is an associate professor at the University of British Columbia, Okanagan Campus, where she teaches sociology. Her areas of interest include the politics of language and the Latin American immigrant experience in Canada; tourism, wine, and migration in the Okanagan Valley; and the effects of neoliberalism in Chile (1973 to the present).

SARA TORRES is a doctoral candidate at the University of Ottawa. Her research is focused on community/lay health worker programs that address health equity for immigrant women in Canada. She has over fifteen years of experience doing research and outreach with multicultural and hard-to-reach populations. Since 2006, she has worked with Denise Spitzer on various studies of live-in caregivers in Canada.

RICARDO TRUMPER is an associate professor at the University of British Columbia, Okanagan Campus, where he teaches sociology. His research interests include migration, mobility, and neoliberalism. He is currently conducting research on mobility, fear, and sport in Chile and on the repercussions of neoliberalism, global mobility, and migration in the Okanagan Valley.

Index